# ZAGAT®

## Chicago
## Restaurants
# 2010/11

Including
Milwaukee

**LOCAL EDITORS**
Alice Van Housen and Ann Christenson
**STAFF EDITOR**
Cynthia Kilian

Published and distributed by
Zagat Survey, LLC
4 Columbus Circle
New York, NY 10019
T: 212.977.6000
E: chicago@zagat.com
www.zagat.com

## ACKNOWLEDGMENTS

We thank Jennifer Olvera, Steven Shukow, Scott Tyree, Thomas Van Housen and Donna Marino Wilkins, as well as the following members of our staff: Caitlin Eichelberger (associate editor), Danielle Borovoy (editorial assistant), Brian Albert, Sean Beachell, Maryanne Bertollo, Jane Chang, Sandy Cheng, Reni Chin, Larry Cohn, Bill Corsello, Carol Diuguid, Alison Flick, Jeff Freier, Michelle Golden, Justin Hartung, Garth Johnston, Natalie Lebert, Mike Liao, Christina Livadiotis, Andre Pilette, Becky Ruthenburg, Jacqueline Wasilczyk, Art Yaghci, Sharon Yates, Anna Zappia and Kyle Zolner.

The reviews in this guide are based on public opinion surveys. The ratings reflect the average scores given by the survey participants who voted on each establishment. The text is based on quotes from, or paraphrasings of, the surveyors' comments. Phone numbers, addresses and other factual data were correct to the best of our knowledge when published in this guide.

# Contents

# Ratings & Symbols

| Zagat Top Spot | Name | Symbols | | Cuisine | Zagat Ratings | | | |
|---|---|---|---|---|---|---|---|---|
| | | | | | FOOD | DECOR | SERVICE | COST |

| Area, Address & Contact | **Z Tim & Nina's ●** *Pizza*     ▽ 23 \| 9 \| 13 \| $15 |
|---|---|
| | **Hyde Park** \| 456 E. Chicago Ave. (Division St.) \| 312-555-3867 \| www.zagat.com |

| Review, surveyor comments in quotes | Hordes of "unkempt" U of C students have discovered this cafeteria-style "24/7 dive", which "single-handedly" started the "deep-dish sushi pizza craze" that's "sweeping the Windy City like a lake-effect storm"; "try the eel-pepperoni-wasabi-mozzarella or Osaka-Napolitano pies" – "they're to die for" – but bring patience, since "T & N never heard of training servers." |
|---|---|

**Ratings**    **Food, Decor** and **Service** are rated on the Zagat 0 to 30 scale.

| 0 – 9 | poor to fair |
|---|---|
| 10 – 15 | fair to good |
| 16 – 19 | good to very good |
| 20 – 25 | very good to excellent |
| 26 – 30 | extraordinary to perfection |
| ▽ | low response \| less reliable |

**Cost**    Our surveyors' estimated price of a dinner with one drink and tip. Lunch is usually 25 to 30% less. For unrated **newcomers** or **write-ins,** the price range is shown as follows:

| I | $25 and below | E | $41 to $65 |
|---|---|---|---|
| M | $26 to $40 | VE | $66 or above |

**Symbols**

| Z | highest ratings, popularity and importance |
|---|---|
| ● | serves after 11 PM |
| 🅂̸ | closed on Sunday |
| 🅼 | closed on Monday |
| 🚫 | no credit cards accepted |

**Maps**    Index maps show restaurants with the highest Food ratings in those areas.

# About This Survey

Here are the results of our **2010/11 Chicago Restaurants Survey,** covering 1,179 eateries in the Chicago area and Milwaukee. Like all our guides, this one is based on input from avid local consumers – 5,701 all told. Our editors have synopsized this feedback and highlighted (in quotation marks within reviews) representative comments. You can read full surveyor comments – and share your own opinions – on **ZAGAT.com,** where you'll also find the latest restaurant news plus menus, photos and more, all for free.

**OUR PHILOSOPHY:** Three simple premises underlie our ratings and reviews. First, we've long believed that the collective opinions of large numbers of consumers are more accurate than the opinions of a single critic. (Consider that, as a group our surveyors bring some 830,000 annual meals' worth of experience to this Survey. They also visit restaurants year-round, anonymously – and on their own dime.) Second, food quality is only part of the equation when choosing a restaurant, thus we ask surveyors to separately rate food, decor and service and report on cost. Third, since people need reliable information in a fast, easy-to-digest format, we strive to be concise and to offer our content on every platform. Our Top Ratings lists (pages 7–16) and indexes (starting on page 187) are also designed to help you quickly choose the best place for any occasion. Milwaukee's Top Ratings and indexes start on pages 243 and 259, respectively.

**ABOUT ZAGAT:** In 1979, we started asking friends to rate and review restaurants purely for fun. The term "user-generated content" had not yet been coined. That hobby grew into Zagat Survey; 31 years later, we have over 375,000 surveyors and cover airlines, bars, dining, fast food, entertaining, golf, hotels, movies, music, resorts, shopping, spas, theater and tourist attractions in over 100 countries. Along the way, we evolved from being a print publisher to a digital content provider, e.g. **ZAGAT.com, ZAGAT.mobi** (for web-enabled mobile devices), **ZAGAT TO GO** (for smartphones) and **nru** (for Android phones). We also produce customized gift and marketing tools for a wide range of corporate clients. And you can find us on Twitter (twitter.com/zagatbuzz), Facebook and other social media networks.

**JOIN IN:** To improve our guides, we solicit your comments; it's vital that we hear your opinions. Just contact us at **nina-tim@zagat.com.** We also invite you to join our surveys at **ZAGAT.com.** Do so and you'll receive a choice of rewards in exchange.

**THANKS:** We're grateful to our local editors, Alice Van Housen, a freelance writer and editor; and Ann Christenson, the dining critic for *Milwaukee Magazine.* We also sincerely thank the thousands of surveyors who participated – this guide is really "theirs."

New York, NY
June 23, 2010

Nina and Tim Zagat

# What's New

The Windy City is weathering the stormy economy with a new crop of affordable eateries. Cantinas, bistros and trattorias are in the ethnic mix, which also includes a sushi and pizza onslaught. There's an izakaya trend blowing in and a nascent food truck scene, all speaking to the 32% of surveyors who report eating in less-expensive places. That said, 60% of participants are willing to pay more for "green" fare, which they're finding at a host of eco-minded newcomers.

**LOCAL HEROES:** The sustainable-food movement continues to grow. Housemade ingredients, locally produced products and a snout-to-tail sensibility characterize the American comfort-meets-fine-dining fare at **Browntrout** in North Center, **Ceres' Table** Uptown and **Cuna** in Lakeview. **Epic** and **Gilt Bar** made the green scene in River North, as did **Gemini Bistro, Kith & Kin** and **Sprout** in Lincoln Park, **Nightwood** (Pilsen), **Prairie Fire** (West Loop) and **Rootstock** (Humboldt Park). And crowds convened at **The Purple Pig** in River North for housemade charcuterie and all manner of pork parts.

 **STAR-CASUAL:** Big-name chefs are branching out with wallet-friendly comfort-food concepts – in sync with the 57% of surveyors seeking out deals. Paul Kahan opened **Big Star,** offering quality tacos, in Wicker Park, and Bill Kim debuted Asian **Belly Shack** in Humboldt Park. Michael Kornick ground out **DMK Burger Bar** in Lakeview and Rick Bayless fired up Mexican street food at **XOCO** in River North.

**CHECKING IN:** Hotel dining is so hot, some hotels doubled up. The Gold Coast's Elysian opened **Balsan** and **Ria,** and the Loop's theWit begat **Cibo Matto** and **State and Lake.** River North welcomed **Elate** (Hotel Felix), while Streeterville debuted **Pelago Ristorante** (Raffaello) and **deca Restaurant + Bar** (the Ritz-Carlton).

**LAST CALL:** We bade farewell to **Don Roth's Blackhawk, Seasons Café** and **Va Pensiero.** Other notable closings included **Aigre Doux, A Mano, Cuatro, FoLLia, Tizi Melloul** and **Vong's Thai Kitchen.**

**WHAT'S BREWING:** Milwaukee hunkered down with recession-era bargains such as extensive happy-hour food deals at **Hinterland** in the Third Ward and nightly specials at **NSB Bar and Grill** in the North Shore. At the same time, the city welcomed its latest "in" spot: **Smyth,** serving American fare with a Midwestern influence in the motorcycle-friendly Iron Horse Hotel, a chic boutique in a historic Walker's Point warehouse. Debuting Downtown is **Harbor House,** a much-anticipated seafooder from restaurateur Joe Bartolotta.

**TALLY-HO:** Though the average Chicago dinner costs $36.97, up from $35.17 in our last Survey, 66% of respondents report eating out as much as or more than two years ago.

Chicago, IL
Milwaukee, WI
June 23, 2010

Alice Van Housen
Ann Christenson

# Most Popular

1. Frontera Grill | *Mexican*
2. Alinea | *American*
1. Topolobampo | *Mexican*
4. Charlie Trotter's | *American*
5. Gibsons | *Steak*
6. Joe's Sea/Steak | *Seafood/Steak*
7. Blackbird | *American*
8. Wildfire | *Steak*
9. Morton's | *Steak*
10. Tru | *French*
11. Spiaggia | *Italian*
12. Everest | *French*
13. avec | *Mediterranean*
14. Shaw's | *Seafood*
15. Lou Malnati's | *Pizza*
16. mk | *American*
17. Chicago Chop House | *Steak*
18. L2O | *Seafood*
19. Capital Grille | *Steak*
20. Giordano's | *Pizza*
21. NoMI | *French*
22. Gene & Georgetti | *Steak*
23. Publican | *American*
24. Maggiano's | *Italian*
25. Hugo's | *Seafood*
26. Bob Chinn's | *Seafood*
27. Hot Doug's | *Hot Dogs*
28. Café Spiaggia | *Italian*
29. Ruth's Chris* | *Steak*
30. Original Gino's | *Pizza*
31. Gage | *American*
32. Orig./Walker Pancake | *Amer.*
33. Les Nomades | *French*
34. Japonais | *Japanese*
35. Coco Pazzo | *Italian*
36. Catch 35 | *Seafood*
37. Cheesecake Factory | *American*
38. Arun's | *Thai*
39. Rosebud* | *Italian*
40. David Burke's | *Steak*
41. Francesca's | *Italian*
42. Cafe Ba-Ba-Reeba! | *Spanish*
43. Naha | *American*
44. Bistro 110 | *French*
45. Harry Caray's* | *Italian/Steak*
46. Heaven/Seven* | *Cajun/Creole*
47. Pizzeria Uno/Due | *Pizza*
48. North Pond | *American*
49. Brasserie Jo | *French*
50. Le Colonial* | *Vietnamese*

It's obvious that many of the above restaurants are among the Chicago area's most expensive, but if popularity were calibrated to price, we suspect that a number of other restaurants would join their ranks. Thus, we have added two lists comprising 80 Best Buys on page 16.

---

* Indicates a tie with restaurant above

# KEY NEWCOMERS

Ceres' Table
LAKE MICHIGAN
Chicago O'Hare Intl. Airport (ORD)
LAWRENCE AVE.
Schiller Park
Browntrout
IRVING PARK RD.
Franklin Park
DMK Burger Bar
River Grove
Revolution Brewing
Elmwood Park
FULLERTON AVE.
Accanto
Belly Shack
Northlake
Rootstock
Melrose Park
Big Star
River Forest
Oak Park
Chicago
FOR DETAIL SEE BELOW
Bellwood
Maywood
Forest Park
Berwyn
WASHINGTON BLVD.
EISENHOWER EXPWY.
Hillside
Broadview
ROOSEVELT RD.
CERMAK AVE.
Nightwood
North Riverside
OGDEN AVE.
La Grange Park
Brookfield
Riverside
Lyons
Stickney
STEVENSON EXPWY.
ARCHER AVE.
PERSHING RD.
Western Sprs.
47TH ST.
55TH ST.
La Grange
Countryside
Summit
Chicago Midway Intl. Arpt. (MDW)
63RD ST.
MARQUETTE RD.
71ST ST.
79TH ST.
Justice
Bridgeview
Burbank
87TH ST.
Evergreen Park

---

Division St.
E. Division St.
SEWARD PARK
NEAR NORTH
Halsted
Chicago
WASHINGTON SQUARE PARK
MOODY BIBLE INSTITUTE
Ria
Pelago
LOYOLA UNIV.
SENECA PARK
LAKE SHORE PARK
W. Chicago Ave.
E. Chicago Ave.
MAGNIFICENT MILE
Elate
NORTHWESTERN UNIV. Medical School
M Burger
Orleans
La Salle
State
Michigan
RIVER NORTH
Milwaukee
Grand Ave.
E. Grand Ave.
STREETERVILLE
XOCO
Purple Pig
Gilt Bar
Mercadito
Chicago River
Prairie Fire
N. Wacker Dr.
Wacker Dr.
NEW EAST SIDE
MARKET DISTRICT
Cibo Matto
E. Randolph St.
Randolph St.
E. Wacker Dr.
W. Madison St.
Washington St.
E. Washington Blvd.
E. Madison St.
MILLENNIUM PARK
THE LOOP
Karyn's on Green
Adams St.
Terzo Piano
GREEKTOWN
Jackson St.
E. Adams St.
E. Jackson
Canal
W. Congress Pkwy.
E. Congress Dr.
UNIVERSITY VILLAGE
PRINTERS ROW
GRANT PARK
UNIVERSITY OF ILLINOIS
State
Michigan
Columbus
DEARBORN PARK
EAST-WEST UNIV
SOUTH LOOP
Chicago River South Branch
Roosevelt Rd.
ROOSEVELT PARK
E. Roosevelt Rd.

Menus, photos, voting and more – free at ZAGAT.com

# Key Newcomers

Our editors' take on the year's top arrivals. See page 229 for a full list.

**Accanto** | *Italian* | Logan Square destination dining

**Belly Shack** | *Asian* | From the Urban Belly gang in Humboldt Park

**Big Star** | *Mexican* | Quality tacos in Wicker Park via Paul Kahan

**Browntrout** | *American* | Farm-to-table fare in North Center

**Ceres' Table** | *American* | Seasonal cuisine Uptown

**Cibo Matto** | *Italian* | Trendy Loop dining in theWit hotel

**DMK Burger Bar** | *Burgers* | Patties with a pedigree in Lakeview

**Elate** | *American* | Innovative fare in an eco-friendly setting in River North

**Gilt Bar** | *American* | Elevated gastro grub in River North

**Karyn's on Green** | *American/Vegan* | Organic-chic in Greektown

**M Burger** | *Burgers* | Fast food in Streeterville from Lettuce Entertain You

**Mercadito** | *Mexican* | NYC import in River North

**Nightwood** | *American* | Funky Pilsen sibling to Lula Cafe

**Pelago** | *Italian* | Creative cuisine in a tasteful hotel setting in Streeterville

**Prairie Fire** | *American* | West Loop comfort food

**Purple Pig** | *Mediterranean* | Heavy-on-pork plates to share in River North

**Revolution Brewing** | *Pub Food* | A hip brewpub in Logan Square

**Ria** | *American* | White-tablecloth dining in the Gold Coast's Elysian hotel

**Rootstock** | *American* | A Humboldt Park wine and beer bar

**Terzo Piano** | *Italian* | Spiaggia sibling in the Art Institute

**XOCO** | *Mexican* | Chef Rick Bayless does street food in River North

---

Coming down the Chicago restaurant pipeline, River North will beef up with **Chicago Cut Steakhouse** and **Mastro's,** with other neighborhood newcomers including **Eatt** (an American comfort-food addition to the **Rosebud** chain) and **grahamwich,** Graham Elliot Bowles' take on the chef-driven sandwich trend. In the Loop, **The Gage** spins off **Henri** (named for architect Louis Henri Sullivan), which will offer seasonal American fare right next door, and in the West Loop, *Top Chef* Stephanie Izard plans Mediterranean small plates at **The Girl & the Goat. Chizakaya** is bringing the Japanese pub concept to Lakeview, Streeterville is gaining a yet-to-be-named American in the former **DeLaCosta** space and Rogers Park will welcome American cuisine from **Act One Cafe** in the former Morse Theater. Up on the Northwest Side, BBQ-piggery **Pork Shoppe** is debuting from the (former) **Tizi Melloul** team. And perhaps most intriguing, **Alinea's** Grant Achatz will be taking flight with **Next Restaurant,** which will sell tickets in advance on its website like an airline booking, plus a bar called **Aviary.**

# Top Food

29 Les Nomades | *French*
Alinea | *American*
Schwa | *American*

28 Arun's | *Thai*
Topolobampo | *Mexican*
Michael | *French*
Tallgrass | *French*
Tru | *French*

27 L2O | *Seafood*
Blackbird | *American*
Oceanique | *French/Seafood*
Carlos' | *French*
Naha | *American*
Vie | *American*
Charlie Trotter's | *American*
mk | *American*
Katsu | *Japanese*
Spring | *American/Seafood*
Everest | *French*
sushi wabi | *Japanese*
Frontera Grill | *Mexican*
Moto | *Eclectic*
Riccardo | *Italian*
NoMI | *French*
Hot Doug's | *Hot Dogs*

Spiaggia | *Italian*
Seasons | *American*

26 Joe's Sea/Steak | *Sea./Steak*
avec | *Mediterranean*
Kuma's Corner | *American*
Bonsoirée | *American/French*
one sixtyblue | *American*
Avenues | *American*
Takashi | *American/French*
Green Zebra | *Vegetarian*
a tavola | *Italian*
Mia Francesca | *Italian*
Morton's | *Steak*
Smoque BBQ | *BBQ*
Crofton on Wells | *Amer.*
Le Titi/Paris | *French*
Lula Cafe | *Eclectic*
Cafe 28 | *Cuban/Mexican*
Salpicón | *Mexican*
Mercat | *Spanish*
Gibsons | *Steak*

25 Zealous | *American*
Adelle's | *American*
Barrington Country | *French*
Yoshi's Café | *French/Japane*

## BY CUISINE

### AMERICAN (NEW)
29 Alinea
Schwa
27 Blackbird
Naha
Vie

### AMERICAN (TRAD.)
26 Kuma's Corner
25 Keefer's
24 Hot Chocolate
Bongo Room
TABLE fifty-two

### ASIAN
25 Shanghai Terrace
23 Belly Shack
Sunda
22 China Grill
20 Joy Yee

### BARBECUE
26 Smoque BBQ
24 Smoke Daddy

23 Twin Anchors
Fat Willy's
22 Carson's Ribs

### CAJUN/CREOLE
23 Heaven on Seven
21 Pappadeaux
Wishbone
19 Davis St. Fish
Dixie Kitchen

### CHINESE
24 Lao
23 Phoenix
Emperor's Choice
21 Hai Yen
Three Happiness

### COFFEE SHOP/DINER
24 Glenn's Diner and Seafood
Original/Walker Pancake
23 Lou Mitchell's
Manny's
Milk & Honey

Excludes places with low votes.

Menus, photos, voting and more – free at ZAGAT.com

## ECLECTIC

27 Moto
26 Lula Cafe
22 Uncommon Ground
21 ZED 451
   HUB 51

## FRENCH

29 Les Nomades
28 Michael
   Tallgrass
   Tru
27 Oceanique

## FRENCH (BISTRO)

25 Barrington Country
   Bistro Campagne
   Kiki's
24 Cafe Central
   Le Bouchon

## GREEK

22 Artopolis
   Costa's
21 Parthenon
   Santorini
   Roditys

## HOT DOGS/BURGERS

27 Hot Doug's
23 Al's #1 Beef
22 DMK Burger Bar
   Epic Burger
21 Wiener's Circle

## INDIAN

25 India House
23 Marigold
22 Hema's Kitchen
   Gaylord
   Vermilion

## ITALIAN

27 Riccardo
   Spiaggia
26 a tavola
   Mia Francesca
25 Coco Pazzo

## JAPANESE

27 Katsu
   sushi wabi
25 Yoshi's Café
   Mirai Sushi
   Sai Café

## MEDITERRANEAN

26 avec
25 mado
24 Pita Inn
   Café/Architectes
23 Turquoise

## MEXICAN

28 Topolobampo
27 Frontera Grill
26 Cafe 28
   Salpicón
25 Mixteco Grill

## MIDDLE EASTERN

24 Pita Inn
23 Turquoise
20 A La Turka
18 Andies
   Aladdin's Eatery

## PIZZA

24 Lou Malnati's
23 Aurelio's
   Piece
   Chicago Pizza/Oven
   Spacca Napoli

## SEAFOOD

27 L2O
   Oceanique
   Spring
26 Joe's Sea/Steak
24 Catch 35

## SMALL PLATES

26 avec
   Green Zebra
25 BOKA
24 Browntrout
21 Quartino

## SPANISH/TAPAS

26 Mercat
24 Emilio's Tapas
   La Tasca
   Tapas Gitana
23 Mesón Sabika

## STEAKHOUSES

26 Joe's Sea/Steak
   Morton's
   Gibsons
25 Capital Grille
   Rosebud Prime/Steak

## THAI

28 Arun's
23 Thai Pastry
22 Butterfly
20 Star of Siam

## VEGETARIAN

26 Green Zebra
23 Ethiopian Diamond
22 Hema's Kitchen
   Chicago Diner
21 Blind Faith

# BY SPECIAL FEATURE

## BREAKFAST

26 Lula Cafe
25 M. Henry
24 Hot Chocolate
   Bongo Room
23 Ina's

## BRUNCH

27 Frontera Grill
26 Cafe 28
   Salpicón
25 Yoshi's Café
   North Pond

## BUSINESS DINING

29 Les Nomades
   Alinea
28 Topolobampo
   Michael
27 L2O

## CHILD-FRIENDLY

27 Hot Doug's
26 Smoque BBQ
24 Lou Malnati's
   Lawry's
   Original/Walker Pancake

## HOTEL DINING

27 L2O (Belden-Stratford Hotel)
   NoMI (Park Hyatt Chicago)
   Seasons (Four Seasons Hotel)
26 Avenues (Peninsula Hotel)
   Mercat (Blackstone Hotel)

## LATE DINING

26 avec
   Kuma's Corner
   Gibsons
24 Coast Sushi/South Coast
   Agami

## MEET FOR A DRINK

27 mk
   Frontera Grill
   NoMI
26 Joe's Sea/Steak
   one sixtyblue

## NEWCOMERS

25 XOCO
24 Cibo Matto
   Browntrout
23 Belly Shack
   Nightwood

## PEOPLE-WATCHING

27 Blackbird
   Naha
   mk
   Spring
   NoMI

## WINNING WINE LISTS

29 Les Nomades
   Alinea
28 Arun's
   Topolobampo
   Michael

## WORTH A TRIP

28 Michael
   Winnetka
27 Oceanique
   Evanston
   Carlos'
   Highland Park
   Vie
   Western Springs
25 Barrington Country
   Barrington

# BY LOCATION

## ANDERSONVILLE/ EDGEWATER

25 M. Henry
Anteprima
23 Ethiopian Diamond
Hopleaf
Jin Ju

## BUCKTOWN

26 Takashi
25 mado
24 Coast Sushi
Hot Chocolate
Le Bouchon

## CHINATOWN

24 Lao
23 Phoenix
Emperor's Choice
Al's #1 Beef
21 Three Happiness

## GOLD COAST

27 NoMI
Spiaggia
Seasons
26 Morton's
Gibsons

## GREEKTOWN

23 Giordano's
22 Artopolis
21 Parthenon
Santorini
Roditys

## LAKEVIEW

26 Mia Francesca
Yoshi's Café
Mixteco Grill
sola
24 Tango Sur

## LINCOLN PARK

29 Alinea
27 L2O
Charlie Trotter's
Riccardo
25 BOKA

## LINCOLN SQUARE/ UPTOWN

25 Bistro Campagne
24 Agami

## LITTLE ITALY

23 Pizza D.O.C.
Marigold
Tank Sushi

24 Chez Joël
23 Al's #1 Beef
22 Francesca's
Rosebud
Tuscany

## LOOP

27 Everest
26 Morton's
25 Rosebud Prime/Steak
24 Catch 35
Palm

## RIVER NORTH

28 Topolobampo
27 Naha
Frontera Grill
26 Joe's Sea/Steak
Avenues

## STREETERVILLE

29 Les Nomades
28 Tru
25 Capital Grille
Rosebud Prime/Steak
Emilio's Tapas

## SUBURBS

28 Michael
Tallgrass
27 Oceanique
Carlos'
Vie

## WEST LOOP

27 Blackbird
sushi wabi
Moto
26 avec
one sixtyblue

## WICKER PARK

29 Schwa
27 Spring
25 Mirai Sushi
24 Smoke Daddy
Bongo Room

# Top Decor

| 28 | NoMI | | Lovells/Lake Forest |
|----|------|---|---------------------|
| | L2O | | Vie |
| | Shanghai Terrace | | 33 Club |
| 27 | Avenues | | Pump Room |
| | Alinea | | Eve |
| | Sixteen | | N9ne Steak |
| | Les Nomades | | Café/Architectes |
| | Tru | 24 | Mercat |
| | Everest | | Il Mulino |
| | Spiaggia | | Naha |
| 26 | Signature Room | | Sunda |
| | North Pond | | Alhambra Palace |
| | Cibo Matto | | SushiSamba rio* |
| | Japonais | | Zealous* |
| | RL | | Topolobampo |
| | Carlos' | | Atwood Cafe |
| 25 | Carnivale | | Marché |
| | Seasons | | one sixtyblue |
| | Charlie Trotter's | | Capital Grille |
| | Le Colonial | | ZED 451 |

## OUTDOORS

| 28 | NoMI | | Bistro Campagne |
|----|------|----|-----------------|
| | Shanghai Terrace | 21 | Park Grill |
| 26 | Japonais | 20 | Fulton's |
| 23 | Piccolo Sogno | | Mia Francesca |
| 22 | Smith & Wollensky | 19 | Athena |

## ROMANCE

| 27 | Les Nomades | | Eve |
|----|-------------|----|-----|
| | Everest | 24 | Il Mulino |
| 26 | Cibo Matto | | Sunda |
| | Japonais | 20 | Geja's Café |
| 25 | Le Colonial | 18 | Café Absinthe |

## ROOMS

| 27 | Alinea | | mk |
|----|--------|----|-----|
| | Everest | 22 | Keefer's |
| 24 | Mercat | | Brasserie Jo |
| | Naha | 21 | Gioco |
| | one sixtyblue | | Gibsons |

## VIEWS

| 28 | NoMI | 26 | Signature Room |
|----|------|----|----------------|
| | Shanghai Terrace | | North Pond |
| 27 | Sixteen | 22 | Smith & Wollensky |
| | Everest | | Riva |
| | Spiaggia | 21 | Park Grill |

# Top Service

# Best Buys

In order of Bang for the Buck rating.

1. Superdawg
2. Hot Doug's
3. Margie's Candies
4. Potbelly Sandwich
5. Wiener's Circle
6. 90 Miles
7. Al's #1 Beef
8. Mr. Beef
9. Hannah's Bretzel
10. Pita Inn
11. Five Guys
12. Gold Coast Dogs
13. Epic Burger
14. Belly Shack
15. Yolk
16. Billy Goat Tavern
17. Julius Meinl
18. Aurelio's
19. Lou Mitchell's
20. Original/Walker Pancake
21. Art of Pizza
22. Breakfast Club
23. M. Henry
24. Penny's Noodle
25. Pompei Bakery
26. Ann Sather
27. Artopolis
28. Toast
29. Bongo Room
30. XOCO
31. Nookies
32. Milk & Honey
33. Irazu
34. Hamburger Mary's
35. Counter
36. Kuma's Corner
37. Kitsch'n/K-Cafe
38. Aladdin's Eatery
39. DMK Burger Bar
40. Piece

## OTHER GOOD VALUES

Andies
Army & Lou's
Art of Pizza
Bagel
Birchwood Kitchen
Chicago Diner
Chicago Pizza/Oven
Chickpea
Crêpe Crave
Depot
Edzo's
fRedhots
Hot Woks
Icosium
Joy Yee
Kroll's
Las Tablas
Leo's Coney Island
Lou Malnati's
Maiz

Nosh
Old Oak Tap
Orange
Over Easy
Pasta Palazzo
Perry's Deli
Phò Xe Tång
Pomegranate
Reza's
Roti
Russell's BBQ
Smoque BBQ
Taco Fuego
Tango Sur
Thai Classic
Tre Kronor
Tweet
Victory's Banner
Vito & Nick's
Wishbone

Menus, photos, voting and more – free at ZAGAT.com

# CHICAGO
# RESTAURANT
# DIRECTORY

| | FOOD | DECOR | SERVICE | COST |
|---|---|---|---|---|

### Abigail's ☒Ⓜ *American*     24 | 20 | 19 | $40

**Highland Park** | 493 Roger Williams Ave. (St. Johns Ave.) | 847-849-1009 | www.abigails493.com

"Surprisingly fresh and interesting" fare displaying "some actual risks being taken" lures North Suburbanites to this "reasonably priced" seasonal New American "hot spot" in Highland Park; the "small space" and "no-reservations policy" result in "crowds" (summer sidewalk tables help) and some say the "terrible acoustics" make it "too noisy to digest" – but friends note "they're working on it."

### 🆕 Accanto *Italian*     - | - | - | E

**Logan Square** | 2171 N. Milwaukee Ave. (Talman Ave.) | 773-227-2727 | www.accanto-chicago.com

Respected Milan-born chef Domenico Acampora oversees the contemporary, fusion-style Italian menu at this destination-dining (read: expensive) arrival in Logan Square; the modern, intimate milieu is done up in sophisticated neutral tones, and also features leather seating, rustic wood beams and stainless dome light fixtures.

### Adelle's Ⓜ *American*     25 | 23 | 25 | $42

**Wheaton** | 1060 College Ave. (bet. President St. & Stoddard Ave.) | 630-784-8015 | www.adelles.com

"Fresh", "consistent", "well-prepared" New American "comfort food with character" woos West Suburbanites to this "quaint" Wheaton "getaway" that's "worth seeking out" "for a special night" ("you'd go twice a week if it weren't as pricey"); additional assets include a "wonderfully accommodating staff" and a "pleasant" ambiance with a gas fireplace when it's cold and "gorgeous outside terrace" "when it's warm"; N.B. there's live jazz on Thursdays.

### Adobo Grill *Mexican*     21 | 19 | 20 | $32

**Old Town** | 1610 N. Wells St. (North Ave.) | 312-266-7999
**Wicker Park** | 2005 W. Division St. (Damen Ave.) | 773-252-9990
www.adobogrill.com

"Colorful surroundings" add to the "festive atmosphere" at this duo that amigos call a "solid choice for upper-scale Mexican" fare with "occasional flashes of wonderful" ("tableside guacamole" and "premium tequila cocktails" are "highlights"); while party-poopers snipe they're "living on reputation", "hand-shaken margaritas" and "easy-to-swallow prices" "are worth the negatives"; P.S. Old Town is "ideally close to Second City", and both locations offer seasonal outdoor dining.

### Agami ◖ *Japanese*     24 | 23 | 21 | $43

**Uptown** | 4712 N. Broadway St. (Leland Ave.) | 773-506-1845 | www.agamisushi.com

"Innovative rolls" are an "unexpected" find in the "restaurant-barren" Uptown location of this "spacious" Japanese "lifesaver" that also pours an "exciting sake" selection amid its "entertaining" "underwater fantasy decor"; while service can be "a bit uneven", it's still "perfect for dinner before a concert at the Green Mill or Riviera."

|  | FOOD | DECOR | SERVICE | COST |
|---|---|---|---|---|

### Ai Sushi Lounge ◑ *Japanese*  | 24 | 21 | 20 | $43 |

**River North** | 358 W. Ontario St. (Orleans St.) | 312-335-9888 |
www.aichicago.us

"Creative sushi" with "beautiful presentations" (plus a "small number
of exciting entrees") pair with an "extensive selection of sakes" at
this "romantic" River North Japanese from the owners of Ringo and
Tsuki; the "knowledgeable" staff and "modern, trendy" decor are
pluses – and an improved Food score indicates it "just keeps getting
better" – so that even if it's a "little pricey", most "would return,
especially for drinks in the back lounge" or the "Sunday all-you-
can-eat" special.

### aja *Asian*  | – | 22 | 20 | M |

**River North** | Dana Hotel & Spa | 660 N. State St. (Erie St.) |
312-202-6050 | www.danahotelandspa.com

Changing to a "less-expensive format", the Dana Hotel's former
pricey steakhouse is now this midpriced Asian small plates and
sushi specialist offering "unique flavor combinations" plus weekend
brunch, sakes by the glass and signature cocktails; the bar area's
new seating includes a communal table, otherwise the "fabulous
decor" remains the same – soaring walls of windows, a steel mesh
scrim and silk wall treatments plus two gas fireplaces, an outdoor
patio and a rooftop lounge – all perfect for "people-watching."

### Akai Hana *Japanese*  | 21 | 14 | 17 | $28 |

**Wilmette** | 3223 W. Lake Ave. (Skokie Rd.) | 847-251-0384 |
www.akaihanasushi.com

"Hidden in a Wilmette strip mall", this "solid" North Suburban
"player" serves "straightforward sushi" and Japanese "cooked
dishes" ("don't look for gourmet touches, but everything is fresh
and tasty") in a "spartan", "kid-friendly" "barn" (the "decor needs
some work"); tipsters deem it "dependable" (though not quite the
"deal it was"), and though service can be "perfunctory", it's so "popular" there's sometimes a "wait on weekend nights."

### Aladdin's Eatery *Mideastern*  | 18 | 13 | 18 | $17 |

**Lincoln Park** | 614 W. Diversey Pkwy. (Clark St.) | 773-327-6300 |
www.aladdinseatery.com

Along with a "large variety" of "fresh, reliable Middle Eastern fare"
including vegetarian dishes, this "casual", "reasonably priced"
Lincoln Park outpost of a "popular chain" also offers "fast and efficient" service (plus beer and wine) beneath its pita bread–shaped
fixtures; even detractors dubbing it merely "decent" deem it "fine to
grab a bite before or after a movie" and "for lunch or takeout."

### A La Turka *Turkish*  | 20 | 18 | 20 | $27 |

**Lakeview** | 3134 N. Lincoln Ave. (bet. Barry & Belmont Aves.) |
773-935-6101 | www.alaturkachicago.com

Enthusiasts who "have enjoyed" this midpriced Lakeview Turkish
"place to eat and be entertained" "for years" are "sure to go" Friday or
Saturday "when the belly dancers are there"; the "whimsical", "romantic setting" works "best for a group" or as a "date spot", and

though some call it "predictable", it's "charming in its own way";
N.B. there's a hookah lounge upstairs.

### NEW Aldino's *Italian* — | — | — | M

**Little Italy** | 626 S. Racine Ave. (Harrison St.) | 312-226-9300 |
www.aldinoschicago.com

Chef Dean Zanella (most recently of 312 Chicago) and Francesca's
founder Scott Harris collaborated on this spiffy Little Italy storefront
spot serving affordable, fresh multiregional Italian comfort food
made with locally sourced ingredients; the warmly lit main room is
all wood-on-wood with earth tones, a tin ceiling and exposed wine
storage, and there's also an intimate bar area and a market for
takeout and specialty foods.

### Alhambra Palace Restaurant *Mideastern* 16 | 24 | 16 | $34

**West Loop** | 1240 W. Randolph St. (bet. Elizabeth St. & Racine Ave.) |
312-666-9555 | www.alhambrapalacerestaurant.com

It's "welcome to the Arabian Nights" for adventurers "entertained"
by the Middle Eastern "dinner and a show" at this "over-the-top"
West Looper with "fanciful, opulent decor", a "huge menu and portions", and a "belly-dancing spectacle" on weekends; faulters find
"better and cheaper" chow elsewhere, and gripe that they "cannot
service the large space" ("lots of drinks" help); P.S. "diners are in-
vited to join in the belly dancing" though "some should decline."

### Z Alinea M *American* 29 | 27 | 28 | $199

**Lincoln Park** | 1723 N. Halsted St. (bet. North Ave. & Willow St.) |
312-867-0110 | www.alinearestaurant.com

"World-famous for its vision and creativity", "genius" Grant Achatz's
"progressive" New American "gastronirvana" provides "amazing"
"avant-garde food" in a "labor-intensive" multicourse "wild ride" that
"incorporates all the senses" and includes cleverly "engineered"
serving pieces ("acupuncture needles", "trapezes", "pillows",
"branches", "rubber tablecloths"); "*Get Smart* automatic doors"
give way to the "luxurious, minimalistic" Lincoln Park setting where
a "professional" staff (rated No. 1 for Service) provides "personal"
attention "with some humor", completing an "unforgettable",
"shock-and-awe experience" – albeit a "fiscally challenging" one
that's "not for the faint of culinary heart"; P.S. "if you can afford it",
choose the "incredible wine pairings."

### Al Primo Canto M *Brazilian/Italian* 24 | 23 | 25 | $40

**NEW River North** | 749 N. Clark St. (bet. Chicago Ave. & Superior St.) |
312-280-9090 🖼

**Northwest Side** | 5414 W. Devon Ave. (Central Ave.) | 773-631-0100
www.alprimocanto.com

"Brazilian meets Italian in an unlikely setting" on the Northwest Side at
this "friendly", "family-run" spot (with a River North sibling) where
specialties such as rotisserie chicken are a "deal"; "old-world service"
operates under a domed wooden ceiling in a "huge room" that's "a
bit too noisy at times" – especially when the "live music" kicks up on
Fridays and Saturdays; N.B. an à la carte menu has been added.

| | FOOD | DECOR | SERVICE | COST |
|---|---|---|---|---|

## ☒ Al's #1 Italian Beef  *Sandwiches* — 23 | 9 | 17 | $11

**River North** | 169 W. Ontario St. (Wells St.) | 312-943-3222 ◗
**Lincoln Park** | 5636 W. Fullerton Ave. (Parkside Ave.) | 773-237-2100
**Chinatown** | 5441 S. Wentworth Ave. (Garfield Blvd.) | 773-373-4700 ◗
**Little Italy** | 1079 W. Taylor St. (Aberdeen St.) | 312-226-4017 ☒↲
**Evanston** | 622 Davis St. (Chicago Ave.) | 847-424-9704
**Niles** | 5948 W. Touhy Ave. (Lehigh Ave.) | 847-647-1577
**Park Ridge** | 33 S. Northwest Hwy. (bet. Euclid & Prospect Aves.) |
847-318-7700
**Chicago Heights** | 551 W. 14th St. (Division St.) | 708-748-2333
**Tinley Park** | 7132 183rd St. (Harlem Ave.) | 708-444-2333
**Downers Grove** | 992 Warren Ave. (Highland Ave.) | 630-964-3222 ◗
www.alsbeef.com
Additional locations throughout the Chicago area

"Get it dipped with hot peppers, eat, repeat" instruct devotees of the Windy City's "champ of beef on a bun", a "cheap and fast" chain also prized for "sausage sandwiches", "fabulous" "hand-cut french fries" and "classic Chicago dogs"; though locations vary from the "bare-bones" Little Italy "original" ("still the best, still the ugliest"), overall they leave chompers cheering for their "messy, sloppy, fabulous" eats ("Philly can keep its cheesesteak") and advising "if you want decor, take it home with you."

## Amber Cafe ☒Ⓜ  *American* — 22 | 20 | 20 | $41

**Westmont** | 13 N. Cass Ave. (Burlington Ave.) | 630-515-8080 |
www.ambercafe.net

Westmont's "snazzy" "local spot for fish" presents "an interesting twist on New American" while offering "quality" fare and service in a woody, brick-walled setting; though "often crowded" and "perhaps a bit overpriced", it's a "reasonable choice" that devotees dub "among the best" in the area; P.S. the "outside is hopping in the summertime" for cocktails and "alfresco dining."

## American Girl Place Cafe  *American* — 16 | 22 | 21 | $29

**Streeterville** | American Girl Place, Water Tower Place Mall |
835 N. Michigan Ave. (bet. Chestnut & Pearson Sts.) |
312-943-9400 | www.americangirlplace.com

"Take your little girl and her favorite doll" to Streeterville's "charming" "fairyland" where each "gets their own place setting" for a "tea" of "dainty sweets and sandwiches"; service is "efficient", but some "squealing" and merely "decent" fare are to be expected, and if it's a bit "pricey", just "watch the delight in the kids' eyes"; P.S. the new location in Water Tower Place "is not as quaint as the former."

## Amitabul Ⓜ  *Korean* — 21 | 11 | 19 | $21

**Northwest Side** | 6207 N. Milwaukee Ave. (Huntington St.) |
773-774-0276

"Completely unique" "vegan fusion" fare is dished out at this Northwest Side Korean that "operates under a spiritual [Buddhist] theme" while delivering "mammoth portions" of "fresh", affordable organic eats with "fast service"; some snipe the "extremely casual" space is "quite uninviting", and a few earnest omnivores who "want to like it" "find it wanting", but all agree it's a "must try for vegetarians"; N.B. no alcohol is served but BYO is welcome.

### Andalous *Moroccan*

22 | 17 | 20 | $23

**Lakeview** | 3307 N. Clark St. (Aldine Ave.) | 773-281-6885 | www.andalous.com

"Terrific" tagines meet up with a smattering of Spanish and Middle Eastern–accented specialties at this Lakeview Moroccan, also beloved for its wallet-friendly BYO policy; fans find it a refreshing "change from the ordinary", with "welcoming", if occasionally "slow", service, and a lively, artifact-decked interior completing the package.

### Andies *Mediterranean/Mideastern*

18 | 15 | 18 | $22

**Andersonville** | 5253 N. Clark St. (Berwyn Ave.) | 773-784-8616
**Ravenswood** | 1467 W. Montrose Ave. (Greenview Ave.) | 773-348-0654
www.andiesres.com

"Reliable" is the word on these "friendly" "neighborhood" twins in Andersonville and Ravenswood turning out "tasty" Middle Eastern and Mediterranean eats, with plenty of vegetarian options; though some find the fare "nothing to write home about", both earn kudos for their "cheap" tabs and "quick" service, as well as a "casual" atmosphere kicked up by patio seating that's especially pleasant in "summer."

### Angelina Ristorante *Italian*

21 | 19 | 21 | $30

**Lakeview** | 3561 N. Broadway St (Addison St.) | 773-935-5933 | www.angelinaristorante.com

A "charming" stop on the Lakeview dining circuit, this longtime "favorite" "holds up well" what with its "authentic" Southern Italian cuisine served in a "quaint" candlelit interior; "bargain prices" sweeten the deal, as do weeknight specials like Tuesday's prix fixe and Wednesday's locals' discount.

### NEW Angin Mamiri Ⓜ *Indonesian*

- | - | - | I

**West Rogers Park** | 2739 W. Touhy Ave. (bet. California & Washtenaw Aves.) | 773-262-6646 | www.anginmamirichicago.com

"If you're jonesing for Jakarta", this inexpensive West Rogers Park newcomer "fills the bill" with "authentic" Indonesian delicacies like sates, curries and gado gado; the pale-green space doesn't offer much in the way of atmosphere, so "bring some friends" to liven things up, and bring a bottle too, as it's BYO.

### Anna Maria Pasteria *Italian*

24 | 17 | 22 | $31

**Ravenswood** | 4400 N. Clark St. (Montrose Ave.) | 773-506-2662 | www.annamariapasteria.com

"Just what you want" in a "neighborhood" restaurant, this Ravenswood entry charms guests with "excellent" takes on "traditional" Italian recipes; the "warm" atmosphere is helped along by modest tabs, Tuscan-style furnishings and a "friendly" staff that "makes you feel at home."

### Ann Sather *American/Swedish*

21 | 15 | 20 | $18

**Andersonville** | 5207 N. Clark St. (Foster Ave.) | 773-271-6677
**Lakeview** | 909 W. Belmont Ave. (Clark St.) | 773-348-2378

*(continued)*

### Ann Sather Café *American/Swedish*

**Lakeview** | 3411 N. Broadway St. (Roscoe St.) | 773-305-0024
**Lakeview** | 3410 N. Southport Ave. (Roscoe St.) | 773-404-4475
www.annsather.com

A Chicago brunchtime "icon", this "bustling" daytime chainlet is famed for its "addictive", "ooey gooey" cinnamon buns that kick off "huge" helpings of "fantastically caloric" Swedish-American "comfort food"; even if some score the sustenance "pedestrian", it remains an area "standby", with "prompt" service and "reasonable" tabs making the perpetual "waits" on weekends easier to stomach.

### Anteprima *Italian*  25 | 19 | 22 | $38

**Andersonville** | 5316 N. Clark St. (bet. Berwyn & Summerdale Aves.) | 773-506-9990 | www.anteprimachicago.net

"Inspired" Italian cooking with a "farm-to-table" bent awaits at this "destination"-worthy Andersonville "treasure", also cherished for its "outstanding", "affordable" stash of wines; "crowds" are a regular occurrence, but a "knowledgeable" staff keeps the mood "homey" no matter how "cramped" and "noisy" it gets; P.S. the Sunday–Thursday prix fixe "is one of the best deals in Chicago" ($29 for three courses).

### Antica Pizzeria *Italian/Pizza*  23 | 15 | 22 | $25

**Andersonville** | 5663 N. Clark St. (Hollywood Ave.) | 773-944-1492

"Delicious", "thin-crust" "Neapolitan-style" pizzas transport you right "back to Italy" at this Andersonville BYO also pumping out "well-made" pastas, salads and such at "great-value" tabs; it's not fancy, but the "small", rustic space is made more "cozy" by a wood-burning oven and an affable owner chock-full of "old-world charm."

### Antico Posto *Italian*  22 | 20 | 21 | $30

**Oak Brook** | Oakbrook Center Mall | 118 Oakbrook Ctr. (Rte. 83) | 630-586-9200 | www.leye.com

Weary shoppers rely on this "suburban" Italian outpost in the Oakbrook Center, a "relaxing find" for an "eclectic" array of well-priced wines, pastas and other "consistently good" nibbles capped by housemade gelato; if "nothing's ever bad", it's "not ever outstanding" either, though it works for a "reliable" bite at the mall.

### Aria *Asian*  24 | 23 | 23 | $53

**Loop** | Fairmont Chicago Hotel | 200 N. Columbus Dr. (bet. Randolph St. & Wacker Dr.) | 312-444-9494 | www.ariachicago.com

"They strive for excellence and it shows" at this "upscale" enclave "hidden inside" the Loop's Fairmont Hotel and turning out "excellent", "innovative" Asian cuisine with a focus on fine sushi; the "sophisticated" surroundings make it a natural for "business lunches", and the "pricey" tabs mean it's "best on an expense account."

### Army & Lou's *Southern*  26 | 16 | 23 | $24

**Far South Side** | 422 E. 75th St. (Martin Luther King Dr.) | 773-483-3100 | www.armyandlous.com

"The premier soul food eatery in the city", this "well-established" (since 1945) Far "South Side treasure" is the "real deal" assures an army of admirers advocating "ribs that melt off their bones", "the best fried chicken", "authentic peach cobbler" and a "Southern brunch chow down"; "down-home, friendly service" is a plus and there's live jazz on Fridays, so if the "decor hasn't been updated in years" surveyors say so what – "neither have the prices"; P.S. "no liquor" but BYO is fine.

### Art of Pizza, The  *Pizza*
22 | 7 | 15 | $13

**Lakeview** | 3033 N. Ashland Ave. (Nelson St.) | 773-327-5600
Patrons "see and pick" from "mouthwatering" "slices or full pizzas" ("deep dish, thin-crust or in-between") at this "reasonably priced", "laid-back" Lakeview "self-serve", where supporters swear "some of the best" pie is served; those deeming the "zero ambiance" "painful" simply "fly in and fly out" – while a few holdouts wonder "what all the fuss is about."

### Artopolis Bakery, Cafe & Agora ● *Greek/Mediterranean*
22 | 20 | 17 | $19

**Greektown** | 306 S. Halsted St. (Jackson Blvd.) | 312-559-9000 | www.artopolischicago.com
Regulars "relax" over "wonderful" breads, "satisfying" salads, sandwiches and "fresh-baked" pastries at this "casual" Greektown purveyor of "affordable" Hellenic-Med eats; occasionally "haphazard" service is a drawback, but it's open into the wee hours, making it well-suited for a "late-night" bite.

### Z Arun's ⓜ *Thai*
28 | 23 | 27 | $96

**Northwest Side** | 4156 N. Kedzie Ave. (bet. Irving Park Rd. & Montrose Ave.) | 773-539-1909 | www.arunsthai.com
"Who says Thai can't be upscale?" ask admirers of Arun Sampanthavivat's "unforgettable" Northwest Side jewel where a "top-notch" staff rolls out "exquisite" prix fixe meals composed of "unusual", "delicious little dishes" that "just keep on coming"; it's set in "simple" digs, although more than a few "wish they'd upgrade the space" to match the "splurge"-worthy prices.

### Z a tavola ⊠ *Italian*
26 | 20 | 25 | $44

**Ukrainian Village** | 2148 W. Chicago Ave. (bet. Hoyne Ave. & Leavitt St.) | 773-276-7567 | www.atavolachicago.com
It's "like eating at someone's home" at this "wonderfully cozy" Ukrainian Village "gem" turning out "fabulous" Northern Italian dishes including some "amazing" gnocchi ("like eating a cloud"); "reasonable" prices and "attentive" service suit the overall "low-key" vibe, and there's also a "lovely" patio in summer.

### Athena ● *Greek*
21 | 19 | 20 | $32

**Greektown** | 212 S. Halsted St. (Adams St.) | 312-655-0000 | www.athenarestaurantchicago.com
Amid a gaggle of Greektown eateries, this "family-owned" Hellenic stands out for its "authentic" eats served on a "lush", landscaped patio in summer; inside sports two fireplaces, lots of candles and a bustling bar so you can really "eat well" here for cheap any time of year.

## Atwater's American/French

20 | 22 | 21 | $44

**Geneva** | Herrington Inn | 15 S. River Ln. (State St.) | 630-208-7433 | www.herringtoninn.com

Guests laud this "romantic" respite in the Herrington Inn with a "cozy, old-fashioned" feel and linen-topped tables overlooking the Fox River; even if the tasty" New American–French menu is "not too adventurous" (and on the pricey side to boot), it offers loads of "choices" for diners, and service sometimes "shines" too.

## Atwood Cafe American

22 | 24 | 22 | $39

**Loop** | Hotel Burnham | 1 W. Washington St. (State St.) | 312-368-1900 | www.atwoodcafe.com

"Comforting" Traditional American fare including Sunday brunch (and holiday season tea service) befits the Loop's "beautifully re-stored" "historic" Hotel Burnham, where the "quirky", "whimsical decor" "feels old-Chicago and very now all at once"; "shoppers", "theater or CSO" patrons and "hotel guests" fill the "odd chairs" (which some find "uncomfortable") while dining on midpriced fare with service that's "gracious" but "inconsistent"; N.B. a recent chef change is not reflected in the Food score.

## Aurelio's Pizza Pizza

23 | 15 | 20 | $17

**Loop** | Holiday Inn | 506 W. Harrison St. (Canal St.) | 312-994-2000
**Addison** | Centennial Plaza | 1455 W. Lake St. (Lombard Rd.) | 630-889-9560
**Chicago Heights** | 1545 Western Ave. (15th St.) | 708-481-5040
**Homewood** | 18162 Harwood Ave. (183rd St.) | 708-798-8050
**South Holland** | 601 E. 170th St. (Park Ave.) | 708-333-0310
**Palos Heights** | 6543 W. 127th St. (Ridgeland Ave.) | 708-389-5170
**Tinley Park** | 15901 Oak Park Ave. (Rte. 6) | 708-429-4600
**Downers Grove** | 940 Warren Ave. (Highland Ave.) | 630-810-0078
**Naperville** | 931 W. 75th St. (Plainfield-Naperville Rd.) | 630-369-0077
**Oak Brook** | 100 E. Roosevelt Rd. (Summit Rd.) | 630-629-3200
www.aureliospizza.com
Additional locations throughout the Chicago area

"Real no-nonsense pizza" at these wallet-loving South Suburban "joints" is "a religion" to disciples who "remember" "growing up with" the "sweet and tangy sauce" of the "killer" "thin-crust, deep-dish and individual" pies; service is "friendly and efficient" and there's a "basic", "family-oriented" feel to some, but the Homewood "original" really "feels like home" to regulars who ask for their order "baked in the old oven" for optimal "crispness"; N.B. some of the franchised locations are pickup and delivery only.

## ☒ avec ● Mediterranean

26 | 21 | 23 | $44

**West Loop** | 615 W. Randolph St. (Jefferson St.) | 312-377-2002 | www.avecrestaurant.com

Blackbird's vino-focused "casual yet classy" next-door cafe is a West Loop "chef hangout" where surveyors say Koren Grieveson's "imaginative", "chef-driven" Mediterranean small plates and "gour-met charcuterie" features "flavor combinations that make you re-think life"; while some who "wish the prices were as minimal as the portions" "could do without cuddling up to a stranger" in the "uncomfortable", "communal" setting reminiscent of a "Swedish sauna", "extroverts" "squeeze in and have a ball" with "wonderful wine experiences" prompted by "savvy servers."

### ☑ Avenues ⊠Ⓜ *American*    26 | 27 | 27 | $102

**River North** | Peninsula Hotel | 108 E. Superior St. (bet. Michigan Ave. & Rush St.) | 312-573-6754 | www.peninsula.com

Curtis Duffy's "superb, creative" New American "cuisine with artful design and surprising flavor combinations" meets "sublime service" in the "beautifully serene atmosphere" of the Peninsula Hotel's "formal" dining room at this "understated, elegant" River North "special-occasion" place; an "excellent view" featuring the historic Water Tower and "impressive wine list" add to an "experience" that's "simply stunning" and "tremendously expensive"; N.B. jackets are suggested.

### Azucar ●Ⓜ *Spanish*    ▽ 22 | 18 | 20 | $42

**Logan Square** | 2647 N. Kedzie Ave. (Milwaukee Ave.) | 773-486-6464 | www.azucartapasrestaurant.com

Raters "run to this" "tiny" Logan Square "treasure" for "fresh, inventive and lovingly prepared" if slightly "pricey" Spanish tapas with "big flavor" and specialty drinks wielded by a "warm staff"; N.B. there's also late-night service (till 2 AM on weekends) and seasonal sidewalk seating.

### Bacchanalia ⍧ *Italian*    24 | 16 | 23 | $33

**Southwest Side** | 2413 S. Oakley Ave. (bet. 24th & 25th Sts.) | 773-254-6555 | www.bacchanaliainchicago.com

"True" "homestyle Italian" earns enthusiasts for this "old-school" Southwest Side "favorite" with a "menu selection from North to South" of "simple", "refreshing" fare; tables are "packed in tightly" under the big mural of Bacchus, but "fair prices" for generous portions and "warm welcomes" make fans "feel like family"; P.S. it's convenient "before or after White Sox games."

### Bacino's *Italian*    22 | 15 | 19 | $25

**Lincoln Park** | 2204 N. Lincoln Ave. (Webster Ave.) | 773-472-7400
**West Loop** | 118 S. Clinton St. (Adams St.) | 312-876-1188 ⓢ
www.bacinos.com

### Bella Bacino's *Italian*

**Loop** | 75 E. Wacker Dr. (Upper Michigan Ave.) | 312-263-2350
**La Grange** | 36 S. La Grange Rd. (Harris Ave.) | 708-352-8882 Ⓜ
www.bellabacinos.com

"Loyal"-ists "keep going back" to this "casual", "friendly" and affordable Italian quartet that's a "dependable" choice for "delicious deep-dish", thin-crust and "personal"-size pizzas; though some dub them "ordinary", most find them "perfect" "for large groups with children"; P.S. the Bellas "concentrate more on pasta and 'fancier' fare", with a "good wine selection for this sort of eatery."

### Bagel, The *Deli*    19 | 12 | 18 | $18

**Lakeview** | 3107 N. Broadway St. (Belmont Ave.) | 773-477-0300

*(continued)*

## Bagel, The

**Skokie** | Westfield Shoppingtown | 4999 Old Orchard Ctr. (Skokie Blvd.) | 847-677-0100
www.bagelrestaurant.com

Among "the few genuine delis left" in Chicago, these Skokie and Lakeview contenders "fill a need" "when you're hankering for a shmear" and other "old-time favorites" like "chopped liver, gefilte fish and chocolate phosphates" ("free pickles don't hurt either"); "witty servers", "matzo ball soup that heals all ills" and "comically large portions" for which the "price is right" find more fans than foes, so just "ignore" the "time-warp decor."

## NEW Bakin' & Eggs *American*   19 | 21 | 18 | $16

**Lakeview** | 3120 N. Lincoln Ave. (bet. Barry & Belmont Aves.) | 773-525-7005 | www.bakinandeggschicago.com

Lakeview's "upscale" American diner with "modernistic decor" featuring "bright turquoise walls" and reclaimed church pews projects a "lively", "youthful feel" and lives up to its name with "inventive", "well-flavored egg dishes" and a "bacon flight", plus a "bakery and espresso counter"; even those joking it "needs a few more minutes in the oven" acknowledge it has "a lot of potential"; N.B. it's BYO and closes at 4 PM daily with weekends offering brunch-only and lunch served weekdays.

## NEW Balsan *European*   - | - | - | E

**Gold Coast** | The Elysian | 11 E. Walton St. (bet. Rush & State Sts.) | 312-646-1400 | www.balsanrestaurant.com

"Upscale" yet "informal", this Modern European bistro in the Gold Coast's "stunning Elysian hotel" serves "pricey", "refined rustic" fare (including charcuterie, raw bar items and "tarte flambé almost too good to be true") with "sharp service" amid "chic decor" recalling 1920s Paris; surveyors suggest it's "way better than it needs to be", drawing a "hip and interesting crowd" while also offering a late-night menu and weekend brunch.

## Bandera *American*   22 | 20 | 20 | $35

**Streeterville** | 535 N. Michigan Ave., 2nd fl. (bet. Grand Ave. & Ohio St.) | 312-644-3524 | www.hillstone.com

Southwestern-style American "comfort food" with "just enough of a twist" meets "attentive service without the 'tude" at this Streeterville "oasis" that fans claim "sets the standard for chain" links; a "limited menu" that's "a little pricey" is trumped by "live nightly jazz" and "low lighting", creating a "cozy, warm atmosphere" and making it "so worth it"; P.S. "get there early for a window seat" "overlooking the Magnificent Mile."

## Bank Lane Bistro ⊠ *American*   23 | 21 | 22 | $45

**Lake Forest** | 670 N. Bank Ln. (bet. Deerpath Rd. & Market Sq.) | 847-234-8802 | www.banklanebistro.com

Boosters bank on a "well-prepared, thoughtful meal" of "ambitious" New American fare "that mostly meets its mark" and is served by a

| | FOOD | DECOR | SERVICE | COST |
|---|---|---|---|---|

"pleasant staff" at this North Suburban "quaint little getaway in Lake Forest" complete with a wood-burning oven for fresh bread; though foes find it "overpriced", friends advise "ask for a table on the balcony for a view" of the "historic market square."

### Bar Louie ● *Pub Food*    16 | 15 | 16 | $22

**River North** | 226 W. Chicago Ave. (Franklin St.) | 312-337-3313
**Wrigleyville** | 3545 N. Clark St. (Addison St.) | 773-296-2500
**Hyde Park** | 5500 S. Shore Dr. (55th St.) | 773-363-5300
**Printer's Row** | 47 W. Polk St. (Dearborn St.) | 312-347-0000
**Little Italy** | 1321 W. Taylor St. (bet. Ashland & Racine Aves.) | 312-633-9393
**West Loop** | 741 W. Randolph St. (Halsted St.) | 312-474-0700
**Evanston** | 1520 Sherman Ave. (Grove St.) | 847-733-8300
**Orland Park** | 14335 LaGrange Rd. (143rd St.) | 708-873-9999
**Naperville** | 22 E. Chicago Ave. (Washington St.) | 630-983-1600
**Oak Park** | 1122 Lake St. (Harlem Ave.) | 708-725-3300
www.restaurants-america.com
Additional locations throughout the Chicago area

"Decent" American "bar grub" "without a huge price tag" draws "friends" who "hang out" from lunch to "happy hour" to "late-night" for "people-watching" or "watching sports" at this chain that "always manages to net a good time"; the fare and "service is consistently average", and some who say there are "better local places" only "go for the drinks", which include "excellent" "monster martinis"; N.B. outdoor seating and entertainment vary by location.

### ☑ Barrington Country Bistro ☒ *French*    25 | 23 | 25 | $46

**Barrington** | Foundry Shopping Ctr. | 700 W. Northwest Hwy. (Hart Rd.) | 847-842-1300 | www.barringtoncountrybistro.com

"It's worth the drive to Barrington" for "French fare better than at pricier" places assure *amis* of this "surprise find" that rates as the "best bistro in the Chicago area"; a "lovely country setting" (despite being "in a shopping mall"), "gracious service" and seasonal "outdoor seating" all contribute to the feeling of "a little slice of France."

### Basil Leaf Café *Italian*    18 | 17 | 18 | $29

**Lincoln Park** | 2465 N. Clark St. (Fullerton Pkwy.) | 773-935-3388 | www.basilleaf.com

Lincoln Parkers satisfied by this "reliable", "standard neighborhood Italian" cite its "friendly staff", "unpretentious", "rustic-chic" "charm" and "European bistro feel"; less-smitten surveyors call the fare "unimaginative – although there is a lot of it" at "reasonable" prices.

### Bella Notte *Italian*    21 | 16 | 21 | $35

**West Loop** | 1374 W. Grand Ave. (Noble St.) | 312-733-5136 | www.bellanottechicago.com

"Be prepared to share or to have lots of leftovers", because the "solid", midpriced "traditional" Southern Italian dishes come in "enormous portions" at this "lively", "family-owned" West Looper that lures the faithful "off the beaten path" (especially "before United Center games"); the mahogany-accented setting is generally "relaxing" with "attentive service", just "don't bring a crowd on a Saturday night."

| | FOOD | DECOR | SERVICE | COST |
|---|---|---|---|---|

## NEW Belly Shack Ⓜ Asian

23 | 16 | 18 | $16

**Humboldt Park** | 1912 N. Western Ave. (Homer St.) | 773-252-1414 | www.bellyshack.com

The "Urban Belly gang" begat this "fast", "zingy" Asian with "Latin-fusion" touches that's "always interesting" ("where else can you get a bulgogi sandwich with an order of tostones") in a "casual, hip" Humboldt Park setting with "industrial decor" that's "gritty on purpose"; "low prices and BYO attract a young crowd" – as if "soft-serve ice cream" isn't "reason enough."

## Benihana  Japanese/Steak

18 | 18 | 20 | $36

**Wheeling** | 150 N. Milwaukee Ave. (Dundee Rd.) | 847-465-6021
**Schaumburg** | 1200 E. Higgins Rd. (bet. Meacham Rd. & National Pkwy.) | 847-995-8201
**Lombard** | 747 E. Butterfield Rd. (Meyers Rd.) | 630-571-4440
www.benihana.com

"Bring on the onion volcano" clamor customers who count on an "entertaining" "show" for "all ages" (even "jaded teenagers") at this Japanese steakhouse chain where tableside teppanyaki chefs perform "knife-juggling" feats while delivering "reliable" eats, including sushi and other "updated" items; critics call it "tired", "tacky" and "overpriced", but it works as a place to "take the kids and still have an edible meal."

## NEW Benny's Chop House  Italian/Steak

- | - | - | E

**River North** | 444 N. Wabash Ave. (Grand Avenue) | 312-626-2444 | www.bennyschophouse.com

From the owner of Volare, this upscale steakhouse in River North offers a pricey menu that includes prime beef, seafood and raw-bar selections, the requisite sides and a handful of pastas and lunch sandwiches; the white-tablecloth setting boasts rich, traditional decor with warm lighting, a champagne cart, live piano on weekends and a handsome bar issuing elaborate cocktails and an affordable wine list.

## Ben Pao  Chinese

21 | 22 | 21 | $34

**River North** | 52 W. Illinois St. (Dearborn St.) | 312-222-1888 | www.benpao.com

Lettuce Entertain You's "upscale" River Norther offers a "carefully thought-out and well-prepared" blend of China's regional cuisines plus "delicious cocktails" amid "soothing", "stylish" "decor that avoids the most hackneyed clichés" with its huge pillars and waterfalls; while some pout about "tourist-friendly" "Americanized" dishes that are "slightly overpriced", others say the "homemade ginger ale" alone is "worth the trip", adding "if you want authentic, go to Chinatown."

## Berghoff Restaurant/Cafe Ⓩ German

18 | 16 | 17 | $25

**Loop** | 17 W. Adams St. (bet. Dearborn & State Sts.) | 312-427-7399
## Berghoff Cafe  German
**O'Hare Area** | O'Hare Int'l Airport | Concourse C (I-190) | 773-601-9180
www.theberghoff.com

"You can still" "enjoy" a "truncated menu" of "standard German fare" "or choose from more modern (lighter) items" and a "great selection of suds" amid "old-world decor" at this redo of the former Loop "landmark" ("owned by an actual Berghoff"); "nostalgic" noshers "miss" the "grumpy Teutonic waiters" and contend that this "shadow" of the "historic site" is "banking on the reputation" (and "higher prices", though there is a weekday-only "lunch deal" in the downstairs Cafe); P.S. the O'Hare outpost is "better than most airport eateries, but not like the real one."

### Bice Ristorante  *Italian*   21  19  20  $50
**Streeterville** | 158 E. Ontario St. (bet. Michigan Ave. & St. Clair St.) | 312-664-1474 | www.bicegroup.com

"Quite upscale for a chain", this "trusted", "expensive" Streeterville Italian (founded in Milan) provides "delicious" food in "lovely" environs that host a "real business scene" at lunch and after work; though some doubters dub it "overrated" and a bit "snooty", most find it "excellent" all around.

### Big Bowl  *Asian*   20  18  20  $25
**River North** | 60 E. Ohio St. (Rush St.) | 312-951-1888
**Gold Coast** | 6 E. Cedar St. (State St.) | 312-640-8888
**Lincolnshire** | 215 Parkway Dr. (Milwaukee Ave.) | 847-808-8880
**Schaumburg** | 1950 E. Higgins Rd. (Rte. 53) | 847-517-8881
www.bigbowl.com

"Fast and easy" Asian fare with a "contemporary" spin includes "noodles your way" from the "compose-it-yourself stir-fry bar" and other "tasty", "solid performers" at this "busy" sustainable-leaning Lettuce Entertain You chainlet that "satisfies" "families", "groups" and "out-of-town guests"; the "theme" decor is "cute" and the outlay "can be cost-effective", plus even those who find it "unremarkable" admit "the housemade ginger ale rocks."

### Big Jones  *Southern*   21  19  21  $32
**Andersonville** | 5347 N. Clark St. (bet. Balmoral & Summerdale Aves.) | 773-275-5725 | www.bigjoneschicago.com

For an "upscale", "coastal" "Southern fix" built around "hospitality, flair" and a "seasonal" menu "without too much fried" fare, surveyors head to this midpriced Andersonviller that's "devoted to sustainable products" served in a room that's airy and contemporary; weekend brunch is "fabulous" (the weekday version offers a smaller menu), so even diners who "don't know if it's authentic" wash it all down with "syrupy sweet tea" and agree it's "never boring."

### NEW Big Star  ●♥ *Mexican*   23  17  17  $26
**Wicker Park** | 1531 N. Damen Ave. (bet. Pierce & Wicker Park Aves.) | 773-235-4039

"Quality" tacos plus "tequila and whiskey" have surveyors asking "where do I sign up" for this cash-only, budget-loving Wicker Park Mexican from Paul Kahan (Blackbird, The Publican) that's "more of a bar" with "outstanding" fare backing up "unique cocktails" and "minimalist decor"; it's "consistently packed" and "noisy" (the seasonal patio should help), but provides some of the "best people-watching" around; P.S. there's a "take-out window" too.

| | FOOD | DECOR | SERVICE | COST |
|---|---|---|---|---|

### Bijan's Bistro ◐ *American*  | 19 | 17 | 19 | $31 |

**River North** | 663 N. State St. (Erie St.) | 312-202-1904 |
www.bijansbistro.com

"In a town that closes up a bit too early", this midpriced River North "neighborhood hangout" "mix of bistro and sports bar" is "almost always open" serving New American fare that's "a smidgen above bar food" (though most takers are "too tired to care what they're eating at 3 AM"); there's also "super-late – or is it early" – "people-watching" and if you're up, lunch and weekend brunch.

### Billy Goat Tavern *American*  | 17 | 12 | 15 | $12 |

**Loop** | 309 W. Washington St. (Franklin St.) | 312-899-1873 🖼🖼
**Loop** | 330 S. Wells St. (Van Buren St.) | 312-554-0297 🖼
**River North** | Merchandise Mart | 222 Merchandise Mart (bet. Orleans & Wells Sts.) | 312-464-1045
**River North** | 430 N. Lower Michigan Ave. (bet. Hubbard & Illinois Sts.) | 312-222-1525 ◐🖼
**Streeterville** | Navy Pier | 700 E. Grand Ave. (Lake Shore Dr.) | 312-670-8789
**O'Hare Area** | O'Hare Field Terminal 1 | Concourse C (I-190) | 773-462-9368
**West Loop** | 1535 W. Madison St. (Ogden Ave.) | 312-733-9132 🖼
www.billygoattavern.com

"Characters abound" at these "quintessential Chicago" "greasy spoons" "famous" for their *SNL* legacy", "cheap" "hangover" grub, "verbal abuse" and an "owner who perpetrated the 'curse of the goat' on the Cubs"; the newer locations made to "look like old-school neighborhood dives" don't compare to the "delightful" 1934 "dungeon" "under the sidewalk" in River North, and butt-inskis bleat that there's "more bun" than beef on this "cheezborger."

### Bin 36 *American*  | 21 | 20 | 21 | $40 |

**River North** | 339 N. Dearborn St. (Kinzie St.) | 312-755-9463 |
www.bin36.com

### Bin Wine Café *American*

**Wicker Park** | 1559 N. Milwaukee Ave. (Damen Ave.) | 773-486-2233 |
www.binwinecafe.com

Champions of this River North American/wine shop with a Wicker Park sibling cite the "chic" confines "convenient for breakfast, lunch, drinks and dinner" plus "fabulous flights" of vino and "sublime" choices for the "cheese obsessed", all at "fair prices" – though sour grapes include "excessive noise" and service that veers from "knowledgeable" to "mixed bag"; the more casual cafe serves as a "pleasant" "date spot or after-work hangout", while the original also offers classes for budding oenophiles and fromage fiends.

### Birchwood Kitchen 🅼 *Sandwiches*  | 23 | 16 | 19 | $16 |

**Bucktown** | 2211 W. North Ave. (bet. Bell Ave. & Leavitt St.) |
773-276-2100 | www.birchwoodkitchen.com

They "take pride in what they do" at this "welcoming", "bright and airy" counter-service Bucktown BYO offering "truly unique sand-wiches" on the "limited menu" of "comfy meals" (including weekend brunch), all "lovingly prepared" from "locally sourced ingredients"; add "accommodating" service and "reasonable prices" and wags "wish they would open a place in my kitchen"; P.S. it "gets crowded", but there's a "lovely courtyard" patio in warm weather.

### NEW Bistro Bordeaux M *French*                                 - | - | - | E

**Evanston** | 618 Church St. (Chicago Ave.) | 847-424-1483 | www.lebistrobordeaux.com

"Interesting" "classic bistro dishes" delivered by a "knowledgeable" staff under the "watchful eye of an enthusiastic owner" position this newcomer as a "keeper" on the "Evanston dining scene"; the "warm, intimate space" features burgundy velvet curtains, leather banquettes and vintage posters, and additional assets include Sunday brunch and sidewalk seating.

### Z Bistro Campagne *French*                                 25 | 22 | 23 | $42

**Lincoln Square** | 4518 N. Lincoln Ave. (bet. Sunnyside & Wilson Aves.) | 773-271-6100 | www.bistrocampagne.com

You can go "light and subtle" or "decadent" at Lincoln's Square's "charming little bistro" where chef-owner Michael Altenberg's "locally grown" approach results in "good value" for "high-quality" French fare with "seasonal specials" that are especially "lovely"; an "outstanding beer menu", sustainable-minded wine list and "personable" staff add to the allure, and while some call the "warm" quarters "intimate" and others say "crowded", all agree the "garden" is "magical."

### Bistro 110 *French*                                 21 | 20 | 21 | $42

**Gold Coast** | 110 E. Pearson St. (bet. Michigan Ave. & Rush St.) | 312-266-3110 | www.bistro110restaurant.com

"After two decades", this French "standby" still delivers "delicious" "everyday" "bistro fare" to patrons who "love the roasted garlic with crusty bread", "relaxing" Sunday "jazz brunch", "wonderful bar" and "Magnificent Mile milieu"; if the resistance reckons it's "tired, touristy" and "a bit pricey", others find the tabs "reasonable", service "competent" and note "in summer, you can sit outside and watch the beautiful people walk by."

### Bistrot Margot *French*                                 20 | 20 | 20 | $39

**Old Town** | 1437 N. Wells St. (bet. North Ave. & Schiller St.) | 312-587-3660 | www.bistrotmargot.com

Supporters of this "cozy Old Town institution" with "classic French bistro cooking" "swear by" its "pleasant", "reliable" fare and staff, "neighborhood" vibe, "reasonably priced wine list" and "lunch and brunch"; frustrated followers feel it "could be better", but the "friendly bar for after work" and "one of the best sidewalk cafes" draw an "interesting clientele."

### Bistrot Zinc *French*                                 21 | 21 | 21 | $38

**Gold Coast** | 1131 N. State St. (bet. Cedar & Elm Sts.) | 312-337-1131 | www.bistrotzinc.com

"Authentic" "Parisian ambiance" starts with the titular zinc bar at this "consistent" Gold Coast "neighborhood" "oasis" for "well-made" French bistro "comfort food" including "weekend brunch" and "amazing lunch specials"; "friendly service" adds to the "value in an area where most choices are expensive", and people-watchers note that come summer, "window walls are opened right onto State Street."

### ⚅ **Blackbird** ⚃ *American*　27 | 22 | 25 | $66

**West Loop** | 619 W. Randolph St. (bet. Desplaines & Jefferson Sts.) | 312-715-0708 | www.blackbirdrestaurant.com

The West Loop's "bold" "destination" "flagship of the [Paul] Kahan empire" flies an "outstanding", "ever-changing menu" from chef Mike Sheerin that's "crafted in the finest tradition of New American" cuisine and coupled with an "unbelievable wine list" and "skillful service" in "sleek, stark" surroundings; while "priced for a special occasion", it delivers a vaunted "value-quality ratio" (wallet-watchers might "come for lunch"), and if the other "diners are so close you're practically wearing each other's clothes", the "high noise and energy level is part of the plan", so just "eat" and "talk later."

### **Blind Faith Café** ⚃ *Vegetarian*　21 | 16 | 19 | $22

**Evanston** | 525 Dempster St. (bet. Chicago & Hinman Aves.) | 847-328-6875 | www.blindfaithcafe.com

"Tasty", "healthy" meals make this Evanston's "solid" "old faithful" – "especially for vegans and vegetarians" – where affordable tabs meet a "comfortable", certified green setting and a staff that's "genuinely interested in pleasing"; P.S. omnivores not sharing the "spirit" bet on the "bakery" and weekend brunch.

### **Bluebird, The** ⦿ *American*　20 | 21 | 19 | $31

**Bucktown** | 1749 N. Damen Ave. (Willow St.) | 773-486-2473 | www.bluebirdchicago.com

New American small plates like "cheese and charcuterie" and "flatbreads that rule" served amid "cool decor" featuring "repurposed doors and windows" and a fireplace make this mid-priced Bucktown "neighborhood hangout" a "cozy" "place for an early evening date" or "late-night dining"; P.S. service can be spotty, so "locals in-the-know" eat "at the bar" and order from the "extensive wine and beer selections."

### **NEW** **Blue Ocean** *Japanese*　▽ 23 | 22 | 24 | $42

**Ravenswood** | 4650 N. Clark St. (Leland Ave.) | 773-334-6288 | www.blueoceanchicago.com

Tucked into the corner of a Ravenswood residential complex, this storefront "neighborhood gem" serves signature rolls in full and half sizes (including creative vegetarian options) "always with a twist" plus Japanese small plates; its eye-popping, psychedelic-colored setting includes 'tinsel' ball light fixtures, a sushi bar and swanky banquette seating.

### **Blue 13** ⦿⚃ *American*　24 | 23 | 25 | $44

**River North** | 416 W. Ontario St. (bet. Kingsbury & Orleans Sts.) | 312-787-1400 | www.blue13chicago.com

"Creative" New American dishes including the signature "steak and eggs on acid" are partnered with service that's "attentive (in a good way)" at this upscale, "cozy" River Norther decked out with exposed brick and candlelight; it's "hip, but never tries to be hipper than its customers", with a house "filthy martini", selection of beers and "reasonably priced wine list" keeping fans lubricated till "late night."

### ⊠ Bob Chinn's Crab House  Seafood    23 | 14 | 20 | $40

**Wheeling** | 393 S. Milwaukee Ave. (bet. Dundee & Willow Rds.) | 847-520-3633 | www.bobchinns.com

"Fresh" fanatics can "check the air bills on the wall" at this "long-time" North Suburban "standard" for "amazing seafood" that has "little sophistication" but comes with moderate prices and "powerful cocktails"; expect a "rowdy", "efficient" "production line", "plastic plates" and "wharfish 1980s seaside" surroundings, plus you may have to "control your server" to not feel "rushed"; but while some who tag it "tired" and "overpriced" don't get the "hype", the fact is "people have been waiting in line since the day they opened."

### Bob San ◑  Japanese    24 | 19 | 21 | $36

**Wicker Park** | 1805 W. Division St. (Wood St.) | 773-235-8888 | www.bob-san.com

Wicker Park's "warm and welcoming" midpriced Sushi Naniwa sibling is a Japanese "mainstay" offering "so many options" of "fresh" sushi and sashimi (the best of which can "stop all conversation") served in "generous portions"; an "understated atmosphere" and "courteous service" are additional reasons it suits for a "casual date."

### BOKA  American    25 | 23 | 25 | $58

**Lincoln Park** | 1729 N. Halsted St. (Willow St.) | 312-337-6070 | www.bokachicago.com

"Talented" chef Giuseppi Tentori has turned this "casually elegant" Lincoln Park "escape" "near the Halsted theater" into a "distinctive fine-dining" destination featuring "cutting-edge" New American cuisine "from raw to small plates to entrees" and "some of the best desserts" in a "cool" setting with "sails" on the ceiling and "a great buzz" (plus an "adorable" enclosed patio); a few reticent raters say some of the "very creative presentations" "work better than others" and it's "a bit pricey" – but all agree it's still "special" (wallet-watchers might try the "early prix fixe" Sunday–Thursday).

### NEW Bolat African Cuisine Ⓜ  African    - | - | - | I

**Lakeview** | 3346 N. Clark St. (bet. Buckingham Pl. & Roscoe St.) | 773-665-1100

Thanks to a recent "makeover", this former "cabbie-style Lakeview joint" is now a "hip, contemporary" and "authentic" regional African eatery with "bold", "delicious" fare (emphasis on small plates and sustainable seafood); the "tastefully done" setting with "traditional art painted on the walls" and affordable tabs help surveyors to "overlook" the "somewhat unprofessional service."

### Bongo Room  American    24 | 16 | 18 | $19

**Wicker Park** | 1470 N. Milwaukee Ave. (Honore St.) | 773-489-0690
**South Loop** | 1152 S. Wabash Ave. (Roosevelt Rd.) | 312-291-0100

Fans are "bonkers" about "some of the best breakfast eats in town" (plus "interesting salads and sandwiches" for lunch) at this "reasonably priced" Wicker Park "crack pancake" palace and its South Loop sister that are "a cut above the usual diner"; weekend brunch "crowds" and occasional "rude service" deter some, but most deem the "decadent" "twists on savory and sweet" sustenance "worth the wait"; P.S. they don't serve dinner, but with these "portions", "you won't need it."

### NEW Bonsai Café Asian
- | - | - | I

**Evanston** | 2916 Central St. (Lincolnwood Dr.) | 847-866-7498
"Well-prepared", "affordable Asian specialties" – from potstickers and crab Rangoon to Thai curry to sushi – come at "very reasonable prices" and pair with beverages including fresh ginger ale and bubble tea at this "cozy" BYO corner storefront in Evanston; while doubters "aren't sure about the authenticity, there's a wide variety" and "portions tend toward the generous"; N.B. a patio is in the works.

### Z Bonsoirée M American/French
26 | 19 | 25 | $76

**Logan Square** | 2728 W. Armitage Ave. (Fairfield Ave.) | 773-486-7511 | www.bon-soiree.com
Initiates insist a "terrific", "strictly degustation" New American–New French "sensory adventure" awaits at this "tiny", "onetime secret" Logan Square "storefront" where "you can wear jeans and have truffles shaved over your plate" by "thoughtful servers"; Saturday dinners are invitation-only through the website, Sunday's menu is a market-driven surprise, and while it's prix fixe only and on the "pricey" side, most feel it's a "bargain" considering the no-corkage BYO policy ("bring your best vino" or arrange for delivery at no charge).

### Boston Blackies Burgers
19 | 14 | 18 | $20

**Loop** | 120 S. Riverside Plaza (bet. Adams & Monroe Sts.) | 312-382-0700 Ⓢ
**Streeterville** | 164 E. Grand Ave. (St. Clair St.) | 312-938-8700
**Lincoln Park** | 1962 N. Halsted St. (Armitage Ave.) | 773-661-5555
**Deerfield** | 405 Lake Cook Rd. (Rte. 43) | 847-418-3400
**Glencoe** | Hubbard Woods Plaza | 73 Green Bay Rd. (Scott Ave.) | 847-242-9400
**Skokie** | 9525 Skokie Blvd. (Golf Rd.) | 847-673-9800
**Arlington Heights** | 222 E. Algonquin Rd. (Tonne Dr.) | 847-952-4700 ◗
**Naperville** | 916 S. Rte. 59 (Ogden Ave.) | 630-717-5555
www.bostonblackies.com
"Reliable for burgers and affordable American" fare (with kudos for the "garbage salad", "onion rings" and "coleslaw"), this "decent chain" of "busy pubs" also offers a "selection of brews", "no-nonsense service" "from central casting" and a dose of "nostalgia"; decor varies by location, but whether it's "'70s retro" or "faux art deco", it's "typically Chicago atmosphere."

### Branch 27 American
17 | 20 | 20 | $36

**West Town** | 1371 W. Chicago Ave. (Noble St.) | 312-850-2700 | www.branch27.com
West Town's "cozy", "casual" New American in a "converted former branch of the Chicago Public Library" wields "upscale bar food" and "brews" that are "priced appropriately" ("nothing extraordinary, but

there's something for everyone"); a "twenty-thirtysomething crowd" in "groups" or with "dates" fills the brick-lined space and "back atrium with beautiful lighting from the glass ceiling"; N.B. the Food score may not reflect a chef change at the Survey's start.

### Brasserie Jo  *French*                           22  22  21  $43

**River North** | 59 W. Hubbard St. (bet. Clark & Dearborn Sts.) | 312-595-0800 | www.brasseriejo.com

"Classic" "French brasserie fare" "leans toward hearty Alsatian" dishes with a "wine list to match" and a "huge selection of beers" at River North's *"jeune frère* to Everest" ("without the glitz or the price") that's "authentic" down to its zinc bar; rapt regulars say it's "just like Paris" – "including service" that some call "indifferent", others "unfussy" – but all in all it's "dependable" and "still can't be beat."

### Brazzaz  *Brazilian/Steak*                      22  20  22  $55

**River North** | 539 N. Dearborn St. (Grand Ave.) | 312-595-9000 | www.brazzaz.com

One of the "eat-until-you-pass-out Brazilian" churrascarias, this "comfortable", "modern" River North rendition parades a prix fixe "cascade of carne" ("served by young, energetic gaucho-types") and offers a "terrific salad bar" with a "plentiful" buffet of "both hot and cold dishes" including seafood; for those who find it "a little pricey" "for the quality", there's always the "lower-priced lunch."

### Breakfast Club, The  *American*                  20  13  21  $16

**Near West** | 1381 W. Hubbard St. (Noble St.) | 312-666-2372 | www.chicagobreakfastclub.com

Near West "locals" laud this "out-of-the-way", "old-school" "breakfast joint" for its "excellent omelets", "killer" "stuffed French toast" and "Bloody Marys" served by a "pleasant staff" in a "homey atmosphere" with "pink accents" reminiscent of a "grandma's country kitchen"; it all adds up to "great value" – in other words, "be prepared to wait awhile on the weekends" (though "tables turn fairly quickly").

### Bricks  *Pizza*                                  22  15  17  $22

**Lincoln Park** | 1909 N. Lincoln Ave. (Wisconsin St.) | 312-255-0851

### Bricks on the Run  *Pizza*

**NEW** **Bucktown** | 1940 N. Elston Ave. (bet. Armitage Ave. & Homer St.) | 773-252-2220
www.brickschicago.com

Fans "forget the basement" "dungeonlike location" with the "first bite" of this Lincoln Park pizzeria's "creative concoctions" made with "not-too-thick, not-too-thin crusts" that are "right on the mark" "when you don't want a manhole-cover–size pie"; "long waits" are endurable thanks to a "friendly staff", "reasonably priced" "craft beers" and an "inexpensive wine list"; N.B. a Bucktown location has opened.

### Briejo  ☒  *American/Eclectic*              ▽  14  18  15  $38

**Oak Park** | 211 Harrison St. (Lombard Ave.) | 708-848-2743 | www.briejo.com

Hopefuls had "high expectations" for this midpriced Eclectic–New American "tucked away" in "Oak Park's cool little art district", given its pedigree (one of the owners is from the former Tomboy), "interesting" menu and "wonderful ambiance" with warm tones and low lighting; so while some are "disappointed" with "mediocre" fare and "service that could use better training", they add that it's "trying" and "not bad for the neighborhood."

### Brio Tuscan Grille  *Italian*          22 | 23 | 21 | $33

**Lombard** | Shops on Butterfield | 330 Yorktown Ctr. (Butterfield Rd.) | 630-424-1515 | www.brioitalian.com
"Varied and tasty" Italian menu choices including weekend brunch "at a decent price" sate Butterfield shoppers at this "lively", "comfortable" and "kid-friendly" Lombard chain link; "when you get the right service person", it's an even better "experience", enhanced by a "warm" Tuscan villa setting that includes two fireplaces in the lounge.

### Bristol, The  *American*          23 | 19 | 21 | $40

**Bucktown** | 2152 N. Damen Ave. (bet. Shakespeare & Webster Aves.) | 773-862-5555 | www.thebristolchicago.com
"Believers" in Bucktown's "worthy", "locavore" New American gastropub say it "cranks out" an "ever-changing seasonal menu" including "delectable and distinctive dishes" in the "nose-to-tail" "school of cooking" ("eat parts you never knew were edible") ferried by a "welcoming", "informed staff"; naysayers note it's "noisy" with "packed tables" and "communal seating" that's "not for everyone", plus the "no-reservations policy is the pits" – but "phenomenal" "custom" cocktails and "many beers and ales" help "while you wait."

### Broadway Cellars  *American*          21 | 17 | 20 | $32

**Edgewater** | 5900 N. Broadway St. (Rosedale Ave.) | 773-944-1208 | www.broadwaycellars.net
Edgewater denizens "date and dine" at this "jazzy", "comfortable" "neighborhood" "brick-exposed cellar" with "consistently" "delicious" New American fare (including "excellent brunch"), "pick-your-own wine flights" from a "creative list" and a "welcoming staff"; added attractions are "occasional live music", seasonal outdoor seating and weeknight deals for "specials, wine-flight dinners and prix fixe."

### NEW Browntrout  *American*          24 | 17 | 22 | $35

**North Center/St. Ben's** | 4111 N. Lincoln Ave. (bet. Belle Plaine & Warner Aves.) | 773-472-4111 | www.browntroutchicago.com
"It's worth swimming upstream" for this midpriced North Center contemporary American where the "delicious, creative" "farm-to-table" fare comes in "small and large plates" with "big flavors"; fans of "communal tables" find the warm-hued modern digs "tastefully decorated" while others peg it as "plain Jane", though most are "impressed" by the "sustainable", "green approach" and "heartfelt chef-iness"; N.B. there's also Sunday brunch and sidewalk seating.

### Bruna's Ristorante  *Italian*          26 | 12 | 21 | $32

**Southwest Side** | 2424 S. Oakley Ave. (24th Pl.) | 773-254-5550
"One of Chicago's oldest continuously operated restaurants" (opened 1933), this moderately priced Southwest Side "neighborhood

stalwart" is an "oasis" of "classic family Italian" dining complete with an "old-world staff"; it may "look like a typical red-sauce" place "but the quality is much better" say aficionados who aver it's "always a pleasure (despite the ancient decor)", plus it's "not a tourist" spot.

## Buona Terra Ristorante Ⓜ *Italian*  24 | 17 | 22 | $31

**Logan Square** | 2535 N. California Ave. (bet. Fullerton Ave. & Logan Blvd.) | 773-289-3800 | www.buona-terra.com

"*Va bene*" cheer champions of this "unpretentious", "popular" Logan Square haunt offering "enjoyable" Northern Italian fare "with some unusual touches" and "caring service" in a "homey" surround including a mural of a Tuscan scene; regulars especially "love the spread for the bread" and the "Thursday prix fixe" "bargain" that offers the run of the menu; N.B. there's garden dining in summer.

## Butterfly Sushi Bar & Thai Cuisine *Japanese/Thai*  22 | 16 | 19 | $23

**West Loop** | 1156 W. Grand Ave. (bet. May St. & Racine Ave.) | 312-563-5555
**West Town** | 1421 W. Chicago Ave. (bet. Bishop & Noble Sts.) | 312-492-9955
www.butterflysushibar.com

A "young, hip crowd" flits to this "lively", often "packed" West Loop and West Town duo for a "diverse menu" of "fresh, tasty" "Thai and sushi classics" including a "dizzying array of rolls" at "fair prices" with a "no-corkage" "BYO to boot"; but while some praise "quick service", others feel "rushed out the door."

## Cab's Wine Bar Bistro *American*  24 | 21 | 25 | $40

**Glen Ellyn** | 430 N. Main St. (Duane St.) | 630-942-9463 | www.cabsbistro.com

Situated in "old Downtown Glen Ellyn", this midpriced "casual" "neighborhood" "landmark" offers seasonal New American "fine dining" with "wonderful wine" (focusing on Cal Cabernets) and a "friendly" vibe in an "unassuming storefront"; though some lobby for "more specials", live music most weekends strikes the right chord.

## Café Absinthe Ⓜ *American*  23 | 18 | 21 | $42

**Bucktown** | 1954 W. North Ave. (Damen Ave.) | 773-278-4488 | www.cafeabsinthechicago.com

To absinthe-minded admirers of this "charming" Bucktown "old standard", the seasonal American cuisine is "consistently interesting and delicious" (if "a bit pricey") and the confines confer a "cool vibe" for "dressed-up or casual" occasions; diners taking a dimmer view suggest bringing a "flashlight" for the "dark" ambiance and mention the "noise" factor, though a "wine list with some boutique options" might help you "tolerate" that.

## Cafe Ba-Ba-Reeba! *Spanish*  22 | 19 | 20 | $32

**Lincoln Park** | 2024 N. Halsted St. (Armitage Ave.) | 773-935-5000 | www.cafebabareeba.com

After 25 years, LEYE's Lincoln Park "pioneer" of the genre still serves "some of the most reliable" "tapas (small dishes) and pinxtos (even smaller dishes)" in a "lively", "loud" setting (where "varieties" of "sangria make everyone even louder"); service is usually "active and efficient", but nitpickers note "some highlights and some mediocre" menu options, and warn it "can get expensive" ("$3 tapas at the bar is a great bargain" at varying times); P.S. "unique Sunday brunch", "three-bite desserts" and "outdoor seating" are added lures.

### Café Bernard  *French*               19 | 15 | 20 | $41

**Lincoln Park** | 2100 N. Halsted St. (Dickens Ave.) | 773-871-2100 | www.cafebernard.com

A Lincoln Park "institution" since 1972 for "well-prepared" "traditional French cooking" including "game specials", this "dimly lit", "tried-and-true" "favorite" is also appreciated for its "terrific, well-priced wine list"; a few who feel it's "faded from its former glory" note it "needs a makeover", while others prefer the "atmosphere" of the less-expensive back-room wine bar and cafe called the Red Rooster.

### Café Bionda  *Italian*               22 | 17 | 20 | $31

**South Loop** | 1924 S. State St. (Archer Ave.) | 312-326-9800 | www.cafebionda.com

*Amici* of this "cozy" South Loop Italian are drawn to its "hearty" "traditional" fare dished out in "large quantities" with "friendly service" amid a "neighborhood ambiance"; "fair prices" add to the allure, including the "Sunday special" platter that's a "terrific bargain" of meatballs, sausages and veal braciole.

### Cafe Central  Ⓜ *French*              24 | 19 | 24 | $38

**Highland Park** | 455 Central Ave. (bet. Linden & St. Johns Aves.) | 847-266-7878 | www.cafecentral.net

Highland Park's "unpretentious" "kissing cousin" to the "extremely upscale Carlos'" is the "go-to place" for "consistent", "classic [French] bistro" fare in a "casual", "colorful" setting; though the "tables are close" there's "outdoor seating in summer", plus tabs are "reasonable" and kids are welcome too – just allow for a policy of "no reservations after 6:30."

### Café des Architectes  *French/Mediterranean*    24 | 25 | 24 | $53

**Gold Coast** | Sofitel Chicago Water Tower | 20 E. Chestnut St. (Wabash Ave.) | 312-324-4063 | www.cafedesarchitectes.com

"Seasonal, local and flavorful" New French–Mediterranean meals with "beautiful presentations" from "noteworthy" chef Martial Noguier come with "excellent service to match" (that's earned a ratings boost) at this "*très* European" eatery in the Sofitel Chicago Water Tower; the "civilized" setting projects "modern luxury" through vibrant colors and mood lighting, and if "prices can be a bit high", the "prix fixe special is a steal" and the "fantastic breakfast" is a "great value."

### Café Iberico  ❶ *Spanish*            22 | 16 | 18 | $29

**River North** | 739 N. LaSalle Dr. (bet. Chicago Ave. & Superior St.) | 312-573-1510 | www.cafeiberico.com

Boosters of this "boisterous" River North taparia cheer the "well-rounded selection" of "tasty" Spanish "small plates to share" plus

FOOD | DECOR | SERVICE | COST

"some of the best paella" around, all at "recession-proof prices" that "pack" the large, "cafeteria-like" digs with "groups" and other diners "on a budget"; just expect "deafening" "noise" and "prepare to drink a lot of sangria while waiting for your table", as reservations aren't accepted after 3 PM on Friday or Saturday.

### Café la Cave 🛂Ⓜ Continental

21 | 20 | 20 | $52

**Des Plaines** | 2777 Mannheim Rd. (bet. Higgins Rd. & Touhy Ave.) | 847-827-7818 | www.cafelacave.net

It's "déjà vu all over again for the old-fashioned expense-account dinner" at this "romantic, dark, quiet" Des Plaines Continental offering "formal dining" with "tableside preparations" and a "cave"-like bar area; modernists say it's "stuffy", "so-so" and "overpriced", but diehards deem it "still a winner if entertaining those flying through O'Hare."

### NEW Cafe Marbella Ⓜ Spanish

- | - | - | I

**Jefferson Park** | 5527 Milwaukee Ave. (bet. Bryn Mawr & Catalpa Aves.) | 773-853-0128 | www.cafemarbella.com

Relocated from its former Peterson Avenue digs, this budget-friendly Jefferson Park BYO turns out an extensive menu of hot and cold Spanish tapas and a fair number of entrees beyond the usual paella, all served in modest digs with booths and cafe tables, tile floor and arched windows; N.B. during the fixed-price Spanish 'dim sum' brunch, available all day Sunday, bring bubbly and the restaurant will squeeze the OJ.

### Cafe Matou Ⓜ French

23 | 19 | 23 | $44

**Bucktown** | 1846 N. Milwaukee Ave. (bet. Leavitt St. & Oakley Ave.) | 773-384-8911 | www.cafematou.com

Charlie Socher's "gracious", "quiet" Bucktown "neighborhood spot" is "a bit off the beaten track" and "flies under the radar" with a "sophisticated", "thoughtfully prepared" "seasonal" French menu that "changes daily" and "won't bankrupt you", plus "prix fixe meals" and "monthly cellar raids"; though a few holdouts call it "hit-or-miss", most deem it "dependable" with a "respectable wine list, knowledgeable staff" and "comfortable", "chic" setting with high ceilings and leather upholstery sealing the deal.

### Café 103 Ⓜ American/Eclectic

- | - | - | E

**Far South Side** | 1909 W. 103rd St. (Walden Pkwy.) | 773-238-5115 | www.cafe103.com

"Small and intimate", this "upscale" bistro is a "wonderful Far South Side treat" in an "otherwise food-challenged" area; New American–Eclectic eats arrive by "attentive" servers for lunch, dinner and Sunday brunch, and the alcohol policy is BYO only , with a small corkage fee.

### Cafe Pyrenees Ⓜ French

21 | 19 | 20 | $36

**Libertyville** | Adler Square Shopping Plaza | 1762 N. Milwaukee Ave. (Buckley Rd./Rte. 137) | 847-362-2233 | www.cafepyrenees.com

Libertyville locals laud this "lovely", "family-run" "traditional French bistro" for its "simple but tasteful" midpriced menu (with some

American additions), "interesting", "affordable wines" and "warm" "cafe atmosphere" where "once inside, you quickly forget you're in a strip mall"; some gripe that service can be "standoffish", but positives include patio seating and periodic live music.

### Café Selmarie *American* | 23 | 17 | 19 | $26 |

**Lincoln Square** | 4729 N. Lincoln Ave. (bet. Lawrence & Leland Aves.) | 773-989-5595 | www.cafeselmarie.com

Patrons of this "neighborhood" "favorite" praise its "mom-and-pop air" yet "professional" service while dishing out "well-prepared" New American "comfort food" and "fantastic desserts" at moderate prices; it offers "wonderful summer dining outside on Lincoln Square" and is a "quick place for afternoon tea", weekend brunch, lunch or light dinner – and some surveyors suggest it's an even "better bakery."

### ☑ Café Spiaggia *Italian* | 25 | 23 | 25 | $56 |

**Gold Coast** | 980 N. Michigan Ave., 2nd fl. (Oak St.) | 312-280-2750 | www.cafespiaggia.com

"More intimate" than its "formal" and "more-expensive big brother" "next door", this "lively", "upscale" Gold Coast cafe lures "Magnificent Mile cruisers" with "luscious", "slightly more rustic" Italian fare ("particularly the fresh pastas"), a "top-notch wine list" and "warm but professional service"; add in a "chichi" setting "overlooking Michigan Avenue" and cafe-goers say that it "never fails to please", just expect a "hefty bill."

### NEW Café Touché Ⓜ *French* | ▽ 25 | 23 | 22 | $36 |

**Northwest Side** | 6731 N. Northwest Hwy. (Oshkosh Ave.) | 773-775-0909 | www.cafetouche.com

Situated "in a neighborhood full of" dining "hits" on "Edison Park's Restaurant Row", this Northwest Side "casual French bistro" "find" is becoming a "local favorite" for its "flavorful", "quality" fare "at reasonable prices"; a dark-wood and brick-lined room with ceiling fans plus seasonal sidewalk seating and free valet parking stoke the "terrific" vibe.

### Cafe 28 *Cuban/Mexican* | 26 | 20 | 22 | $30 |

**North Center/St. Ben's** | 1800-1806 W. Irving Park Rd. (Ravenswood Ave.) | 773-528-2883 | www.cafe28.org

North Center's "neighborhood" "treasure" earns enthusiasm for its "well-seasoned", "well-priced" and "mouthwatering" Cuban and Mexican fare with a "contemporary twist" that's built with "extremely fresh ingredients" and delivered by a "dedicated staff"; "wonderful brunch", "house mojitos" and "big-city buzz" heighten the appeal, though a "no-reservations" policy begets "weekend waits"; P.S. "when the weather's nice, try the patio seating."

### Campagnola Ⓜ *Italian* | 25 | 20 | 23 | $45 |

**Evanston** | 815 Chicago Ave. (Washington St.) | 847-475-6100 | www.campagnolarestaurant.com

"Upscale but not fancy", this Evanston Italian with rustic decor and "lots of character" is a "date-night locale" that draws a "devoted fol-

FOOD · DECOR · SERVICE · COST

lowing" for its seasonal, "unique takes on typical" fare with a focus on "sustainable" and "locally grown" ingredients; if it's a bit "expensive", a "modest yet excellent wine list" and "friendly, competent staff" (with improved Service scores) add to the "value"; N.B. the patio is popular in summer.

### Cape Cod Room  *Seafood*    22 | 22 | 23 | $60

**Streeterville** | Drake Hotel | 140 E. Walton St. (Michigan Ave.) | 312-787-2200 | www.thedrakehotel.com

Serving Streeterville since 1933, this "dark, clubby" "institution" "tucked away in the Drake Hotel" offers "classy seafood" to "sentimental" types who recall its "historical" heyday and appreciate "old-time classics" such as "Bookbinder's soup with sherry on the side" served by "seasoned professionals"; naysayers knock the "nautical decor" as "stuffy" "in spite of an update", but old salts find it "elegant yet comfortable", adding it's "expensive" and "worth every penny."

### Z Capital Grille, The  *Steak*    25 | 24 | 25 | $63

**Streeterville** | 633 N. St. Clair St. (Ontario St.) | 312-337-9400
**Rosemont** | 5340 N. River Rd. (Balmoral Ave.) | 847-671-8125
**Lombard** | 87 Yorktown Shopping Ctr. (Highland Ave.) | 630-627-9800
www.thecapitalgrille.com

Fans "feel like power brokers" after being "fortified" by "stellar" steaks (and "getting lubricated at the wonderful bar pre-dinner") at these "heavyweight" contenders among the "big hunka meat restaurants" situated in Chicago's city and suburbs as well as Downtown Milwaukee; they remain "true to the national brand with highly professional service and reliable menus" of "traditional steakhouse fare" served in a "clubby", "upscale atmosphere", though a few carnivores call them "somewhat corporate" with "no differentiating features"; P.S. if you're not on an "expense account", "lunch is the best bet pricewise."

### Z Carlos'  *French*    27 | 26 | 27 | $92

**Highland Park** | 429 Temple Ave. (Waukegan Ave.) | 847-432-0770 | www.carlos-restaurant.com

"Still near the top of the charts" after some 30 years, Highland Park's New French "destination" offers "amazing, approachable gourmet" cuisine and an "incredible, if pricey, wine list" accompanied by service "with grace and a sense of humor"; the "conversation-friendly", "intimate space" adds to the feeling of "understated elegance" (jackets are required) and "you pay a premium", but it's "perfect" for even the "most special of occasions."

### Carlos & Carlos  Ⓜ *Italian*    ▽ 24 | 20 | 23 | $33

**Arlington Heights** | 115 W. Campbell St. (Vail Ave.) | 847-259-5227 | www.carlosandcarlosinc.com

"Imaginative" French-influenced Italian fare with a "selection that accommodates all tastes" offers real "value" – complete with a "fair-priced wine list" – at this Arlington Heights reprise of a one-time Bucktown "original"; regulars praise the service and "comfortable surroundings" of the "small, friendly room."

|  | FOOD | DECOR | SERVICE | COST |
|---|---|---|---|---|

### Carlucci  *Italian*

| 19 | 21 | 19 | $36 |

**Downers Grove** | 1801 Butterfield Rd. (I-355) | 630-512-0990 |
www.carluccirestaurant.com

This Downers Grove Italian provides a "wide variety of classics" plus
some "inventive" dishes in a pleasant (even "romantic") contemporary setting; maybe it's "not gourmet" but it's "solid", with "good
service and value", "great outdoor seating" and occasional live
entertainment as pluses.

### Carlucci  *Italian*

| 20 | 19 | 20 | $41 |

**Rosemont** | Riverway Complex | 6111 N. River Rd. (Higgins Rd.) |
847-518-0990 | www.carluccirosemont.com

Expect "well-prepared" Northern Italian fare, "both traditional and
with small twists", at this "upscale" Rosemont fixture with a Tuscan-
style interior plus patio seating; it's "convenient to O'Hare" and a
"safe bet" for business meals with "perfectly timed" service, though
a few critics find it "predictable" and geared for "expense accounts."

### Carmichael's Chicago Steak House  *Steak*

| 22 | 19 | 20 | $50 |

**West Loop** | 1052 W. Monroe St. (bet. Aberdeen & Morgan Sts.) |
312-433-0025 | www.carmichaelsteakhouse.com

Carnivores come to this "solid" West Loop "neighborhood" meatery
for a "business lunch" or a "classic Chicago-style steak dinner" with
"large portions" but "without the attitude"; the clubby "old-school
masculine decor" features large booths, and there's also outdoor
seating; P.S. it's "convenient for United Center games."

### Carmine's  ❶ *Italian*

| 22 | 18 | 20 | $43 |

**Gold Coast** | 1043 N. Rush St. (bet. Bellevue Pl. & Cedar St.) |
312-988-7676 | www.rosebudrestaurants.com

"Step past the Lamborghinis, Hummers and Ferraris" to enter this
Gold Coast Italian of the "Rosebud franchise" that's "popular" for
"generous" "portions of red-sauce goodness"; even those who warn of
a "Viagra Triangle" vibe and a "cookie-cutter" menu that "costs too
much" admit the scene at the "huge bar", "live piano" and "patio"
perch for "people-watching" the "Rush Street crowd" "can't be beat."

### ❷ Carnivale  *Nuevo Latino*

| 23 | 25 | 21 | $41 |

**Loop** | 702 W. Fulton Mkt. (Union Ave.) | 312-850-5005 |
www.carnivalechicago.com

Jerry Kleiner's "extravagant", "slightly pricey" Nuevo Latino on the
fringe of the Loop boasts "bright" "flavors and even brighter decor" for
a "wonderful sensory overload" fueled by "funky servers" and "daring
drinks"; just know the "atmosphere is true to its name" (it can be
"deafening"), though there is seasonal dining on the patio.

### Carson's Ribs  *BBQ*

| 22 | 16 | 20 | $34 |

**River North** | 612 N. Wells St. (Ontario St.) | 312-280-9200
**Deerfield** | 200 Waukegan Rd. (bet. Kates & Lake Cook Rds.) |
847-374-8500
www.ribs.com

"One of the Chicago originals", this River North rib "reliable" and its
Deerfield double have their boosters for "some of the best" baby-

| | FOOD | DECOR | SERVICE | COST |

back barbecue, "fabulous, artery-clogging potato sides" and "free chopped liver" served in confines that are "comfortable" if "nothing fancy"; some surveyors find the fare "a bit pricey" and sour on the "sweet sauce", but at least service is "speedy."

**Z Catch 35** *Seafood*  24 | 23 | 23 | $49

**Loop** | Leo Burnett Bldg. | 35 W. Wacker Dr. (bet. Dearborn & State Sts.) | 312-346-3500
**Naperville** | 35 S. Washington St. (bet. Benton & Van Buren Aves.) | 630-717-3500
www.catch35.com

Fish fans are hooked on "wonderfully fresh seafood" "with an Asian twist" at the "high-volume" Loop "location by the Chicago River" (also offering "enjoyable" "live entertainment") and its Naperville schoolmate; finicky types label the "casual modern" settings "cold" and find it a bit "overpriced", but service that's "attentive to time issues" makes Downtown a "staple" for a "business lunch" or "pre-theater dining."

**NEW Cellar at**  ∇ 21 | 21 | 18 | $36
**The Stained Glass, The** 🅢 *Eclectic*

**Evanston** | 820 Clark St. (bet. Benson & Sherman Aves.) | 847-425-5112 | www.thecellarevanston.com

Valued for its "varied", "generous and tasty" Eclectic small plates and wine offerings both "priced and sized right", this "baby-bistro of the Stained Glass" in Evanston is "not too formal nor too casual" and "cozier than" its parent "around the corner" in its brown-hued digs with plaid banquettes; N.B. bargain specials include two-for-one micro burgers and $1 mini fish tacos after 9 PM Sunday–Thursday.

**NEW Ceres' Table** 🅢 *American*  - | - | - | M

**Uptown** | 4882 N. Clark St. (bet. Ainslie St. & Lawrence Ave.) | 773-878-4882 | www.cerestable.com

Named for the Roman goddess of agriculture, this smart, stylish Uptown New American features seasonal fare crafted by Giuseppe Scurato (ex BOKA, Topaz Café) from local and imported ingredients; the spartan-chic space is decked out in slate-gray and light-blue walls, with a bar, banquette and table seating and romantic pendant lighting – decidedly upscale considering the moderate prices.

**Chalkboard** *American*  22 | 19 | 21 | $42

**Lakeview** | 4343 N. Lincoln Ave. (bet. Montrose & Pensacola Aves.) | 773-477-7144 | www.chalkboardrestaurant.com

"Creative" chef-owner Gilbert Langlois writes his "changing menu" of "slightly exotic" New American "comfort food" "across a chalkboard" dominating a wall of this "cozy", kid-friendly Lakeview spot that also serves weekend "afternoon tea" and Sunday brunch; even if it's "probably a bit overpriced for the neighborhood", surveyors note a "local, organic" bent plus "welcoming service" and say it's "lovely" "for a special night out."

| | FOOD | DECOR | SERVICE | COST |
|---|---|---|---|---|

### ☑ Charlie Trotter's 🖻🅼 *American*    | 27 | 25 | 27 | $140 |

**Lincoln Park** | 816 W. Armitage Ave. (bet. Dayton & Halsted Sts.) |
773-248-6228 | www.charlietrotters.com

Regulars revere "the original celebrity chef's palace of haute cuisine"
as the "pinnacle" of "precision", where a "memorable" "three-hour
homage" to New American "gastronomic bliss" "showcases flavors
in new intensities and sometimes surprising combinations" alongside
selections from an "encyclopedic wine list"; "formal", "professional
service" befits the "staid" Lincoln Park setting, and though some patrons are "put off" by "pretense" and "petite portions", the faithful
insist "go at least once in your lifetime", especially if you can "find
someone with an expense account."

### Châtaigne 🖻 *Continental/Eclectic*    | - | - | - | M |

**Near North** | Cooking & Hospitality Institute of Chicago |
361 W. Chestnut St. (Orleans St.) | 312-873-2032 | www.chic.edu

"Friendly" "future chefs" from the Cooking & Hospitality Institute
concoct the "imaginative" Continental-Eclectic prix fixe menus at
this Near North "gem" named for the French word for 'chestnut' and
staffed by the students; eaters enjoy a "blue-jeans" meal "with
business-suit food" and "earnest" service, overlooking the occasional "glitch" given the budget-friendly bills; N.B. they serve beer
and wine (or BYO), and the schedule is based on the school's curric-
ulum, so confirm before you go.

### ☑ Cheesecake Factory *American*    | 19 | 19 | 18 | $28 |

**Streeterville** | John Hancock Ctr. | 875 N. Michigan Ave. (bet. Chestnut St. &
Delaware Pl.) | 312-337-1101 ●

**Lincolnshire** | Lincolnshire Commons | 930 Milwaukee Ave.
(Aptakisic Rd.) | 847-955-2350

**Skokie** | Westfield Shoppingtown | 4999 Old Orchard Ctr. (Skokie Blvd.) |
847-329-8077

**Schaumburg** | Woodfield Shopping Ctr. | 53 Woodfield Rd. (Golf Rd.) |
847-619-1090

**Oak Brook** | Oakbrook Center Mall | 2020 Spring Rd. (bet. Harger Rd. &
22nd St.) | 630-573-1800

www.thecheesecakefactory.com

With outposts in Chicago and Milwaukee, this "raucous" Traditional
American chain offers "one of the largest menus known to man" and
"serving sizes" that "never fail to amaze" "from breakfast dishes to
fabulous desserts"; boosters bet "you could eat here every day and
get something different" "without breaking the bank", praising the
"offbeat decor" and "enthusiastic staff", and though haute culinary
types call it "hyper-commercialized", "tacky and touristy", masses
willingly brave the "two-hour waits", "loud" conditions with "cranky
kids" and service that's "slow when busy."

### Chef's Station 🅼 *American*    | 24 | 20 | 22 | $51 |

**Evanston** | Davis Street Metro Station | 915 Davis St. (Church St.) |
847-570-9821 | www.chefs-station.com

"Hidden away" in a 1920 building "under the tracks" of the Davis
Street Metro is where fans find this New American "gem" with an

"enthusiastic" "host-proprietor" and chef who always has "something different to look forward to" on his menu; "personal service", "inventive, comfortable" decor and a seasonal patio add to the "quality-to-value quotient", though it's "not cheap."

### Chens  *Chinese/Japanese*   22 | 17 | 18 | $23

**Wrigleyville** | 3506 N. Clark St. (Addison St.) | 773-549-9100 | www.chenschicago.com

Wrigleyville's "civilized" "local" Chinese-Japanese hybrid offers a "quality" menu that "works for even the pickiest of eaters" (and includes "fresh sushi") plus an "impressive martini and cocktail list"; the "decor and music are not exactly what you'd expect, but that's a good thing" – as are affordable prices.

### Chez Joël  Ⓜ *French*   24 | 20 | 22 | $43

**Little Italy** | 1119 W. Taylor St. (May St.) | 312-226-6479 | www.chezjoelbistro.com

"Right at home in Little Italy", this "welcome exception" of a French "charmer" features a "classic bistro experience" with "authentic" fare and "friendly, helpful service" in a "comfortable neighborhood setting"; it's considered a "value" by surveyors who also note an "outdoor space that's quite special."

### ⓩ Chicago Chop House  *Steak*   25 | 21 | 23 | $66

**River North** | 60 W. Ontario St. (bet. Clark & Dearborn Sts.) | 312-787-7100 | www.chicagochophouse.com

Carnivores concur "steak becomes an experience, not just a meal" at River North's "classic Chicago" "bastion of big beef" (and "fabulous fish") complete with a "piano player" and pictures of local celebrities "on the wall"; the "old men's-club vibe" may be better for "business" than "romance", especially given the "expense-account" tariff, and though most call the staff "professional", some say what's most "legendary" is the "wait" to be seated.

### Chicago Curry House  *Indian/Nepalese*   25 | 18 | 21 | $28

**South Loop** | 899 S. Plymouth Ct. (9th St.) | 312-362-9999 | www.curryhouseonline.com

"Delicious" and "authentic", the Indian-Nepalese cuisine goes beyond "excellent curries" to include "some unusual dishes" (such as momo dumplings) say South Loopers who've sampled this "wonderful" "neighborhood" spot's midpriced menu with an "extra spin"; the "polite" staff "goes out of its way to please" in the "pleasant", "simple space", and the "lunch buffet is a fantastic value."

### Chicago Diner, The  *Diner/Vegetarian*   22 | 14 | 19 | $21

**Lakeview** | 3411 N. Halsted St. (Roscoe St.) | 773-935-6696 | www.veggiediner.com

"'Meat-free since '83' is the catchy slogan" at this Lakeview longtimer touted as a "safe haven" serving "innovative", "value"-priced vegetarian fare "with all sorts of dietary needs met" amid decor that "looks like a diner" because "that's what it is"; "servers are a little too cool for school" and omnivores opine "if you aren't vegan, it's hit-or-miss", but the "back patio is beautiful in the summer."

|  | FOOD | DECOR | SERVICE | COST |
|---|---|---|---|---|

### Chicago Firehouse  *American*
20 | 21 | 21 | $45

**South Loop** | 1401 S. Michigan Ave. (14th St.) | 312-786-1401 | www.chicagofirehouse.com

With its "unusual ambiance" "In a cleverly remodeled old fire-house" (circa 1905) as a "definite draw", this Traditional American "delivers" "one of the classiest" dining experiences "in the South Loop" to a brigade of believers who "enjoy" the "classic dishes" and "wonderful steaks"; though wet blankets deem it "just ok for the cost", generally "professional service" and a "summer patio" fan the flames.

### Chicago Pizza & Oven Grinder Co. ✈ *Pizza*
23 | 16 | 20 | $22

**Lincoln Park** | 2121 N. Clark St. (bet. Dickens & Webster Aves.) | 773-248-2570 | www.chicagopizzaandovengrinder.com

"Pizza in a bowl? oh yes, my friend" affirm fans of Lincoln Park's "unique Chicago" "dive-gem" famed for its affordable "pot pie" 'za and "ginormous subs" with "fresh ingredients" served in a "cuckoo" "'70s ski lodge" setting; there are "no credit cards and no reservations, so come prepared to pay cash and wait" warn patient patrons who insist "that guy who remembers where we are in line 40 minutes later" must have a "photographic memory."

### Chickpea ✈ *Mideastern*
22 | 18 | 19 | $15

**West Town** | 2018 W. Chicago Ave. (bet. Damen & Hoyne Aves.) | 773-384-9930 | www.chickpeaonthego.com

West Town's "friendly" oasis offers "healthy, delicious" "home-cooked" Middle Eastern and "authentic Palestinian" fare – prepared by the owner's mother – in a "cool space" with a "warm" vibe and budget-coddling prices (including the $1 BYO corkage fee); N.B. it's cash-only and there are no reservations.

### Chief O'Neill's  *Pub Food*
18 | 18 | 17 | $24

**Northwest Side** | 3471 N. Elston Ave. (Albany Ave.) | 773-583-3066 | www.chiefoneillspub.com

"Solid, hearty" fare – including "tasty, traditional" Emerald Isle favorites and a Sunday brunch buffet "deal" – goes down easy with a "terrific Guinness pour" and "Irish musical entertainment" (Sundays and Tuesdays) at this "comfortable", wallet-friendly Northwest Side "neighborhood pub"; a staff with "personality" and "one of the best beer gardens in the city" add to the allure; N.B. Saturday breakfast has been added.

### NEW Chilam Balam ✈ *Mexican*
25 | 14 | 21 | $31

**Lakeview** | 3023 N. Broadway St. (bet. Barry & Wellington Aves.) | 773-296-6901 | www.chilambalamchicago.com

Diners "crowd" into this "teeny" Lakeview "basement" for "adventurous", "delicious" "Mexican small plates" with "huge flavor" (plus some larger plates) served in a "funky" setting with "lively artwork"; "you may have to wait for a table" and it's "not cheap", but the "BYO policy helps keep the price down" (margarita mix is available); P.S. it's "cash-only."

|  | FOOD | DECOR | SERVICE | COST |
|---|---|---|---|---|

### China Grill  *Asian*  —  22 | 22 | 20 | $55

**Loop** | Hard Rock Hotel | 230 N. Michigan Ave. (Lake St.) |
312-334-6700 | www.chinagrillmgt.com

"Hip", "contemporary" and "loud", this Loop chain link in the Hard
Rock Hotel dishes out a "diverse, upscale" Asian menu and "amazing concoctions at the bar" in a setting featuring red lacquer walls;
while some surveyors are "pleasantly surprised" by the fare (if not
so much the spotty service), others are "shocked by the price" and
"eliminate it as an option" unless "with a group" so the "large portions" "can be shared."

### Chinn's 34th St. Fishery  *Seafood*  —  25 | 15 | 23 | $37

**Lisle** | 3011 W. Ogden Ave. (Fender Ave.) | 630-637-1777 |
www.chinns-fishery.com

"Delicious fresh fish" (flown in daily) is "reasonably priced" at this
"hopping" Lisle seafooder where "signature mai tais" and "addictive
garlic rolls" add zest to a "bland" nautical setting; "service is always
'on'" and it's "kid-friendly", so most don't mind the lack of "inventive
recipes" (as evidenced in improved scores across the board).

### C-House  *Seafood*  —  21 | 22 | 21 | $56

**Streeterville** | Affinia Chicago Hotel | 166 E. Superior St. (St. Clair St.) |
312-523-0923 | www.c-houserestaurant.com

Chef Marcus Samuelsson (NYC's Aquavit) has "brought his
skills to the Windy City" to a mixed reception at this Streeterville
seafood house – one school calls the "creative fresh take on
small plates" served amid "modern, simplistic" decor "wonderful and innovative", while another pegs the edibles "erratic" at
prices that are "a bit much" (granted it's in an "expensive area");
service, however, is "welcoming."

### NEW Ciao Napoli Pizzeria  Ⓜ  *Pizza*  —  - | - | - | M

**Logan Square** | 2607 N. Milwaukee Ave. (Kedzie Ave.) |
773-278-7300

A hand-built brick pizza oven fires the Neapolitan 'za crafted from
imported ingredients by a native pizzaiolo at this midpriced Logan
Square arrival also known for fresh pasta, Italian doughnuts and artful cocktails; the warm, urban-rustic setting combines exposed
brick, wood, lots of windows and a bar where you can keep your eye
on the pies.

### NEW Cibo Matto  Ⓢ  *Italian*  —  24 | 26 | 23 | $53

**Loop** | theWit Hotel | 201 N. State St. (Lake St.) | 312-239-9500 |
www.eatcibomatto.com

"Trendy" types testify the "hype is justified" at this "elegant but happening" Italian in theWit Hotel where "ultramodern decor" with
"swanky booths" is the setting for "inventive", "beautifully presented" seasonal cuisine accompanied by "informed service"; while
the "see-and-be-seen" atmosphere makes for a special "night out",
it's "expensive", so wallet-watchers "list it for lunch in the Loop";
N.B. chef Todd Stein also oversees the small-plates menu at Roof,
the indoor-outdoor rooftop lounge.

| | FOOD | DECOR | SERVICE | COST |
|---|---|---|---|---|

### Cité *American*
| | 20 | 26 | 20 | $71 |

**Streeterville** | Lake Point Tower | 505 N. Lake Shore Dr., 70th fl.
(Navy Pier) | 312-644-4050 | www.citechicago.com
City-dwellers and "tourists" alike seek out this "quiet", "elegant"
(jackets suggested) New American – towering 70 stories above
Streeterville since 1969 – "for a romantic dinner or special occasion" complete with a "phenomenal" 360-degree panorama; grudg-
ing graders who call the service and "expensive" fare "not fantastic"
grump "you can't eat the view."

### NEW CityGate Grille ☒ *American/Mediterranean*
| | - | - | - | M |

**Naperville** | CityGate Ctr. | 2020 Calamos Ct. (Westings Ave.) |
630-718-1010 | www.citygategrille.com
West Suburban Naperville's LEED-certified CityGate Centre is home
to this New American with Mediterranean underpinnings that
serves lunch and dinner (there's a bar menu too), accompanied by
signature cocktails and a Cal-Med wine list; the smart, handsome
space boasts walls of windows and tiered pendant light fixtures, and
there's live music on Fridays and Saturdays.

### Clubhouse, The *American*
| | 21 | 21 | 20 | $40 |

**Oak Brook** | Oakbrook Center Mall | 298 Oakbrook Ctr. (Rte. 83) |
630-472-0600 | www.theclubhouse.com
Surveyors swinging into this "upscale American" in Oak Brook's
mall for a "business lunch, happy hour" or "break from shopping"
find "comfort food" in "large portions" (including "monster-
sized salads" and "massive desserts"); service might be "hit-or-
miss", but the place offers "something for everyone in both cuisine
and price", including a Sunday brunch with "value"; P.S. the bar
is "always buzzing" with "singles" but the "upstairs is quieter" and
patio seating has expanded.

### Club Lucky *Italian*
| | 19 | 16 | 20 | $30 |

**Bucktown** | 1824 W. Wabansia Ave. (Honore St.) | 773-227-2300 |
www.clubluckychicago.com
"Old-time homestyle Italian" fare "in a new-wave neighborhood"
lures Bucktowners to this '40s-style "supper club" that pours some
of the "best martinis in town"; service is "attentive", and while most
call the "red-sauce" fare "satisfying" and "lots for the buck", even
those "underwhelmed" by it admit the "red-checkered tablecloths
and wall-to-wall cool vibe" "keeps you coming back."

### Coalfire Pizza ☒ *Pizza*
| | 23 | 13 | 18 | $20 |

**West Loop** | 1321 W. Grand Ave. (bet. Ada & Elizabeth Sts.) |
312-226-2625 | www.coalfirechicago.com
"Excellent East Coast–style" pie wins "thin-crust" fans for this
"funky little" affordable West Loop "joint" with a "kick-ass coal-
burning" oven "so hot the pizza always comes out a little" "charred"
(which some "love" and others call "burnt"); "now that they have
their liquor license" regulars reckon "the only thing holding them
back" is the somewhat "remote" locale.

|  | FOOD | DECOR | SERVICE | COST |
|---|---|---|---|---|

### Coast Sushi Bar ◑ *Japanese*     24 | 20 | 18 | $36

**Bucktown** | 2045 N. Damen Ave. (bet. Dickens & McLean Aves.) |
773-235-5775 | www.coastsushibar.com

### South Coast *Japanese*

**South Loop** | 1700 S. Michigan Ave. (bet. 16th & 18th Sts.) |
312-662-1700 | www.southcoastsushi.com

Fin fans attest this Bucktown Japanese "BYO treasure" (with a South
Loop sibling that serves wine) offers "extremely fresh" fish and a
"wide variety" of "creative rolls" while "keeping costs down and
quality high"; it's not only a suitable "place for friends to eat" or a
"date", but even for losing one's "sushi virginity" – thanks to a
"knowledgeable staff" and "loungey" feel.

### ⛝ Coco Pazzo *Italian*     25 | 22 | 24 | $52

**River North** | 300 W. Hubbard St. (Franklin St.) | 312-836-0900 |
www.cocopazzochicago.com

Surveyors are "still crazy after all these years" for this "sophisticated, simple and not snooty" River Norther whether "for business
dining, pre-theater" or a "quick and classy lunch" of "remarkable",
"*delizioso*" "seasonal" Northern Italian cuisine; the all-Italy "long
and varied wine list", "elegant" "loft" setting with "white tablecloths" and "consummately professional staff" complete a "Tuscan
experience" that's "expensive" and "worth it."

### Coco Pazzo Café *Italian*     22 | 19 | 20 | $40

**Streeterville** | Red Roof Inn | 636 N. St. Clair St. (Ontario St.) |
312-664-2777 | www.cocopazzocafe.com

*Amici* of "Coco Pazzo's unassuming but overachieving little brother"
consider it a Streeterville "gem" by virtue of its "simple", "moderately priced" menu including "authentic pastas" and "delicious anti-
pasti" served in "smart casual" surroundings with a "contemporary
European feel" right down to the "alfresco" patio; if "service is a cut
below" its "upscale sibling" and one rater's "cozy" is another's
"crowded", most dub it "always satisfying."

### NEW Conoce     - | - | - | I
### Mi Panama Ⓜ *Central American*

**Logan Square** | 3054 W. Armitage Ave. (bet. Albany Ave. & Whipple St.) |
773-252-7440 | www.conocemipanama.weebly.com

Hearty plates of Panamanian cuisine with Costa Rican and Caribbean
accents lure Logan Square locals to this inexpensive BYO (beer and
wine only), which also offers vegetarian and vegan options plus non-
alcoholic beverages and coffees; the little brick storefront has a casual yet warm feel with hot-hued walls, photographs of Panama and
catchy island background music.

### Coobah Ⓜ *Filipino/Nuevo Latino*     17 | 17 | 17 | $32

**Lakeview** | 3423 N. Southport Ave. (bet. Newport Ave. & Roscoe St.) |
773-528-2220 | www.coobah.com

"Eclectic" Nuevo Latino–Filipino "flavor combinations" and
"delicious" weekend brunch in a "sexy", "clubby" and "dark" setting
are the draw at this midpriced Lakeview lair; though downbeat din-

ers dish the "drinks are better than the food" and "service has op-
portunity for improvement", the "upbeat vibe" trumps all for many.

### NEW Corner 41 Bar & Grill *American*  - | - | - | M

**North Center/St. Ben's** | 4138 N. Lincoln Ave. (bet. Berteau &
Warner Aves.) | 773-327-3500 | www.corner41.com

This upscale North Center bar and grill offers a midpriced American
menu including prime beef, a lengthy sandwich list and some Italian-
Med fare, plus full-bar service and local beers from Half Acre Brewery;
there's a rustic-industrial feel to the open, loftlike room with open
ductwork and warm lighting, and you can eat outdoors as well.

### NEW Co-Si-Na Grill Ⓜ *Mexican*  - | - | - | I

**Andersonville** | 1706 W. Foster Ave. (Paulina St.) | 773-271-7103

"Authentic", affordable Mexican fare and "complex, flavorful moles"
draw Andersonville denizens for lunch and dinner to this "appealing
little storefront" with a simple, colorful interior including a painted
concrete floor; P.S. "BYO is encouraged" (with virgin piña coladas
plus strawberry daiquiri and flavored margarita mixes on hand).

### Costa's *Greek*  22 | 19 | 20 | $37

**Oakbrook Terrace** | 1 S. 130 Summit Ave. (Roosevelt Rd.) | 630-620-1100 |
www.costasdining.com

While the Greektown mainstay has closed due to a fire (repairs are
pending), fans attest this midpriced Oakbrook Terrace outpost serves
"traditional, satisfying" Greek fare "in the suburbs" along with a selection of wines from Greece in a "relaxed atmosphere" where "you'll
be treated like family"; N.B. there's live entertainment on weekends.

### Counter, The *Burgers*  20 | 15 | 19 | $19

**Lincoln Park** | 666 W. Diversey Pkwy. (bet. Clark & Orchard Sts.) |
773-935-1995 | www.thecounterburger.com

"Customize" your ("huge") burger and toppings from a "great variety" of "combinations" (including a "bunless bowl") at this Lincoln
Park chain link that also offers "shakes and shareable sides of fries"
in a "hip, dinerlike environment"; some think it's "overpriced for
what it is" but the brew crew likes the "beers on tap."

### Courtright's Ⓜ *American*  25 | 26 | 25 | $66

**Willow Springs** | 8989 S. Archer Ave. (Willow Springs Rd.) |
708-839-8000 | www.courtrights.com

"Overlooking a forest preserve", the "view is always spectacular" at
this "upscale, pricey" Southwest Suburban "fine-dining spot" where
the "wonderful", "inventive" New American cuisine is accompanied by
an "excellent wine list", all served by a "knowledgeable" staff; the
Arts and Crafts setting contributes additional "warmth" and "elegance" to a "night to remember", "especially with the tasting menu."

### NEW Crêpe Crave *Crêpes*  - | - | - | I

**Wicker Park** | 1752 W. North Ave. (bet. Hermitage Ave. & Wood St.) |
773-698-8783 | www.crepecrave.com

Wicker Park's affordable "neighborhood" "quick-service" BYO offers
"tasty crêpes" ("sweet, savory, breakfast – they've got it covered")

and the option to choose "one of their suggested combos or make up your own"; add in a "personable" "counter staff", plus gelato and coffee, and the colorful setting is suitable "for takeout or dine-in."

## Crêpes Cafe Ⓩ *Crêpes* | - | - | - | I

**Loop** | 410 S. Clark St. (Van Buren St.) | 312-341-1313 | www.crepescafe.net

For "French food without attitude", pancake-loving locals seek out this Loop BYO and its "fantastic" sweet and savory crêpes; the cozy quarters are decorated with travel posters, completing an affordable Eastern European–style cafe experience where "you can't go wrong."

## NEW Crêpe Town *Crêpes* | - | - | - | I

**Lakeview** | 3915 N. Sheridan Rd. (Dakin St.) | 773-248-8844

Creative savory, sweet and breakfast crêpes make for budget-friendly bites at this upscale-casual Lakeview counter-service storefront with bright, modern decor in gray and green; you can take out or grab a table, where you can BYO or enjoy a smoothie or coffee.

## Ⓩ Crofton on Wells Ⓩ *American* | 26 | 21 | 25 | $60

**River North** | 535 N. Wells St. (bet. Grand Ave. & Ohio St.) | 312-755-1790 | www.croftononwells.com

Suzy Crofton's "refined", "inventive" New American fare featuring "impressive local ingredients" (including "fabulous vegetarian options") compensates for the "drab decor" at this "steady" River North "treasure" tended by a "professional" staff; patrons who declare it "doesn't get the hype of others but is just as tasty" plead "please don't tell anyone"; P.S. it's "expensive, but worth the price."

## Crust *Pizza* | 19 | 15 | 15 | $23

**Wicker Park** | 2056 W. Division St. (Hoyne Ave.) | 773-235-5511 | www.crustorganic.com

Michael Altenberg's "cool", "casual" Wicker Park pizzeria turns out "gourmet" seasonal pies with a "special", "thin and crispy crust" for patrons who praise the "natural and organic offerings" in both the fare and the "many beers"; "infused vodkas" help take the edge off spotty service, and tabs are "quite reasonable"; P.S. fresh-air fiends gravitate to "one of the large outdoor spaces", front or back.

## Cucina Paradiso *Italian* | ▽ 20 | 20 | 21 | $36

**Oak Park** | 814 North Blvd. (Oak Park Ave.) | 708-848-3434 | www.cucinaoakpark.com

Oak Park's "neighborhood" *cucina* "charms" with "pasta classics with a twist" and other "delicious" Italian fare served in a warm, modern setting with brick and yellow walls hung with posters and photos; "accommodating" service adds to the "experience", and a new patio and moderate prices help make it "worth a visit."

## NEW Cuna Ⓜ *Eclectic* | - | - | - | M

**Lakeview** | 1113 W. Belmont Ave. (bet. Clifton & Seminary Aves.) | 312-224-8588 | www.cunasupperclub.com

The affordable menu at this Lakeview Eclectic gently globe-hops from mini pork belly sandwiches to grilled Amish chicken (plus two levels of tasting menus), with an equally diverse range of wines and specialty cocktails; set in a former art gallery, the hip, architectural space blends brick and concrete, space-age red scoop barstools, Pop Art, water sculpture and a loungey den.

**Curry Hut Restaurant** *Indian/Nepalese* 20 | 15 | 19 | $25
**Highwood** | 410 Sheridan Rd. (bet. Walker & Webster Aves.) | 847-432-2889 | www.curryhutrestaurant.com
Surveyors "welcome" the "change of taste" and "value" at this "kid-friendly" Highwood hut that offers a "unique combination of Nepal and India" and "even Indian wines" and beers; the "run-of-the-mill" decor doesn't need to impress given "attentive" service and an "extensive" "lunch buffet worth coming for" on the budget-loving scene.

**Custom House Tavern** *American* 25 | 23 | 25 | $58
**Printer's Row** | Hotel Blake | 500 S. Dearborn St. (Congress Pkwy.) | 312-523-0200 | www.customhouse.cc
A broader menu of "wonderful new items" (including a tavern menu in the lounge) is replacing the former meat-centric concept at this Hotel Blake New American where "pleasant, efficient service" and a "wine list without the usual suspects" help make the "modern, elegant" quarters suitable "for a business lunch or dinner" and "well worth beating a path to" Printer's Row; N.B. the Food score may not reflect a recent chef change.

**Cyrano's Bistrot & Wine Bar** 🗷 *French* 22 | 19 | 20 | $42
**River North** | 546 N. Wells St. (Ohio St.) | 312-467-0546 | www.cyranosbistrot.com
"Authenticity has made" this River North respite a "keeper" for its "traditional" French bistro "favorites" ("chef Didier [Durand] cares") complete with "quaint" "character" and "streetscape sidewalk" seating; the "reasonable price lets you eat like a Frenchman without the airfare", making it "suitable for casual, business or romantic" meals.

**Czech Plaza** *Czech* ∇ 22 | 8 | 18 | $19
**Berwyn** | 7016 W. Cermak Rd. (bet. Home & Wenonah Aves.) | 708-795-6555 | www.czechplaza.com
"Generous portions" of "inexpensive", "authentic" fare "not for" lightweights draw big eaters to Berwyn's Czech chowhouse where "meals include soup, dessert" and side dishes plus "good beer and broken English"; furthermore, "you can have supper with every grandma in the neighborhood" amid "simple" decor that "hasn't changed in decades" (possibly since 1962).

**D & J Bistro** Ⓜ *French* 24 | 19 | 23 | $43
**Lake Zurich** | First Bank Plaza Ctr. | 466 S. Rand Rd./Rte. 12 (Rte. 22) | 847-438-8001 | www.dj-bistro.com
Lake Zurich's "bustling" "charmer" is a "solid performer" that "belies its location" "in a strip mall" with a "wonderful", "authentic" "French bistro menu", "personal service" and "very European surroundings" including a "congenial bar area" – all of which make it a local "favorite" "in this price range."

| | FOOD | DECOR | SERVICE | COST |
|---|---|---|---|---|

### Dan McGee ☒ *American*     | - | - | - | M |

**Frankfort** | 330 W. Lincoln Hwy. (bet. Elm & Locust Sts.) |
815-469-7750 | www.danmcgeerestaurant.net

Champions cheer "chef Dan gets it" by dishing out "top-notch",
"amply portioned" "American fare" (including "spot-on desserts")
with "cocktails and service" to match at this Frankfort "find"; "comfortable" yet "sophisticated" "minimalist" decor "rounds out the experience", which South Suburbanites swear "saves the trip
Downtown for comparable cuisine."

### Dave's Italian Kitchen *Italian*     | 17 | 11 | 17 | $19 |

**Evanston** | 1635 Chicago Ave., downstairs (bet. Church & Davis Sts.) |
847-864-6000 | www.davesik.com

Boosters believe they're "back in college" at this "Evanston tradition" "run by really nice folks" "that keeps on keeping on" serving
"standard, huge" "homestyle" Italian dishes "at giveaway prices" in
a "casual" "basement" with "simple decor"; unconvinced eaters say
it's not for "adults looking for real food" but "fine for family dining
with the children."

### ☒ David Burke's Primehouse *Steak*     | 25 | 22 | 23 | $71 |

**River North** | The James Chicago Hotel | 616 N. Rush St. (Ontario St.) |
312-660-6000 | www.davidburke.com

"Magnificent" meat praised for its "depth, power and tang" (including long-"aged masterpieces") plus an "excellent array of
sides and desserts", "expansive wine list" and "wonderful"
weekend brunch win fans for this "classy", "contemporary" River
North "steakhouse with imagination" that's "more hip than its competitors"; the "prices can stop your heart quicker than the cholesterol will", and though a few have their "doubts", most agree that
the fare and service "are worth it."

### Davis Street Fishmarket *Seafood*     | 19 | 16 | 18 | $38 |

**Evanston** | 501 Davis St. (Hinman Ave.) | 847-869-3474 |
www.davisstreetfishmarket.com

Evanston locals hit this "reliable" midpriced "neighborhood"
seafooder for a "wealth of fish choices" (including Cajun) "in a casual
atmosphere", "fresh raw oysters" and "lobster specials that can't be
beat"; service can be "iffy" and nostalgists still "miss the old feel" from
before "it made its upscale move", but they're outnumbered by those
who find the nautical decor "attractive", thus it's "often crowded."

### ☒☒☒ deca Restaurant + Bar *French*     | - | - | - | M |

**Streeterville** | Ritz-Carlton Hotel | 160 E. Pearson St., 12th fl.
(Michigan Ave.) | 312-573-5160 | www.fourseasons.com

As part of a multimillion-dollar renovation, the Ritz-Carlton has debuted this new midpriced French brasserie concept featuring *fruits
de mer* and classic dishes from locally sourced ingredients with 40
wines by the glass (half the list); the open setting in the 12th-floor
lobby features multilevel seating, handsome art deco–inspired decor,
adjustable lighting at each table and a chic bar with a sweeping city
view situated by the famous fountain.

| | FOOD | DECOR | SERVICE | COST |
|---|---|---|---|---|

### de cero ⓜ Mexican
21 | 17 | 16 | $32

**West Loop** | 814 W. Randolph St. (bet. Green & Halsted Sts.) | 312-455-8114 | www.decerotaqueria.com

Patrons praise this "modern" West Loop "taco shop" for its "excellent selection" of "tapas-style Mexican" fare, "outstanding cocktails" and "people-watching" amid "trendy", "design-savvy" digs; naysayers call the noshes "overpriced" and "don't understand why this place is so crowded" to which amigos answer "sitting outside in the summer sipping margaritas with duck nachos is the way to live."

### NEW Decolores Mexican
- | - | - | I

**Pilsen** | 1626 S. Halsted St. (17th St.) | 312-226-9886

Fresh Mexican lunch and dinner fare – including traditional dishes, seafood specialties, housemade moles, three flavors of tres leches and agua frescas – comes at affordable prices at this Pilsen storefront BYO; past the charming brick facade, the simple interior is accented by a giant skull mural and other local artwork, plus skylights and ceiling fans.

### Dee's Asian
19 | 16 | 18 | $29

**Lincoln Park** | 1114 W. Armitage Ave. (Seminary Ave.) | 773-477-1500 | www.deesrestaurant.com

"If you want sushi" plus Mandarin and Sichuan specialties all "in one restaurant", this "upscale" Lincoln Park "institution" fills the bill; its "attractive" space complete with roomy patio, "warm, charming" owner and "live jazz" on Fridays have many calling it dee-lightful, but the less-impressed dismiss it as a "jack of all trades, master of none."

### NEW Dee's Place Soul Food/Southern
- | - | - | I

**Wicker Park** | 2114 W. Division St. (Hoyne Ave.) | 312-348-6117

Not to be confused with Dee's in Lincoln Park, this neighborhood storefront BYO in Wicker Park dishes up hearty, inexpensive Southern and soul-food classics (barbecue from the house pit, fried chicken and catfish, greens, mac 'n' cheese); the funky, casual setting hosts a variety of weekend entertainment, including movies and live jazz and blues.

### Deleece Eclectic
19 | 16 | 19 | $32

**Lakeview** | 4004 N. Southport Ave. (Irving Park Rd.) | 773-325-1710 | www.deleece.com

"For a regular night out", fans of this "welcoming" Lakeview vet favor its "fresh, inventive" Eclectic dishes and "fantastic deals on Mondays and Tuesdays" (three courses for $20), not to mention its "pleasing contemporary" interior heavy on "exposed brick and wood" and "nice patio"; some "disappointed" dinner patrons claim its "aspirations are higher than its reach", but even they "recommend brunch."

### Deleece Grill Pub American
∇ 20 | 15 | 18 | $25

**Lakeview** | 3313 N. Clark St. (bet. Aldine Ave. & Buckingham Pl.) | 773-348-3313 | www.deleecegrillpub.com

A casual counterpart to nearby Deleece, this Lakeview standby offers "tasty", "value"-priced steaks, chops and American "comfort" staples (e.g. "a variety of mac 'n' cheese" iterations), which go down well with its "fantastic" craft beers; "warm" decor "with lots of local art on the walls" is another reason locals keep coming back to this "friendly", pubbish place.

### Del Rio ☒ Italian
20 | 15 | 21 | $39

**Highwood** | 228 Green Bay Rd. (Rte. 22) | 847-432-4608

It "hasn't changed in years" (possibly since 1923) and that pleases fans of this "Highwood stalwart", a fourth-generation family-owned "neighborhood red-sauce Italian" appreciated for its "predictable but good food at reasonable cost" ("when you do something right, stick to it") and "vast" wine cellar; ok, maybe it feels "a little tired", but to most it's a "North Shore classic" all the same; N.B. reservations taken for larger parties only.

### Depot American Diner, The  Diner
- | - | - | I

**Far West** | 5840 W. Roosevelt Rd. (bet. Mayfield & Monitor Aves.) | 773-261-8422 | www.depotamericandiner.com

"Such a deal" swoon supporters of this Far West "pinnacle of diner dining" and its "fresh", low-priced, three-meals-a-day American "comfort" classics; regulars "really like their pot-roast sandwich" and "doughnuts to die for", and the "blue-plate specials", a BYO policy and nifty "'50s" decor are more reasons it's "worth going back to."

### Depot Nuevo  Nuevo Latino
18 | 18 | 18 | $30

**Wilmette** | 1139 Wilmette Ave. (bet. Central & Lake Aves.) | 847-251-3111 | www.depotnuevo.com

Surveyors split over the food at this Wilmette way station – literally, it's housed in a 100-year-old train depot – with some reporting "tasty, contemporary takes on" Nuevo Latino fare but others merely a "mediocre" "North Shore idea" of the same; however, there's consensus regarding the "fabulous" margaritas, "cute" colorful decor and "pleasant porch dining" in summer.

### Devon Seafood Grill  Seafood
21 | 21 | 20 | $46

**River North** | 39 E. Chicago Ave. (Wabash Ave.) | 312-440-8660 | www.devonseafood.com

"Your choice of preparations" of fish ordered from a "diverse" menu is the deal at this "solid", "subtly elegant" River North link of an "upscale" seafood chain; the "main floor" and its "crowded" bar boasts plenty of "buzz", while the downstairs dining room's "cozy booths" are "better for conversation" – either way most rate the overall package "nicely done"; P.S. check out the "great happy-hour specials."

### Dining Room
at Kendall College, The ☒ French
23 | 20 | 22 | $40

**Near West** | Kendall College | 900 N. North Branch St. (Halsted St.) | 312-752-2328 | www.kendall.edu

At this "special, hidden" Near West learning ground, Kendall College students prepare the New French "fine-dining" fare, which is served by "nervous, dewy-eyed" trainees in "simple, elegant" digs elevated by "sweeping" skyline views; it's a "nice deal" for lunch or dinner, and a "great way to support" the "next generation of American chefs"; P.S. "they now serve wine."

### Dinotto Ristorante  *Italian*  | 19 | 17 | 19 | $36 |

**Old Town** | 215 W. North Ave. (Wells St.) | 312-202-0302 | www.dinotto.com

Old Towners tout this "charming, comfortable neighborhood favorite" for its "tasty" Italian cooking at "reasonable prices", "great" wine list and "cozy", "traditionally appointed" space augmented with a "wonderful patio"; a few who feel it "needs new menu items" shrug "nothing special", but they're in the minority; P.S. it's well located for dining "pre–Second City or Zanies."

### Di Pescara  *Italian/Seafood*  | 19 | 16 | 19 | $36 |

**Northbrook** | Northbrook Court Shopping Ctr. | 2124 Northbrook Ct. (Lake Cook Rd.) | 847-498-4321 | www.leye.com

"Better-than-average mall grub" satisfies "shoppers", "families" and "ladies who lunch" at this Italian seafooder from the Lettuce group that's especially appreciated given "Northbrook Court's limited selection" of eating options; sure, plenty are "unimpressed", citing an "uninspired" menu and "uneven" service, but it's "always crowded" (and "noisy") nonetheless – so "come early or make a reservation."

### Distinctive Cork  🛇 *American*  | ▽ 21 | 22 | 21 | $35 |

**Naperville** | 192 W. Gartner Rd. (Washington St.) | 630-753-9463 | www.distinctivecork.com

Naperville's "off-the-beaten-path" "gem" of a wine bar offers a "short menu" of "bistro-style" New American small plates and entrees, all designed to go well with the wines available "by the taste, glass, flight or bottle"; it's equally suited for a "light, casual" get-together with friends or a "quiet, romantic" dinner, with weekend jazz and sidewalk dining in summer to further boost the mood.

### Dixie Kitchen & Bait Shop  *Cajun/Southern*  | 19 | 18 | 19 | $23 |

**Evanston** | 825 Church St. (bet. Benson & Sherman Aves.) | 847-733-9030
**Lansing** | 2352 E. 172nd St. (Torrence Ave.) | 708-474-1378
www.dixiekitchenchicago.com

"When a trip to New Orleans isn't in the cards", hit these "casual", "funky" Cajuns in Evanston and Lansing that are "reliable" sources for "Southern-style" sustenance in "generous", "low-priced" portions (including pleasingly "spiced-up breakfast"); the overall experience is "full of fun and flavor", enhanced by "super-kitschy" setups and "prompt", "friendly" service.

### NEW DMK Burger Bar  Ⓜ *Burgers*  | 22 | 17 | 19 | $20 |

**Lakeview** | 2954 N. Sheffield Ave. (Wellington Ave.) | 773-360-8686 | www.dmkburgerbar.com

Restaurateurs David Morton and Michael Kornick "take burgers to another level" at this "trendy" Lakeview spot whose "carefully sourced, grass-fed" beef patties (plus lamb, turkey and veggie versions) come with a bevy of "interesting" topping and fry options, as well as an "extensive craft beer list"; the majority declares it "awesome", but a few humbuggers aver "nothing special" and gripe about "loud" acoustics and "lackluster" service; P.S. "definitely try the milkshakes."

### Don Juan's  *Mexican*  20 | 14 | 19 | $31

**Edison Park** | 6730 N. Northwest Hwy. (Oshkosh Ave.) | 773-775-6438 | www.donjuanschicago.com

An Edison Park "classic" for "many years now" (since 1984), this affordable Mexican is appreciated for its "killer margaritas", 40-plus-label tequila selection and "authentic", seasonal *comida* ordered from "two menus": one features "top-notch standards", the other more "distinctive, creative" dishes; the unenthused cite "dingy" digs and food they claim has gone "downhill" recently, but the fact that it's often "crowded" speaks for itself.

### Dorado  ☒ *French/Mexican*  23 | 13 | 19 | $36

**Lincoln Square** | 2301 W. Foster Ave. (bet. Claremont & Oakley Aves.) | 773-561-3780

"Wonderful", "sophisticated" and definitely "not your run-of-the-mill Mexican", this colorful Lincoln Square standout offers "upscale" yet "reasonably priced" south-of-the-border fare with French influences; factor in the BYO policy, and you've got an "incredible value" – and even if there are often "waits" and service can be "slow", to most it's a "great find in the 'hood."

### NEW Dos Diablos ● *Tex-Mex*  - | - | - | I

**River North** | 15 W. Hubbard St. (bet. Dearborn & State Sts.) | 312-245-5252 | www.dosdiabloschicago.com

Devilish temptations at this River North newcomer include mid-priced Tex-Mex fare for lunch, dinner and late-night, plus plenty of margaritas and other Mexican cocktails; the sprawling, clubby saloon setting features distressed wood and brick, funky light fixtures and a big bar.

### Double Li  *Chinese*  - | - | - | I

**Chinatown** | 228 W. Cermak Rd. (bet. Archer & Wentworth Aves.) | 312-842-7818

A "good alternative" to the usual suspects, this under-the-radar player is touted as "one of the real treasures of Chinatown" by those few surveyors who've discovered it; the "genuine", "spicy" Sichuan fare prepared with "fresh ingredients" is delivered in unpretentious environs, and there's a BYO policy to keep the already-low price down.

### Drake Bros.'  *American*  - | - | - | M

**Gold Coast** | Drake Hotel | 140 E. Walton St. (Michigan Ave.) | 312-932-4626 | www.thedrakehotel.com

This former steakhouse inside the Drake Hotel has undergone some changes of late, and now serves a revamped menu of mid-priced Traditional American fare during the day only (no dinner), including an "outstanding Sunday brunch buffet"; luckily the "fabulous" dark wood–lined setting retains its stellar views out over Lake Michigan.

| | FOOD | DECOR | SERVICE | COST |
|---|---|---|---|---|

### Drawing Room, The ●⊠Ⓜ *American*  ▽ 23 | 24 | 20 | $41

**Gold Coast** | 937 N. Rush St. (bet. Oak & Walton Sts.) | 312-266-2694 | www.thedrchicago.com

Maybe "a restaurant attached to a club is the last place you'd expect to find good food", but this Gold Coast eatery connected to Le Passage (and now owned by Three Headed Productions) exceeds expectations with its "innovative" New American cuisine matched with some of the "most creative cocktails in town", mixed "tableside" upon request; better still, this "place to chill" is open into the wee hours.

### Duchamp Ⓜ *American*  17 | 19 | 17 | $36

**Bucktown** | 2118 N. Damen Ave. (Charleston St.) | 773-235-6434 | www.duchamp-chicago.com

"Fun, creative" New American dishes with a "global reach" from Zealous chef Michael Taus and "attitude-free" service are assets at this Bucktown gastropub, where the "cubist" confines are equipped with communal tables ("convivial" to some, "could be an issue" for others); the jury's still out on the kitchen's "inconsistent" output, however, but all agree that the terrace is "one of Chicago's most beautiful and inviting" outdoor dining options.

### NEW Duckfat Tavern & Grill *American*  - | - | - | M

**Forest Park** | 7218 Madison St. (Elgin Ave.) | 708-488-1493 | www.duckfatgrill.com

Named for its signature duckfat fries, this West Suburban neighborhood tavern serves a midpriced menu of Traditional American and pub food favorites with an upscale slant – think calamari with tequila cocktail sauce, Kobe sliders with truffle butter and four-cheese mac cooked in a skillet; the warm, wood-on-wood setting includes a big bar and seasonal outdoor seating.

### NEW Duck Walk *Thai*  19 | 12 | 15 | $20

**Lakeview** | 919 W. Belmont Ave. (bet. Clark St. & Wilton Ave.) | 773-665-0455

**Lincoln Park** | 1217 W. Fullerton Ave. (bet. Racine Ave. & Surrey Ct.) | 773-327-6200

www.duckwalkchicago.com

"Good, cheap, basic" Thai fare and "sweet" service add up to "solid" neighborhood standby status for this "nothing-fancy" Lakeview original and its Lincoln Park sequel; "speedy delivery" ("it's like the food is beamed to you") and a BYO policy are icing on the cake.

### Duke of Perth *Scottish*  20 | 16 | 18 | $22

**Lakeview** | 2913 N. Clark St. (Oakdale Ave.) | 773-477-1741 | www.dukeofperth.com

Lakeview's longtime Scottish pub offers "authentic" eats (including an "all-you-can-eat fish fry" on Wednesdays and Fridays), "some exotic U.K. beers" and an "outstanding selection of single malts"; there's a "patio in the rear", and the "friendly corner bar atmosphere" with "no TV" and lots of antiques makes it ideal for a "blustery winter night", plus the "price is right."

| | FOOD | DECOR | SERVICE | COST |
|---|---|---|---|---|

**Ed Debevic's** *Diner*  � 15 | 19 | 18 | $22

**River North** | 640 N. Wells St. (Ontario St.) | 312-664-1707
**Lombard** | Yorktown Shopping Ctr. | 157 Yorktown Shopping Ctr.
(Highland Ave.) | 630-495-1700
www.eddebevics.com

Good sports dutifully "doo-wop" at these "true-blue American"
"classic diners" "serving burgers, fries and malts" in River North and
Lombard, where "service means the sassy waitress" gets "rude" and
"dances on the countertop" ("be prepared to become part" of the
"sideshow"); jaded jurors say the "'50s concept" makes for a "cli-
chéd tourist trap" and call the prices "bloated", but others "never
tire" of the "colorful" "shtick"; P.S. "bring the kiddies" – the "place
will match their energy."

**Edelweiss** *German*  19 | 21 | 22 | $32

**Norridge** | 7650 W. Irving Park Rd. (Overhill Ave.) | 708-452-6040 |
www.edelweissdining.com

"When it's good, it's wunderbar" at this "cozy", affordable Norridge
German "neighborhood favorite" that's a "solid" option for "hearty"
"schnitzel and wurst" plus "liters of brews" including Bavarian
beers; the alpine-themed setting is complete with "oompahs from a
live band" on weekends.

**Edwardo's Natural Pizza** *Pizza*  20 | 11 | 15 | $19

**Gold Coast** | 1212 N. Dearborn St. (Division St.) | 312-337-4490 |
www.edwardos.com
**Lincoln Park** | 2662 N. Halsted St. (Wrightwood Ave.) | 773-871-3400 |
www.edwardosonhalsted.com
**Hyde Park** | 1321 E. 57th St. (Kimbark Ave.) | 773-241-7960 |
www.edwardos.com
**South Loop** | 521 S. Dearborn St. (bet. Congress Pkwy. & Harrison St.) |
312-939-3366 | www.edwardos.com
**Skokie** | 9300 Skokie Blvd. (Gross Point Rd.) | 847-674-0008 |
www.edwardos.com
**Wheeling** | 401 E. Dundee Rd. (Milwaukee Ave.) | 847-520-0666 |
www.edwardos.com
**Oak Park** | 6831 W. North Ave. (Grove Ave.) | 708-524-2400 |
www.edwardos.com

"Pie oh my" gush partial patrons of this chain they call "still one
of the best" for "fresh", "flavorful" "stuffed or thin pizzas" plus a
"nice selection of pasta and sandwiches"; the "digs are nothing
special" but "you don't go for the ambiance or any other frills" –
and some stick to "takeout" to bypass "questionable service"
at some locations.

**NEW Edzo's Burger Shop** Ⓜ *Burgers*  - | - | - | I

**Evanston** | 1571 Sherman Ave. (bet. Davis & Grove Sts.) | 847-864-3396 |
www.edzos.com

"Fresh-ground burgers" with a "variety of toppings" and hand-cut
fries done 10 "different ways" "are the big draw" at this budget-loving
lunch-only Evanston "burger joint" "with a little extra flair"; counter
service is "friendly and efficient", "the milkshakes are for real" and
"it's noisy, crowded and worth the trip."

| | FOOD | DECOR | SERVICE | COST |
|---|---|---|---|---|

### EJ's Place  Italian/Steak
22 | 16 | 19 | $49

**Skokie** | 10027 Skokie Blvd. (Old Orchard Rd.) | 847-933-9800 |
www.ejsplaceskokie.com

"Gene and Georgetti's north, if you will" ("the same family, the same meat"), this Skokie Italian steakhouse "standby" lures neighborhood loyalists who "love" its "terrific" beef and seafood and "Wisconsin roadhouse" atmosphere; penurious patrons would prefer "half the portions at half the price" but "brusque service seems to fit the setting."

### NEW Elate  American
∇ 21 | 21 | 16 | $41

**River North** | Hotel Felix | 111 W. Huron St. (Clark St.) | 312-202-9900 |
www.elatechicago.com

This "comfy bar/restaurant" in River North's Hotel Felix offers an "interesting menu" of "appealing" New American plates that most find "innovative yet not intimidating" served in an eco-friendly contemporary setting sporting reclaimed wood tables; prices are "reasonable" and service is "relaxed", but some say the "kitchen is slow", so it's best to be in "no rush."

### Eleven City Diner  Diner
19 | 17 | 17 | $20

**South Loop** | 1112 S. Wabash Ave. (11th St.) | 312-212-1112 |
www.elevencitydiner.com

Surveyors "craving enormous deli sandwiches or matzo ball soup" head to this "cool, retro" "Jewish-American" "cross between a diner and a deli" that's a "welcome oasis in the South Loop" for the "comfort-food" "standards"; added treats are a full soda fountain ("Green River soda – enough said") and "it's open late", though "Michigan Avenue pricing" and occasional "management attitude" influence "hit-or-miss" experiences.

### ☒ Emilio's Tapas  Spanish
24 | 19 | 21 | $32

**Hillside** | 4100 Roosevelt Rd. (Mannheim Rd.) | 708-547-7177

### ☒ Emilio's Tapas Sol y Nieve  Spanish
**Streeterville** | 215 E. Ohio St. (St. Clair St.) | 312-467-7177
www.emiliostapas.com

Doling out an "interesting variety" of "well-prepared and flavorful" "traditional tapas" "to share with friends", these Streeterville and Hillside haunts appeal with "comfortable settings" (both also have a "nice patio") and "reasonable prices"; "unobtrusive, non-pushy service" enhances the experience, and "sangrias go down nicely" too; N.B. the Lincoln Park and Wheaton locations have closed.

### Emperor's Choice ◑ Chinese
23 | 12 | 20 | $27

**Chinatown** | 2238 S. Wentworth Ave. (Cermak Rd.) |
312-225-8800

"Sound Cantonese cooking" including "flawless seafood" and "unusual dishes" draws "gourmets" and adventurers alike to this Chinatown "haven" with a "quiet, intimate ambiance", "crisp white-linen tablecloths" and a saltwater fish tank; it might be "a bit pricier" than its neighbors, but "it's worth it"; N.B. open till midnight except Sunday (when it closes at 11 PM).

| | FOOD | DECOR | SERVICE | COST |
|---|---|---|---|---|

## Entourage on American Lane *American*

**20** | **23** | **20** | **$48**

**Schaumburg** | 1301 American Ln. (bet. Meacham Rd. & National Pkwy.) | 847-995-9400 | www.entourageventures.com

Perhaps a "notch below the best", this Schaumburg American steakhouse wins fans with its "upscale atmosphere" "in the 'burbs" complete with a "great bar", two fireplaces and many wines by the glass; prices are "somewhat reasonable" for the genre, but perfectionists point out the fare and service "would benefit from further refinement."

## NEW Epic Ⓩ *American*

**-** | **-** | **-** | **E**

**River North** | 112 W. Hubbard St. (bet. Clark & LaSalle Sts.) | 312-222-4940 | www.epicrestaurantchicago.com

At this swanky River Norther, chef Stephen Wambach (most recently of Laurent Tourondel's restaurant group) concocts New American fine dining utilizing classic French technique and housemade ingredients – all paired with a serious, well-rounded wine list and signature cocktails; a dramatic winding staircase separates a second-floor dining room with soaring windows from an informal first-floor lounge (with a different menu) and seasonal outdoor dining on a vast rooftop.

## Epic Burger *Burgers*

**22** | **14** | **15** | **$13**

**Loop** | 517 S. State St. (Congress Pkwy.) | 312-913-1373 | www.epicburger.com

"Eco-conscious" quick bites in the Loop earn enthusiasm for this "spacious, modern" "counter-service" concept where a "juicy", "delicious", "well-priced" "burger binge" involves "local ingredients" ("add a fried egg from a free-range chicken" or "nitrate-free bacon"), "sinful milkshakes" and "fast, friendly service"; patty partisans sniffing it's "not as 'epic' as depicted" are outnumbered by those who are "wow"-ed.

## Erie Cafe *Italian/Steak*

**22** | **19** | **23** | **$54**

**River North** | 536 W. Erie St. (Kingsbury St.) | 312-266-2300 | www.eriecafe.com

"It may not be chic" but the "nothing-fancy" "solid steaks" and chops and "old-school staff" make this Italian "standby" "off the beaten path" in River North a "man's kind of place"; with its "pseudo" "Sinatra-era" vibe, "it's nostalgia on a plate, albeit a pricey one"; P.S. there's a "great view on the river[side] patio."

## erwin, an american cafe & bar Ⓜ *American*

**23** | **19** | **21** | **$39**

**Lakeview** | 2925 N. Halsted St. (Oakdale Ave.) | 773-528-7200 | www.erwincafe.com

Namesake chef Erwin Drechsler was "using local seasonal ingredients before it was cool" at his "reliable" contemporary American "Boys Town fixture" that's "popular with young and old alike" for its "tasty, inventive" dishes and "comfort-food" "favorites" (and "one of the best brunches"); it all comes at "value"-minded prices in a "warm and cozy" dining room with a "funky rooftop mural", where patrons happily "talk without shouting."

|  | FOOD | DECOR | SERVICE | COST |
|--|------|-------|---------|------|

## Essence of India *Indian* | 21 | 19 | 20 | $30 |

**Lincoln Square** | 4601 N. Lincoln Ave. (Wilson Ave.) | 773-506-0002 | www.essenceofindiachicago.com

Though "south of Devon", this Lincoln Square subcontinental "does a good job" with its "traditional Indian dishes" (you can even "choose your own spice level") in a "cozy", "pleasing" setting hung with tapestries; quibblers peg it "on the pricier side for the portions", but on the plus side it serves beer and wine and has a summer patio.

## Estrella Negra ☑ *Mexican/Nuevo Latino* | - | - | - | I |

**Logan Square** | 2346 W. Fullerton Ave. (bet. Oakley & Western Aves.) | 773-227-5993 | www.estrellanegra.com

From tacos to tamales, pozole to pomegranate-seed guacamole, this inexpensive, "funky, bohemian" Logan Square spot serves Mexican and "contemporary Latin cuisine with unexpected flair" (including brunch every day) in exposed-brick environs with "*Dia de los Muertos*-inspired art"; even those who find the decor "freaky weird" agree "there's nothing scary about the food or the BYO policy."

## ☒ Ethiopian Diamond *Ethiopian* | 23 | 16 | 20 | $24 |

**Edgewater** | 6120 N. Broadway St. (Glenlake Ave.) | 773-338-6100 | www.ethiopiandiamondcuisine.com

"Still the spot" for "authentic" "finger food" (since "you eat with your hands"), this affordable Edgewater Ethiopian "diamond in the rough" is a "vegetarian's delight" while also "pleasing meat eaters"; it's a "great place for an introduction" to using "sour pancakelike" injera bread instead of utensils as "they will guide you" through the "experience"; P.S. "enjoyable" "live" jazz plays on Fridays.

## ☒ Eve *American* | 22 | 25 | 20 | $56 |

**Gold Coast** | 840 N. Wabash Ave. (Chestnut St.) | 312-266-3383 | www.evechicago.com

"Chic clientele" adorn this "gorgeous", "upscale" Gold Coast New American where a "luxe", "romantic" setting with mirrors and brown suede curtains is the backdrop for "elegant dining" on "innovative", "sophisticated" fare featuring "local and natural" ingredients; "professional service" befits the "pricey" experience, though some say "the best thing" is "the room itself"; P.S. there's also an "attractive front patio."

## ☒ Everest ⓢ Ⓜ *French* | 27 | 27 | 27 | $106 |

**Loop** | One Financial Pl. | 440 S. LaSalle St., 40th fl. (Congress Pkwy.) | 312-663-8920 | www.everestrestaurant.com

"High expectations" (and "stratospheric prices") "reflect the name" of this Loop "special-occasion" French perched on the 40th floor of the Chicago Stock Exchange that surveyors hail as the "summit" for "sublime", "classic white-linen" dining on the "inventive menus" of Jean Joho; an "unbelievable" ("in size and price") "wine binder" with "excellent half-bottles" enhances an experience that's completed with "pomp", "formal" service and a "view that seems to stretch to Iowa"; N.B. jacket suggested.

| | FOOD | DECOR | SERVICE | COST |
|---|---|---|---|---|

### Evergreen  *Chinese*
▽ 23 | 16 | 21 | $33

**Chinatown** | 2411 S. Wentworth Ave. (24th St.) | 312-225-8898
"Excellent", "authentic" "mostly Cantonese cuisine with very fresh ingredients" is "prepared with imagination" at this Chinatown stalwart where "the Peking duck is something to quack about"; "good service" makes this "one of the better" choices in the area – and "one of the best values."

### NEW Fame da Lupo  *Pizza*
- | - | - | I

**Uptown** | 1463-65 W. Leland Ave. (bet. Clark & Dover Sts.) | 773-334-9800 | www.pizzafamedalupo.com
Hand-tossed thin pizzas with extensive topping choices are the claim to fame at this budget-friendly Uptown BYO, which also offers pastas with homemade sauces, sandwiches, salads and desserts; the casual, low-lit neighborhood setting features citrus-colored walls and polished wood tables.

### Fat Willy's Rib Shack  *BBQ/Southern*
23 | 11 | 16 | $22

**Logan Square** | 2416 W. Schubert Ave. (Western Ave.) | 773-782-1800 | www.fatwillysribshack.com
"Satisfied" fans say this Logan Square Southern shack provides "authentic", "greasy" BBQ including "tasty, tangy" ribs "with a lot of verve" (and "don't forget the mac 'n' cheese") "in an appropriate dive setting"; patrons "never feel rushed" whether "inside or outside", plus it's "convenient" for a "movie across the street" and "carryout."

### Feast  *American*
19 | 16 | 17 | $29

**Gold Coast** | 25 E. Delaware Pl. (bet. State & Wabash Sts.) | 312-337-4001
**Bucktown** | 1616 N. Damen Ave. (North Ave.) | 773-772-7100
www.feastrestaurant.com
An "expansive menu of" "fresh, delicious" contemporary American fare, a "martini list" and "reasonable prices" lure feasters to these "casual" Bucktown and Gold Coast "hangouts" that are open all day and "accommodating to kids"; however, what some call "international dishes" are "all over the map" to others, who also suggest service can be "lacking"; P.S. both locations have "outdoor" settings "worth the wait" "in season."

### NEW Felony Franks  *Hot Dogs*
- | - | - | I

**West Loop** | 229 S. Western Ave. (Jackson Blvd.) | 312-243-0505 | www.felonyfranks.com
It's cash only at this casual West Loop hot dogger where offerings include the Felony Frank and the Misdemeanor Weiner; loyalists who "like the concept a lot" attest "you'll get lunch" or budget-friendly dinner while "supporting a business that helps a population so many ignore" – namely the ex-convicts providing the "good service."

### Fiddlehead Café  Ⓜ  *American*
20 | 19 | 21 | $33

**Lincoln Square** | 4600 N. Lincoln Ave. (Wilson Ave.) | 773-751-1500 | www.fiddleheadcafe.com
Fans of this midpriced Lincoln Square "casual", "neighborhood" New American applaud the "well-prepared, imaginative" "seasonal

menu", "wonderful wine and cheese pairings" and "fantastic beer flights"; though nigglers say the "decor could be more interesting", a "warm environment" and "friendly", "attentive service" help make it "genuinely enjoyable."

### Fifty/50, The ● *American* — 21 | 17 | 16 | $23

**Wicker Park** | 2047 W. Division St. (bet. Damen & Hoyne Aves.) | 773-489-5050 | www.thefifty50.com

"Bar food and outside dining" fill this "cool and entertaining" Wicker Park American with a drinking crowd aiming to "catch a game and grab a bite"; despite three levels and 18 flat-screens, it gets "crowded and loud", but service is "adequate" and affordable grub including "teriyaki boneless wings" and "fabulous sweet-potato fries" also has its fans.

### Filippo's *Italian* — ∇ 24 | 18 | 23 | $40

**Lincoln Park** | 2211 N. Clybourn Ave. (Webster Ave.) | 773-528-2211 | www.filipposristorante.com

Lincoln Parkers agree this "solid neighborhood Italian" is "still great after all these years" as they "chill out" while dining on "basic", "delicious" midpriced fare in the "cozy", rustic quarters; it can get "crowded" – "especially on weekends" – though there are "rarely ridiculous waits", and besides, a mostly Boot-centric wine list stokes the "sanctuary" vibe.

### Fiorentino's Cucina Italiana *Italian* — 22 | 17 | 21 | $36

**Lakeview** | 2901 N. Ashland Ave. (George St.) | 773-244-3026 | www.fiorentinoscucina.com

"Traditional" "Southern Italian cuisine" in "plentiful" portions combines with a "romantic atmosphere" to make this "off-the-beaten-track" Lakeview trattoria a "wonderful neighborhood" "gem"; P.S. "in the summer" patrons "welcome" the "outdoor patio option", and moderate prices add to reasons they "leave happy" year-round.

### 545 North *American* — 20 | 19 | 20 | $35

**Libertyville** | 545 N. Milwaukee Ave. (Lake St.) | 847-247-8700 | www.545north.com

There's a "trendy city feeling" in the Northern Suburbs at this "intimate" midpriced Libertyville New American combining "small-scale charm" with "upscale touches" and "enjoyable" fare (including steaks), where "locals" linger and the "bar is usually packed with action"; entertainment "guarantees a lively weekend" and if some dub it "loud" and say service can be "lacking", others call it "happening" with its fireplace-equipped, "summer patio" ("nirvana") and late bar hours (2 AM nightly, 3 AM Friday and Saturday).

### Five Guys *Burgers* — 20 | 10 | 16 | $11

**Lincoln Park** | 2140 N. Clybourn Ave. (Wayne Ave.) | 773-327-5953
**NEW** **Lincoln Park** | 2368 N. Clark St. (bet. Belden Ave. & Fullerton Pkwy.) | 773-883-8930
**NEW** **Rogers Park** | The Morgan at Loyola Station | 6477 N. Sheridan Rd. (Arthur Ave.) | 773-262-9810

*(continued)*

(continued)

## Five Guys

**Naperville** | 22 E. Chicago Ave. (Washington St.) | 630-355-1850
**Oak Park** | 1115 W. Lake St. (bet. Harlem Ave. & Marion St.) |
708-358-0856
www.fiveguys.com

"Juicy, greasy, tasty" burgers "with all the trimmings" "blow away" the
competition according to fans of this "presidential favorite" that's
also prized for its "farm-to-fryer" fries and "free peanuts while you
wait"; so even if doubters "don't get the hype", these "bare-bones"
but "clean and cheery" franchises are "taking the world by storm."

## Flat Top Grill  *Asian*                        20 | 15 | 17 | $21

**NEW** Loop | 30 S. Wabash Ave. (bet. Madison & Monroe Sts.) |
312-726-8400
**Lakeview** | 3200 N. Southport Ave. (Belmont Ave.) | 773-665-8100
**Old Town** | 319 W. North Ave. (Orleans St.) | 312-787-7676
**West Loop** | 1000 W. Washington Blvd. (Carpenter St.) | 312-829-4800
**Evanston** | 707 Church St. (bet. Orrington & Sherman Aves.) |
847-570-0100
**Lombard** | Shops on Butterfield | 305 Yorktown Ctr. (Highland Ave.) |
630-652-3700
**Naperville** | 218 S. Washington St. (bet. Chicago & Jefferson Aves.) |
630-428-8400
**Oak Park** | 726 Lake St. (Oak Park Ave.) | 708-358-8200
www.flattopgrill.com

"Get exactly what you want" at this "fast-casual chain" by "creating
a stir-fry" from a "stunning array" of "vegetables, protein and
sauces" (or else "use their combinations") for dishes that are
"cooked on a flat top"; holdouts hint it's best "if you're not too particular", but fans counter it can be "relatively healthy and cheap",
adding "you don't come here for the service."

## Flatwater  *Eclectic*                          16 | 20 | 14 | $35

**River North** | 321 N. Clark St. (bet. Kinzie St. & Wacker Dr.) |
312-644-0283 | www.flatwater.us

"Take your boat and tie up next to your table" at this "romantic",
Eclectic River North eatery prized for its "river scenery" and "wonderful patio" that's an especially "picturesque" waterside perch for
"alfresco brunch" or "drinks" on a "summer evening"; since "service
could improve" and the fare "isn't exciting", some claim you "pay for
the view" – but that "can't be beat" "on a sunny day."

## Fleming's Prime                               23 | 23 | 22 | $60
## Steakhouse & Wine Bar  *Steak*

**Near North** | 25 E. Ohio St. (bet. State & Wabash Sts.) |
312-329-9463
**Lincolnshire** | Lincolnshire Commons | 960 Milwaukee Ave.
(Aptakisic Rd.) | 847-793-0333
www.flemingssteakhouse.com

"Swanky", "upscale" and "reliable", these city and suburban steakhouses, part of a national chain, please patrons who seek the classics "done well" along with an "enormous selection of wines by the

| | FOOD | DECOR | SERVICE | COST |
|---|---|---|---|---|

glass" (100) and "happy hour in the bar"; "service is super", but since "everything is à la carte" it's best "on the company tab."

### Flight ⊠ *Eclectic*                           17 | 16 | 17 | $38

**Glenview** | 1820 Tower Dr. (Patriot Blvd.) | 847 729-9463 | www.flightwinebar.com

Surveyors buckle up for Eclectic "small plates to pair" with an "excellent wine selection" (150 bottles, 80 by the glass) at this "refreshing" Glenview "independent in a land of chains"; but "Downtown prices", "inconsistency" and "lackluster" decor leave undecideds up in the air.

### Flo Ⓜ *American*                           22 | 17 | 19 | $20

**West Town** | 1434 W. Chicago Ave. (bet. Bishop & Noble Sts.) | 312-243-0477 | www.eatatflo.com

West Towners advise "run don't walk" to this "cozy, laid-back" "neighborhood joint" that's "designed like a rustic general store" and serves "dependable" Traditional and Southwestern American fare including weekend "brunch with a little kick"; prices are affordable and service is "accommodating and brisk" – but since "breakfast is a mob scene", less patient types "go for dinner."

### NEW Flo & Santos                           - | - | - | I
### Pizza & Pub *Pizza/Pub Food*

**South Loop** | 1310 S. Wabash Ave. (bet. 13th & 14 Sts.) | 312-566-9817 | www.gloandsantos.com

The likes of thin-crust pizzas, wings and a 'Polska sampler' meet on the menu at this South Loop amalgam of pub, pizzeria and Polish-Italian restaurant, with full bar service highlighting brews on tap and Polish vodkas; despite the culinary melting pot, the casual setting is industrial pub, with bare wood tables, open ductwork, dangling bulbs, multiple TVs and historic black-and-white photos of the bygone Chicago Coliseum.

### Fogo de Chão *Brazilian/Steak*                           24 | 20 | 24 | $59

**River North** | 661 N. La Salle Dr. (Erie St.) | 312-932-9330 | www.fogodechao.com

"Serious carnivores" "pig out" at this River North churrascaria, a Brazilian "house of meat on a sword" offering an "obscene amount" of "grilled and BBQ" cuts plus an "off-the-charts salad bar"; it's "a little stagey", but service that's "fast and furious" from a "friendly staff" makes it "enjoyable" "especially for a group" – just come "hungry" as the tab "puts your cardiologist's kids through college."

### NEW Folklore ☽ *Argentinean/Steak*                           - | - | - | M

**Ukrainian Village** | 2100 W. Division St. (Hoyne Ave.) | 773-292-1600

A hipster version of Tango Sur hits Ukrainian Village, offering a similar affordable Argentinean steakhouse menu (with the addition of organic and grass-fed beef options) plus – unlike its BYO sibling – a full bar issuing specialty cocktails; the intimate, candlelit setting features a tin ceiling, reclaimed wood accents and a colorful exterior mural.

| | FOOD | DECOR | SERVICE | COST |
|---|---|---|---|---|

**Fonda del Mar** *Mexican/Seafood* | 25 | 17 | 20 | $33 |

**North Center/St. Ben's** | 3908 N. Lincoln Ave. (bet. Byron St. & Larchmont Ave.) | 773-348-7635 | www.fondaonfullerton.com
Compadres compliment this casual North Center Mexican's "first-rate" "creative seafood combinations", "reasonable prices" and "genuinely pleasant servers", though you might need a scorecard to keep up with the changes, as the original Fullerton location briefly turned into a now defunct taco stand, and the 'del mar' menu moved to this location, which housed the short-lived fdm offshoot.

**NEW Fonda Isabel** *Mexican* | - | - | - | M |

**Lombard** | 18 W. 333 Roosevelt Rd. (bet. Church & Luther Aves.) | 630-691-2222 | www.fondaisabel.com
Lombard lays claim to this traditional Mex whose midpriced lunch and dinner offerings are augmented by an all-inclusive set-price menu and a variety of signature margaritas, sangrias and tropical cocktails; painted in rich colors, its two cozy dining rooms are decorated with white tablecloths, vintage-inspired light fixtures and a few art objects.

**Fontana Grill** *Italian* | - | - | - | M |

**Uptown** | 1329 W. Wilson Ave. (bet. Beacon & Malden Sts.) | 773-561-0400 | www.fontanagrill.com
Dishing out moderately priced Italian fare including pizza, plus a "must-try" specialty of *cevapi* (Sarajevo-style grilled beef, lamb sausages and onions in pita), this "cute place with friendly service" is a "treat to have Uptown" and a "hidden neighborhood gem" that "really shines in summer" with its "spacious, flower-lined patio"; P.S. there's also a "thoughtful list of wines" priced at $1 or $2 per ounce.

**foodlife** *Eclectic* | 19 | 13 | 15 | $17 |

**Streeterville** | Water Tower Pl. | 835 N. Michigan Ave. (bet. Chestnut & Pearson Sts.) | 312-335-3663 | www.leye.com
Streeterville's Eclectic "self-serve" "world's fair" of fare is "what a mall food court should be", whether you're "shopping alone" at Water Tower Place or in a "group with no consensus on what to eat" seeking a "decent", "fast and efficient" solution; the "chaos" becomes somewhat "organized" with a "charge card" "payment concept" (you "settle up" on exiting) – still, despite "reasonable prices" you can "end up spending more" than planned.

**Fornetto Mei** *Chinese/Italian* | 20 | 18 | 18 | $38 |

**Gold Coast** | The Whitehall Hotel | 107 E. Delaware Pl. (bet. Michigan Ave. & Rush St.) | 312-573-6300 | www.thewhitehallhotel.com
Though it's "not on most people's radar", this "intimate, well-appointed" hotel eatery "close to Michigan Avenue shopping" "in the heart of the Gold Coast" offers an "interesting combination of Italian and Chinese" such as "thin-crust", "wood-fired pizza" plus "limited" Asian choices including potstickers and egg rolls – some say it's an "odd combo, but they do it well", with "attentive service" and at "decent prices."

| | FOOD | DECOR | SERVICE | COST |
|---|---|---|---|---|

### NEW Fountainhead *Pub Food*

| | - | - | - | M |
|---|---|---|---|---|

**Ravenswood** | 1968-70 W. Montrose Ave. (Damen Ave.) |
773-697-8204 | www.fountainheadchicago.com

Upscale American pub food pairs with a big list of draft microbrews (including two hand-pumped beer engines) and brown liquors at this cozy, midpriced Ravenswood corner spot where booths, a mahogany bar, a fireplace and warm lighting from vintage-inspired light fixtures create a rustic tavern feel; N.B. summer brings a sprawling seasonal roof garden with street lamps and a fountain.

### 1492 Tapas Bar *Spanish*

| | 21 | 19 | 20 | $35 |
|---|---|---|---|---|

**River North** | 42 E. Superior St. (Wabash Ave.) | 312-867-1492 |
www.1492tapasbar.com

Surveyors explore an array of "flavorful", "authentic" tapas at this "cozy" "little" River North "hideaway" "in an old brownstone" where "not overly pricey" Spanish "small-ish plates" are washed down with "varieties of sangria"; though some find the "traditional" decor "nondescript" and service "somewhat spotty" and "slow", friends call the "sidewalk tables" "pleasant" for a "date during summer."

### Francesca's Bryn Mawr *Italian*

| | 22 | 19 | 21 | $35 |
|---|---|---|---|---|

**Edgewater** | 1039 W. Bryn Mawr Ave. (Kenmore Ave.) | 773-506-9261

### Francesca's by the River *Italian*
**St. Charles** | 200 S. 2nd St. (Illinois St.) | 630-587-8221

### Francesca's Campagna *Italian*
**West Dundee** | 127 W. Main St. (2nd St.) | 847-844-7099

### Francesca's Famiglia *Italian*
**Barrington** | Cook Street Plaza | 100 E. Station St. (Hough St.) |
847-277-1027

### Francesca's Fiore *Italian*
**Forest Park** | 7407 W. Madison St. (Harlem Ave.) | 708-771-3063

### Francesca's Forno *Italian*
**Wicker Park** | 1576 N. Milwaukee Ave. (North Ave.) | 773-770-0184

### Francesca's Intimo *Italian*
**Lake Forest** | 293 E. Illinois Rd. (Western Ave.) | 847-735-9235

### Francesca's on Chestnut *Italian*
**NEW Streeterville** | Seneca Hotel | 200 E. Chestnut St. (Dewitt Pl.) |
312-482-8800

### Francesca's on Taylor *Italian*
**Little Italy** | 1400 W. Taylor St. (Loomis St.) | 312-829-2828

### La Sorella di Francesca *Italian*
**Naperville** | 18 W. Jefferson Ave. (bet. Main & Washington Sts.) |
630-961-2706
www.miafrancesca.com
Additional locations throughout the Chicago area

Regulars regard this "reliable", "growing" "local chain" (about to go national) as a "very satisfying experience" with its "rotating menu" of "simple, tasty" "less-traditional Italian" fare at "excellent-value" tabs, "better-than-average service" and "sophisticated, informal" "bistro"-like quarters; even if some locations at peak times "can be as noisy as a soccer match in Milan", fans feel there's "no downside."

|  | FOOD | DECOR | SERVICE | COST |
|---|---|---|---|---|

### Francesco's Hole in the Wall  *Italian*  | 24 | 13 | 20 | $34 |

**Northbrook** | 254 Skokie Blvd. (bet. Dundee & Lake Cook Rds.) |
847-272-0155

Northbrook's "venerable", "one-of-a-kind local hangout" is known
for "ample portions" of "excellent" "traditional Italian fare" "at very
reasonable prices" from a "changing nightly menu", "chummy service" and "lines out the door" ("the trick to getting seated is to go
early or late"); they still don't take reservations, but "good news,
they are now accepting credit cards!"

### Frankie's Scaloppine &  | 18 | 14 | 19 | $27 |
### Fifth Floor Pizzeria  *Italian/Pizza*

**Gold Coast** | 900 Shops | 900 N. Michigan Ave., 5th fl. (bet. Delaware &
Walton Pls.) | 312-266-2500 | www.leye.com

"Exceeding expectations" "for mall eats", this "solid", "reasonably
priced" Lettuce Entertain You Gold Coaster purveys "traditional,
flavorful Italian fare" and "perfectly crispy", "thin-crust pizza" delivered by "friendly" staffers in a setting with "autographed dinner
plates along the walls"; noshers naming it "nothing special" maintain it "will do when you're shopping", though boosters say it's
"worth checking out" anytime.

### NEW  Franks 'N' Dawgs  *Hot Dogs*  | - | - | - | I |

**Lincoln Park** | 1863 N. Clybourn Ave. (bet. Willow & Wisconsin Sts.) |
312-281-5187 | www.franksndawgs.com

Seasonal, foodie-friendly franks and sausages are offered in catego-
ries including 'wild', 'global' and 'haute' at this Lincoln Park dog
house that also boasts artisanal French-style rolls, gourmet condi-
ments and fresh hand-cut fries; the modern, casual diner setting
features dark-wood booths, lots of quilted steel and funky artwork.

### Frasca Pizzeria & Wine Bar  *Pizza*  | 20 | 14 | 17 | $26 |

**Lakeview** | 3358 N. Paulina St. (Lincoln Ave.) | 773-248-5222 |
www.frascapizzeria.com

"Better-than-average" "wood-fired", "brick-oven" pizza made with
"high-end ingredients" lures Lakeview locals to this "neighborhood
wine bar" that also offers "great antipasto" and other Italian fare in
a setting with leather banquettes and large windows; "excellent"
"drink and dinner specials" ("including two-for-one" pies on
Wednesdays), "friendly service" and moderate prices make it
a "repeat performer."

### fRedhots & Fries  *Hot Dogs*  | 21 | 10 | 20 | $10 |

**Glenview** | 1707 Chestnut Ave. (Waukegan Rd.) | 847-657-9200 |
www.fredhots.com

"An interesting selection" of "tubular meats" from "Chicago hot
dogs" to "eclectic gourmet" "specialty sausages" plus "outstanding
garnishes" and "superior fries" ("real Belgian frites with aïoli") are
the draw at this Glenview "shack" with "friendly, efficient service";
some "disappointed" dogcatchers "don't know what all the fuss is
about", but a litter of loyalists lauds the budget-loving grub as
the "real deal."

### Fred's *American*  19 | 24 | 19 | $44

**Gold Coast** | Barneys New York | 15 E. Oak St. (Rush St.) |
312-596-1111 | www.barneys.com

"Well-heeled" "beautiful people" come to "see and be seen" at this "cosmopolitan" Gold Coast "fashionista capital of Chicago" where "accommodating service" accompanies New American fare that's "reasonably priced" "for the location" inside Barneys department store; additional assets include a "small but well-selected wine list", a "fabulous view" "down Oak Street to the lake" and outdoor terrace seating "on a beautiful day."

### Froggy's French Cafe ⊠ *French*  22 | 20 | 23 | $50

**Highwood** | 306 Green Bay Rd. (Highwood Ave.) | 847-433-7080 |
www.froggysrestaurant.com

"They have maintained their Escoffier standards (and their butter content)" since 1980 at Highwood's "civilized" "traditional French restaurant" where "service is consistent and personable" and "kitschy paintings contribute" to the "old-style" ambiance; while "everything tastes the same as it has for years", diners divide on whether "that's a good thing" or it's "getting a little dated", but you can dine here "without breaking the bank."

### ☑ Frontera Grill ⊠ M *Mexican*  27 | 22 | 23 | $45

**River North** | 445 N. Clark St. (bet. Hubbard & Illinois Sts.) |
312-661-1434 | www.fronterakitchens.com

"Magnificent" Mexican cuisine from celebrity chef Rick Bayless is a "revelation" at this River North "temple", voted Chicago's Most Popular and touted for its "bold", "complex flavors" ("he won *Top Chef Masters* for a reason"), "drinks as spectacular as" the fare and "colorful decor" with "museum-quality artwork"; the "first-come, first-served" "crowds can be daunting, but it's worth the wait" to a "cultish following" that boasts "you have to believe Mexico is jealous" and calls the prices "totally reasonable"; P.S. "hint: sit at the bar for the same food but faster service."

### Fuego Mexican
### Grill & Margarita Bar M *Mexican*  24 | 19 | 23 | $30

**Logan Square** | 2047 N. Milwaukee Ave. (Armitage Ave.) | 773-252-1122 |
www.fuegomexicangrill.com

"Upscale" and "large", this midpriced Logan Square cantina is a "notch above your average Mexican" say locals who promise it "will exceed your expectations" for service and food with its "sophisticated moles and seafood preparations"; "outstanding margaritas" are also in the mix, and it's all served in an "upbeat, lively yet not-too-crowded atmosphere"; N.B. there's a lounge and nightclub upstairs.

### Fulton's on the River ⊠ *Seafood/Steak*  19 | 20 | 18 | $47

**River North** | 315 N. La Salle Dr. (Wacker Dr.) | 312-822-0100 |
www.fultonsontheriver.com

Fin fans are lured to River North's "solid corporate seafood cousin of Disney's Orlando place" with its "excellent variety" of "fresh" fish,

| | FOOD | DECOR | SERVICE | COST |

"tender steaks" and "classy decor" featuring a "big bar" and a "beautiful setting on the river"; the less-enchanted cite "inconsistent service" and "pretty standard fare", saying it's best "in the summer if you can sit outside", while wallet-watchers recommend lunch as "more affordable."

### ☒ Gabriel's ☒☒ French/Italian — 25 | 23 | 25 | $72
**Highwood** | 310 Green Bay Rd. (Highwood Ave.) | 847-433-0031 | www.egabriels.com

Gabriel Viti "runs a hands-on operation" at his "intimate", "romantic" Highwood restaurant, which devotees dub a "mecca for exceptional eats" for its "wonderful take on Italian" with an "obvious French influence", "outstanding wine list" and "excellent", "personal service"; though some surveyors call it "too pricey", and others lobby for "some new dishes", all agree it's a "first-class night out."

### Gaetano's ☒ Italian — 24 | 19 | 23 | $48
**Forest Park** | 7636 Madison St. (bet. Ashland & Lathrop Aves.) | 708-366-4010 | www.gaetanos.us

"Bringing Italy to the western suburbs", this Forest Park "surprise" offers "imaginative, tradition-based *cucina*" with "fresh ingredients" that's "reasonably priced" for the quality, along with an excellent selection of wines; the "small" setting with art-adorned walls can be "a bit cramped, but it's lovely" and the "staff is friendly and professional."

### ☒ Gage, The American — 22 | 22 | 22 | $40
**Loop** | 24 S. Michigan Ave. (bet. Madison St. & Monroe Dr.) | 312-372-4243 | www.thegagechicago.com

"Inventive" New American "comfort food" at "upscale prices" stays "in step with the season" at this gastropub "gem along Michigan Avenue" that's set in a "historic" Loop building with "beautiful decor and details" "right across from Millennium Park" (a "perfect location" for "hitting the Art Institute or going to the orchestra"); "servers know their stuff", and there's a "sidewalk cafe" and a "fantastic" "beer and spirits selection" plus a "lively" 50-ft. mahogany bar – just know it's "hard to park" and the "acoustics" can be "deafening."

### Gale Street Inn American — 22 | 15 | 21 | $30
**Jefferson Park** | 4914 N. Milwaukee Ave. (Lawrence Ave.) | 773-725-1300 | www.galestreet.com
**Mundelein** | 935 Diamond Lake Rd. (Rte. 45) | 847-566-1090 | www.galest.com ☒

Rib wranglers feel like they're "in a supper club" when they "walk through the door" of these separately owned "old-school" Americans in Jefferson Park and Mundelein "famous for" "reasonably priced", "perfectly seasoned" "fall-off-the-bone" slabs of meat and "fantastic side dishes"; those who've had it on their "'reliable list' for years" say the fare and "friendly service" "will keep you coming back."

### Gaylord Fine Indian Cuisine Indian — 22 | 19 | 21 | $34
**Gold Coast** | 100 E. Walton St. (bet. Michigan Ave. & Rush St.) | 312-664-1700

*(continued)*

### Gaylord Fine Indian Cuisine

**Schaumburg** | 555 Mall Dr. (Higgins Rd.) | 847-619-3300
www.gaylordll.com

"Lots of interesting", "delicious" Indian dishes "that aren't too spicy" –
plus an "inexpensive lunch buffet" with an "often-changed selection" –
are wielded by "welcoming" servers at this midpriced city and
suburban duo; the Gold Coast location has "quite attractive decor",
and Schaumburg features a "woodwork bar with an Indian theme."

### Geja's Cafe  *Fondue*                    | 21 | 20 | 20 | $50 |

**Lincoln Park** | 340 W. Armitage Ave. (Orleans St.) | 773-281-9101 |
www.gejascafe.com

Lincoln Parkers liken this "folksy" fondue "throwback" to "'60s-era"
spots "where romance blossomed in the dark" while dunking into
melted "wonderful chocolate" and classic "Gruyère cheese" (plus a
"variety of seafood and meat"); it's "a little pricey", but there are "well-
chosen" wines (50 by the glass), and daters declare "if couples can't
enjoy soft lights and live flamenco guitar" (weekends only) while
dipping dinner, "it's breakup time"; N.B. no kids under age 10.

### NEW  Gemini Bistro  Ⓜ *American*        | 21 | 20 | 20 | $39 |

**Lincoln Park** | 2075 N. Lincoln Ave. (Dickens Ave.) | 773-525-2522 |
www.geminibistrochicago.com

Patrons of this "quality neighborhood Lincoln Park bistro" situated
on a "desolate stretch of Lincoln Avenue" praise Jason Paskewitz's
"well-prepared", moderately priced New American fare, "ever-
changing menu" and "lively atmosphere" in a "mature", "glamorous
yet understated" setting; a few note service, while "accommodating", is "less than polished" and it's "hard to hear at peak dining
hours", "still", it's "worth a visit."

### ☑ Gene & Georgetti  ⓈＳ *Steak*         | 24 | 17 | 22 | $63 |

**River North** | 500 N. Franklin St. (Illinois St.) | 312-527-3718 |
www.geneandgeorgetti.com

Carnivores who "like their steak with a step back in time" plead
"save me a seat" at River North's "Chicago cow classic" "under the
el tracks" – a "masculine" meatery with "melt-in-your-mouth" beef,
"garbage salad and strong drink"; sentimental surveyors "savor" the
"old-school" decor "untouched by interfering interior decorators"
and "grumpy service that's part of the shtick", but modernists who
muse it "must have been something in its day" mostly leave it to the
"regulars who get special treatment."

### ☑ Gibsons Bar & Steakhouse  ◑ *Steak*   | 26 | 21 | 24 | $64 |

**Gold Coast** | 1028 N. Rush St. (Bellevue Pl.) | 312-266-8999
**Rosemont** | Doubletree Hotel | 5464 N. River Rd. (bet. Balmoral &
Bryn Mawr Aves.) | 847-928-9900
www.gibsonssteakhouse.com

"Waiters show you the slabs before they're cooked" at these "brash"
city and suburban "speakeasy-styled steakhouses" serving "big",
"succulent" steaks, "big side dishes" and "big desserts" at "big

prices"; the "professional service" is "terrific" and "they pour a righteous drink", while the "people-watching" is peppered with "celebrities", "pro athletes", "cougars and sugar daddies" (especially in the "piano bar"), and if the Rosemont offshoot is "not quite the same" as the "Rush Street cornerstone", on the plus side it's also open till midnight most nights.

### NEW Gilt Bar ⌧Ⓜ American                          - - - M

**River North** | 230 W. Kinzie St. (Franklin St.) | 312-464-9544
Elevated New American gastro grub fashioned from artisanal ingredients gives new life to the former Aigre Doux space in River North, where French Laundry and Alain Ducasse veteran Brendan Sodikoff is turning out a midpriced menu complemented by classic cocktails, microbrews and a compact global wine list; the funky-chic surroundings are adorned with ornate antique mirrors, a hammered brass bar and vintage streetlamps.

### Gioco Italian                                  25 21 22 $42

**South Loop** | 1312 S. Wabash Ave. (13th St.) | 312-939-3870 | www.gioco-chicago.com
For "quality" dining in the South Loop, surveyors look to the "excellent" seasonal Northern Italian fare ("nothing trendy or silly") including "heavenly pasta with wild boar sauce" at this "happening" "former speakeasy" from Jerry Kleiner (Marché, Red Light, 33 Club); "it's a little expensive", but the "warm", "urban" "exposed-brick decor" with "open kitchen" is home to a "noisy fun atmosphere" and "friendly, competent service"; P.S. it's also "near the Convention Center."

### ⊠ Giordano's Pizza                             23 15 18 $22

**Loop** | 135 E. Lake St. (Upper Michigan Ave.) | 312-616-1200 ◑
**Loop** | 225 W. Jackson Blvd. (Franklin St.) | 312-583-9400
**River North** | 730 N. Rush St. (Superior St.) | 312-951-0747 ◑
**Lakeview** | 1040 W. Belmont Ave. (Kenmore Ave.) | 773-327-1200
**Edison Park** | 5927 W. Irving Park Rd. (Austin Ave.) | 773-736-5553
**Northwest Side** | 2855 N. Milwaukee Ave. (Wolfram St.) | 773-862-4200
**Hyde Park** | 5311 S. Blackstone Ave. (53rd St.) | 773-947-0200
**Southwest Side** | 5159 S. Pulaski Rd. (Archer Ave.) | 773-582-7676 ◑
**Southwest Side** | 6314 S. Cicero Ave. (63rd St.) | 773-585-6100 ◑
**Greektown** | 815 W. Van Buren St. (Halsted St.) | 312-421-1221
www.giordanos.com
Additional locations throughout the Chicago area
"Stuffed and satisfied customers" of "all ages" crave the "delicious prototypical" "Chicago deep-dish" at this family of affordable local pie palaces, which is "why there's usually a wait"; those who claim the spots are "unfairly maligned by pizza snobs" add so what if "service and decor are unremarkable" – you're "there for" the pie.

### ⊠ Glenn's Diner and Seafood House Diner   24 14 21 $29

**Ravenswood** | 1820 W. Montrose Ave. (Honore St.) | 773-506-1720 | www.glennsdiner.com
An "eclectic crowd" gathers for "bargains on excellent fresh fish" that's "well prepared with restraint" plus Traditional American diner

fare including "breakfasty meals" served all day at this Ravenswood "local dive" and "hidden treasure" where "service is attentive and friendly" and "fair corkage for BYO is a bonus" (it has "limited bar offerings"); gregarious graders suggest it for "some old-fashioned noise and prices", while conspiratorial types whisper "let's keep this" "a secret"; P.S. Tuesday's "all-you-can-eat crab legs is a steal."

## Glen Prairie *American*  23 | 21 | 21 | $34

**Glen Ellyn** | Crowne Plaza Glen Ellyn | 1250 Roosevelt Rd. (Finley Rd.) | 630-613-1250 | www.glenprairie.com

"Surprising for a suburban hotel restaurant", this "green"-minded "find" in the Crowne Plaza Glen Ellyn incorporates "fresh selections from local purveyors" in its "reasonably priced" New American cuisine and offers a "modest", "interesting wine list with organic selections"; a "knowledgeable staff" and "beautiful" "prairie-style decor" featuring recycled wood and earth tones underscore the "sustainable" scene, even if "they're not reinventing the wheel."

## Gold Coast Dogs *Hot Dogs*  19 | 6 | 13 | $10

**Loop** | 159 N. Wabash Ave. (bet. Lake & Randolph Sts.) | 312-917-1677
**Loop** | Union Station | 225 S. Canal St. (bet. Adams St. & Jackson Blvd.) | 312-258-8585
**Loop** | Ogilvie Transportation Ctr. | 500 W. Madison St. (Canal St.) | 312-715-9488 🗷
**O'Hare Area** | O'Hare Int'l Airport | Concourse L (I-190) | 773-462-7700 ◑
**O'Hare Area** | O'Hare Int'l Airport | Terminal 3 (I-190) | 773-462-9942
**O'Hare Area** | O'Hare Int'l Airport | Terminal 5 (I-190) | 773-462-0125
**Rosemont** | Rosemont Market Pl. | 7084 Mannheim Rd. (Touhy Ave.) | 847-759-1520
**Southwest Side** | Midway Int'l Airport | 5700 S. Cicero Ave. (55th St.) | 773-735-6789 ◑
www.goldcoastdogs.net

Patrons "woof!" their approval for this "quintessential" series of "stands" dispensing the "true Chicago dog" – "and don't forget the peppers" – "at a good price"; admirers warn "service with a smile this is not" and suggest "forget the decor" (just "what do you expect?"), and though some surveyors report "underwhelming" eats at what was once their "go-to", most insist it's "a must when you're in town."

## Goose Island Brewing Co. *Pub Food*  17 | 16 | 18 | $23

**Wrigleyville** | 3535 N. Clark St. (Addison St.) | 773-832-9040
**Lincoln Park** | 1800 N. Clybourn Ave. (Sheffield Ave.) | 312-915-0071
www.gooseisland.com

"You can't beat their brews" and the "basket of homemade chips" at these affordable "local" Lincoln Park and Wrigleyville "staple stop-off" microbreweries appealing to "young singles, families and beer snobs" alike; even if the suds "outshine" the "upscale bar food" and "service could use some work", it's a "must" for "all pub crawls" – tip: have the "sampler if someone else is driving."

## Gordon Biersch
**Brewery Restaurant** *Pub Food*

| 16 | 17 | 18 | $27 |

**Bolingbrook** | Promenade Bolingbrook | 639 E. Boughton Rd. (Janes Ave.) | 630-739-6036 | www.gordonbiersch.com

"If you can't find a true local microbrewery", this affordable Bolingbrook chain link is a "fine substitute" serving up "delicious" "craft beers" that "beat" the "decent" American pub grub (though all hail the "amazing" garlic fries); an "enjoyable happy-hour kinda place", it's not particularly "exciting", but the "relaxed" atmosphere is well suited to "kicking back with friends."

## Grace O'Malley's *Pub Food*

| 18 | 20 | 18 | $21 |

**South Loop** | 1416 S. Michigan Ave. (14th St.) | 312-588-1800 | www.graceomalleychicago.com

Known as a "nice Irish pub in the South Loop" where the Celtic and Traditional American "grub" is "fairly priced" "and the beer is cold" (so "what else do you want" from a bar?), this "low-key" "place to hang out with friends" is considered a "keeper" by "locals"; the "on-tap selection" adds to reasons regulars "return."

## graham elliot ⊠Ⓜ *American*

| 24 | 22 | 22 | $70 |

**River North** | 217 W. Huron St. (bet. Franklin & Wells Sts.) | 312-624-9975 | www.grahamelliot.com

"Cult followers" who favor Graham Elliot Bowles' "trendy" "deconstructed" New American "comfort" cuisine "mingling junk food and high ingredients" laud his "low-key" River North "passion project" as "kooky, innovative and totally delicious"; with its hefty tabs, some diners pan it as "pretentious" and say "substance" is often "drowned out by style" and "deafening music", but proponents of the "warm, inviting" setting and "down-to-earth staff" dub it "fantastic in every way"; N.B. grahamwich sandwich shop is in the works.

## Grand Lux Cafe *Eclectic*

| 20 | 21 | 19 | $29 |

**River North** | 600 N. Michigan Ave. (Ontario St.) | 312-276-2500 | www.grandluxcafe.com

Offering "pages and pages of options", this "classier counterpart" to the Cheesecake Factory located in River North serves "nicely done" Eclectic dishes in a "loud", somewhat "over-the-top" "high-ceilinged" setting inspired by European grand cafes; portions are as "ridiculously large" as the original's (but a bit "more expensive"), so there's still "no room" for the "decadent" desserts.

## Great Lake ⊠Ⓜ *Pizza*

| 23 | 11 | 11 | $22 |

**Andersonville** | 1477 W. Balmoral Ave. (bet. Clark St. & Glenwood Ave.) | 773-334-9270

Andersonville's "cramped", controversial "artisanal pizza" "hole-in-the-wall" divides diners into fans who warrant it's "worth the wait" for pies that are "more of an art form than most" with "daily choices reflecting local foods", and doubters who claim it may be "above-average" but is "overpriced" with "inflexible" service and "does not live up to the hype"; P.S. open only for dinner Wednesday through Saturday, "and don't forget a bottle of wine as it's BYO."

### Greek Islands  *Greek*

21 | 19 | 21 | $31

**Greektown** | 200 S. Halsted St. (Adams St.) | 312-782-9855 ☽
**Lombard** | 300 E. 22nd St. (Highland Ave.) | 630-932-4545
www.greekislands.net

"Jovial crowds" cheer this "anchor of Greektown" (with a Lombard sibling) as "authentic to a degree" with "consistently well-prepared" "Greek favorites" and "fresh seafood that lifts it" "above most of its *'opa!'*-shouting neighbors"; "flaming cheese and people-watching" in "friendly" if somewhat "kitschy" confines are additional pluses, even as contrarians call out "standard" sustenance and service that swings from "speedy" to "slow."

### ☑ Green Zebra  *Vegetarian*

26 | 23 | 24 | $53

**West Town** | 1460 W. Chicago Ave. (Greenview Ave.) | 312-243-7100 | www.greenzebrachicago.com

"No one will miss the meat" with the "best vegetarian dining in Chicago" at Shawn McClain's "brilliant" West Town "innovator" where the "high-end", "creative, edgy" small plates are "almost totally veggie" and boast "plenty of flavors, a variety of influences" and "seasonal ingredients"; specialty "libations", "excellent brunch" and a "lovely staff" complete the "satisfying" supping in this "soothing", "subdued" sage-colored modern setting.

### Grill on the Alley, The  *American*

21 | 21 | 21 | $48

**Streeterville** | Westin Hotel | 909 N. Michigan Ave. (Delaware Pl.) | 312-255-9009 | www.thegrill.com

"Traditional" American chophouse fare and "comfort food in large quantities" – like "delicious steak, seafood", pot pie and "cobbler that's pure joy" – satisfy diners at this somewhat pricey Streeterville branch of the Beverly Hills original set in the Westin Michigan Avenue; the dark-wood and leather dining room is "quiet" with "usually knowledgeable, caring service", while a "warm and comfortable", "lively bar" area adds to the bonhomie.

### Grillroom, The  *Steak*

15 | 16 | 17 | $42

**Loop** | 33 W. Monroe St. (bet. Dearborn & State Sts.) | 312-960-0000 | www.restaurants-america.com

"A wide range" of "typical steakhouse choices with some salads" delivered with "quick service" in a "modern ambiance" makes this Loop lair from the Bar Louie and Midtown Kitchen folks the "place for a power lunch" or other "business dining"; "it's pleasant" and "perfectly adequate", though some say it's "pricey for dinner."

### Gruppo di Amici  Ⓜ *Pizza*

▽ 16 | 16 | 18 | $31

**Rogers Park** | 1508 W. Jarvis Ave. (Greenview Ave.) | 773-508-5565 | www.gruppodiamici.com

"Thin-crust", "wood-fired pizza" and "modern Italian-style entrees" draw "value"-minded Rogers Park regulars to this "warm", "cozy" "neighborhood place"; true, "there aren't a lot of other options" nearby, but "friendly service offsets the average" fare, and "terrific martinis" don't hurt either.

|  | FOOD | DECOR | SERVICE | COST |
|---|---|---|---|---|

### Habana Libre  *Cuban*
▽ 22 | 10 | 18 | $24

**West Town** | 1440 W. Chicago Ave. (bet. Bishop St. & Greenview Ave.) | 312-243-3303

"Tasty pork preparations", empanadas and other "authentic" fare make diners "dream of Cuba" at this West Town "BYO neighborhood joint"; an "attentive staff" and "good value" add to reasons it also suits "for a weeknight date" or a "big group."

### Hachi's Kitchen  *Japanese*
- | - | - | M

**Logan Square** | 2521 N. California Ave. (bet. Fullerton St. & Logan Blvd.) | 773-276-8080 | www.hachiskitchen.com

Sushi so "fresh" it's "like it swam to your plate" (including "delicious original rolls") joins "other Japanese specialties" in luring Logan Square locals to this "beautiful", "high-ceilinged" sibling of Sai Café; acolytes applaud the staff and say there's "rarely a wait", which along with moderate prices and a seasonal patio make it suitable "for friends or a date."

### Hackney's  *Burgers*
18 | 15 | 19 | $22

**Printer's Row** | 733 S. Dearborn St. (bet. Harrison & Polk Sts.) | 312-461-1116

**Glenview** | 1241 Harms Rd. (Lake Ave.) | 847-724-5577

**Glenview** | 1514 E. Lake Ave. (bet. Sunset Ridge & Waukegan Rds.) | 847-724-7171

**Wheeling** | 241 S. Milwaukee Ave. (Dundee Rd.) | 847-537-2100

**Lake Zurich** | 880 N. Old Rand Rd. (Rand Rd.) | 847-438-2103

**Palos Park** | 9550 W. 123rd St. (La Grange Rd.) | 708-448-8300

www.hackneys.net

At this local chain of "good-old burger-joint" "time capsules" (Printer's Row is newer), hankerers hail the "huge" "Hackneyburger" "on dark rye" and "onion rings fried as a brick" as a "guilty pleasure" supplying "all the grease you need for a year"; the "roadhouse atmosphere" and service vary by location, but there's an option to "sit outside" and a "decent beer selection" at all, and though modernists sniff it's just plain "old", it's also "held the line on price."

### Hai Yen  *Chinese/Vietnamese*
21 | 13 | 18 | $23

**Lincoln Park** | 2723 N. Clark St. (Diversey Pkwy.) | 773-868-4888

**Uptown** | 1055 W. Argyle St. (B'way) | 773-561-4077

www.haiyenrestaurant.com

It's "definitely not high-end" joke fans of this duo's "authentic Vietnamese cuisine" (including "steaming bowls of pho") that's mixed with Mandarin Chinese choices and "amazing fresh bubble teas" – all at "reasonable prices"; "bland but pleasant decor" and "so-so service" come with the territory, though cognoscenti call the Uptown location more culinarily "adventurous" than Lincoln Park.

### Half Shell  ⊄  *Seafood*
24 | 7 | 16 | $37

**Lakeview** | 676 W. Diversey Pkwy. (bet. Clark & Orchard Sts.) | 773-549-1773 | www.halfshellchicago.com

Fish lovers fancy this Lakeview "basement" seafooder, a no-reservations "madhouse" where "amazing crab legs and raw bar" options, "beer by the pitcher", "unfriendly service and cheap decor" converge for some of the "best value" dining in town ("just bring cash", they don't take cards); P.S. those not feeling the "dark", "dive" digs are "part of the charm" head for the "outdoor terrace in the summer."

## Hamburger Mary's *Burgers*

17 | 16 | 20 | $18

**Andersonville** | 5400 N. Clark St. (Balmoral Ave.) | 773-784-6969 | www.hamburgermaryschicago.com

"Pleasantly mixed crowds" of "all ages, genders and sexual orientation" convene at Andersonville's "kitsch" "center of activity" for "terrific burgers" and "interesting twists on traditional bar" bites plus "housemade microbrews"; seating options include a "playhouse upstairs", a "rec room with sports bar theme" and "outdoor dining", and if it's "a little bit pricey for what you get", it's also "enjoyable dinner theater" – "how can you beat a drag queen waitress and your bill delivered in a slipper?"

## NEW Hana Restaurant 🍽 *Japanese*

- | - | - | M

**Rogers Park** | 6803 N. Sheridan Rd. (Pratt St.) | 773-338-8815

This affordable, family-owned neighborhood Japanese in Rogers Park specializes in sushi rolls (no sashimi or nigiri) and teriyaki, plus bargain lunch specials, all served in a casual, no-frills storefront space with bare tables, bare walls and bright lighting; N.B. there's no booze, and no BYO.

## 🔲 Hannah's Bretzel 🍽 *Sandwiches*

23 | 13 | 19 | $13

**Loop** | 180 W. Washington St. (bet. La Salle & Wells Sts.) | 312-621-1111
**Loop** | Illinois Ctr. | 233 N. Michigan Ave. (Water St.) | 312-621-1111
www.hannahsbretzel.com

Some of the "best and freshest-tasting sandwiches in the Loop" are served at these twin "Downtown workday spots" that heap "high-end ingredients" on "delicious" "pretzel bread" and offer a "wall" of "fancy chocolate bars" "for dessert"; while the budget brigade bristles that it's "expensive for what you get", most "don't mind paying a bit more" for organic ingredients; N.B. Washington Street has limited seating, while Michigan Avenue has plenty.

## NEW Han 202 *Asian/Eclectic*

∇ 25 | 25 | 25 | $25

**Near South Side** | 605 W. 31st St. (bet. Lowe Ave. & Wallace St.) | 312-949-1314 | www.han202restaurant.com

Near South Siders have taken to this Asian-Eclectic BYO, finding "excellent value" in its prix fixe menu of "interesting, flavorful" fare served by a "friendly", "attentive staff" amid "crisp decor"; P.S. there's "limited seating", but "it's well worth planning ahead."

## NEW Happ Inn Bar & Grill *American*

17 | 19 | 17 | $30

**Northfield** | 305 S. Happ Rd. (Willow Rd.) | 847-784-9200 | www.thehappinn.com

Kindred spirits are "rooting for" this midpriced Carlos' spin-off concept in Northfield that's a "comfortable setting" for American "comfort food" with a "nice outdoor seating area"; some who are "not happy" guess it might be "too popular" (and "noisy") resulting in "uneven" fare and "rocky service", but repeat customers contend it's "getting better."

| | FOOD | DECOR | SERVICE | COST |
|---|---|---|---|---|

## Happy Chef Dim Sum House ● *Chinese*  23 | 8 | 15 | $28

**Chinatown** | 2164 S. Archer Ave. (Cermak Rd.) | 312-808-3689

"Enjoyable dim sum" and Chinese "main dishes" plus "reasonable pricing" keep this Chinatown spot "hopping" with "happy" patrons despite "nondescript decor" and an occasional "language barrier"; service varies from "quick" to "being ignored", but since orders are written "on a menu sheet and brought to your table", "you don't have to flag down carts" for these "bites of heaven."

## Hard Rock Cafe ● *American*  12 | 20 | 14 | $29

**River North** | 63 W. Ontario St. (bet. Clark & Dearborn Sts.) | 312-943-2252 | www.hardrockcafe.com

"Rock memorabilia" is the claim to fame of this "noisy", "nostalgic", music-driven American chain link in River North, and if the food doesn't exactly rock, it's fine for "enjoying a burger and a beer"; but those who deem the concept "so yesterday" ("does anyone still think this is cool?") feel it may be best left to "headbangers", "tourists" and youngsters who "love" those T-shirts.

## Harry Caray's *Italian/Steak*  20 | 20 | 20 | $42

**River North** | 33 W. Kinzie St. (Dearborn St.) | 312-828-0966

**Rosemont** | O'Hare International Ctr. | 10233 W. Higgins Rd. (Mannheim Rd.) | 847-699-1200

**Lombard** | 70 Yorktown Shopping Ctr. (Butterfield Rd.) | 630-953-3400

## Harry Caray's Seventh Inning Stretch *Italian/Steak*

**Southwest Side** | Midway Int'l Airport | 5757 S. Cicero Ave. (55th St.) | 773-948-6300

www.harrycarays.com

To fans who "feel the presence of Harry himself", this phalanx of "fancy sports bars" is "exciting, noisy" and "less stuffy" than the steakhouse staples, with "enjoyable and tasty" (if "not gourmet") "steaks and oversize Italian specialties" plus "great baseball memorabilia" (including the "Bartman ball" Downtown); underwhelmed umps "go for the kitsch" and the "bar scene, especially when the Cubs are on TV", knocking the "overpriced", "mediocre food" and "touristy" tone.

## NEW Havana ☒ *Nuevo Latino*  - | - | - | M

**River North** | 412 N. Clark St. (bet. Hubbard & Kinzie Sts.) | 312-644-1900

River North's former Mambo Grill space has been revived with a similar midpriced Nuevo Latino menu, served for lunch and dinner, along with a slew of specialty cocktails; aglow in natural light by day and golden lighting by night, the setting features dark wood, mirrors, stone tiles and a display of dining-related words snaking around the ceiling edge; there's also seasonal sidewalk seating.

## HB Home Bistro Ⓜ *American*  25 | 20 | 25 | $35

**Lakeview** | 3404 N. Halsted St. (Roscoe St.) | 773-661-0299 | www.homebistrochicago.com

Lakeview locals "keep coming back" to Joncarl Lachman's "small" New American BYO for its "good vibe" and "excellent fine dining"

|  | FOOD | DECOR | SERVICE | COST |

featuring "glorious" "seasonal" "combinations in every dish" served by an "accommodating", "enthusiastic" staff; it's so "affordable" that surveyors say "for the price, we ripped them off"; P.S. "make reservations as the few tables fill up fast."

### Heartland Cafe  *Eclectic/Vegetarian*
| | 16 | 13 | 18 | $21 |

**Rogers Park** | Heartland Bldg. | 7000 N. Glenwood Ave. (Lunt Ave.) | 773-465-8005 | www.heartlandcafe.com

Opened in 1976, this "vegetarian-friendly" Rogers Park "throwback" is an "unwavering institution of hippiedom" offering affordable, "organic and delicious" Eclectic eats plus a "wonderful" "selection of draft beers"; though antis call the fare "hit-or-miss" ("except for breakfast") and declare service "a bit slow", it's an "experience on many levels" with "lots of outdoor seating", entertainment such as music Wednesday–Saturday and "incense-scented shopping in the extreme left-wing gift shop."

### NEW Hearty ☑ *American*
| | - | - | - | M |

**Wrigleyville** | 3819 N. Broadway (Grace St.) | 773-868-9866 | www.heartychicago.com

Food Network stars the Hearty Boys dish out "updated" New American "comfort food" for dinner and brunch along with mid-priced wines and creative cocktails at this "cozy", "friendly" Wrigleyville haunt with exposed brick and bright walls, glass artwork and a "scene" at the mahogany and tile bar; N.B. there's outdoor dining in season.

### ☑ Heaven on Seven  *Cajun/Creole*
| | 23 | 17 | 19 | $26 |

**Loop** | Garland Bldg. | 111 N. Wabash Ave., 7th fl. (Washington Blvd.) | 312-263-6443 ☒⇗

**River North** | AMC Loews | 600 N. Michigan Ave., 2nd fl. (bet. Ohio & Ontario Sts.) | 312-280-7774

**Naperville** | 224 S. Main St. (bet. Jackson & Jefferson Aves.) | 630-717-0777

www.heavenonseven.com

"Soul-satisfied" surveyors swear by the "modestly priced", "comprehensive menu of well-prepared Cajun and Creole specialties" and "hot-sauce kitsch atmosphere" featuring "rows of bottles on the wall" at this "taste of New Orleans in Chicago"; "service isn't much", but a consensus claims the "cash-only" Loop "original" (that's not open for dinner) offers "better" fare and "funkier atmosphere than the spin-offs", hence its "lines down the hall."

### Hecky's Barbecue  *BBQ*
| | 20 | 5 | 14 | $18 |

**Evanston** | 1902 Green Bay Rd. (Emerson St.) | 847-492-1182 | www.heckys.com

"Barbecue as good as it gets" "for miles around" "hits the spot" for most meat eaters at this Evanston BYO that's "been there forever and is usually consistent" for "smoked ribs and sausages", "turkey legs" and "sauce that's not too sweet"; since there's "no decor" and "no real sit-down option", "takeout is the way" to go, but "delivery is a nice touch" too.

### Hema's Kitchen *Indian*  22 | 12 | 16 | $22

**Lincoln Park** | 2411 N. Clark St. (Fullerton Pkwy.) | 773-529-1705
**West Rogers Park** | 2439 W. Devon Ave. (Artesian Ave.) |
773-338-1627
www.hemaskitchen.com

With kitchens in Lincoln Park and West Rogers Park, this "no-frills"
BYO duo issues an "extensive menu" of "authentic dishes from various regions of India" that are "not too spicy unless you want it that
way"; some call it "nothing special" with service that "can be too relaxed" and "decor that's lacking", "but the real attraction" is the
fare, which is also a "godsend for vegetarians."

### Hemmingway's Bistro *American/French*  21 | 19 | 21 | $39

**Oak Park** | The Write Inn | 211 N. Oak Park Ave. (Ontario St.) |
708-524-0806 | www.hemmingwaysbistro.com

"Warm and welcoming", this "neighborhood spot" in the Write Inn
is "in keeping with the Oak Park vibe" and a "comfortable" contender offering "Parisian" "flair" and a "selection of French bistro"
and Traditional American fare along with a bar and "attentive service"; P.S. it's "perfect for a cold winter evening", and there's jazz on
Wednesday nights and at the Sunday brunch buffet.

### Holy Mackerel!  ▽ 21 | 18 | 18 | $58
### American Fish House *Seafood*

**Lombard** | Westin Lombard | 70 Yorktown Shopping Ctr. (Butterfield Rd.) |
630-953-3444 | www.holymackerelseafood.com

"There's a lot" of "good seafood" on the menu at this seafaring spin-
off of the Harry Caray's clan located in the Westin Lombard and
deemed "above average for a suburban hotel restaurant"; some who
suggest the "city prices" "may not quite be justified" by the "portion
size and quality" or "slower-than-expected service" prefer "sticking
to" the steakhouse sibling "next door."

### Honey 1 BBQ Ⓜ *BBQ*  20 | 8 | 15 | $20

**Bucktown** | 2241 N. Western Ave. (Lyndale St.) | 773-227-5130 |
www.honey1bbq.com

"Serious barbecue" boosters praise the "pure, smoky, porky goodness" ("especially the ribs and tips" and "hot links") at this budget-
loving Bucktown 'cue contender; "accommodations are sparse" and
the meals "messy", so it might "not be the place for a first date", but
who needs romance when "you're there for the food."

### Hop Häus ◑ *Burgers*  19 | 15 | 17 | $21

**River North** | 646 N. Franklin St. (Erie St.) | 312-467-4287
**Rogers Park** | 7545 N. Clark St. (Howard St.) | 773-262-3783
www.thehophaus.com

"Burgers and more burgers" both "mini" and "tall" are on a "selection worth seeing" (including exotic game) along with "super-large
salads", "tons of beers from around the world" and weekend brunch
with "skillets and waffles" at these sometimes "noisy" "sports bars"
with "TVs galore and friendly staff"; P.S. Rogers Park has a "lovely
outdoor setting", and River North has live entertainment on Fridays.

| | FOOD | DECOR | SERVICE | COST |
|---|---|---|---|---|

## Hopleaf  *Belgian*    23 | 18 | 18 | $27

**Andersonville** | 5148 N. Clark St. (Foster Ave.) | 773-334-9851 |
www.hopleaf.com

A "hip crowd" (21 and older only) haunts this "authentic" gastropub, a "little bit of Belgium in Andersonville" that "sets the standard for others" say surveyors who explore a "dizzying array of beers" and "unique, delicious" midpriced fare ("don't miss" the moules frites) amid a "biergarten" atmosphere with a "fabulous patio in the summer"; the only complaints concern "staff attitude" and that it's "too popular", thus "hard to get in", but a second location is planned.

## Hot Chocolate  Ⓜ *American*    24 | 19 | 21 | $33

**Bucktown** | 1747 N. Damen Ave. (Willow St.) | 773-489-1747 |
www.hotchocolatechicago.com

"Don't let the name fool you into thinking it's just sweets" at Mindy Segal's "unique", "crowded and loud" Bucktown "locavore" that's "trendy, upscale and down-home" all at once; yes, the "decadent" desserts are "mind-blowing" and the "hot chocolate orgasmic", but the American "savory items are equally delicious" and the "tabs reasonable", making it a "top-to-bottom favorite" despite reports of "average service"; P.S. "take home a box of her cookies."

## Ⓩ Hot Doug's  Ⓢ⑁ *Hot Dogs*    27 | 13 | 20 | $12

**Northwest Side** | 3324 N. California Ave. (Roscoe St.) | 773-279-9550 |
www.hotdougs.com

"Believe what you read" woof wiener hounds hooked on the "mind-boggling" "gourmet" "encased meat" and "amazing fries" (sometimes "fried in duck fat") at this Northwest Sider – voted tops for hot dogs in this Survey – dispensing everything from the "classic" Chicago-style to "adventures in sausageology" including specials such as spicy alligator; "Doug [Sohn] is a mini-celebrity who still mans" the cash-only counter "with a smile", and though "lines are incredibly long" at this colorful space with Elvis memorabilia and outdoor seating, "they keep it moving" and "it's worth the wait"; N.B. open till 4 PM.

## Hot Woks Cool Sushi  *Asian*    23 | 18 | 23 | $22

**NEW** Loop | 30 S. Michigan Ave. (bet. Madison & Monroe Sts.) |
312-345-1234
**Northwest Side** | 3930 N. Pulaski Rd. (Dakin St.) | 773-282-1818
www.hotwokscoolsushi.com

"Decently priced", "dependable sushi, Thai food", "noodle dishes" and other Asian fare make this duo "welcome" to both the Loop and Northwest Side neighborhoods, even if service can be slow; N.B. Downtown serves beer and wine, the northern outpost is BYO.

## House of Fortune  *Chinese*    23 | 13 | 17 | $23

**Chinatown** | 2407 S. Wentworth Ave. (24th St.) | 312-225-0880
Considered a "safe bet, both culinarywise and for overall service", this "consistent" Chinatowner is the choice of those who "know freshness, authenticity and quality"; its "low-key" atmosphere, "af-

fordable" pricing and some of the "best Peking duck in the neighborhood" (which "you don't have to order in advance") are additional "incentives" bringing patrons back "again and again."

### HUB 51 ● American/Eclectic | 21 | 20 | 19 | $34 |

**River North** | 51 W. Hubbard St. (Dearborn St.) | 312-828-0051 | www.hub51chicago.com

"Trendy" "urban" "twentysomethings" tout the New American–"Eclectic food in an electric room" ("where else can you get sushi and Mexican in one place?"), "fabulous cocktails and moderate prices" at this "lively" River North noshery "from the sons of [Lettuce Entertain You] impresario Rich Melman"; it "turns into a nightclub later in the evening" with DJs Thursday–Saturday and "service is appropriate for the venue", but more staid types chalk up the lure to the "cool scene", "not the grub."

### ☑ Hugo's Frog Bar & Fish House ● Seafood | 24 | 21 | 23 | $50 |

**Gold Coast** | 1024 N. Rush St. (bet. Bellevue Pl. & Oak St.) | 312-640-0999
**Naperville** | Main Street Promenade Bldg. | 55 S. Main St. (bet. Benton & Van Buren Aves.) | 630-548-3764
www.hugosfrogbar.com

"Where the locals eat in the Gold Coast", this "hoppin'" "fish companion to Gibsons" "delivers top (albeit pricey) seafood" including "amazing frogs' legs" ("plus steaks" from "next door"), piano nightly and "people-watching"; service is generally "professional", but many experience a "delay even with a reservation" especially "on weekends" (Naperville is somewhat less "noisy" than Downtown).

### Icosium Kafe African | 19 | 15 | 19 | $19 |

**Andersonville** | 5200 N. Clark St. (Foster Ave.) | 773-271-5233

"The lamps, mint tea" and "interesting decor and seating" "practically transport you to North Africa" at this Andersonville "surprise" serving a "delicious" "twist" on "hot crêpes all day" (including a build-your-own option and "dessert" "variations") at an "excellent price"; P.S. service can be "slow, so don't go if you're in a hurry."

### Il Mulino New York Italian | 25 | 24 | 24 | $77 |

**Gold Coast** | 1150 N. Dearborn St. (bet. Division & Elm Sts.) | 312-440-8888 | www.ilmulino.com

Offering "fine Italian dining" complete with a "very good wine list", this Gold Coast "New York import" set in the "intimate", "beautiful Biggs mansion" also boasts an "expert staff" that pleased patrons liken to "flawless performers on stage" delivering a "special evening"; the less-impressed say service "can be overwhelming" and find it all "outrageously expensive", but those seated next to one of the "fireplaces" just call it "wonderful."

### NEW Il Poggiolo Italian | 19 | 21 | 19 | $40 |

**Hinsdale** | 8 E. First St. (bet. Garfield Ave. & Washington St.) | 630-734-9400 | www.ilpoggiolohinsdale.com

Beyond its red-and-white entrance canopy, Jerry Kleiner's "hopping" West Suburban seasonal Italian located in a former silent

|  | FOOD | DECOR | SERVICE | COST |
|--|------|-------|---------|------|

movie theater is "better than expected for a trendy Hinsdale spot", turning out "quality" fare "at reasonable prices"; though some call the service "consistently inconsistent", the "open environment" wins compliments for its "bar setup" and decor featuring a vaulted-ceiling dining room, photography and plush red upholstery.

### Ina's  *American*                                23 | 16 | 22 | $23

**West Loop** | 1235 W. Randolph St. (Elizabeth St.) | 312-226-8227 | www.breakfastqueen.com

"Chicago icon" Ina Pinkney "makes you feel like a guest in her home" at her West Loop New American that's beloved for "breakfast with passion" and "tasty" "comfort food" ("go for the fried chicken") for lunch and dinner (hours vary seasonally); "warm service" amid a "collection of funky salt and pepper shakers" adds to the allure, so expect "long lines" at peak hours (however they "move quickly"); P.S. "you can't beat the free parking in the lot outside the door."

### ⊠ India House  *Indian*                         25 | 18 | 19 | $29

**River North** | 59 W. Grand Ave. (bet. Clark & Dearborn Sts.) | 312-645-9500
**Buffalo Grove** | Buffalo Grove Town Ctr. | 228-230 McHenry Rd. (Lake Cook Rd.) | 847-520-5569
**Schaumburg** | 1521 W. Schaumburg Rd. (Springinsguth Rd.) | 847-895-5501 Ⓜ
**Oak Brook** | 2809 Butterfield Rd. (Meyers Rd.) | 630-472-1500
www.indiahousechicago.com

"Excellent, authentic Indian dishes" keep surveyors "satisfied" at this quartet of midpriced subcontinentals with "accommodating service", where the "delicious, beautifully presented lunch buffets" (price varies by location but they're all a "value") are one reason why regulars say "face it, you are going to overeat" so "enjoy it"; River North is more "elegant" than the outlying locations but suburbanites love that there's "no need to go to Devon."

### Indian Garden, The  *Indian*                    21 | 15 | 18 | $27

**Streeterville** | 247 E. Ontario St., 2nd fl. (Fairbanks Ct.) | 312-280-4910 | www.indiangardenchicago.com
**West Rogers Park** | 2546 W. Devon Ave. (Rockwell St.) | 773-338-2929 | www.indiangardenchicago.com
**Schaumburg** | 855 E. Schaumburg Rd. (Plum Grove Rd.) | 847-524-3007 | www.theindiangardenschaumburg.com  Ⓜ

Surveyors "step into India" at this threesome of "reliable standbys" for a "variety of tasty", "decently spiced" midpriced "standards" and lunch "buffet extravaganzas"; they're separately owned, which might account for service that gets mixed marks and settings that rank somewhere between "nice" and merely "satisfactory."

### Indie Cafe  *Japanese/Thai*                     24 | 18 | 20 | $22

**Edgewater** | 5951 N. Broadway St. (bet. Elmdale & Thorndale Aves.) | 773-561-5577 | www.indiecafe.us

"They are striving to be different" at this "low-key" Edgewater indie with an "extensive menu" of "creative sushi" and other "outstanding" Japanese bites, "luscious curries and Thai dishes", all "presented with a stunning sense of plating aesthetics"; so if the service is "somewhat random" and an "elegant" "city" feel to some is a "lack of decor" to others, everyone agrees you "go for" the "fantastic" fare; P.S. "bring your own wine."

### Inovasi ⓩ *American*                    - | - | - | M

**Lake Bluff** | 28 E. Center Ave. (Scranton Ave.) | 847-295-1000 | www.inovasi.us

At this Lake Bluff New American, John Des Rosiers (ex Bank Lane Bistro) delivers creative, midpriced lunches and dinners in a variety of portion sizes (plus a kids' menu) using local and sustainable seasonal ingredients; the brick corner storefront sets a chic but casual mood with handsome wood and neutral-and-smoky-blue tones.

### Irazu ⓩ⇔ *Costa Rican*              22 | 10 | 18 | $17

**Bucktown** | 1865 N. Milwaukee Ave. (Western Ave.) | 773-252-5687 | www.irazuchicago.com

"Now known by more than [just] the locals", Bucktown's Costa Rican BYO and cash-only "neighborhood gem" dishes out "tasty", "unique" fare that's "super cheap"; it's "casual" and "family-friendly", but there are no reservations and fans say the "only downside is that the space is way too small for its justified popularity" – though you can sometimes "eat outside."

### Irish Oak
### Restaurant & Pub  *Pub Food*          ▽ 19 | 24 | 22 | $23

**Wrigleyville** | 3511 N. Clark St. (Addison St.) | 773-935-6669 | www.irishoak.com

"Guinness and a burger is the name of the game" at this "real", affordable "old-fashioned" "Irish pub" located next to Wrigley Field that "knows how to pour a pint" – and where it's "always a great time for a drinking session"; the decor from the floors up "was brought over from the old sod", and there's live music Thursday through Saturday nights.

### NEW Isacco Kitchen Ⓜ *Italian/Eclectic*     - | - | - | M

**St. Charles** | 210 Cedar St. (bet. 2nd & 3rd Aves.) | 630-444-0202 | www.isaccokitchen.com

Globe-trotting chef Isacco Vitali presides over this affordable West Suburban arrival where Italian culinary concepts get creative, contemporary Eclectic treatments; a former barbecue hut has been transformed into an intimate white-tablecloth dining room with modern Italian furnishings, splashes of bright color, funky art and a variety of seating including a small lounge area and patio.

### Isla Filipino Restaurant Ⓜ *Filipino*      - | - | - | I

**Lincoln Square** | 2501 W. Lawrence Ave. (Campbell Ave.) | 773-271-2988 | www.islapilipina.com

The extensive, budget-friendly Filipino menu "has far more hits than misses" at this "no-frills Lincoln Square BYO" situated in a strip mall; a "sweet staff", local art on the walls and bargain lunch specials add to the appeal.

| | FOOD | DECOR | SERVICE | COST |
|---|---|---|---|---|

### NEW Istanbul Restaurant  *Turkish*   `- | - | - | I`

**Lakeview** | 3613 N. Broadway (bet. Addison St. & Patterson Ave.) | 773-525-0500 | www.istanbulrestaurantchicago.com

Lakeview's "Istanbul-style Turkish grill" serves "appealing", "healthful" and "innovative dishes" (including some Mediterranean choices) plus "fresh-baked breads" at "reasonable prices"; the "staff seems interested in the customers' opinions", so "despite the storefront coffee-shop atmosphere" fans say "if you can't go" to the Middle East, "eat here."

### NEW Italiasia  *Asian/Italian*   `- | - | - | M`

**River North** | Holiday Inn Chicago Mart Plaza | 350 W. Mart Center Dr., 15th fl. (Orleans St.) | 312-836-5000 | www.italiasiarestaurant.com

Italian and Asian cuisine combine at this midpriced River North aerie, where entrees run from chicken Vesuvio to seafood tempura, sweets include won ton cannoli and spumoni, and champagne and sake star on the drink list; its handsome modern setting sports distinctive geometric floor, wall and lighting treatments, and offers great cityscape views from 15th-floor windows.

### Itto Sushi ●☒ *Japanese*   `24 | 14 | 21 | $33`

**Lincoln Park** | 2616 N. Halsted St. (Wrightwood Ave.) | 773-871-1800 | www.ittosushi.com

Regulars "welcome" this "completely unpretentious" Lincoln Park "respite from the trendy sake bars", an "old" (since the '80s) "traditional sushi" "standby" that's "reasonably priced" and the "real deal" for "authentic Japanese" fare served in a simple setting by a "friendly staff"; N.B. open noon to midnight daily.

### Jack Rabbit  *Southwestern*   `- | - | - | I`

**Lincoln Square** | 4603 N. Lincoln Ave. (Wilson Ave.) | 773-989-9000

Lincoln Square locals hop to this Southwestern specialist that delivers "innovative" fare and "awesome margaritas" with "great service", adding up to "enjoyable meals" with affordable tabs to boot; the "small space" features a faux tin ceiling and glass tile bar, and there's also Sunday brunch and sidewalk seating.

### Jack's on Halsted  *American*   `21 | 17 | 19 | $34`

**Lakeview** | 3201 N. Halsted St. (Belmont Ave.) | 773-244-9191 | www.jacksonhalsted.com

Halsted Street's New American "mainstay" is a "cozy", midpriced Lakeview "neighborhood place" with an urban look as a backdrop for a "solid menu", special martinis and "pleasant service"; a "diverse, hipper-than-usual clientele" adds to the "city atmosphere", and it "gets pretty crowded most nights with the Boys Town crew"; P.S. it's "well located for dinner before Briar Street Theatre."

### Jacky's on Prairie ☒ *French*   `21 | 20 | 20 | $48`

**Evanston** | 2545 Prairie Ave. (Central St.) | 847-733-0899 | www.jackysonprairie.com

Though former chef-owner "Jacky [Pluton] doesn't run the place anymore", this "intimate, unpretentious" Evanston homage is still gaining followers with its "delightful" seasonal New French fare (even if it is "a little pricey"); the verdict on the "vibe is more neighborhood cafe than night on the town", though some say the "updated decor" is "less homey" than before and note the "new owners are making changes to the menu."

### Jaipur  *Indian*  | - | - | - | M |

**West Loop** | 847 W. Randolph St. (bet. Green & Peoria Sts.) | 312-526-3655 | www.jaipurchicago.com

For a "taste of real Indian on Restaurant Row", surveyors seek out the "honest", "wonderful" midpriced fare full of "fresh ingredients" at this West Loop eatery where the "service is great" and the "room is quite comfortable"; P.S. a patio and prix fixe lunch (not buffet) add to the "great deal."

### J. Alexander's  *American*  | 20 | 20 | 20 | $32 |

**Lincoln Park** | 1832 N. Clybourn Ave. (bet. Willow & Wisconsin Sts.) | 773-435-1018
**Northbrook** | 4077 Lake Cook Rd. (bet. I-294 & Sanders Rd.) | 847-564-3093
**Oak Brook** | 1410 16th St. (Rte. 83) | 630-573-8180
www.jalexanders.com

This "dependable" Lincoln Park and suburban trio is considered a "competent chain" for its "decent" "all-around" chophouse and Traditional American "comfort food" "at less-than-steakhouse prices" and in a "variety pleasing to all palates"; a "welcoming" staff and "warm", "comfortable" dark-wood confines have commenters noting "no surprises, no complaints."

### NEW  Jam  ⊄ *American*  | ∇ 21 | 16 | 24 | $19 |

**Ukrainian Village** | 937 N. Damen Ave. (bet. Augusta Blvd. & Walton St.) | 773-489-0302 | www.jamrestaurant.com

Ukrainian Villagers note that the "innovative, delicious" breakfast and lunch fare at this New American is "made with trendy ingredients" and "served by hipsters for hipsters" in a "nondescript" minimalist room with an "open kitchen" and "loud rock 'n' roll music playing in the background"; dinner service started post-Survey, so surveyors will have another chance to see if it's "worth all the buzz."

### Jane's  *American/Eclectic*  | 22 | 16 | 18 | $29 |

**Bucktown** | 1655 W. Cortland St. (Paulina St.) | 773-862-5263 | www.janesrestaurant.com

Situated "off the beaten path" in a "traditional Chicago coach house", this "cozy", "adorable" New American–Eclectic "neighborhood joint" is a "longtime Bucktown favorite" rated "reliable" for "consistent, creative and comforting" midpriced comestibles and "friendly service"; N.B. it offers weekend brunch and seasonal outdoor dining.

### ☑ Japonais  *Japanese*  | 24 | 26 | 20 | $59 |

**River North** | 600 W. Chicago Ave. (Larrabee St.) | 312-822-9600 | www.japonaischicago.com

"Lots of young, beautiful people" come to "eat and be seen" at this "swanky", "pricey" River North Japanese with "excellent sushi", a

| | FOOD | DECOR | SERVICE | COST |
|---|---|---|---|---|

"variety" of "inventive" entrees and "lethal signature martinis"; "service is what you'd expect" (some say "aloof"), but most maintain it's "managed to stay trendy" while providing "consistent" fare "for quite some time", plus the "neo-Asian decor" is an "architectural dream" – especially the "sexy downstairs bar with a river view."

### Jerry's  *Sandwiches*  | 22 | 16 | 20 | $24 |

**Wicker Park** | 1938 W. Division St. (Damen Ave.) | 773-235-1006
**West Loop** | 1045 W. Madison St. (bet. Aberdeen & Morgan Sts.) | 312-563-1008
www.jerryssandwiches.com

A Wicker Park "winner" for "super", "interesting sandwiches" from a "menu that goes for days" and includes a "selection of microbrews" and wines by the glass, this inexpensive entry also claims a "convenient location" with a fireplace and sidewalk seating plus a "pleasant staff"; though it "can get a bit loud and crowded on weekends", "during the week it's an extremely relaxing experience"; N.B. the quieter West Loop sib does not stay open late.

### Jilly's Cafe  Ⓜ *American/French*  | 21 | 19 | 21 | $42 |

**Evanston** | 2614 Green Bay Rd. (Central St.) | 847-869-7636 | www.jillyscafe.com

Fans of the "nicely frilly" New American–New French "bistro cuisine" (and brunch with a prix fixe champagne option) at this "quaint little house" in Evanston call it an "undiscovered gem" that "doesn't look like much from street" but is "charming" and "homelike" inside; service adds to the "dependable" experience that's perhaps "a little pricey"; P.S. "only wine and beer are served."

### Jin Ju  *Korean*  | 23 | 20 | 22 | $31 |

**Andersonville** | 5203 N. Clark St. (Foster Ave.) | 773-334-6377 | www.jinjuchicago.com

"It's rare to find a high-end Korean restaurant", and while this "fantastic part of the Andersonville scene" is "not particularly authentic", "it's a pleasure to visit" for its "mouthwatering", "modern take" on the "classics" and "fabulous flavors" of soju martinis that "go down too easily"; add in "casual service" and a weekend lounge and you have a potential "date place."

### 🏆 Joe's Seafood, Prime Steak & Stone Crab  *Seafood/Steak*  | 26 | 22 | 25 | $64 |

**River North** | 60 E. Grand Ave. (Rush St.) | 312-379-5637 | www.joes.net

Surveyors "look forward to" meals at Lettuce Entertain You's "sophisticated", "supper club"–like River Norther – the No. 1 chophouse in this Survey – that emulates the "famous" "Miami original" by serving "extra-fresh seafood in traditional and contemporary dishes" (of course, "stone crabs are the showstopper", even if they're "frozen" when "out of season") but also "outstanding steaks" and "Key lime pie for dessert"; "spot-on service" is "well trained" to handle "families and businessmen alike", and "it's jumping every night" due to "large crowds", the "high density of tables" and the "busy bar" – all in all, "a real treat and worth every wildly expensive penny."

### Joey's Brickhouse  *American*    20 | 16 | 19 | $25

**Lakeview** | 1258 W. Belmont Ave. (Racine Ave.) | 773-296-1300 | www.enterthechef.com

This "friendly neighborhood establishment" in Lakeview cooks up "cool twists" on Traditional American "comfort-food" "classics" in a "casual atmosphere"; there's "something for everyone" on the "reasonably priced" menu and it's both a "family destination" and a "place to watch sports on TV"; N.B. additional assets include weekend brunch, outdoor dining and periodic live entertainment.

### John's Place  Ⓜ *American*    18 | 14 | 19 | $23

**Lincoln Park** | 1200 W. Webster Ave. (Racine Ave.) | 773-525-6670
**Roscoe Village** | 2132 W. Roscoe St. (Hamilton Ave.) | 773-244-6430
www.johnsplace.com

Somehow "family-friendly but still vaguely hip", this Lincoln Park "staple" and its Roscoe Village sibling serve "tasty" Traditional American "comfort food" including a "delicious" weekend brunch at "value" prices; the atmosphere is "pleasant", especially "outdoors in the summer", just be aware that there are usually "lots of young children"; P.S. "lines aren't as long" on Roscoe Street.

### Joy Yee's Noodle Shop  *Asian*    20 | 12 | 15 | $18

**Chinatown** | 2139 S. China Pl. (Archer Ave.) | 312-328-0001
**South Loop** | 1335 S. Halsted St. (bet. Liberty & W. Maxwell Sts.) | 312-997-2128
**Evanston** | 521 Davis St. (bet. Chicago & Hanman Aves.) | 847-733-1900
**Naperville** | Iroquois Ctr. | 1163 E. Ogden Ave. (Iroquois Ave.) | 630-579-6800

### Joy Yee Plus  *Asian*

**NEW** **Chinatown** | 2159 S. China Pl. (Archer Ave.) | 312-842-8928
www.joyyee.com

"Expansive", "inexpensive" Asian menus "encourage experimentation" at this local chain of "quick-fix" BYO "favorites" known for "giant portions" of multicultural "noodle choices for everyone" and "excellent bubble teas and smoothies"; curmudgeons call it a "case of quantity over quality (but the prices are sure right)", plus the speed of service varies by location and the "cafeteria-style" settings "discourage lingering"; N.B. Chinatown's Plus focuses on shabu-shabu and sushi.

### Julius Meinl Café  *Austrian*    21 | 20 | 18 | $17

**Lakeview** | 3601 N. Southport Ave. (Addison St.) | 773-868-1857
**Lincoln Square** | 4363 N. Lincoln Ave. (Montrose Ave.) | 773-868-1876
www.meinl.com

Surveyors seeking a "tranquil", "civilized" "oasis" find it at these Lakeview and Lincoln Square "continental" "*konditoreis*" noted for their "fabulous pastries" and "perfectionist coffee" served "on a tray" plus a "surprising variety" of "coffeehouse" and "authentic Austrian fare" for breakfast, lunch and dinner; it's a little "pricey", and the "European atmosphere" includes "weak service" but also "wonderful live music that is not overwhelming" on weekend nights.

| | FOOD | DECOR | SERVICE | COST |
|---|---|---|---|---|

**Jury's** *Pub Food* | 18 | 12 | 19 | $21 |

**North Center/St. Ben's** | 4337 N. Lincoln Ave. (Montrose Ave.) | 773-935-2255 | www.jurysrestaurant.com

The verdict is in on this "upscale" North Center "neighborhood bar", where the "slmple, excellent burger" causes sold surveyors to forget they "serve something else" – namely American "standards" and "solid steaks and seafood"; decor and service are "old-school" with a "welcoming atmosphere" some liken to "going home for dinner (or lunch) – except you agree to pay the bill"; P.S. there's "outdoor dining in the summer."

**NEW J. Wellington's** *Burgers* | - | - | - | I |

**Wicker Park** | 2045 W. North Ave. (bet. Damen & Hoyne Aves.) | 773-687-9142

Named for Popeye's 'Wimpy' burger finagler, this wallet-friendly Wicker Park quick-serve offers a variety of burger combos (or a build-your-own option), along with fries, Traditional American comfort foods like chili and mac 'n' cheese, and traditional and craft sodas (you can also BYO); the interior is smart for the category, with warm, earthy colors, wood tables, a leather banquette and soft lighting.

**Kamehachi** *Japanese* | 21 | 16 | 18 | $38 |

**Streeterville** | 240 E. Ontario St. (bet. Fairbanks Ct. & St. Clair St.) | 312-587-0600
**Old Town** | 1400 N. Wells St. (Schiller St.) | 312-664-3663 ☽
**Northbrook** | Village Green Shopping Ctr. | 1320 Shermer Rd. (bet. Meadow & Waukegan Rds.) | 847-562-0064
www.kamehachi.com

"One of the original Japanese restaurants in the city" (the Old Town location) is the founding member of this chainlet where "traditional sushi" and "light fare" including "teriyaki and tempura dishes" are "well-priced" and "consistently delicious", and come with "good service" "regardless of location" (unlike the variable decor); even adventurous eaters who deem it "unimaginative" vet it as "solid."

**Kansaku** *Japanese* | ▽ 22 | 18 | 18 | $42 |

**Evanston** | 1514 Sherman Ave. (Grove St.) | 847-864-4386 | www.kansakusushi.com

"Top-quality fish" in "fresh, inventive and tasty" presentations paired with a "list of premium sakes" have fin-fans flagging this dimly lit, slightly pricey Evanston Japanese as a "place to wind down as well as to celebrate" (especially with saketinis) seven days a week; P.S. it's now also "open for lunch on weekends."

**Kan Zaman** *Lebanese* | - | - | - | I |

**River North** | 617 N. Wells St. (Ontario St.) | 312-751-9600 | www.kanzamanchicago.com

"If you like to eat while sitting on pillows", this budget-friendly River North Lebanese BYO has got the goods (and table seating too) for dining on "tasty" "Middle Eastern meals" at lunch or dinner; on weekend nights, the "enjoyable experience is highlighted by live belly dancing."

| | FOOD | DECOR | SERVICE | COST |
|---|---|---|---|---|

### Karma *Asian*

| 23 | 27 | 23 | $46 |

**Mundelein** | Doubletree Libertyville-Mundelein | 510 E. Il. Rte. 83 (Rte. 45) | 847-970-6900 | www.karmachicago.com

"Surprised" surveyors swear "you'd never guess that this gorgeous" "oasis of Zen" is in Mundelein's Doubletree hotel, what with its Asian "fine" dining and "awesome cocktails" amid "darkly miminal-ist", "romantic" surroundings; it's a little pricey but "has that edge you're looking for when it's a special occasion."

### Karyn's Cooked *Vegan*

| 20 | 16 | 20 | $28 |

**River North** | 738 N. Wells St. (Superior St.) | 312-587-1050

### Karyn's Fresh Corner *Vegetarian*

**Lincoln Park** | 1901 N. Halsted St. (Armitage Ave.) | 312-255-1590 www.karynraw.com

"Vegans and vegetarians" vouch for this "friendly" "midpriced" duo's "refined", "savory cuisine" "for the compassionate eater" accompanied by a "selection of healthy non-alcoholic drinks", all brought by a "helpful staff"; River North's "modern yet cozy" Cooked fits the bill "whenever you need to get your 'veg' on" (it also offers organic wine and beer), and though fans of Lincoln Park's fountain-filled Fresh say "raw never tasted so good", the less adventurous "really want to like it but . . ."

### 🆕 Karyn's on Green *American/Vegan*

| – | – | – | M |

**Greektown** | 130 S. Green St. (bet. Adams & Monroe Sts.) | 312-226-6155 | www.karynsongreen.com

Raw-foodist Karyn Calabrese (Karyn's Cooked, Karyn's Fresh Corner) has given Greektown an organic-chic dining destination with an all-vegan New American menu – some raw items, some reinterpreted comfort food – plus a bar program of sustainable sips and spirits (spirulina mojito, anyone?); the ultramodern setting has an open, airy feeling with a lofty mezzanine, waterfall sculpture and communal table, and there's also a small take-out and retail area.

### 🆕 Katakana & Koko Sushi Bar *Japanese*

| – | – | – | M |

**Logan Square** | 2829 W. Armitage Ave. (Mozart St.) | 773-235-2199 | www.kokosushibar.com

A long, affordable menu featuring traditional Japanese soups, sushi and cooked entrees – plus bento box lunch bargains – is on offer at this Logan Square BYO arrival; a sushi bar divides the sprawling double-storefront space decorated with brick walls, polished wood floors and tables, plasma TVs and reproductions of Picasso murals.

### 🅩 Katsu Japanese Ⓜ *Japanese*

| 27 | 16 | 23 | $52 |

**Northwest Side** | 2651 W. Peterson Ave. (bet. Talman & Washtenaw Aves.) | 773-784-3383

Fish fanatics "skip the tony and more-publicized sushi boutiques and head" to the Northwest Side's "hidden gem", the "best Japanese restaurant in Chicago" where "caring owners" offer the "freshest", "most delectable" seafood and "traditional" hot fare that's "often exquisite", accompanied by "attentive service" and an "excellent sake selection" in a "conversation-friendly", "elegant, traditional" atmosphere; cost is also "top of the line" but most maintain it's "worth the money."

### ☑ Keefer's ☒ *American*                     25 | 22 | 24 | $59

**River North** | 20 W. Kinzie St. (Dearborn St.) | 312-467-9525 | www.keefersrestaurant.com

A "favorite" for many chop lovers, this "high-end", "adult" River Norther offers "consistent", "excellent" Traditional American steakhouse cuisine (chef "John Hogan does wonders with meat") and seafood (including "some of the best Dover sole") paired with a winning "wine list" and "warm yet professional" service; add the "contemporary, comfortable decor" and "summer patio" and it's "worth the trip" and "expense-account" tabs.

### Kiki's ☒ *French*                     25 | 22 | 24 | $48

**Near North** | 900 N. Franklin St. (Locust St.) | 312-335-5454 | www.kikisbistro.com

"When the mood for country bistro food hits", "satisfied" Francophiles swear by the "fine traditional" fare and "affordable French wine" at this "adult" Near North "stalwart" where the atmosphere "oozes cozy" and service is "excellent under the watchful eye of owner" Georges 'Kiki' Cuisance; though a few nigglers say it "needs some spunk", for most, this "perennial winner" is "reassuring" "like a favorite pair of jeans."

### NEW Kin Sushi &                     - | - | - | I
### Thai Cuisine *Japanese/Thai*

**River West** | 1132 N. Milwaukee Ave. (bet. Haddon Ave. & Thomas St.) | 773-772-2722 | www.kinchicago.com

Sushi-Thai fusion finds its way to River West by way of this hip, inexpensive BYO serving classics from both cuisines (including a hearty selection of specialty maki); the modern, black-and-blond-wood setting features bare wood tables with benches, a sushi bar and plastic bubble seats in the lounge area that comes complete with a clubby decibel level.

### Kinzie Chophouse *Steak*                     22 | 19 | 22 | $48

**River North** | 400 N. Wells St. (Kinzie St.) | 312-822-0191 | www.kinziechophouse.com

Champions cheer a "quality" "Chicago steak without the steakhouse arrogance" at this River North "unsung hero" with a "cozy" if "typical chophouse atmosphere", where you can "sit outside in the summer overlooking the [Merchandise] Mart and the el" tracks; while a few feeders can't find anything that "stands out about it", fans deem it "friendly" and "well priced."

### NEW Kith & Kin ◐ *American*                     - | - | - | E

**Lincoln Park** | 1119 W. Webster Ave. (bet. Clifton & Seminary Aves.) | 773-472-7070 | www.kithandkinchicago.com

Cognoscenti concur this Lincoln Park New American "neighborhood find" "is going to go far" thanks to "outstanding" cuisine from Grant Achatz protégé David Carrier that's "reasonably priced" given the "high quality"; "attentive" "servers are quite knowledgeable", and the former La Canasta space has a clean, "casual" feel with a tin ceiling and a working fireplace in winter.

### Kit Kat Lounge & Supper Club ●Ⓜ Eclectic
16 | 19 | 19 | $32

**Lakeview** | 3700 N. Halsted St. (Waveland Ave.) | 773-525-1111 | www.kitkatchicago.com

"Bachelorettes" advise "be prepared for killer drinks" ("it's the martini menu that sets this place apart"), "amazing desserts and men with better legs than you" at this "distinctive, glamorous" Lakeview supper club where you "come for" the "amazing drag show", not the mostly "disappointing" Eclectic dining (and leave the kiddies at home); N.B. it offers seasonal outdoor seating.

### Kitsch'n on Roscoe Eclectic
19 | 19 | 18 | $20

**Roscoe Village** | 2005 W. Roscoe St. (Damen Ave.) | 773-248-7372
### K-Cafe Eclectic
**River North** | 600 W. Chicago Ave. (Larrabee St.) | 312-644-1500
www.kitschn.com

"Fun, tasty", affordable Eclectic eats like "green eggs and ham" "or chicken and waffles" come "with a '70s twist" at this "cool", "amusing" Roscoe Village "favorite" that's "laid-back in extremis"; while some call the service "excellent" and others say it's "less than ideal", it's hard not to "like any restaurant that has Tang on the menu"; N.B. the River North location morphed into a counter-service cafe post-Survey.

### Klay Oven Indian
20 | 16 | 17 | $31

**River North** | 414 N. Orleans St. (Hubbard St.) | 312-527-3999
**Oak Park** | 734 Lake St. (bet. Euclid & Oak Park Aves.) |
708-386-3999
www.klayovenrestaurant.com

"A lovely mix" of "well-spiced", "classically prepared" Indian dishes with "complex flavors" has diners saluting these River North and Oak Park offerings as "solid" citizens (including the service); though a few partakers peg it "a little pricey for not dazzling" dining, both locations have an "excellent, cheap and well-attended lunch buffet."

### NEW Klopa Grill & Cafe Serbian
- | - | - | I

**Lincoln Square** | 4835d N. Western Ave. (bet. Gunnison St. & Lawrence Ave.) | 774-745-5672 | www.klopagrill.com

The name of this Serbian BYO in Lincoln Square is slang for 'good food', and that's exactly what the affordable lunch and dinner menus strive to deliver – think sweet and savory crêpes, steaks, kebabs and barbecued meats, along with fruit juices and pungent coffee; mirrors and food photography accent the casual neighborhood setting.

### NEW (k)new Ⓢ American/Eclectic
- | - | - | E

**Logan Square** | 2556 W. Fullerton Ave. (Rockwell St.) | 773-772-7721 | www.knewrestaurant.com

In Logan Square, the latest "location for the husband-and-wife" team behind the defunct Think lures a "loyal following" for their hospitality and "innovative" New American and Eclectic menu with "promise";

though doubters dish that the "decor doesn't match" the "expensive prices", the "wow"-ed crowd assures "BYO keeps overall costs down."

### Koda Bistro Ⓜ *French*    | - | - | - | E |

**Far South Side** | 10352 S. Western Ave. (bet. 103rd & 104th Sts.) | 773-445-5632 | www.kodabistro.com

Still a "neighborhood secret" in Beverly, this French bistro boasts an "inventive chef" who crafts a "limited menu" of "fabulous", "beautifully presented" seasonal fare that's coupled with an "excellent wine list"; the "warm, welcoming" setting with upscale decor and a "business casual dress code" further elevate an experience that's "worth the trip" to the Far South Side ("don't worry, you won't fall off if you cross Pershing").

### Koi *Asian*    | 21 | 20 | 18 | $36 |

**Evanston** | 624 Davis St. (bet. Chicago & Orrington Aves.) | 847-866-6969 | www.koievanston.com

Evanston locals find "fancy", "fair-priced" Asian cuisine at this "light and airy", "contemporary Chinese and Japanese" spot with a "fine sushi bar", a "wonderful array of drinks" and an "always helpful" staff; still, despite "lots of options for fussy eaters", a few frown over some "bland renditions", saying they "should focus on one cuisine."

### Kroll's *American*    ∇ | 19 | 18 | 21 | $20 |

**South Loop** | 1736 S. Michigan Ave. (18th St.) | 312-235-1400 | www.krolls-chicago.com

Graded a "great neighborhood sports bar" "for a burger, beer and ballgame", this Wisconsin import qualifies as "an oasis" in its South Loop location, dishing out "decent food, sandwiches, pizza, wings, etc." in an "upscale bar/grill atmosphere"; there are "no drunk twentysomethings" in the "friendly, diverse crowd", which seals it as a "favorite" for folks who "love" it.

### ☑ Kuma's Corner ● *American*    | 26 | 15 | 17 | $20 |

**Logan Square** | 2900 W. Belmont Ave. (Francisco Ave.) | 773-604-8769 | www.kumascorner.com

You'll find "about the best" "mind-blowing" burgers in Chicago (and a mac 'n' cheese that some call the real "star") at this Logan Square "heavy metal bar – really!" where the staff is "as friendly as it is tattooed" and "body-pierced", and the "rock-star atmosphere" includes "way too loud" music and "crazy", "long lines"; luckily, the "tables turn quickly", and in summer, you can "sit outside" and escape the noise.

### Kuni's *Japanese*    | 24 | 14 | 22 | $44 |

**Evanston** | 511-A Main St. (bet. Chicago & Hinman Aves.) | 847-328-2004

"Traditional, unpretentious Japanese" lures loyalists to "Kunisan's" "old-fashioned" Evanston shop serving "beautifully cut", "classic" "sushi the way it should be" – "no trendy rolls" – as well as teriyakis, tonkatsu and sukiyaki "for over 20 years"; "reasonable prices" are appreciated, but lingerers warn "the cost can run up" if you stick with the raw fish and sake all night.

### La Bocca della Verità *Italian* | 22 | 13 | 19 | $31 |

**Lincoln Square** | 4618 N. Lincoln Ave. (bet. Lawrence & Wilson Aves.) | 773-784-6222 | www.laboccachicago.com

This Lincoln Square "friendly, neighborhood ristorante" "isn't well known" "but it should be" say fans of its "authentic Italian" cooking combining "old-world tradition" and "new-world flair"; although a few are bothered by "slow" service, the comfortable "bistro" feel and sidewalk seating in summer make lingering pleasant.

### La Cantina ● *Italian/Seafood* | ▽ 21 | 22 | 22 | $34 |

**Loop** | Italian Vill. | 71 W. Monroe St. (bet. Clark & Dearborn Sts.) | 312-332-7005 | www.lacantina-chicago.com

A "typical" if "not inspiring" Northern Italian menu with a "flair for seafood", a massive wine list and a basement space with "twinkling lights" and "seasoned waiters" satisfy visitors to this Loop location in the 55-year-old Italian Village complex; it's "definitely recommended for a large family" or "a great late-night" outing since the kitchen is open till midnight daily.

### La Casa de Isaac *Mexican* | 20 | 11 | 18 | $26 |

**Highland Park** | 431 Temple Ave. (Waukegan Ave.) | 847-433-5550 | www.lacasadeisaac.com

"What do two nice Jewish boys know about tacos?" ask loyalists of this "festive" Highland Park "neighborhood" Mexican – "apparently enough to turn out good ones" as well as classic items (chicken in red mole sauce, enchiladas) and breakfast selections; "it's pretty loud" and sticklers snap it's "not really authentic" (there's no pork and it's "closed Friday nights" until "sundown on Saturday"), but the salsa gets "special kudos" and you can "sit outside" guzzling "great margaritas" in summer.

### **NEW** La Ciudad *Mexican* | - | - | - | I |

**Uptown** | 4515 N. Sheridan Rd. (bet. Sunnyside & Windsor Aves.) | 773-728-2887

Serving a mix of Mexican classics and street food, this Uptowner is sleeker than its low prices would suggest, the contemporary storefront setting decorated in the red, white and green of the Mexican flag and sporting moody black-and-white photographs; N.B. it's BYO, and the staff will mix you a margarita in a salt-rimmed glass if you bring the tequila and mixer.

### La Cocina de Frida *Mexican* | ▽ 20 | 18 | 20 | $31 |

**Andersonville** | 5403 N. Clark St. (Balmoral Ave.) | 773-271-1907

### Frida's *Mexican*

**NEW** **Lakeview** | 3755 N. Southport Ave. (Grace St.) | 773-935-2330 | www.lacocinadefrida.com

"The decor really makes you think of Frida" Kahlo at this colorful "semi-upscale" Andersonville "neighborhood Mexican" and its Lakeview sister featuring affordable "traditional fare with occasional twists" ("tortas and tamales are particular" favorites, "chips and margaritas are exceptional"); P.S. both sites serve up "alfresco" patio dining.

**La Crêperie**  *Crêpes/French*  21 | 17 | 19 | $27

**Lakeview** | 2845 N. Clark St. (bet. Diversey Pkwy. & Surf St.) | 773-528-9050 | www.lacreperieusa.com

A "charming little gem of a restaurant" that "whisks" diners "back to France", this Lakeview "oasis" offers "inexpensive", "amazing" and "authentic" sweet and savory crêpes; the "cozy, candlelit tables" and "surprising outdoor back garden" are "romantic" enough for "anniversaries" and "laid-back" enough for a bite before or "after a movie at the Landmark."

**La Fonda del Gusto**  *Mexican*  − | − | − | I

**Wicker Park** | 1408 N. Milwaukee Ave. (bet. Evergreen & Wolcott Aves.) | 773-278-6100 | www.lafondadelgusto.com

"Delicious family recipes" become "affordable", "high-quality" fare at this casual, "attentive" Wicker Park BYO Mexican, run by a husband-and-wife team; the red-brick storefront space features an open kitchen and multiple dining rooms with booth seating and lacquered wood tables.

**La Fonda Latino** *Colombian*  − | − | − | M

**Andersonville** | 5350 N. Broadway St. (Balmoral Ave.) | 773-271-3935

"Authentic", affordable Colombian fare in "good-size portions" accompanied by "fabulous margaritas" and served by "friendly, knowledgeable" staffers earn points for this Andersonville eatery; the bi-level space – with its share of Latin tchotchkes – "gets loud" when it's busy, however, so take advantage of sidewalk seating in summer.

**Z La Gondola** *Italian*  24 | 13 | 20 | $25

**Lakeview** | Wellington Plaza | 2914 N. Ashland Ave. (Wellington Ave.) | 773-248-4433 | www.lagondolachicago.com

"Huge servings" of "consistently fantastic", "made-to-order" "classic Italian" and "great thin pizza" presented by an "Italian family" lure Lakeview locals to this "quaint", "teensy room in a shopping mall"; it's "relatively unknown", which is surprising given the "reasonable" tabs and the "welcoming" staff that runs it; P.S. avoid the "crowded seating area" and "order takeout."

**La Madia** *Italian/Pizza*  23 | 20 | 21 | $31

**River North** | 59 W. Grand Ave. (bet. Clark & Dearborn Sts.) | 312-329-0400 | www.dinelamadia.com

Expect "gourmet", "brick-oven", "thin-crust" pies, supported by "strong salads and sandwiches" and "extensive wines by the glass", at this "reasonably priced" River North "find"; equally appropriate for a "business lunch" or a "cozy" date beside the "crackling fireplace", it errs only when it comes to what a few call "slow service."

**Landmark** *American*  20 | 21 | 22 | $42

**Lincoln Park** | 1633 N. Halsted St. (North Ave.) | 312-587-1600 | www.landmarkgrill.net

"They pay attention to detail" at this Lincoln Park "hot spot" known for "comforting" New American noshes and "delicious seasonal cocktails" perfect for "pre-theater dining" or "late-night bar" hopping; the "huge" space still "manages to feel intimate" thanks to its "many rooms", but it gets "clubby after 10 PM", so "dine early if you want to hear your tablemates."

**NEW Lan's China Bistro ◐** *Chinese*  — | — | — | I

**Old Town** | 1507 N. Sedgwick St. (bet. Blackhawk St. & North Ave.) | 312-255-9888 | www.lansoldtown.com

Behind grand red doors worthy of Chinatown, this Old Town Chinese "BYO gem" maintains a budget-friendly menu of MSG-free Mandarin, Sichuan and dim sum faves, as well as hot pots steamed at the dining bar; the setting is minimalist Asian.

**Ⓩ Lao Beijing** *Chinese*  24 | 10 | 16 | $24

**Chinatown** | Chinatown Mall | 2138 S. Archer Ave. (Cermak Rd.) | 312-881-0168

**Ⓩ Lao Sze Chuan ◐** *Chinese*

**Chinatown** | 2172 S. Archer Ave. (Princeton Ave.) | 312-326-5040
**Downers Grove** | 1331 W. Ogden Ave. (Oakwood Ave.) | 630-663-0303
www.tonygourmetgroup.com

This trio of regional Chinese chow houses serves "long menus" of "genuine", "standard and exotic" dishes in "minimal" "hole-in-the-wall" dining rooms that draw "lines out the door"; the servers "often don't speak English" so you "must be comfortable not knowing for sure what you're eating", but spice-heads believe it's always a good sign when their "mouth is burning two days later"; N.B. Beijing is BYO, city Sze Chuan serves beer and wine only and suburban Sze Chuan has a full bar.

**la petite folie Ⓜ** *French*  24 | 21 | 21 | $49

**Hyde Park** | Hyde Park Shopping Ctr. | 1504 E. 55th St. (Lake Park Blvd.) | 773-493-1394 | www.lapetitefolie.com

"Straightforward, classic French cooking" and a "superb" all-French wine list meet in this "elegant", "civilized" Hyde Parker that locals call a "neighborhood gem"; while some take issue with the "sometimes slow" service, most say "it's so pleasant, one hardly cares."

**La Sardine Ⓩ** *French*  24 | 20 | 23 | $45

**West Loop** | 111 N. Carpenter St. (bet. Randolph St. & Washington Blvd.) | 312-421-2800 | www.lasardine.com

If you like "excellent", "moderately priced", "traditional French bistro" fare served in an "intimate", "romantic" room by a "uniformly friendly staff" that "knows when to leave you alone", then this West Loop "gem" and sister to Le Bouchon "is the real goods"; in fact, there's "not a thing wrong with this place" unless you count the "crowds" of "friendly repeat customers" who make it "noisy" at times; P.S. the "prix fixe on Tuesdays" is the "best deal."

**La Scarola** *Italian*  24 | 14 | 21 | $35

**River West** | 721 W. Grand Ave. (bet. Halsted St. & Union Ave.) | 312-243-1740 | www.lascarola.com

"Entrees feed two" at this "old-school" River West "neighborhood" Italian with the "obligatory red-checkered tablecloths" and a staff that "treats you like family"; the setting is "dumpy", but judging from the "crowded atmosphere" (you may have to wait "even with reservations"), it's the "full-flavored", "fairly priced" dishes that everyone cares about.

### Las Palmas *Mexican*     21 | 16 | 22 | $27

**Bucktown** | 1835 W. North Ave. (Honore St.) | 773-289-4991
**Buffalo Grove** | 86 W. Dundee Rd. (Old Buffalo Grove Rd.) | 847-520-8222
www.laspalmaschicago.com

These upscale sibs of a more casual local chain serve "interesting", "fairly authentic" Mexican food along with "great cocktails" in a "bright and cheerful environment"; Bucktown has nightly live entertainment and an "outdoor patio" that "can't be beat on a summer day", while Buffalo Grove offers music on weekend nights.

### Las Tablas *Colombian/Steak*     20 | 16 | 20 | $29

**Lakeview** | 2942 N. Lincoln Ave. (Wellington Ave.) | 773-871-2414
**Northwest Side** | 4920 W. Irving Park Rd. (bet. Lamon & Laporte Aves.) | 773-202-0999
www.lastablas.com

At once "exotic and familiar", these Colombian steakhouse sibs in Lakeview and the Northwest Side feature "fantastic, flavorful" steak and "perfectly seasoned grilled chicken served on a wood plank"; the "fun", "friendly" atmosphere includes live weekend entertainment, and the Lincoln Avenue branch relocated post-Survey to a larger space and acquired a liquor license.

### La Tache *French*     22 | 19 | 20 | $44

**Andersonville** | 1475 W. Balmoral Ave. (bet. Clark St. & Glenwood Ave.) | 773-334-7168

Andersonville's "serviceable", "neighborhood standby" serves "above-average", "simple" French bistro fare (Lyonnaise salad, steak frites) for brunch and dinner; even if it loses points for "average surroundings" and sometimes "inattentive" service, "you'll still feel you've got your money's worth" – especially if you hit Monday's "three-course deal"; P.S. head to the "little outdoor tables" in summer.

### La Tasca *Spanish*     24 | 20 | 21 | $34

**Arlington Heights** | 25 W. Davis St. (Vail Ave.) | 847-398-2400 | www.latascatapas.com

"Right off the train line" in Arlington Heights, this "lively" veteran offers a seemingly "never-ending" choice of "delicious" tapas for "sharing" as well as "great paellas and fish dishes"; "reservations are a must", but "you're never rushed out", plus the "tasty sangria" and periodic "live entertainment" are "worth the trip" alone.

### NEW Laurel Mediterranean Grill *Mediterranean*     - | - | - | M

**Naperville** | 1163 E. Ogden Ave. (bet. East & E. Iroquois Aves.) | 630-946-6656 | www.laurelgrill.com

Fare from Turkey, Greece and Lebanon mingle on the midpriced menu at this Naperville strip-mall Med, where the small plates and grilled fare are accompanied by a limited wine list and other beverage options like ouzo, Turkish coffee and Moroccan tea; the setting is open and airy, with Aegean blue-and-white walls, bare-wood cafe tables, a fireplace and lots of windows.

### Lawry's The Prime Rib  *American/Steak*   24 | 22 | 23 | $53

**River North** | 100 E. Ontario St. (Rush St.) | 312-787-5000 | www.lawrysonline.com

"Slabs of tender prime rib with equally desirable sides" (and that "famous spinning salad") explain the enduring appeal of this Beverly Hills–based steakhouse chain (including the River North outpost), that's also known for its "unique table service" from "rolling carts"; it's a bit "touristy" and "pricey", but committed customers don't mind, calling it a serious "contender for a last meal."

### LB Bistro & Patisserie  *American*   - | - | - | M

**Streeterville** | Sheraton Chicago Hotel & Towers | 301 E. North Water St. (Columbus Dr.) | 312-329-5900 | www.sheratonchicago.com

World Pastry Championship winner Laurent Branlard helms this handsome French-American bistro inside the Streeterville Sheraton, where midpriced breakfast and lunch fare – including build-your-own omelets, parfaits, salads, sandwiches, crêpes and sweets – is served in an upscale, modern deco setting with warm wood, a glass-mosaic floor, a water wall and a view of the Chicago River.

### Le Bouchon  🗷 *French*   24 | 19 | 21 | $46

**Bucktown** | 1958 N. Damen Ave. (Armitage Ave.) | 773-862-6600 | www.lebouchonofchicago.com

Bucktown bistro-goers are "brought back to Paris" with Jean Claude Poilevey's "wonderful French food at a reasonable price" "served up by focused servers" in a "cozy, fast-paced dining room"; it's "authentic" right down to the occasional "attitude" and "tiny" with a "huge following" (so "be prepared to wait even if you have a reservation because no one wants to leave"); P.S. "the prix fixe menu is a great bargain."

### 🗷 Le Colonial  *Vietnamese*   24 | 25 | 22 | $50

**Gold Coast** | 937 N. Rush St. (bet. Oak & Walnut Sts.) | 312-255-0088 | www.lecolonialchicago.com

"Terrific" Vietnamese cuisine "with a French hand" enchants enthusiasts of this "exotic-elegant", "pricey", "exquisite oasis" where an "attentive" staff navigates a "sexy" Gold Coast setting that's a "visual snapshot of pre-war Vietnam with ceiling fans and palms, white tablecloths and orchids"; "be prepared to be elbow-to-elbow with self-aware beautiful people" (it's "a little cramped for Chicago, ok for Saigon") or head for the bar area and "sit on the second story balcony overlooking" the "entertaining show" along Rush Street.

### Lee Wing Wah  *Chinese*   - | - | - | I

**Chinatown** | 2147 S. China Pl. (bet. Princeton Ave. & Wells St.) | 312-808-1682 | www.leewingwah-chicago-chinese.com

"Consistently fresh, delicious" fare and "fast, efficient service" make this "Chinatown favorite" Cantonese and seafood specialist a

## L'Eiffel Bistrot & Crêperie  *Crêpes/French*     21 | 22 | 22 | $37

**South Barrington** | Arboretum Mall | 100 W. Higgins Rd. (Rte. 59) |
847-428-4783 | www.leiffelbistrot.com

South Barrington's "charming", "pleasantly surprising mall" bistrot with a bar delivers French fare (including "wonderful crêpes") and "wine for a very reasonable price"; the "warm, friendly" setting's "eye candy" includes Parisian-style "artistic details" and "lovely outdoor dining."

## Lem's BBQ ●⧧ *BBQ*     ▽ 25 | 8 | 16 | $22

**Far South Side** | 311 E. 75th St. (bet. Calumet & Prairie Aves.) |
773-994-2428

"You can smell the smoke blocks away" at this budget-loving Far South Side "staple" where fans of the "outstanding" barbecue chow down on some of the "best ribs anywhere"; "zero decor" and no seating are part of the package, leaving some praising the "quick in-and-out" experience for "carryout"; N.B. open till 2 AM and closed Tuesdays.

## Leonardo's Ristorante Ⓜ *Italian*     - | - | - | M

**Andersonville** | 5657 N. Clark St. (Hollywood Ave.) |
773-561-5028

An Andersonville "neighborhood" "favorite", this "hidden gem" pleases patrons by serving "terrific", "sophisticated" Northern Italian fare "at a good price" and "with enough menu changes to keep repeat diners intrigued"; the "wine selection", "helpful service" and "friendly atmosphere" are additional reasons locals contend it's not "just another" rustic-looking trattoria.

## NEW Leo's Coney Island  *Hot Dogs*     - | - | - | I

**Wrigleyville** | 3455 N. Southport Ave. (Cornelia Ave.) | 773-281-5367 |
www.leoschicago.com

Challenging the local dog dynasty, this Detroit import on a Wrigleyville corner impudently heaps grilled franks with no-bean chili, onions and mustard; the menu expands with other affordable fast-food items including burgers, wings, nachos and potato skins, along with an extensive roundup of breakfast fare and American and Greek diner classics, all served in a casual setting with table seating and takeout, ketchup-colored accents and a Chicago skyline mural.

## Le P'tit Paris  *Continental/French*     20 | 19 | 21 | $50

**Streeterville** | 260 E. Chestnut St. (Dewitt Pl.) | 312-787-8260
"Hidden" "out of the way" in Streeterville, this "quaint", "wonderful little restaurant" issues "entirely authentic" French-Continental cuisine that patrons find "reasonably priced for the quality"; though detractors deem the decor "a bit outdated", Francophiles who "love" the "old-school" setting and "knowledgeable, friendly staff" prefer to keep this place their "secret."

| | FOOD | DECOR | SERVICE | COST |
|---|---|---|---|---|

### ☑ Les Nomades ⌖Ⓜ French    `29` `27` `28` `$113`

**Streeterville** | 222 E. Ontario St. (bet. Fairbanks Ct. & St. Clair St.) | 312-649-9010 | www.lesnomades.net

"One of the last bastions of haute cuisine", the No. 1 for Food in Chicago is Streeterville's French "crème de la crème" of "very formal" "fine dining", where chef Chris Nugent's "sophisticated", "beautifully prepared and presented" fare "is en pointe" as is the "extremely attentive service" and "remarkable", "francocentric" wine selection; the "quietly elegant", "clubby townhouse" ("once a private dining club") is a "place out of time and space" with "white linens", an "upstairs fireplace" and "gorgeous flowers", and though it's "*très* pricey", it's "perfect for a special, romantic occasion."

### ☑ Le Titi de Paris Ⓜ French    `26` `24` `25` `$65`

**Arlington Heights** | 1015 W. Dundee Rd. (Kennicott Ave.) | 847-506-0222 | www.letitideparis.com

Chef Michael Maddox's "creative menu" of "superb" "upscale" French fare is "prepared with the utmost care and savoir faire" at this "elegant" eatery "hidden in" Arlington Heights; "friendly service" and a "romantic" setting evoking "Parisian sophistication" with chandeliers, fresh flowers and "even the china" are reasons it remains a "favorite" for "special occasions" "after all these years."

### Le Vichyssois Ⓜ French    `26` `22` `22` `$52`

**Lakemoor** | 220 Rand Rd. (2 mi. west of Rte. 12) | 815-385-8221 | www.levichyssois.com

"It's a journey to another era" at Bernard Cretier's "unexpected wayside inn" in Lakemoor offering "classic country French cuisine" at "reasonable" tabs in an "elegant", "art museum" milieu filled with antiques; smitten surveyors say that "service can be flawless or a little off, but everyone is always kind", making it "well worth" "the hike to the boonies."

### 🆕 Little Bucharest Bistro ◕ European    `-` `-` `-` `M`

**Northwest Side** | 3661 N. Elston Ave. (Addison St.) | 773-604-8500 | www.littlebucharestbistro.com

This Modern European redo of "the original" located in the Northwest Side offers affordable entrees (some with Romanian influences) and shared plates delivered with "friendly service"; the "charming room" attracts an "eclectic clientele", and the "pleasant experience" includes live entertainment Tuesday through Sunday.

### 🆕 LM Ⓜ French    `22` `21` `21` `$48`

**Lincoln Square** | 4539 N. Lincoln Ave. (bet. Sunnyside & Wilson Aves.) | 773-942-7585 | www.lmrestaurant.com

Supporters sum up this "excellent addition to the Lincoln Square" scene as "special-occasion" dining "at an everyday price" with its combination of "complex, innovative and well-prepared" "contemporary French" fare, "polished service" and "extremely tasteful modern design" – but lack of "stuffiness"; P.S. the "cocktails are tasty and strong", and the wine list offers "some good picks."

### Lobby, The  *European/Seafood*    28 | 28 | 28 | $70

**River North** | Peninsula Hotel | 108 E. Superior St., 5th fl.
(bet. Michigan Ave. & Rush St.) | 312-573-6760 | www.peninsula.com
For a "wonderfully civilized" "splurge", raters recommend this River
North Euro seafood specialist in an "amazing" Peninsula Hotel
space that's "well lit" with 20-ft. floor-to-ceiling windows; "genteel"
service and "discreet celebrity-watching" are in the mix, and while
early eaters say "breakfasts are the thing to come for" and the "Sunday brunch" "will please everyone", celebrants suggest "for a special occasion, it's the best tea in town."

### Lockwood  *American*    19 | 25 | 19 | $47

**Loop** | Palmer House Hilton | 17 E. Monroe St. (bet. State St. &
Wabash Ave.) | 312-917-3404 | www.lockwoodrestaurant.com
Following the "trend of putting a great restaurant in a hotel lobby",
this "lovely" Loop "fine-dining" destination in the historic Palmer
House Hilton features an "interesting" New American menu,
"delicious" "breakfast and brunch buffets" and an "outstanding
wine selection"; if service can be "disappointing" and some find it
"overpriced", the decor is "stunning" and it's "a relaxing place to
dine before theater or symphony."

### NEW LOKaL  *European*    - | - | - | M

**Bucktown** | 1904 W. North Ave. (Wolcott St.) | 773-904-8113 |
www.lokalchicago.com
At this edgy Bucktown eatery, "Eastern European–inspired" "contemporary creative comfort food" comes at "value" prices with a
limited but affordable wine list and a handful of house cocktails; the
space's concrete floor, mineral color scheme and massive mesh
light fixtures create a cool urban vibe, and there's an intimate lounge
area; P.S. the "brunch deal" includes "bottomless mimosas
and Bloody Marys."

### NEW Longman & Eagle ☽ *American*    - | - | - | M

**Logan Square** | 2657 N. Kedzie Ave. (Schubert Ave.) | 773-276-7110 |
www.longmanandeagle.com
This Logan Square lair with inn aspirations (it's adding six rooms upstairs) serves a midpriced New American menu loaded with artisanal
ingredients – think wild-boar sloppy joes and duck egg with tongue
hash and truffle vinaigrette – accompanied by specialty cocktails,
microbrews and lots of brown booze; the cozy tavern space features
distressed brick and reclaimed wood, with an open kitchen, drafting-
style barstools, mismatched chairs and a Wurlitzer jukebox.

### Los Moles  *Mexican*    - | - | - | M

**Lakeview** | 3140 N. Lincoln Ave. (bet. Barry & Belmont Aves.) |
773-935-9620 | www.losmoles.net
Chef Geno "Bahena still works his magic" at this midpriced Lakeview
cantina where the "delicious" Mexican food and drink leaves patrons professing "you had me at mole"; there's a "pleasant, relaxed"
vibe and optional "tasting menu" that's an "exceptional value";
P.S. "don't miss the lady making fresh tortillas."

| | FOOD | DECOR | SERVICE | COST |
|---|---|---|---|---|

## ☑ Lou Malnati's Pizzeria  *Pizza*     24 | 14 | 19 | $21

**River North** | 439 N. Wells St. (Hubbard St.) | 312-828-9800
**Lincoln Park** | 958 W. Wrightwood Ave. (Lincoln Ave.) | 773-832-4030
**Southwest Side** | 3859 W. Ogden Ave. (Cermak Rd.) | 773-762-0800
**Evanston** | 1850 Sherman Ave. (University Pl.) | 847-328-5400
**Lincolnwood** | 6649 N. Lincoln Ave. (bet. Devon & Pratt Aves.) | 847-673-0800
**Buffalo Grove** | 85 S. Buffalo Grove Rd. (Lake Cook Rd.) | 847-215-7100
**Elk Grove Village** | 1050 E. Higgins Rd. (bet. Arlington Heights & Busse Rds.) | 847-439-2000
**Schaumburg** | 1 S. Roselle Rd. (Schaumburg Rd.) | 847-985-1525
**Naperville** | 131 W. Jefferson Ave. (bet. Main & Webster Sts.) | 630-717-0700
**Naperville** | 2879 W. 95th St. (Rte. 59) | 630-904-4222  ●☒
www.loumalnatis.com
Additional locations throughout the Chicago area
Legions of loyalists swear by these "deep-dish joints" where the "authentic", "home-grown" Chicago-style pizzas are built with "the right amount of everything" including a "flaky", "buttery crust" and "quality ingredients"; just know that service and surroundings vary by location, the latter from "classic" to "sports bar" to "minimal", and the pies are "cooked to order" so you may have to "wait"; P.S. for "yearners" who "live far away", "life will never be the same" since most surveyors say the "in-restaurant" version outshines the "frozen", "shipped" option.

## Lou Mitchell's  *Diner*     23 | 14 | 21 | $17

**Loop** | 565 W. Jackson Blvd. (Jefferson St.) | 312-939-3111  ⊟
**O'Hare Area** | O'Hare Int'l Airport | Terminal 5 (I-190) | 773-601-8989  ●
www.loumitchellsrestaurant.com
The Loop's "breakfast legend" lives on serving "straight American" "diner-style" morning fare through lunch including "fluffy" "omelets steaming in their own skillets and perfectly done pancakes"; the "old-fashioned" "warmth and character" includes "experienced" staffers who "give out" "Milk Duds and doughnut holes" when there's a "line out the door" to this "cholesterol capital" ("no dieters allowed"); P.S. "get there early and bring cash" (the airport quick-serve takes credit cards).

## ☑ Lovells of Lake Forest  *American*     23 | 25 | 22 | $54

**Lake Forest** | 915 S. Waukegan Rd. (Everett Rd.) | 847-234-8013 | www.lovellsoflakeforest.com
There's "no hurrying" at this "classy place for a North Suburban business lunch or romantic date" in Lake Forest that does "delicious, creative" New American fare in a "quiet" setting filled with "very interesting" "memorabilia" from Apollo 13 astronaut Jim Lovell, the owner's father; the staff is "helpful" and surveyors sum it up as "rather expensive for routine dining but great for special occasions"; P.S. the "Captain's Quarters" downstairs is more "informal with fun bands on the weekends."

| | FOOD | DECOR | SERVICE | COST |
|---|---|---|---|---|

### NEW Loving Hut, The *Vegetarian/Vegan*  | – | – | – | I |
### (fka Alice & Friends)

**Edgewater** | 5812 N. Broadway St. (Ardmore Ave.) | 773-275-8797 |
www.lovinghut.us

Edgewater's former Alice & Friends continues under the same team
as this quirky, inexpensive Asian-vegetarian chain link with a
devoted following for its vegan vittles for lunch and dinner; the spartan remodeled setting features expanded seating and theme photography; N.B. there's no alcohol and no BYO.

### Z L2O *Seafood*   27 | 28 | 27 | $142 |

**Lincoln Park** | Belden-Stratford Hotel | 2300 N. Lincoln Park W.
(Belden Ave.) | 773-868-0002 | www.l2orestaurant.com

It's "nothing but superlatives" for "Chicago's finest seafooder",
Lincoln Park's "inventive, seductive" "artistic triumph" from restaurateurs Lettuce Entertain You and chef Laurent Gras, featuring
"amazing taste sensations" and "surprising techniques" (there's no
shortage of "powders and foam"); add "eye-popping" decor that's
"smart and modern without formality" and "scrupulous" service,
and it amounts to a "truly divine" "escape from everyday life", especially if you "have the wine pairings" and "don't look at the tab";
P.S. gentlemen, "jackets are preferred."

### NEW Lucky Monk Burger,   | – | – | – | I |
### Pizza & Beer Co. *Pizza/Pub Food*

**South Barrington** | 105 Hollywood Blvd. (Studio Dr.) | 847-898-0500 |
www.theluckymonk.com

'Hand-stretched' NYC–style pizza, prime beef burgers and housemade
beers are the tasty trifecta at this chic, sprawling Northwest Suburban
microbrewery whose name is a nod to the monastic Belgian brewing
tradition (order brews in bombers, growlers or kegs to-go); the
upscale-casual, warmly lit environs include an imposing installation
of stone and beer barrels, cushy leather sofas and tastefully scat-
tered TVs, and there's a waterfront terrace with a fire pit.

### Z Lula Cafe *Eclectic*   26 | 19 | 21 | $31 |

**Logan Square** | 2537-41 N. Kedzie Blvd. (bet. Fullerton Ave. & Logan Blvd.) |
773-489-9554 | www.lulacafe.com

Logan Square's "semi-secret" "neighborhood gem" confers "creative, market-driven" Eclectic dishes "with fresh, local organic ingredients" for breakfast, lunch and dinner in an "unpretentious",
"arty environment" with a "quirky staff" that "adds to the milieu";
there are no reservations, so you may encounter a "long wait."

### LuLu's Dim Sum & Then Sum *Asian*   21 | 15 | 19 | $23 |

**Evanston** | 804 Davis St. (Sherman Ave.) | 847-869-4343 |
www.lulusdimsum.com

"Delicious", "reasonably priced" "dim sum–style dishes" and an "extensive menu" of "well-prepared Asian" specialties including various
"all-you-can-eat" specials keep this "fast-food-looking", "longtime
Evanston favorite" with "knowledgeable service" "hopping"; P.S. if
purists pan it as "inauthentic", the "kids" will find it "exotic."

|  | FOOD | DECOR | SERVICE | COST |
|--|------|-------|---------|------|

### Lupita's Ⓜ *Mexican*                21 | 16 | 22 | $25

**Evanston** | 700 Main St. (Custer Ave.) | 847-328-2255 |
www.lupitasmexicanrestaurant.com

"Well-prepared", low-priced Mexican meals are "inventive" or
"standard" depending on who's dining at this Evanston "local" that
flies "under the radar"; but "prompt", "helpful service" and weekend
"nights with music" add to "a pleasant experience."

### LuxBar ◕ *American*                20 | 20 | 21 | $32

**Gold Coast** | 18 E. Bellevue Pl. (Rush St.) | 312-642-3400 | www.luxbar.com
A "diversified" Traditional American menu that's a "step up" from the
"usual bar food" (and a "value for the area") meets a "hipster look"
in a "dark atmosphere" with a "dynamic bar scene" of "drinks and
eye candy", luring loungers to this often "noisy" Gold Coast "neighborhood spot"; with "efficient service", it also works for a "shopping
break", "catching TV sports" or "people-watching", especially in the
"outdoor dining area" or at a seat "overlooking Michigan Avenue";
P.S. the "fireplace" adds appeal "in the winter."

### L. Woods Tap & Pine Lodge *American/BBQ*    20 | 18 | 20 | $31

**Lincolnwood** | 7110 N. Lincoln Ave. (Kostner Ave.) | 847-677-3350 |
www.lwoodsrestaurant.com

From Lettuce Entertain You, this "family-friendly" Lincolnwood
"take" on a "Wisconsin roadhouse" is "dependable" for a midpriced
American "comfort-food" menu "with something for everyone" served
in "casual" confines with "comfortable booths" and "service with a
smile"; what some call "uninspired" others peg as "unassuming."

### Macello *Italian*                – | – | – | M

**West Loop** | 1235 W. Lake St. (bet. Elizabeth St. & Racine Ave.) |
312-850-9870

Fans who admired the "meat-cooler" chic look and "broad,
well-priced menu" at this Market District Italian are no doubt glad
that it's back in business after having closed for a year after a
fire; set in a former butchery, it still has "great glass globes
hanging from the ceiling" and is serving "tasty pizzas" and other
"neighborhood"-friendly fare.

### 🆕 Macku Sushi *Japanese*             – | – | – | M

**Lincoln Park** | 2239 N. Clybourn Ave. (bet. Greenview & Janssen Aves.) |
773-880-8012 | www.mackusushi.com

Chefs from the defunct Kaze are back at this Lincoln Parker, serving a
similar midpriced menu of creative sushi and contemporary Japanese
cuisine along with full bar offerings; the spiffed-up storefront setting is
decorated in exposed brick, mirrors and mixed shades of green,
while seating includes a wall-length banquette and a sushi bar.

### Ⓩ mado Ⓜ *Italian/Mediterranean*      25 | 19 | 23 | $42

**Bucktown** | 1647 N. Milwaukee Ave. (bet. Concord Pl. & North Ave.) |
773-342-2340 | www.madorestaurantchicago.com

Run by a "warm and friendly" "husband-and-wife duo", this Bucktown
"locavore" serves "sinfully good" "farm-to-table" "modern Italian"–

FOOD | DECOR | SERVICE | COST

Mediterranean "food with a conscience" in a rustic setting with chalkboard menus on brick walls; the selection might be "limited" and "a little pricey", but it's "never the same twice" as offerings are "chosen daily from current market availability", while service is "enthusiastic but unpretentious"; P.S. if you want wine "you can – indeed must – bring your own."

### ☑ Maggiano's Little Italy  *Italian*    20 | 19 | 21 | $32

**River North** | 516 N. Clark St. (bet. Grand Ave. & Illinois St.) | 312-644-7700
**Skokie** | Westfield Shoppingtown | 4999 Old Orchard Ctr. (Skokie Blvd.) | 847-933-9555
**Schaumburg** | 1901 E. Woodfield Rd. (Rte. 53) | 847-240-5600
**Naperville** | 1847 Freedom Dr. (E. Diehl Rd.) | 630-536-2270
**Oak Brook** | Oakbrook Center Mall | 240 Oakbrook Ctr. (Rte. 83) | 630-368-0300
www.maggianos.com

"Giant", "family-style" feeds of "Americanized" "comfort food" are the attraction at this ever-expanding, Chicago-bred "franchise" of "Italian-themed" eateries where "kid-friendly" quarters with red-checkered tablecloths are home to generally "timely" service; naysayers nag they're too "noisy" and "generic", but *amici* insist they're "predictably good" and there's "always leftovers", concluding you "can't beat the value, especially for larger groups and families."

### Magnolia Cafe  Ⓜ *American*    22 | 17 | 22 | $38

**Ravenswood** | 1224 W. Wilson Ave. (Magnolia Ave.) | 773-728-8785 | www.magnoliacafeuptown.com

A "small, refined menu" of "wonderful" New American cuisine that's "fresh and attractively" plated with "seasonal selections" calls to fans of this "conversation-friendly", midpriced Ravenswood "hidden gem" where they "don't try to do too much, but what they do, they do well"; though the brick-walled, candlelit room is "small", diners "don't feel hemmed in", with the service adding to their "delight" as does a bar that's a "great place to meet."

### Maijean  Ⓜ *French*    ▽ 28 | 24 | 26 | $47

**Clarendon Hills** | 30 S. Prospect Ave. (Park Ave.) | 630-794-8900 | www.maijean.com

"You may be transported to Paris" – or "certainly out of the 'burbs" – at this "lovely little bistro" in Clarendon Hills that's a "consistent" conveyor of "excellent" "French-inspired cuisine" and "wines by the glass" plus an "unusual selection of cheeses", all at "good prices"; "top-flight service", an "art deco atmosphere" and "outdoor tables in the summer" complete the scene.

### 🆕 Main Street Smokehouse  ☒ *BBQ*    ─ | ─ | ─ | I

**Libertyville** | 536 N. Milwaukee Ave. (School St.) | 847-247-4330 | www.mainstreetsmokehouse.com

Regional American barbecue from a rotisserie smoker – babybacks, brisket, pulled pork and chicken, all with a choice of five sauces – lures the 'cue crowd to this casual, dine-in and take-out Libertyville lair decorated with reclaimed barn wood and brick; other options on the budget-friendly menu include quesadillas, sweet potato fries and blueberry-peach cobbler, and there's beer too.

### Maiz ☒✍ *Mexican* ▽ 23 | 15 | 21 | $25

**Humboldt Park** | 1041 N. California Ave. (Cortez St.) | 773-276-3149

Humboldt Parkers looking for a "change from your average taqueria" head for this cantina specializing in "inexpensive, homey" Mexican fare with a focus on "fascinating" corn-based "little dishes, any of which you are likely to enjoy" in the space decked out in pastel colors and terra-cotta; P.S. "be sure to get the [signature] guacamole."

### Makisu Sushi Lounge & Grill *Japanese* - | - | - | M

**Skokie** | Village Crossing Shopping Ctr. | 7150 Carpenter Rd. (Touhy Ave.) | 847-677-9030 | www.makisu-sushi.com

A "beautiful" Asian milieu awash with jazzy music belies the Skokie strip-mall setting of this "amazing sushi oasis" where "super-fresh" modern maki, small plates and grilled fare (including steaks) round out the creative midpriced Japanese menu supplemented by "bento box lunch specials", sake and specialty martinis; seating includes a swanky lounge and a sushi bar with stone backdrop, in a setting of dark wood and neutral leather, giant bamboo and botanicals, and panorama windows.

### MANA Food Bar *Eclectic/Vegetarian* 27 | 21 | 22 | $28

**Wicker Park** | 1742 W. Division St. (bet. Paulina & Wood Sts.) | 773-342-1742 | www.manafoodbar.com

"Fantastic" "feats of creativity with vegetables" attract a "loving" following to this "cute little" Wicker Park Eclectic-vegetarian small plates specialist with a "no-fake-meat policy" and "cocktail options" to boot; it's "very reasonable for the quality" and in season you can "sit outside and watch the world go by on Division Street" – now if they'd just "accept reservations" or "expand."

### Mandarin Kitchen *Chinese* - | - | - | M

**Chinatown** | 2143 S. Archer Ave. (bet. Princeton & Wentworth Aves.) | 312-328-0228

Those hankering for "hot pots" "highly recommend" this Chinatown midpriced "alternative" for what they call some of "the best" "savory soups" in Chicago, along with noodle "dishes that hold their own" against the competition; N.B. beer is available, but no reservations.

### NEW Manghal *Mediterranean/Kosher* - | - | - | M

**Evanston** | 1805 Howard St. (bet. California & Washtenaw Aves.) | 847-859-2681 | www.manghalgrill.com

Evanston locals keep it kosher at this midpriced Med featuring Israeli-style spit-roasted meats on massive skewers and other fresh fare including falafel, shawarma and salads (a blackboard menu lists to-go items), all served in a simple setting with polished wood tables and chairs, a ceramic tile floor and a fire pit for baking flatbreads; N.B. in keeping with tradition, it's closed Friday and Saturday, and if you opt to BYO, make sure it's kosher.

FOOD | DECOR | SERVICE | COST

## Manny's  *Deli*

23 | 7 | 14 | $18

**South Loop** | 1141 S. Jefferson St. (bet. Grenshaw St. & Roosevelt Rd.) | 312-939-2855 ⑤
**Southwest Side** | Midway Int'l Airport | 5700 S. Cicero Ave. (55th St.) | 773-948-6300
www.mannysdeli.com

For "attitude" with a side of "cardiac arrest", this "no-frills", affordable South Loop deli "icon" delivers "patter on the cafeteria line" to rival the "big-as-your-head sandwiches" and "incredible variety" of "choices from the steam table"; "everybody is right out of central casting", from the "loudmouthed", "old-style Chicago countermen" to the "sociological panorama" of patrons; as for ambiance, acolytes ask "you want decor – the corned beef isn't enough?"; P.S. insiders insist Midway is a "mere shadow of the main restaurant."

## Marché  *French*

23 | 24 | 21 | $42

**West Loop** | 833 W. Randolph St. (Green St.) | 312-226-8399 | www.marche-chicago.com

"Theatrical fine dining" in an "over-the-top" setting prompts surveyors to "march to" this "original pioneer" of the Market District from Jerry Kleiner (Red Light, Gioco) that's "still going strong" with its "delicious" French bistro–style fare dished out in a "lively" atmosphere with an "open kitchen", "lots of velvet trimmings" and prime "people-watching" ("including the cute staff"); P.S. "reasonable prices" include weekday prix fixe lunch "bargains."

## ⚡ Margie's Candies  *American*

22 | 13 | 16 | $11

**Bucktown** | 1960 N. Western Ave. (Armitage Ave.) | 773-384-1035 ◗
**Ravenswood** | 1813 W. Montrose Ave. (Ravenswood Ave.) | 773-348-0400

"Go for" the "outrageously colored Ice creams" and "big creamy sundaes" "served in plastic clamshells" with both "hot fudge sauce" and "nostalgia on the side" say surveyors who tend to "take a pass on the rest" of the Traditional American fare at these affordable "classic old-time" "ice cream and candy" "emporiums"; the 1921 Bucktown "original" has all the "kitschy" decor but you "can often get into" the "more modern" Ravenswood repeat without the long "wait."

## Marigold  Ⓜ *Indian*

23 | 19 | 22 | $38

**Uptown** | 4832 N. Broadway St. (bet. Ainslie St. & Lawrence Ave.) | 773-293-4653 | www.marigoldrestaurant.com

"Truly innovative", "upscale" Indian "fusion cooking" with "nuanced flavors" plus "great cocktails" draw devotees to this "hip", "fairly affordable" Uptowner with "friendly, understated" service; the sleek, warm-colored setting is "elegant" yet "comfortable" and suitable for a romantic meal as "you can even hear to talk."

## Market  ◗ *American*

18 | 19 | 12 | $28

**West Loop** | 1113 W. Randolph St. (bet. Aberdeen & May Sts.) | 312-929-4787 | www.marketbarchicago.com

Cheerleaders champion this West Looper's "creative menu" of moderately priced Traditional American fare that's "surprisingly" "tasty" for an "upscale" "sports bar" and served with an "ample cocktail list" in a "hip" "open room with multiple levels" featuring "lots of TVs"; "outdoor spaces" including a "beer garden" and "rooftop lounge" win favor, though not "slow", "inattentive" service that's just "not up to speed."

## Markethouse *American* ▽ 21 | 15 | 18 | $41

**Streeterville** | Doubletree Hotel | 611 N. Fairbanks Ct. (bet. Ohio & Ontario Sts.) | 312-224-2200 | www.markethousechicago.com
Regulars are rooting for this "hidden" Streeterville "gem" in the Doubletree where the "carefully prepared" New American menu is built on a "theme of market-fresh, seasonal" and organic ingredients and also features a "wonderful cheese selection"; "service is attentive" and "attention to detail" is evident throughout – though some are less thrilled by an atmosphere that understandably "feels like a hotel"; N.B. they serve an all-you-can-eat breakfast buffet daily.

## NEW Masu Izakaya ⓩ *Japanese* - | - | - | M

**Lincoln Park** | 1969 N. Halsted St. (bet. Armitage Ave. & Willow St.) | 773-435-9314 | www.masuchicago.com
A Japanese version of a gastropub, this Lincoln Park small plates-and-sake specialist from the owner of the former Tsunami serves midpriced snacks, skewers, tempura and traditional sushi; the space is done up for minimal Asian effect in sophisticated neutrals and wood – a nod to the masu (the square wooden sake cup), which you can personalize here and they'll keep till your return – with bar and table seating; N.B. a sake selection rounded out with Japanese whiskeys and beers awaits the liquor license.

## Maya Del Sol *Nuevo Latino* 23 | 22 | 24 | $33

**Oak Park** | 144 S. Oak Park Ave. (bet. Pleasant St. & South Blvd.) | 708-358-9800 | www.mayadelsol.com
"Appealing to all ages", this Oak Park "high-end" Nuevo Latino offers a "broad range of menu items from modest snacks to a full meal" (including Sunday brunch) at "reasonable prices"; there's "an excellent drink menu" with a "crazy selection of 'ritas and specialty tequilas", and the "friendly atmosphere" features an "outdoor garden you won't want to leave."

## May Street Market ⓩ *American* 24 | 20 | 22 | $45

**West Loop** | 1132 W. Grand Ave. (May St.) | 312-421-5547 | www.maystreetmarket.com
"Excellent", "creative" New American fare comes with a "beautiful", "arty presentation" at this West Loop "find" with "fair prices" and "friendly service"; while the "understated" modern chic setting is at times "a little loud", patrons appreciate that "you can talk"; P.S. there's also patio seating and a "reasonably priced, interesting wine list."

## Maza *Mideastern* 21 | 15 | 21 | $32

**Lincoln Park** | 2748 N. Lincoln Ave. (Diversey Pkwy.) | 773-929-9600 | www.mazarestaurant.net
"Authentic", "innovative" Lebanese small plates made with "uncommon finesse" come with a "welcoming" vibe and prices fans

|  | FOOD | DECOR | SERVICE | COST |
|---|---|---|---|---|

consider a "bargain" at this Lincoln Park Middle Eastern that's a "solid neighborhood" "standby"; "helpful service" adds to the attraction in the casual room.

### NEW M Burger *Burgers*

| | - | - | - | I |

**Streeterville** | 161 E. Huron St. (bet. Michigan Ave. & St. Clair St.) | 312-254-8500 | www.mburgerchicago.com

The Lettuce Entertain You team is behind this tiny Streeterville counter-serve offering inexpensive made-fresh burgers, skin-on fries, shakes and a few sandwiches; the über-simple, white-tiled space features just a handful of seats, a few of them outdoors, and a window in the wall provides a view of LEYE's Tru next door.

### McCormick & Schmick's *Seafood*

| | 21 | 20 | 21 | $48 |

**Loop** | 1 E. Wacker Dr. (bet. State St. & Wabash Ave.) | 312-923-7226
**Gold Coast** | 41 E. Chestnut St. (Rush St.) | 312-397-9500
**Skokie** | Westfield Shoppingtown | 4999 Old Orchard Ctr. (Skokie Blvd.) | 847-763-9811
**Schaumburg** | 1140 E. Higgins Rd. (bet. Del Lago Dr. & National Pkwy.) | 847-517-1616
**Oak Brook** | 3001 Butterfield Rd. (Meyers Rd.) | 630-571-3700
www.mccormickandschmicks.com

An "enjoyable" choice for "business and pleasure", this "upscale" seafood chain offers a "daily changing" menu of "freshly caught" fare in an "upbeat" atmosphere; though it feels too "stamped-out-of-a-mold" for some, its "professional" service is a plus and the "happy-hour bar menu" wins over the after-work crowd.

### Medici on 57th *American*

| | 17 | 13 | 16 | $19 |

**Hyde Park** | 1327 E. 57th St. (bet. Kenwood & Kimbark Aves.) | 773-667-7394 | www.medici57.com

Hyde Park's "funky, retro" BYO "local hangout" offers "something for every taste" on its affordable American menu including "great burgers", "breakfasts" and "thin-crust" and "pan pizzas" – plus a "bakery next door"; "nostalgia" reigns in the "scribbles on the walls and tables (including Obama's)", helping make it a "University of Chicago" "fixture", though antis dub it "average" fare for a "captive clientele."

### Meiji ⑤ *Japanese*

| | 25 | 22 | 23 | $52 |

**West Loop** | 623 W. Randolph St. (bet. Desplaines & Jefferson Sts.) | 312-887-9999 | www.meijirestaurant.com

"Sleek, spare" and "stylish", this "hipster" West Loop Japanese sushi source supplies a selection of "fresh", "imaginative" maki (traditionalists "avoid the rolls and just ask for the best fish") plus a "list of sake" and "attentive" service; meal tickets are "expensive" but mostly considered "worth the splurge."

### NEW Melanthios
### Greek Char House *Greek/Steak*

| | - | - | - | M |

**Lakeview** | 3114 N. Broadway St. (bet. Barry Ave. & Briar Pl.) | 773-360-8572

Greek classics, steaks and chops, whole-roasted lambs and pigs (on weekends) and a fair number of vegetarian dishes pair with Greek

FOOD | DECOR | SERVICE | COST

and Italian wines and ouzo at this Lakeview newcomer; the cozy interior features an open kitchen, fireplace, low-lit iron chandeliers and banquettes, while the white brick and rustic wood facade looks transported from the homeland.

## Melting Pot  Fondue
### 19 | 18 | 19 | $44
**River North** | Millennium Center Towers | 609 N. Dearborn St. (bet. Ohio & Ontario Sts.) | 312-573-0011 ◐
**Buffalo Grove** | 1205 W. Dundee Rd. (Arlington Heights Rd.) | 847-342-6022
**Schaumburg** | 255 W. Golf Rd. (bet. Higgins & Roselle Rds.) | 847-843-8970 ◐
www.meltingpot.com

"It's all about sharing" and "cooking your own food" at this chain serving "every kind of fondue", including "delicious" chocolate pots; while it's a "romantic" "treat" for "younger couples" and "fun to do with a group", critics contend it's "overpriced" and "pretentious", and would prefer a "more casual" setup; P.S. go with a large party if you want "two burners."

## NEW Mercadito ◐ Mexican
### 22 | 22 | 17 | $38
**River North** | 108 W. Kinzie St. (bet. Clark & LaSalle Sts.) | 312-329-9555 | www.mercaditorestaurants.com
Enlivening "the competitive River North neighborhood", this mid-priced Mexican Manhattan import issues a "terrific" "upscale take on tacos" and "street food" small plates plus "eclectic, amazing margaritas"; despite "inconsistent food and service", the "cool feel" and "funky decor" create an atmosphere that's "perfect for happy hour", "girl groups" and "dudes who want a little eye candy"; N.B. seating options include a communal table and sidewalk dining.

## Z Mercat a la Planxa  Spanish
### 26 | 24 | 22 | $53
**South Loop** | Blackstone Hotel | 638 S. Michigan Ave. (Balbo Ave.) | 312-765-0524 | www.mercatchicago.com
"Upbeat and swank", this "soaring space" "reminiscent of Barcelona" revitalizes the "former ballroom" of the South Loop's historic Blackstone Hotel, where Jose Garces' "dizzying array" of "adventurous" Catalan tapas (a "cut above the usual" in both "selection and price") and entrees including "roast pig for a large group" is the top-rated Spanish cuisine in this Survey; "gracious service", "outstanding" wine selections and "unusual sangrias" please patrons who praise the "beautiful", "Gaudi"-esque setting with a "busy bar scene" and an "amazing view" of Grant Park.

## Merle's Smokehouse  BBQ
### 19 | 16 | 18 | $29
**Evanston** | 1727 Benson Ave. (bet. Church & Clark Sts.) | 847-475-7766 | www.merlesbbq.com
"Bargain prices" and "big portions" of "tasty" "barbecue of any kind" plus "interesting sides" and beer have the 'cue crowd queuing up at Evanston's "rib joint" with a "'50s Texas atmosphere" complete with "Elvis memorabilia"; while a few commenters complain about "consistency" issues and "spotty service", most "leave happy."

| | FOOD | DECOR | SERVICE | COST |
|---|---|---|---|---|

### Merlo la Salumeria Ⓜ *Italian*   24 | 21 | 22 | $57

**Lincoln Park** | 2638 N. Lincoln Ave. (Wrightwood Ave.) |
773-529-0747

### Merlo on Maple  *Italian*

**Gold Coast** | 16 W. Maple St. (bet. Dearborn & State Sts.) |
312-335-8200

### La Trattoria Del Merlo  *Italian*

**Lincoln Park** | 1967 N. Halsted St. (Armitage Ave.) | 312-951-8200
www.merlochicago.com

The Maple Street Merlo maintains its standing as an "upscale" purveyor of "exquisite", "beautifully prepared" "Italian cuisine with some of the best" "fresh pasta" around, a "wonderful wine list" and "professional service" in a "quaint", "quiet" "converted" Gold Coast "brownstone"; "prices are quite high" but suitable for a "special evening"; P.S. neither the "pleasant" Trattoria nor the Salumeria (in the location of the original ristorante) inspire as much praise.

### Mesón Sabika  *Spanish*   23 | 22 | 21 | $37

**Naperville** | 1025 Aurora Ave. (bet. River Rd. & West St.) | 630-983-3000 |
www.mesonsabika.com

### Tapas Valencia  *Spanish*

**South Loop** | 1530 S. State St. (bet. 15th & 16th Sts.) | 312-842-4444 |
www.tapasvalencia.com

Tapas aficionados tout the "huge selection" – from "killer" bacon-wrapped dates to an "extensive" Spanish wine list – at these city and suburban sibs that are popular for "celebrations" and "every other day"; the (sometimes "noisy") original, set in a "historic" "mansion" with a "beautiful patio" in Naperville, is a destination for Sunday brunch, while the "spacious" South Loop hot spot with Miro-esque tile details offers "great value", especially when you "go with a group."

### Mexique Ⓜ *Mexican*   25 | 20 | 23 | $46

**West Town** | 1529 W. Chicago Ave. (bet. Armour St. & Ashland Ave.) |
312-850-0288 | www.mexiquechicago.com

"Masterful" and "stunning" are surveyors' superlatives for the "French twist on Mexican" cuisine, "uniquely appetizing and imaginative" menu and "exceptional sauces" at this "hidden gem" "off the beaten path" in West Town; add in "friendly, knowledgeable service" and "sophisticated decor" and those for whom it's a "favorite" (including the weekend brunch) warrant it's "worth the price"; N.B. it serves beer, wine, sangria, tequila and digestifs but no cocktails.

### NEW Mezé ◗Ⓢ *Eclectic*   - | - | - | M

**West Loop** | 205 N. Peoria St. (Lake St.) | 312-666-6625 |
www.mezechicago.com

A midpriced menu of Eclectic small plates is served with red, white and seasonal sangrias, wines by the glass and more than two dozen brews at this clubby West Loop tapas lounge; the sexy setting gets a warm glow from polished wood and backlit panels of thin-sliced marble, while seating options include plush banquettes, dining tables and a central bar.

|  | FOOD | DECOR | SERVICE | COST |
|---|---|---|---|---|

## M. Henry ⓜ *American*    25 | 18 | 20 | $19

**Andersonville** | 5707 N. Clark St. (Hollywood Ave.) | 773-561-1600 | www.mhenry.net

Fans are "willing to stand in line outside in the cold" for the "original", "delicious" daytime-only dining featuring "seasonal offerings and local products" at this "adorable" and affordable Andersonville BYO American; it's "very popular" – in fact, there's "nothing not to love" except the no-reservations policy and "weekend crowds" (it helps that "summer offers an outdoor patio"); P.S. don't forget to "take home some of their great breads and pastries."

## Ⓩ Mia Francesca *Italian*    26 | 20 | 22 | $35

**Lakeview** | 3311 N. Clark St. (School St.) | 773-281-3310 | www.miafrancesca.com

The Lakeview matriarch of the Francesca's family is an "absolute staple" offering "remarkably consistent", "robust" and "always changing" Italian dishes that are "decently priced" and "neither too fancy nor too plain"; the "fast" and "personable" service works well given the "crowded" setting, but the "decibel level can be frightening" so "make reservations" for this "classic" and "leave your conversation at home."

## Ⓩ Michael ⓜ *French*    28 | 23 | 27 | $67

**Winnetka** | 64 Green Bay Rd. (Fisher Ln.) | 847-441-3100 | www.restaurantmichael.com

Namesake chef and "personality" Michael Lachowicz is "always there, interacting with his guests" at this Winnetka "winner" where his "exceptional", "delicate and flavorful" New French fare with "spot-on wine pairings" is served in an "elegant but casual", "conversation-friendly" room by a staff that "works well together"; it's admittedly "pricey", but "worthwhile for celebrating, relaxing or rewarding a good client."

## Mike Ditka's *Steak*    22 | 21 | 21 | $50

**Gold Coast** | Tremont Hotel | 100 E. Chestnut St. (Rush St.) | 312-587-8989
**Oakbrook Terrace** | 2 Mid America Plaza (bet. 16th & 22nd Sts.) | 630-572-2200 ☻
www.mikeditkaschicago.com

"Kudos to da coach" say supporters of these "upscale" Gold Coast and Oakbrook Terrace sports bars/steakhouses, where "everything is big", "from the drinks to the sides" to the "juicy pork chops" and "thick" slabs of beef "worthy of a linebacker"; football fans who hail it as a "hall-of-fame experience" figure in the "entertainment upstairs" and the "chance" to see "local sports celebrities" and even Mike himself, but the opposition throws a penalty flag on "overpriced", "ordinary" offerings and "spotty" service.

## Milk & Honey *American*    23 | 14 | 15 | $17

**Wicker Park** | 1920 W. Division St. (bet. Damen & Wolcott Aves.) | 773-395-9434 | www.milkandhoneycafe.com

Enthusiasts are enamored of this "casual", "counter-service" New American, saying "every neighborhood" should have a place for

such "delicious" breakfasts and lunches featuring "artisan ingredients" and "amazing baked goods"; the "casual", "cozy" atmosphere
includes "hip" Wicker Park "people-watching" and "lines out the
door" "during hopping weekend brunch", but "they do a nice job of
moving people through"; P.S. if you find the "decor colder than the
old location" "try the patio."

### Miller's Pub ◑ American — 17 | 16 | 19 | $27

**Loop** | 134 S. Wabash Ave. (bet. Adams & Monroe Sts.) |
312-263-4988 | www.millerspub.com
Though it's "close to the Art Institute, symphony" and theater, there's
"nothing arty" about this Loop "legend" that's "classic Chicago all
the way", from the "old warrior surroundings" that include "signed
celebrity photos on the walls" to the "ol'-fashioned American food"
(steaks, ribs, sandwiches, burgers); "you can't beat the prices" or
the "long bar for cocktails until 4 AM", but don't expect more
than "adequate service."

### Mirabell American/German — ▽ 21 | 20 | 20 | $32

**Northwest Side** | 3454 W. Addison St. (bet. Kimball & St. Louis Aves.) |
773-463-1962 | www.mirabellrestaurant.com
A "neighborhood" "holdout" on the Northwest Side, this German-
American "just off the Kennedy Expressway" pulls in savorers of
schnitzel, goulash and bratwurst; the setting includes "murals of
Salzburg", a beer stein display and servers in traditional garb, but
service can be inconsistent.

### Mirai Sushi Japanese — 25 | 19 | 21 | $52

**Wicker Park** | 2020 W. Division St. (bet. Damen & Hoyne Aves.) |
773-862-8500 | www.miraisushi.com
Surveyors praise this "high-end" Wicker Park sushi "hipster" for its
"incredibly fresh fish" and "masterfully prepared" "special rolls that
really *are* special"; whether you "go upstairs" to the sake bar "for a
darker, more loungey feel" or "downstairs for an open, well-lit"
space, the offerings are presented with "flair" by servers who "know
their stuff"; P.S. it "can get a bit expensive", but for the quality, "it's
what you expect."

### Miramar Bistro French — 17 | 19 | 19 | $43

**Highwood** | 301 Waukegan Ave. (Highwood Ave.) | 847-433-1078 |
www.miramarbistro.com
North Shoreites hike to Highwood for "classic French" bistro fare "with
Cuban drinks" ("odd, but it works") at Gabriel Viti's "casual", often
"crowded" eatery manned by a "professional staff"; a "racy weekend
reputation" appeals to some, but less dazzled diners dis the "loud"
conditions, "overpriced" fare and "limited menu"; N.B. chef Roland
Liccioni departed post-Survey.

### Mitchell's Fish Market Seafood — 21 | 18 | 19 | $37

**Glenview** | Glenview Town Ctr. | 2601 Navy Blvd. (Patriot Blvd.) |
847-729-3663 | www.mitchellsfishmarket.com
With "reasonably priced", "dependable" "fresh fish" from a daily
changing catch, along with "consistent" service, this Glenview sea-

food chain link with a nautical theme is "better than expected"; even if the dishes "lack creativity", "they do their best" with "simple" preparations and there are "so many options" to choose from.

### Mity Nice Grill  *American*    17 | 15 | 18 | $29

**Streeterville** | Water Tower Pl. | 835 N. Michigan Ave., Mezzanine level (bet. Chestnut & Pearson Sts.) | 312-335-4745 | www.leye.com

Lettuce Entertain You's "casual" "oasis of calm" in "the wilds" of Streeterville's Water Tower Place is a suitable stop for "comfort food and a stiff martini"; the "homestyle" American menu is "large" and "moderately priced" and the staff is "friendly", but even though it's a "reliable", "convenient" shopping "respite", it's "not a destination."

### Mixteco Grill Ⓜ  *Mexican*    25 | 14 | 22 | $30

**Lakeview** | 1601 W. Montrose Ave. (Ashland Ave.) | 773-868-1601

"Wonderfully creative", "vibrant" "haute Mexican" impresses proponents who "want to mainline the moles" at this Lakeview BYO "gem"; the "basic space" is "always crowded" and "noisy", but the "fantastic" fare and "accommodating" service "make up for it"; P.S. now that they've "expanded", maybe it'll be "possible to get a table on short notice."

### Mizu Yakitori & Sushi Lounge  *Japanese*    24 | 16 | 21 | $31

**Old Town** | 315 W. North Ave. (North Park Ave.) | 312-951-8880

Regulars "keep coming back" to this "reasonably priced" Old Town Japanese for "creative", "well-executed" dishes including "inventive yakitori" and "high-quality" sushi ("they always have cool new rolls"), plus "flights of sake" and "good mixed drinks"; while it "lacks the trendy scene of many others", "it more than makes up for it" with "helpful service" and "consistent" fare.

### Ⓩ mk  *American*    27 | 24 | 26 | $72

**Near North** | 868 N. Franklin St. (bet. Chestnut & Locust Sts.) | 312-482-9179 | www.mkchicago.com

It's continuing "kudos" for Michael Kornick's "classy", "happening" Near North haunt that's "stood the test of time" and still "shines" with "honest", "outstanding", "seasonal" New American cuisine "minus the fussiness"; expect "knockout desserts", a "stellar wine list" and "excellent service all around" in the "spare", "urban-cool", "renovated warehouse" space – in other words, it "meets high expectations" "from start to finish."

### Mon Ami Gabi  *French*    22 | 21 | 22 | $42

**Lincoln Park** | Belden-Stratford Hotel | 2300 N. Lincoln Park W. (Belden Ave.) | 773-348-8886

**Oak Brook** | Oakbrook Center Mall | 260 Oakbrook Ctr. (Rte. 83) | 630-472-1900

www.monamigabi.com

The "terrific" French bistro bites include a "fantastic variety of steak frites" and the "best onion soup ever", plus "wines by the glass" "on a rolling cart" at these "delightful" Lincoln Park and Oak Brook spots from the Lettuce Entertain You chain; "you can't beat the prices" and "service is smooth" in the "traditionally" decorated spaces, but a few call them "cramped" and "predictable"; N.B. both locations offer outdoor dining.

**Montarra** Ⓜ *American*　　　　▽ 24 | 23 | 24 | $44

**Algonquin** | 1491 S. Randall Rd. (County Line Rd.) | 847-458-0505 | www.montarra.com

Diners don't expect this kind of "hidden gem" "all the way out in Algonquin", where a "talented chef" tempts touters with his "internationally influenced" New American steakhouse cuisine paired with an "excellent wine list"; the modern setting with "Chihuly-inspired fixtures" is surprising in a "small, strip-mall" location, but a couple of critics found the service less impressive.

**Moody's Pub** ●⑰ *Pub Food*　　19 | 11 | 15 | $19

**Edgewater** | 5910 N. Broadway St. (Thorndale Ave.) | 773-275-2696 | www.moodyspub.com

A "local crowd" "brings cash" ("no credit cards") to this 51-year-old Traditional American Edgewater "joint" for "reliable", "inexpensive" burgers, "great onion rings", "potent cocktails" and pitchers of beer beside a "warm fire" in winter or in the "wonderful" beer garden with silver oak trees in summer; the "dark", "grubby" interior and "irregular" service, however, can't hold a candle to the fare.

**Moon Palace** *Chinese*　　　　22 | 15 | 20 | $22

**Chinatown** | 216 W. Cermak Rd. (Wentworth Ave.) | 312-225-4081 | www.moonpalacerestaurant.com

Back after a "recent face lift" that "really spruced up the place", this "longtime Chinatown favorite" continues to be a "reliable" resource for Chinese chow with "flavors right on the mark", particularly in its "Shanghai specialties" and "fabulous black mushroom soup"; the "pleasant atmosphere" is buttressed by a "fast", "wonderful" staff.

**NEW Morgan Harbor Grill** *Kosher/Seafood*　– | – | – | M

**Rogers Park** | 2948 W. Devon Ave. (bet. Richmond St. & Sacramento Ave.) | 773-764-8115 | www.morganharborgrill.com

Midpriced, modern kosher parve dining (no meat, dairy or shellfish) includes selections such as sushi, grilled seafood, tempura and salads, done in sophisticated plate presentations that belie the bright, spartan West Rogers Park storefront setting (attached to a longtime fish market) with a handful of tables; N.B. it's BYO (kosher only) and closed for dinner Friday and all day Saturday.

**Ⓩ Morton's The Steakhouse** *Steak*　26 | 22 | 25 | $70

**Loop** | 65 E. Wacker Pl. (bet. Michigan & Wabash Aves.) | 312-201-0410
**Gold Coast** | Newberry Plaza | 1050 N. State St. (Maple St.) | 312-266-4820
**Rosemont** | 9525 Bryn Mawr Ave. (River Rd.) | 847-678-5155
**Northbrook** | 699 Skokie Blvd. (Dundee Rd.) | 847-205-5111
**Schaumburg** | 1470 McConnor Pkwy. (bet. Golf & Meacham Rds.) | 847-413-8771
**Naperville** | 1751 Freedom Dr. (E. Diehl Rd.) | 630-577-1372
www.mortons.com

Carnivores who crown the late Arnie Morton's "old-school" "class act" the "king of the national steakhouse chains" say they're "incredibly consistent" for "fabulous", "prime" "aged beef Chicago-style"; the "ridiculous prices" are offset by "insane amounts of food", a solid wine cellar and "elaborately staged demonstrations" from a staff that "knows how to read the customer", plus the "masculine" spaces – especially at the "original", "clubby" State Street basement – are "classic" "business" settings.

## ℤ Moto ⊠Ⓜ *Eclectic*                    27 | 23 | 27 | $142

**West Loop** | 945 W. Fulton Mkt. (Sangamon St.) | 312-491-0058 | www.motorestaurant.com

Simultaneously "serious and fun", Homaro Cantu's "amazing" West Loop Eclectic is ground zero for "molecular gastronomy", where "nothing looks like what it tastes like" when it comes to the "playful", "cutting-edge" creations; the "expensive" experience includes 10-course tasting menus, "phenomenal service", a "choice wine list" and "stark interiors" that "put the whole focus on the food", so even if a handful find that some of the "gimmicky" dishes "don't quite work", the "mind-bending" "originality" always makes up for it.

## ℤ Mr. Beef ⊠彡 *Sandwiches*              24 | 7 | 16 | $11

**River North** | 666 N. Orleans St. (bet. Erie & Huron Sts.) | 312-337-8500

Meat eaters "bite, drip, wipe, sigh, repeat" at River North's "historic", quick-dining "dump", still the sandwich "champ" for its "wonderfully messy", "best beef" sammie "bar none"; "service and decor couldn't get much worse" – the dining room is a "bunch of picnic tables pushed together" and "you order by yelling at" the "guy behind the counter" – but you come here until the wee hours for "a mouthful of bliss, Chicago-style"; N.B. it's cash only, and the kitchen is open until 5 AM Friday and Saturday nights from April–December.

## Mrs. Murphy & Sons                       22 | 21 | 23 | $31
## Irish Bistro *Pub Food*

**North Center/St. Ben's** | 3905 N. Lincoln Ave. (bet. Byron St. & Larchmont Ave.) | 773-248-3905 | www.irishbistro.com

"Gourmet Irish food? somehow they do it" admit admirers of this "friendly" North Center pub serving an "awesome" brunch and an updated, "traditional" menu (shepherd's pie, corned beef and cabbage, beef and Guinness stew); the setting "in an ex-funeral home" boasts "beautiful stained-glass windows" and an "imposing center bar" "imported from Ireland" that features an "impressive selection of craft, micro and imported beers" plus lots of whiskey choices.

## Mt. Everest Restaurant *Indian*          22 | 16 | 19 | $28

**Evanston** | 630 Church St. (bet. Chicago & Orrington Aves.) | 847-491-1069 | www.mteverestrestaurant.com

"Surprisingly tasty Nepalese options" (including the signature goat dish) back up the "top-notch" Indian fare at this "Evanston standby", deemed "dependable" for "neighborhood" dining "without the hassle of parking on Devon"; the "terrific lunch buffet" where "everything is labeled" is a "great value", but the "outdated" dining room scales no heights.

| | FOOD | DECOR | SERVICE | COST |
|---|---|---|---|---|

### Mundial Cocina Mestiza ⓜ *Eclectic*

| - | - | - | M |

**Pilsen** | 1640 W. 18th St. (bet. Marshfield Ave. & Paulina St.) | 312-491-9908 | www.mundialcocinamestiza.com

Morphed from its Mexican origins, this casual, inexpensive Pilsen spot has a new chef serving "creative" Eclectic cuisine based on seasonal ingredients for brunch, lunch and dinner; set in "an unlikely storefront" with colorful tiled decor that seems to go well with the neighborhood, it's a "real find" "if you can find it"; N.B. it no longer offers live entertainment.

### Myron & Phil Steakhouse ⓜ *Steak*

| 21 | 14 | 23 | $43 |

**Lincolnwood** | 3900 W. Devon Ave. (Springfield Ave.) | 847-677-6663 | www.myronandphil.com

Lincolnwood's "longtime standby" is a "throwback to another era" serving "tasty", "traditional" steakhouse fare with a "free chopped liver" "relish tray" and a "dose of nostalgia" ("nothing has changed in 40 years"); even if the "decor is nothing to write home about", the "well-trained" staff is "caring" and the once mostly "geriatric crowd" "seems to be getting younger"; P.S. there's a "piano bar" on Saturdays.

### Mythos ⓜ *Greek*

| 23 | 16 | 20 | $28 |

**Lakeview** | 2030-32 W. Montrose Ave. (Seeley Ave.) | 773-334-2000

While Lakeview seems like an "unusual location" for Greek, locals feel "lucky" that this "team effort" by two "lovely" sisters is "in the neighborhood" given its "authentic", "homestyle" Hellenic cooking considered "a cut above" Greektown; "wonderful service" and a "congenial atmosphere", along with a BYO policy that "holds tabs down", are further pluses.

### ❷ Nacional 27 Ⓢ *Nuevo Latino*

| 23 | 22 | 21 | $44 |

**River North** | 325 W. Huron St. (Orleans St.) | 312-664-2727 | www.nacional27.net

Loyalists have "lots of fun" at this "neat" River North restaurant-cum-"nightclub" where "delicious and inventive" Nuevo Latino flavors (the name refers to the 27 nations in Latin America) are coupled with a multitude of "mojito and sangria options"; even though some reviewers find the "food and service irregular" and the tapas "expensive", especially given the "casual" vibe, many others flag it their "favorite date night" with "dancing too" (it turns into a "salsa club on weekend nights"); P.S. the "late lunch" is a great "deal."

### 🆕 Nagoya Japanese Seafood Buffet *Japanese*

| - | - | - | M |

**Naperville** | 804 S. Rte. 59 (bet. Aurora & La Fox Aves.) | 630-637-8881 | www.nagoyausa.com

A spin-off of a Baton Rouge original, this sprawling West Suburban sushi castle boasts a midpriced, 140-ft. Asian smorgasbord of all-you-can-eat fish and shellfish – in raw, hibachi and teriyaki preparations – plus dim sum and a variety of other dishes, accompanied by smoothies and full-bar service; the clean and modern, Chinese-inspired setting is decorated in soothing colors with well-spaced tables and TVs playing sports.

| | FOOD | DECOR | SERVICE | COST |
|---|---|---|---|---|

**Ø Naha** Ⓐ *American*   | 27 | 24 | 25 | $64 |

**River North** | 500 N. Clark St. (Illinois St.) | 312-321-6242 |
www.naha-chicago.com

Locals find "the total package" at this "upscale" River North New
American where chef Carrie Nahabedian serves up "perfection on a
plate" with a "world-class" yet "accessible" fusion of "contemporary
styling" and "organic produce" at its "absolute peak"; beyond that,
there's a staff that "anticipates your needs" and a "refined atmosphere" in a "cool, modern" space, so even those bothered by the
"noise" "get over it" given the "spectacular" value.

**Natalino's** Ⓜ *Italian*   | 23 | 19 | 22 | $42 |

**West Town** | 1523 W. Chicago Ave. (Armour St.) | 312-997-3700 |
www.natalinoschicago.com

"Don't tell anyone" about this "worth-the-trip" West Town "jewel"
whisper loyalists or "you'll spoil it for the regulars" who relish the
"wonderful", "reasonably priced" Italian fare, "attentive" hospitality
and clubby, "warm" setting; budget-watchers love the "daily specials", and night owls can "people-watch" until 2 AM.

**NEW Nella Pizzeria Napoletana** *Pizza*   | 22 | 18 | 20 | $26 |

**Lincoln Park** | 2423 N. Clark St. (bet. Arlington Pl. & Fullerton Ave.) |
773-327-3400 | www.pizzerianella.com

"Authentic Neapolitan" "designer" pizza with "fresh toppings" (like
prosciutto di parma, arugula and smoked mozzarella) draw pie-
hards to this "affordable" new Lincoln Parker, where the "awesome"
crust hits a "delicate balance of crunch, chew and char"; a few dissenters say service in the "casual, simple room" is "still being ironed
out", but most are "pleasantly surprised."

**Next Door Bistro** Ⓜ *American/Italian*   | 23 | 13 | 22 | $33 |

**Northbrook** | 250 Skokie Blvd. (Lake Cook Rd.) | 847-272-1491

"Next door to", but no longer affiliated with, Francesco's Hole in the
Wall, this "always crowded", "reasonably priced" Northbrooker
serves a mix of solid Traditional American and Italian eats and rotating daily specials; just "go early" or make reservations; P.S. they
"take credit cards now."

**Nia** *Mediterranean*   | - | - | - | M |

**West Loop** | 803 W. Randolph St. (Halsted St.) | 312-226-3110 |
www.niarestaurant.com

An extensive menu of seasonal small plates, from grilled octopus to
bacon-wrapped dates, is accompanied by signature cocktails and
three different sangrias at this "low-key", midpriced West Loop
Med; "get a seat by the window and watch the world go by" say fans
who find it "worth a visit"; N.B. lunch is served in summer only.

**Niche** Ⓜ *American*   | 28 | 27 | 29 | $63 |

**Geneva** | 14 S. Third St. (bet. James & State Sts.) | 630-262-1000 |
www.nichegeneva.com

"Go west!" urge proponents of this "intimate" Geneva "favorite",
"located adjacent to farm country", where the service is "top-

notch" and the "legacy of 302 West lives on" in Jeremy Lycan's "outstanding" New American fare filled with "quality" "local and sustainable" ingredients; add in a "well-thought-out", "affordable" wine list and it's "comfortable and refined at the same time"; N.D. it now serves Sunday brunch.

## Nick's Fishmarket 🗷 Seafood
**23 | 21 | 22 | $62**

**Rosemont** | O'Hare International Ctr. | 10275 W. Higgins Rd. (Mannheim Rd.) | 847-298-8200 | www.nicksfishmarketchicago.com
While bereft boosters were "sorry to see the Downtown [location] close", the Rosemont branch offers the same "excellent seafood", including "fresh fish flown in daily"; the "old-fashioned" room "designed for Vegas" and peopled by "tuxedoed waiters" strikes some as the perfect "special-occasion" spot, but those who knock the "fair" service and "bloated prices" tolerable only when "someone else is buying" sigh maybe it worked "30 years ago, but not now."

## NEW Nightwood American
**23 | 21 | 21 | $47**

**Pilsen** | 2119 S. Halsted St. (21st St.) | 312-526-3385 | www.nightwoodrestaurant.com
"Unique, trendy" and "friendly", Lula's Pilsen sib proffers a "funky" and "ever-changing" New American menu of "inventively presented" local and organic ingredients and a "well-chosen, value-oriented wine list"; the "welcoming" space, with a "great patio" in summer and a "fireplace in winter", is "a bit on the loud side", but most rank it worthy of "a repeat" visit; N.B. they've added Sunday brunch.

## ☑ N9ne Steakhouse 🗷 Seafood/Steak
**24 | 25 | 22 | $63**

**Loop** | 440 W. Randolph St. (Canal St.) | 312-575-9900 | www.n9ne.com
"Yeah baby" exclaims the "lively", "arm candy"–filled crowd at this "flashy" Loop steakhouse where the "inventive" offerings and "creative presentations" include "marvelous seafood" dishes coupled with a "fantastic wine list that won't break the bank"; the service is "fine, but not the reason you come", while the "slick", "disco" decor leaves some surveyors "cold", but the majority finds it "stunning" "for business and romance."

## NEW 90 Miles Cuban Cafe Cuban
**22 | 16 | 21 | $13**

**Lakeview** | 3101 N. Clybourn Ave. (Barry Ave.) | 773-248-2822
**Logan Square** | 2540 W. Armitage Ave. (Rockwell St.) | 773-227-2822
www.90milescubancafe.com
Diners curb cravings for "authentic, tasty" "Cuban sandwiches", "empanadas, tostones and ropa vieja" at this "friendly", "funky", "no-frills" duo offering a "very casual", "quick, cheap bite" with "cafe cubano" that packs an "unmatchable jolt"; if "parking" and (especially at Lakeview) "seating are at a minimum", outdoor tables provide additional dining space at both locations; P.S. "don't forget it's BYO."

## Niu Japanese Fusion Lounge Asian
**19 | 20 | 18 | $37**

**Streeterville** | 332 E. Illinois St. (bet. Columbus Dr. & McClurg Ct.) | 312-527-2888 | www.niusushi.com
With "huge portions" of "interesting, modern" Japanese fusion that includes "adventurous" and "classic" sushi presented "like edible

| | FOOD | DECOR | SERVICE | COST |
|---|---|---|---|---|

works of art", this "crowded" Streeterville "neighborhood" "hot spot" is showing "no [signs of a] recession"; even if diners disagree on whether the dishes are "more style than substance", they concur the service is usually "prompt."

### ☑ NoMI *French* 27 | 28 | 26 | $75

**Gold Coast** | Park Hyatt Chicago | 800 N. Michigan Ave. (Chicago Ave.) | 312-239-4030 | www.nomirestaurant.com

Voted No. 1 for Decor in the Chicago Survey, this "romantic" Gold Coast "fine dining" destination is "first class all the way"; each item on "amazing chef" Christophe David's New French menu is "a work of art", the "wine list is excellent", "service is beautifully executed" and the "gorgeous", "sophisticated" setting includes a "cool" rooftop deck in summer, but the "million-dollar" Mag Mile view comes with a tab that makes it best for a "memorable" "splurge"; P.S. there's a sushi station and a "to-die-for" brunch that some say is even "better than dinner."

### Nookies *Diner* 20 | 12 | 20 | $17

**Old Town** | 1746 N. Wells St. (bet. Lincoln & North Aves.) | 312-337-2454

### Nookies Too *Diner*

**Lincoln Park** | 2114 N. Halsted St. (bet. Dickens & Webster Aves.) | 773-327-1400

### Nookies Tree ◑ *Diner*

**Lakeview** | 3334 N. Halsted St. (bet. Buckingham Pl. & Roscoe St.) | 773-248-9888
www.nookiesrestaurants.net

For "solid", "affordable" Traditional American "mom food" in "massive portions" "at all hours of the day" (including 24-hour weekend breakfast at Too and Tree, and all-day eats at the Old Town original), this BYO trio of "busy", "convenient" "neighborhood" diner "hangouts" with "just-right" service fills the bill; families who can't "handle the wait" come "with kids before 9."

### Noon-O-Kabab *Persian* 25 | 18 | 21 | $24

**Northwest Side** | 4661 N. Kedzie Ave. (Leland Ave.) | 773-279-8899 | www.noonokabab.com

"This place has everything" praise proponents whose "mouths start watering just thinking" about the "fantastic", "reasonably priced" Persian fare ("awesome kebabs", "addicting" basmati rice) served at this "welcoming" Northwest Side Middle Eastern; it's "easy to access" by CTA and even by car since it's in a "neighborhood without meters."

### ☑ North Pond Ⓜ *American* 25 | 26 | 23 | $65

**Lincoln Park** | 2610 N. Cannon Dr. (bet. Diversey & Fullerton Pkwys.) | 773-477-5845 | www.northpondrestaurant.com

Loyalists "love" to "sup on the season's freshest ingredients" from "excellent" chef Bruce Sherman's "dynamic" New American menu at this "romantic" Arts and Crafts "cabin in the woods" set in "an old ice-skating warming house" on Lincoln Park's North Pond; it's "kind of hard to find, but worth the trouble", though reviewers agree more on the "unparalleled setting" than on the "precious portions" and hit-or-miss service since a few detect "attitude" that "needs to be addressed"; N.B. it serves Sunday brunch as well as lunch on summer weekdays.

## Nosh  *Eclectic*  ∇ 24 | 16 | 23 | $21

**Geneva** | 211 James St. (3rd St.) | 630-845-1570
"The best West Suburban breakfast/lunch" spot "for foodies", this Geneva daytime destination is "definitely not cookie-cutter" thanks to its "creative, Eclectic" sweet and savory eats fashioned from "high-quality ingredients" and delivered in "beautiful plate presentations"; there's a short wine list and patio dining as well, so it's small wonder that most "wish it were open for dinner."

## Oak Tree  *American*  17 | 17 | 16 | $25

**Gold Coast** | Bloomingdale's Bldg. | 900 N. Michigan Ave., 6th fl. (bet. Delaware & Walton Pls.) | 312-751-1988
Traditional American eats including "great breakfast", "sandwiches and salads" along with "terrific views of Michigan Avenue" make this Gold Coast coffee shop/diner in the Bloomie's building a popular "pit stop" for both "business" folks and the "ladies who lunch" (it closes at 5 PM daily); although "service can be great or poor" and dollar-watchers deem it "expensive" for "upscale mall food", the "new decor is lovely."

## NEW Oba Contemporary  - | - | - | M
## Japanese  *Japanese*

**Des Plaines** | 1285 Elmhurst Rd. (Algonquin Rd.) | 847-228-8810 | www.obasushi.net
A tiny Northwest Suburban strip mall houses this contemporary sushi spot serving elaborately presented hot and cold signature maki, nigiri and sashimi, classic rolls and cooked Japanese fare (plus bargain lunches under $10); the clean, modern space includes banquette and table seating, semi-private booths with blinds and a bar serving beer, wine and sake only.

## Z Oceanique  *French/Seafood*  27 | 22 | 27 | $63

**Evanston** | 505 Main St. (bet. Chicago & Hinman Aves.) | 847-864-3435 | www.oceanique.com
Mark Grosz's "memorable", "magnifique" Evanston eatery offers some of the "best seafood in the city", serving "superb new fusion and old-school dishes" with "unique" "combinations of French and Asian flavors" along with a "fantastic wine list"; the "fancy", "formal" setting and "top-notch service" further elevate the experience (and the prices), but "you get what you pay for" – though you can pay less at the weeknight prix fixe.

## Old Jerusalem  *Mideastern*  19 | 9 | 15 | $20

**Old Town** | 1411 N. Wells St. (bet. North Ave. & Schiller St.) | 312-944-0459 | www.oldjerusalemrestaurant.com
Old Town's "no-frills", BYO "neighborhood" "mom-and-pop" proffers "simple", "affordable" Middle Eastern eats like "homemade hummus", tabbouleh, grape leaves and falafel; the "friendly staff"

can't do anything about the "basic decor", so "carry out" or sit "outdoors, weather permitting."

### Old Oak Tap ● *Pub Food* — 20 | 23 | 19 | $21

**Ukrainian Village** | 2109 W. Chicago Ave. (Hoyne Ave.) | 773-772-0406 | www.theoldoaktap.com

"Pretend your corner bar got hip and had a sense of humor" and it'd be much like this Ukrainian Village "neighborhood" "hangout" where the New American pub fare "goes above and beyond" ("delicious" homemade pretzels with cheddar stout fondue) and the "solid" international beer selection features a dozen types on tap; with a "modern" space that includes "high ceilings", two fireplaces and a "terrific" partially enclosed patio, as well as service that "clicks", it's a "worthy destination."

### NEW Old Town Social *American* — ▽ 18 | 18 | 16 | $32

**Old Town** | 455 W. North Ave. (Cleveland Ave.) | 312-266-2277 | www.oldtownsocial.com

While this "hip" new Old Town "meat market" "for the social crowd" "seems to want to be several different things", most maintain "it pulls that off nicely"; an "interesting" New American menu of "items meant to be shared", including "delicious cheeses" and charcuterie, plus "personable bartenders", make it "a welcome addition."

### One North ⊠ *American* — 15 | 17 | 18 | $41

**Loop** | UBS Bldg. | 1 N. Wacker Dr. (Madison St.) | 312-750-9700 | www.restaurants-america.com

"Location" may be it's strong suit propose pre-theater diners and "power"-lunchers at this New American in a Loop office building, since the "average" menu "needs a refresh" and the "noise levels are higher than on stage at the opera across the street"; luckily, you can eke out a conversation during the warmer months, when "pleasant" outdoor dining is available.

### ☑ one sixtyblue ⊠ *American* — 26 | 24 | 25 | $66

**West Loop** | 1400 W. Randolph St. (Ogden Ave.) | 312-850-0303 | www.onesixtyblue.com

Fans of this "first-class" West Loop "favorite", owned in part by former basketball star Michael Jordan, cite chef Michael McDonald's "exceptional" and "unique" New American dishes, the "expansive wine list" and the "helpful, but not intrusive, service", deeming it "modern-chic but warm", "gourmet but comfortable" and "tucked-away but accessible"; sure, it's also "pricey", so look for "bargains on various nights"; P.S. perfect for "dinner on the way to United Center."

### OPA Estiatorio *Greek* — 25 | 22 | 25 | $33

**Vernon Hills** | 950 Lakeview Pkwy. (Hawthorn Pkwy.) | 847-968-4300 | www.oparestaurant.com

For "a little bit of Greece in Vernon Hills", try this "relaxing" outpost with "large portions" of "authentic Greek cuisine" including "excellent seafood dishes", like "fantastic octopus", and a solid Hellenic wine selection; it's all served in a "light, whitewashed, airy room" or on a "delightful patio" overlooking Bear Lake.

| | FOOD | DECOR | SERVICE | COST |
|---|---|---|---|---|

### Opera *Asian* | 20 | 22 | 19 | $41 |

**South Loop** | 1301 S. Wabash Ave. (13th St.) | 312-461-0161 |
www.opera-chicago.com

Jerry Kleiner's (Gioco, Red Light) "upscale", "energetic" South Loop Asian has diners singing a duet, with one part pleased by "high-concept", "vigorously spiced", "tasty and satisfying" "twists on traditional dishes" in a "funky", "trendy" setting, and the other brought down by "gaudy" "slightly pretentious" environs and "over-priced", "Americanized" fare that "lacks nuance"; at least the "fun" staff "doesn't rush you."

### Orange *Eclectic* | 20 | 14 | 17 | $19 |

**NEW River North** | 738 N. Clark St. (bet. Chicago Ave. & Superior St.) | 312-202-0600

**Lakeview** | 3231 N. Clark St. (Belmont Ave.) | 773-549-4400

**Lincoln Park** | 2413 N. Clark St. (Fullerton Pkwy.) | 773-549-7833

**NEW Near West** | 730 W. Grand Ave. (bet. Halsted St. & Union Ave.) | 312-942-0300

**NEW Glenview** | 1834 Glenview Rd. (bet. Church & Pine Sts.) | 847-832-1901

### Orange on Roscoe *Eclectic*

**Roscoe Village** | 2011 W. Roscoe St. (Damen Ave.) | 773-248-0999
www.orangerestaurantchicago.com

Those for whom there's "always something original to try" at this fruitful family of "funky" breakfast-brunch joints don't mind paying "modestly premium prices" for "green eggs and ham", "pancake flights" and "fruit sushi" washed down with "create-your-own" fresh juices and "orange-infused coffee" (alcohol service varies by location); "service is friendly, if occasionally harried", but grumpy graders who grumble over the "gimmicky" grub wonder "why is everybody waiting to get in?"; N.B. they've added several new locations post-Survey, including in Near West, River North and North Suburban Glenview.

### Z Original Gino's East, The *Pizza* | 22 | 15 | 17 | $22 |

**River North** | 633 N. Wells St. (Ontario St.) | 312-943-1124

**Streeterville** | 162 E. Superior St. (Michigan Ave.) | 312-266-3337

**Lincoln Park** | 2801 N. Lincoln Ave. (Diversey Pkwy.) | 773-327-3737

**O'Hare Area** | 8725 W. Higgins Rd. (bet. Cumberland & East River Rds.) | 773-444-2244

**Libertyville** | 820 S. Milwaukee Ave. (bet. Condell & Valley Park Drs.) | 847-362-1300

**Rolling Meadows** | 1321 W. Golf Rd. (Algonquin Rd.) | 847-364-6644

**Orland Park** | 15840 S. Harlem Ave. (159th St.) | 708-633-1300

**Naperville** | 1807 S. Washington St. (bet. Foxcroft & Redstart Rds.) | 630-548-9555

**St. Charles** | Tin Cup Pass Shopping Ctr. | 1590 E. Main St. (Tyler Rd.) | 630-513-1311

**Wheaton** | 315 W. Front St. (West St.) | 630-588-1010
www.ginoseast.com
Additional locations throughout the Chicago area

Regulars reckon "there's a reason for the multiple locations and rep" of this "relaxed" longtime, Chicago-style deep-dish pizza chain – namely the "ooey-gooey layers of pure indulgence" over "cornmeal crusts to die for"; just be forewarned: "service is what you'd expect at a big feeder", the "non-pie menu items are weak" and the "out-of-town" "crowds" make them feel a bit like "tourist traps"; P.S. "don't forget a marker" for "writing on the walls, tables, floors, chairs, bathrooms – and even the servers if you ask nicely."

**Z Original Pancake House, The** *American* | 24 | 16 | 20 | $17 |

**Streeterville** | 22 E. Bellevue Pl. (bet. Michigan Ave. & Rush St.) | 312-642-7917
**Lincoln Park** | 2020 N. Lincoln Park W. (Clark St.) | 773-929-8130
**Hyde Park** | Village Ctr. | 1517 E. Hyde Park Blvd. (bet. 51st St. & Lake Park Blvd.) | 773-288-2323
**Oak Forest** | 5148 W. 159th St. (bet. Laramie & Le Claire Aves.) | 708-687-8282
www.originalpancakehouse.com

**Z Walker Bros. Original Pancake House** *American*

**Lincolnshire** | 200 Marriott Dr. (Milwaukee Ave.) | 847-634-2220
**Glenview** | 1615 Waukegan Rd. (bet. Chestnut & Lake Aves.) | 847-724-0220
**Highland Park** | 620 Central Ave. (2nd St.) | 847-432-0660
**Wilmette** | 153 Green Bay Rd. (Isabella St.) | 847-251-6000
**Arlington Heights** | 825 W. Dundee Rd. (bet. Arlington Heights Rd. & Rte. 53) | 847-392-6600
**Lake Zurich** | Lake Zurich Theatre Development | 767 S. Rand Rd. (June Terr.) | 847-550-0006
www.walkerbroso.net
Additional locations throughout the Chicago area

"Well-prepared, hearty breakfasts" earn this "always-packed", "old family favorite" American chain status as a "shrine" to carbs – especially pancakes, including a "Dutch Baby to live for" and a flapjack that's "the reason apples were invented"; while naysayers "don't understand the attraction" of "long waits" and "screaming children", patrons point out "attentive service" and "low-cost" "belly-busting of the highest order"; N.B. not all locations are open for dinner.

**NEW Orvieto Pizzeria & Wine Bar** *Pizza* | – | – | – | M |

**Lincoln Park** | Green Dolphin Street | 2200 N. Ashland Ave. (Webster Ave.) | 773-395-0066 | www.jazzitup.com
Located inside Lincoln Park's Green Dolphin Street jazz club (diners get a discount for the club), this casual pizzeria/sports bar offers thin-crust pies accompanied by a big selection of moderately priced Italian classics; there's also a separate lounge menu and a fairly brief wine list, and it's all served in a handsome space with drum lighting and plenty of flat-screen TVs.

**Osteria Via Stato** *Italian* | 23 | 20 | 22 | $39 |

**River North** | 620 N. State St. (Ontario St.) | 312-642-8450
**Pizzeria Via Stato** *Italian*
**River North** | 620 N. State St. (Ontario St.) | 312-337-6634
www.leye.com
It's "not just a red-sauce menu" at Lettuce Entertain You's "affordable" River North Italian osteria where you can "stuff yourself silly" if you order the prix fixe "cavalcade" of "hearty" dishes to share or go à la

carte with options like slow-roasted pork shank; the "homey", Tuscan-style room works for "groups" as well as "romance", and the "family-friendly" adjoining pizzeria fires up "terrific thin-crust" pies.

### Otom ⊠ American
22 | 21 | 25 | $59

**West Loop** | 951 W. Fulton Mkt. (bet. Morgan & Sangamon Sts.) | 312-491-5804 | www.otomrestaurant.com

Moto's "hip" New American sibling in the West Loop conjures up "fancy comfort food" – pork belly croquettes, German potato salad gnocchi – and pairs it with "inventive drinks" and an "excellent" wine list; "attentive servers" "notice the details" in the modern, "minimalist" digs that include white-oak floors, orange resin chairs, a fireplace and seasonal sidewalk seating.

### Over Easy Café Ⓜ American
27 | 21 | 23 | $17

**Ravenswood** | 4943 N. Damen Ave. (bet. Ainslie & Argyle Sts.) | 773-506-2605

"Resolve to wake up earlier" and "kick-start your day" at this "cute" Ravenswood BYO breakfast, brunch and luncher, where the "creative" choices range from "decadent stuffed French toast" and "outrageous" apple pancakes to grilled Brie-cheese-and-apple sandwiches; the waits can be "long and tedious", however, so it's a good thing the "welcoming" staff pours "free coffee outside on weekends."

### Oysy Japanese
20 | 18 | 19 | $33

**River North** | 50 E. Grand Ave. (bet. Rush St. & Wabash Ave.) | 312-670-6750
**South Loop** | 888 S. Michigan Ave. (9th St.) | 312-922-1127
**Northbrook** | 315 Skokie Blvd. (Dundee Rd.) | 847-714-1188
www.oysysushi.com

The name of this "stylish" Japanese trio means "delicious" – and the majority of reviewers says it applies to the "tasty", "reasonably priced" sushi offerings, "complex rolls" and small plates brought to table by the "eye-candy waitresses"; but finicky fin-atics point to "dull combinations" and "inconsistent" service that make them "nothing special"; P.S. the South Loop locale offers "brilliant outdoor dining" "opposite Grant Park" in the summer and live music on weekends.

### Palette Bistro Ⓜ American
- | - | - | M

**Lakeview** | 2834 N. Southport Ave. (Wolfram St.) | 773-477-2565 | www.paletteonsouthport.com

"A bit off the beaten path", this "little" "gem" in Lakeview is "especially appropriate" for an "intimate, romantic" dinner or weekend brunch; the "gorgeous corner space" features "numerous windows and French doors , "warm woods" and a "showpiece carved bar", and both the "delicious" American menu and the wine list are "as low-key or upscale" "as you want"; N.B. there's summer sidewalk seating.

### Palm, The Steak
24 | 21 | 23 | $67

**Loop** | Swissôtel | 323 E. Wacker Dr. (bet. Lake Shore Dr. & Michigan Ave.) | 312-616-1000 | www.thepalm.com

"Perfect" lobster, "superb" steaks and "hefty" cocktails are the signatures of this "bustling", "special-occasion" chophouse chain with a "dark men's-club" look and "wonderful atmosphere" enhanced by "caricatures of celebs" (and "locals") covering the walls; "impeccable", "old-school" service seals the deal, so while it's "not cheap", most conclude it's "worth it."

## Pane Caldo  *Italian*  23 | 21 | 21 | $62

**Gold Coast** | 72 E. Walton St. (bet. Michigan Ave. & Rush St.) | 312-649-0055 | www.pane-caldo.com

"Superb" Italian fare, a solid wine list and generally "knowledgeable" service are on offer at this "quaint", "romantic" Gold Coast "gem" that "feels like Milan" with its amber-hued walls and dark-blue ceilings; but the "intimate" setting strikes some as "cramped", while others feel their wallet's pain from "overpricing."

## ☒ Pappadeaux Seafood Kitchen  *Seafood*  21 | 19 | 19 | $35

**Arlington Heights** | 798 W. Algonquin Rd. (Golf Rd.) | 847-228-9551
**Westmont** | 921 Pasquinelli Dr. (Oakmont Ln.) | 630-455-9846
www.pappas.com

Suburbanites who swim to these "buzzing", "casual" sibs for seafood with a Cajun-Creole "flair" are content with the "huge portions", "wide variety of sauces", "piquant flavors" and "popular Sunday brunch" buffet; dissenters who won't make a return lap, however, cite the "mixed service", "semi-industrial setting" and "unimaginative", "middling" fare that's "more fried than fish."

## Paramount Room, The  *American*  ▽ 24 | 17 | 23 | $22

**Near West** | 415 N. Milwaukee Ave. (bet. Hubbard & Kinzie Sts.) | 312-829-6300 | www.paramountroom.com

Its sign is "a beacon" along a "dark stretch of Milwaukee Avenue" say denizens drawn to this bi-level Near West "neighborhood" noshery set in a former speakeasy, where the "surprisingly diverse menu" of "simple", "delicious" New American pub fare includes Kobe burgers that drip juice "down your arm" and a Reuben with house-cooked and -cured corned beef; the "bartenders know their stuff" too, mixing "excellent drinks" in a tavern space with distressed floors and lofted ceilings.

## NEW Paris Café  *Pub Food*  - | - | - | M

**River North** | 810 N. Clark St. (bet. Chestnut St. & Chicago Ave.) | 312-255-0811

Bistro classics and pub faves like burgers and a Philly cheesesteak blend on the midpriced menu at this casual River Norther with full bar service (including specialty martinis) and weekend breakfast; an upscale tavern feel is created with rustic brick, romantic lighting, an elaborate tiled bar with multiple TVs and seating options including high-top tables, banquettes and lounge groupings.

## Parkers' Restaurant & Bar  *American*  23 | 22 | 24 | $43
(fka Parkers' Ocean Grill)

**Downers Grove** | 1000 31st St. (Highland Ave.) | 630-960-5701 | www.selectrestaurants.com

A post-Survey name change and menu retool (not reflected in the Food score) shifted the emphasis from seafood to New American fare, including wood-fired pizzas, at this Western Suburbs spot, but it retains its "comfortable", "corporate" atmosphere and "accommodating staff"; the "well-spaced tables" work for "business" or "romance", so while some admit the "common man might find the prices a bit steep", admirers believe its assets "make up for it."

### Park 52 *American*  19 | 21 | 21 | $46

**Hyde Park** | 5201 S. Harper Ave. (52nd St.) | 773-241-5200 | www.park52chicago.com

While the Traditional American menu may "not be adventurous", seasonal "specials are usually more interesting" at this Hyde Park spot decorated in the "vibrant colors" and "elaborate furnishings" that are the signature of restaurateur Jerry Kleiner (Opera, Red Light); supporters say the neighborhood "needs more places like this", but judging from complaints over "food that could be better" and service that merely "tries hard", this eatery's still "not quite good enough"; N.B. it serves Sunday brunch.

### Park Grill *American*  20 | 21 | 19 | $37

**Loop** | Millennium Park | 11 N. Michigan Ave. (bet. Madison & Washington Sts.) | 312-521-7275 | www.parkgrillchicago.com

With a "wonderful setting" "under 'the bean'" in Millennium Park, this "friendly", "stylish restaurant" serves up a "view of the ice skaters in winter" and a "delightful" "patio scene in summer"; but while some park here for "tasty" New American fare, including "the best burgers", spoilsports who skewer "inconsistent", "good-to-pedestrian" eats and a staff that "can't handle the lunch crowds" label it "for tourists."

### NEW Park Place *American/Eclectic*  - | - | - | M

**Northwest Side** | 6733 N. Olmsted Ave. (Oshkosh Ave.) | 773-631-8100 | www.parkplacediningandevents.com

This vast Northwest Side noshery serves a mix of midpriced Traditional American and globally inspired dishes along with specialty cocktails, daily specials, family-style Sunday dinners and weekend brunch; the bustling, upscale sports-bar atmosphere is enlivened with warm lighting, colorful tiled floors, vintage album covers, guitars and other musical motifs.

### Parrot Cage, The Ⓜ *American*  - | - | - | M

**Far South Side** | South Shore Cultural Ctr. | 7059 S. South Shore Dr. (71st St.) | 773-602-5333

What a "find on the [Far] South Side" say gourmands of this "creative" New American that's part of the Washburne Culinary Institute and manned by student-cooks who produce "excellent", "reasonably priced" steak, lamb and fish and "interesting vegetarian options", all accompanied by a "bargain wine list" (and a low-corkage BYO policy); the "bright and peachy" space has outdoor seating, a "gorgeous" view of the lake and is surrounded by parrots' nests, but it's too bad the "pleasant" service "can be spotty"; P.S. cognoscenti concur the Wednesday–Thursday "three-course meal is a real deal."

| | FOOD | DECOR | SERVICE | COST |
|---|---|---|---|---|

## Parthenon ● *Greek*

| | 21 | 17 | 21 | $30 |

**Greektown** | 314 S. Halsted St. (bet. Jackson Blvd. & Van Buren St.) | 312-726-2407 | www.theparthenon.com

"A consistent favorite" for more than 40 years, this Greektown "staple" has a "triple-A" Grecian formula: "huge portions" of "authentic, affordable, appetizing" eats served "family-style" from 11 AM to midnight, seven days a week, service with a "sense of humor" and a "fun", "casual" space "broken up into smaller rooms"; however, critics advise "don't focus on the surroundings", which are "somewhat campy."

## NEW Pasha ⑤ *Spanish*

| | - | - | - | M |

**West Loop** | 802 W. Randolph St. (Halsted St.) | 312-243-4442 | www.pashachicago.com

Creative Spanish small and main plates using local and organic ingredients, specialty libations and a predominantly Spanish wine list mark this Market District revival of the defunct River North haunt; the cozy, low-lit lair features white linens, candlelight and a bar with backlit booze bottles, and the Latin band Bandoleros (who are also co-owners) perform on Thursdays and Saturdays.

## Pasta Palazzo *Italian*

| | ▽ 22 | 15 | 19 | $19 |

**Lincoln Park** | 1966 N. Halsted St. (Armitage Ave.) | 773-248-1400 | www.pastapalazzo.com

Lincoln Park locals "love" this "cozy" Italian with "attentive service" and "reasonable prices" for "pasta and more pasta" (try the jalapeño gnocchi), "great salads" and "excellent apps"; the "casual" setting can be "loud", but most say it's an "enjoyable stop for a neighborhood" lunch or dinner; N.B. no reservations, but they now accept credit cards.

## Pegasus ● *Greek*

| | 20 | 17 | 18 | $28 |

**Greektown** | 130 S. Halsted St. (bet. Adams & Monroe Sts.) | 312-226-4666

## Pegasus on the Fly ● *Greek*

**Southwest Side** | Midway Int'l Airport | 5700 S. Cicero Ave. (55th St.) | 773-581-1522
www.pegasuschicago.com

"In the heart of Greektown", this "favorite" features a "wide range" of "terrific dishes" including "classic" spanakopita, broiled whole fish and "yummy" Greek tapas brought to table by "accommodating" servers; a "bright", "cozy" interior "with painted Mykonos windmills" and a summertime rooftop with "views of the Chicago skyline" and live music on weekends elevate this one "a step above other restaurants in the area"; N.B. the Midway fly-by is open 24/7.

## NEW Pelago Ristorante *Italian*

| | ▽ 26 | 24 | 27 | $53 |

**Streeterville** | Raffaello Hotel | 201 E. Delaware Pl.
(Mies Van Der Rohe Way) | 312-280-0700 | www.pelagorestaurant.com

Chef-owner Mauro Mafrici "knows how to cook" pronounce proponents of the "superb", "creative" Italian at his new Streeterville dining room serving breakfast, lunch and dinner; it's "worth seeking out" in a "hidden hotel" off Michigan Avenue, given the "winning" dishes, "outstanding service" and "tastefully decorated" space with porcelain chandeliers, white leather chairs and a mother of pearl fireplace; N.B. there's seasonal patio seating.

### Penny's Noodle Shop  *Asian*
20 | 12 | 17 | $15

**Lakeview** | 3400 N. Sheffield Ave. (Roscoe St.) | 773-281-8222 Ⓜ
**Lincoln Park** | 950 W. Diversey Pkwy. (Sheffield Ave.) | 773-281-8448
**Wicker Park** | 1542 N. Damen Ave. (North Ave.) | 773-394-0100 Ⓜ
**Northfield** | 320 S. Happ Rd. (Mt. Pleasant St.) | 847-446-4747
**Oak Park** | 1130 Chicago Ave. (Harlem Ave.) | 708-660-1300
www.pennysnoodleshop.com

Champions of "cheap", "palate-pleasing", "predictable" Asian dishes defer to this "casual", "quick-service", "no-frills" string of noodle shops for a "wide variety" of "simple dishes" with "fresh ingredients" and "lots of vegetarian options"; some sophisticated palates pooh-pooh "bland", "faux" fare, but penny-savers praise the "plentiful" portions that are "perfect for recessionary times"; N.B. Lakeview and Northfield are BYO, the others offer beer and wine.

### Perennial  *American*
24 | 22 | 24 | $55

**Lincoln Park** | Park View Hotel | 1800 N. Lincoln Ave. (Clark St.) | 312-981-7070 | www.perennialchicago.com

"Elegant, well-crafted plates" and "friendly, but not intrusive, service" meet in a "terrific Lincoln Park location" "across from the Green City Market" where chef Ryan Poli procures the "fresh ingredients" for his "superb", "seasonal" New American menu; the "lively" and "hip" rustic-modern space in the Park View Hotel – with a "lovely terrace" and a fireplace lounge serving "exceptional cocktails" – attracts a "beautiful" crowd that revels in this "wonderful" "addition to the neighborhood"; P.S. there's an "outstanding" Sunday brunch.

### Perry's Deli  *Deli*
26 | 12 | 17 | $11

**Loop** | 174 N. Franklin St. (bet. Lake & Randolph Sts.) | 312-372-7557 | www.perrysdeli.com Ⓢ
**University Village** | 719 W. Maxwell St. (bet. Halsted St. & Union Ave.) | 312-372-7557

"One of the best deli spots in town", the Loop original in this simple duo gets so crowded you may have to "fight for a table" after you order one of the "huge", "tasty" sandwiches "piled high" with house-cooked meats; you're not going for the atmosphere (takeout may be better) or the quirky service ("leave your cell phone outside" cause if you use it "Perry himself will yell at you"), but "it's worth it" for sammies "so big you can only eat half"; N.B. a recent offshoot offers the same sustenance in University Village.

### Pete Miller's Seafood & Prime Steak  *Seafood/Steak*
22 | 21 | 21 | $51

**Evanston** | 1557 Sherman Ave. (bet. Davis & Grove Sts.) | 847-328-0399 ☻
**Wheeling** | 412 N. Milwaukee Ave. (bet. Dundee & Lake Cook Rds.) | 847-243-3700
www.petemillers.com

These "suburban steakhouses" are considered "friendly", "clubby" connections for a "basic menu" of "high-quality" "prime" steaks and "even better seafood" in a "dark" setting reminiscent of "the mid '40s"; while most agree the service is usually "reliable", scorers are split over whether the "live jazz" every night (except Sunday in Evanston) is "great" or so "loud" it's "difficult to tolerate."

### Petterino's  *American*  | 19 | 19 | 21 | $42 |

**Loop** | Goodman Theatre Bldg. | 150 N. Dearborn St. (Randolph St.) | 312-422-0150 | www.petterinos.com

"Theatergoers" and the "business crowd" fill this Lettuce Entertain You Loop American in the Goodman Theatre building, where "snappy" service (both in speed and, sometimes, "attitude") keeps the "clubby", "bustling" room under control; the straightforward fare is generally "dependable" – and the "after-7 prix fixe" is a "bargain" – but tougher critics suspect something's "missing in the kitchen" given the "lackluster" offerings.

### P.F. Chang's China Bistro  *Chinese*  | 20 | 19 | 19 | $31 |

**River North** | 530 N. Wabash Ave. (Grand Ave.) | 312-828-9977
**Northbrook** | Northbrook Court Shopping Ctr. | 1819 Lake Cook Rd. (Northbrook Court Dr.) | 847-509-8844
**Schaumburg** | Woodfield Mall | 5 Woodfield Mall (Frontage & Golf Rds.) | 847-610-8000
**Orland Park** | Orland Park Crossing | 14135 S. La Grange Rd. (Southwest Hwy.) | 708-675-3970
**Lombard** | 2361 Fountain Square Dr. (bet. Butterfield & Meyers Rds.) | 630-652-9977
www.pfchangs.com

"Light, delicious", "Americanized" Chinese food keeps fans "coming back" – especially for the "standout" lettuce wraps – to this "trendy", "stylish" chain; though not everyone is convinced ("overpriced", "ordinary", "loud"), the "consistent" service is a plus, as is the "smart" menu "catering to people with allergies" and other needs.

### Philly G's  *Italian*  | 21 | 22 | 23 | $37 |

**Vernon Hills** | 1252 E. Hwy. 45 (Rte. 21) | 847-634-1811 | www.phillygs.com

"People of all ages enjoy" this "welcoming" Vernon Hills Italian where "you feel like you're at someone's home" dining on "authentic", old-school fare like "veal francese", chicken cacciatore and pasta carbonara; the "reliable service" gets it right in the "sprawling", "old-mansion" space with an "enclosed outdoor porch" and live weekend entertainment.

### Phil Stefani's 437 Rush  Ⓢ *Italian/Steak*  | 24 | 21 | 24 | $48 |

**River North** | 437 N. Rush St. (Hubbard St.) | 312-222-0101 | www.stefanirestaurants.com

Traditionalists tout the "upper-end", "Chicago-style fine-dining" experience at Phil Stefani's "classic white-tablecloth Italian steakhouse" that works well for "business" folks "sealing a deal" and "titled ladies comparing vacation plans"; the food "doesn't blow away" everyone, but the "cheerful and knowledgeable service", including a "roving maitre d'/tenor who takes requests", certainly creates an "inviting" vibe in a River North location that's "convenient to many hotels."

| | FOOD | DECOR | SERVICE | COST |
|---|---|---|---|---|

**NEW Pho & I** *Thai/Vietnamese* — — — I

**Lakeview** | 2932 N. Broadway (Oakdale Ave.) | 773-549-5700 |
www.phoandichicago.com

A hybrid Vietnamese-Thai, this budget-friendly Lakeview BYO
serves apps, buns, curries, noodles and rice dishes in addition to the
namesake soup; the upscale-casual storefront boasts spare, modern design with bare white tables, warm wood, recessed lighting and
a red accent wall.

**Z Phoenix** *Chinese* 23 12 17 $26

**Chinatown** | 2131 S. Archer Ave., 2nd fl. (Wentworth Ave.) |
312-328-0848 | www.chinatownphoenix.com

While "best known for" its "large variety" of "daily dim sum"
"from the commonplace to the weird", this "huge" moderately
priced Chinatowner is also sought out for "gourmet Chinese dinners" (the "Peking duck is always available"); service swings
from a "paragon of efficiency" to "hit-and-miss", "fluent English
is at a premium" and the surroundings are "drab", yet it remains
"extremely popular", so just remember to "come early" or "be prepared for a wait" "on weekends."

**Pho 777** *Vietnamese* 21 8 15 $15

**Uptown** | 1065 W. Argyle St. (bet. Kenmore & Winthrop Aves.) |
773-561-9909 | www.pho777.com

Whether it's "delicious" or merely "decent", surveyors suggest
the "authentic", "tasty Vietnamese" fare – including an "amazing number of phos" plus noodles, "fresh spring rolls and shrimp
paste on sugar cane" – at this Uptown BYO is "hot", "satisfying"
and "maybe one of the best values in all of Chicago", even if
decor and service are "no-frills"; N.B. the menu is offered midmorning through late evening.

**Phò Xe Tång** *Vietnamese* 26 8 13 $13

**Uptown** | 4953-55 N. Broadway (Argyle St.) | 773-878-2253 |
www.tanknoodle.com

"In the land of pho", "this is one of the best" say satisfied slurpers at
this "always-busy" budget Uptown BYO (aka Tank Noodle) that's a
"reliable" source for "excellent", "fresh" Vietnamese fare delivered
with "quick service"; there's "zero atmosphere" at communal round
tables, but devotees declare the "constant wait is a testament"
to "broad appeal."

**Piazza Bella** *Italian* 21 17 19 $30

**Roscoe Village** | 2116 W. Roscoe St. (bet. Damen & Western Aves.) |
773-477-7330 | www.piazzabella.com

"Delicious" midpriced Italian cooking in a "comfortable", "casual"
setting with "cute", "authentic" atmosphere draws Roscoe Villagers
to this "neighborhood" trattoria for a "date" or "family" outing; nitpickers note that "service could use some improvement", but at
least an "expansion" "has alleviated the crowding" and there's also
an "outdoor dining area"; P.S. "don't miss the Sunday brunch
with unlimited mimosas."

| | FOOD | DECOR | SERVICE | COST |
|---|---|---|---|---|

### Piccolo Sogno  *Italian*

| 24 | 23 | 22 | $50 |

**Near West** | 464 N. Halsted St. (Grand Ave.) | 312-421-0077 |
www.piccolosognorestaurant.com

Even the most "avid" fans of Northern Italian cuisine say Tony Priolo
(ex Coco Pazzo) "pushes the boundaries" "of quality and authenticity" at this "visually beautiful" Near West "treasure" with "wine
choices" so vast and "reasonably priced" they make "an oenophile
weep for joy"; "in summertime" a "glorious" garden is "heaven" to
habitués, so if "service is inconsistent" and it can be "a bit noisy",
most still insist it's "truly a little dream."

### Piece  *Pizza*

| 23 | 14 | 19 | $20 |

**Wicker Park** | 1927 W. North Ave. (Damen Ave.) | 773-772-4422 |
www.piecechicago.com

"New Haven thin-crust pizza in a stuffed-crust town" scores with
surveyors at this "cavernous" Wicker Park "sports bar" serving "customized" pies (choose your "sauce" and "top your 'za with everything from clams to mashed potatoes") and "interesting" "fresh"
microbrews, all at "decent prices"; "service is serviceable" but the
setting has "screens all over tuned to various" games, and if it's
"crowded" and "loud" (like during the "live-band karaoke" on Saturday
nights), Piece Out does delivery and takeout next door.

### Pierrot Gourmet  *French*

| 20 | 20 | 18 | $35 |

**River North** | Peninsula Hotel | 108 E. Superior St. (bet. Michigan Ave. &
Rush St.) | 312-573-6749 | www.peninsula.com

"It costs more than other places to have a coffee, croissant, lunch"
or early dinner, but not as much as a "trip abroad" at this "serene"
River North "oasis" featuring "flatbreads, sandwiches, salads,
quiches" and other French bistro fare crafted from "high-quality ingredients" and proffered by generally "professional service" in an
"upscale" "Continental cafe"–space that's "part of the Peninsula
Hotel"; N.B. they have a seasonal patio and close earlier in winter.

### NEW Piggery, The  *BBQ*

| - | - | - | I |

**Lakeview** | 1625 W. Irving Park Rd. (Marshfield Ave.) | 773-281-7447 |
www.thepiggerychicago.com

This little piggy comes to Lakeview with a passel of budget-loving
porcine proferrings; ribs are a mainstay, and there's pork in every
conceivable comfort-food dish (and replacing other proteins in
items like pot roast, salad, poppers and nachos), all served
with craft beers on tap in an upscale sports-bar setting with high-
tops, reclaimed wood floors and lighting that still flatters at 2 AM
(nightly closing time, though the kitchen closes earlier).

### Pine Yard  *Chinese*

| 18 | 11 | 16 | $23 |

**Evanston** | 1033 Davis St. (Oak St.) | 847-475-4940 |
www.pineyardrestaurant.com

"Delicate Cantonese, spicy Sichuan" and Mandarin dishes secure
supporters for this enduring Evanston Chinese where the "hot,
fresh" fare comes at "reasonable prices" in a simple, contemporary
setting; while naysayers lament it's a "shadow of its old self", fans

favor the prix fixe "lunch specials" and note that service is so "prompt" you're "served practically before you've read the menu."

**pingpong** ● *Asian*  | 20 | 17 | 17 | $28 |

**Lakeview** | 3322 N. Broadway St. (bet. Aldine Ave. & Buckingham Pl.) | 773-281-7575 | www.pingpongrestaurant.com

"Cute and tiny", this "local" Boys Town "scene" "keeps it interesting" with a mix of "delicious", "above-average" Asian eats ("i.e. Japanese, Korean, Thai" and others) plus cocktails in a "lively" atmosphere with "loud music" and sometimes a movie projected "on the wall"; the "stark white", "fashionista" setting includes a seasonal patio.

**Pinstripes** *American/Italian*  | 17 | 18 | 17 | $28 |

**Northbrook** | 1150 Willow Rd. (bet. Patriot Blvd. & Waukegan Rd.) | 847-480-2323

**Barrington** | 100 W. Higgins Rd. (Rte. 59) | 847-844-9300
www.pinstripes.com

Some regulars roll into these "classy", "comfortable" suburban "bowling-alley restaurants" for their "reasonably priced", "tasty" traditional American-Italian bistro fare and "Sunday buffet brunch" with special children's stations, while sporty types and revelers consider them a "blast" for "bowling, bocce, booze", "outings and birthday parties"; P.S. seating options include "leather sofas" or "inviting patios."

**☑ Pita Inn** *Mediterranean/Mideastern*  | 24 | 9 | 17 | $12 |

**Glenview** | 9854 N. Milwaukee Ave. (bet. Central & Golf Rds.) | 847-759-9990

**Skokie** | 3910 Dempster St. (Crawford St.) | 847-677-0211

**Wheeling** | 122 S. Elmhurst Rd. (Dundee Rd.) | 847-808-7733
www.pita-inn.com

Offering "healthy" fare "as delicious as it is cheap", this trio of "dependable" Med and Middle Eastern "self-service standbys" earns accolades as "one of the best deals around" for an "alternative to fast food"; "frenzied but efficient" "counter" service controls "crowds" of "loyal pita, hummus" and falafel fans, and while there's "zero atmosphere", the "decor is simple and functional"; P.S. the prix fixe "businessperson's lunch" "is hard to beat."

**NEW Pitchfork** *BBQ*  | - | - | - | I |

**North Center/St. Ben's** | 2922 W. Irving Park Rd. (Richmond St.) | 773-866-2010 | www.pitchforkchicago.com

This low-cost North Center arrival slings barbecue essentials plus sandwiches, salads, wings and chili mac to accompany its rotating chalkboard menu of over 35 bourbons and whiskeys; the stylishly casual brick-and-wood space is outfitted with a tin ceiling, taxidermy, framed stained glass and antique gaslights, plus multiple plasmas and dartboards for entertainment.

**Pizza Capri** *Pizza*  | 20 | 12 | 16 | $22 |

**Lakeview** | 962 W. Belmont Ave. (Sheffield Ave.) | 773-296-6000

**Lincoln Park** | 1733 N. Halsted St. (Willow St.) | 312-280-5700

*(continued)*

*(continued)*

## Pizza Capri

**Hyde Park** | 1501 E. 53rd St. (Harper Ave.) | 773-324-7777
www.pizzacapri.com

"Unique and delicious" "crispy, thin pizza" and a "variety" of "creative salads and pasta dishes" add up to a "tasty meal at a fair price" at this trio of "atypical Italian" eateries where the "decor is institutional" but "friendly" "service makes it a pleasant dining experience"; N.B. Lincoln Park is BYO, the others offer beer and wine.

## Pizza D.O.C. *Pizza*

23 | 15 | 20 | $25

**Lincoln Square** | 2251 W. Lawrence Ave. (bet. Bell & Oakley Aves.) | 773-784-8777 | www.mypizzadoc.com

"One of the pioneers in the wood-fired pizza revolution", this "happening" Lincoln Square Italian woos with "wonderful" "Neapolitan" "thin pizza with a wide variety of toppings" including "egg" and "potato" ("but don't overlook the rest of the menu", like "excellent spaghetti carbonara"); the "family-friendly" "bistro atmosphere" can be "noisy", and while the "excellent pies" are "not cheap", they're "always satisfying"; N.B. it serves all-you-can-eat Sunday brunch.

## NEW Pizzeria Serio *Pizza*

- | - | - | M

**Roscoe Village** | 1708 W. Belmont Ave. (bet. Paulina St. & Ravenswood Ave.) | 773-525-0600 | www.pizzeriaserio.com

Roscoe Villagers now have a New York–style pizza option in the form of this spiffy midpriced storefront serving chewy thinnish crust (but not skinny) pies made from hand-stretched dough in an 800-degree brick oven; the brick theme extends to the facade and walls, with the loftlike feel enhanced by wood floors and exposed ductwork.

## Pizzeria Uno ❶ *Pizza*

22 | 14 | 16 | $23

**River North** | 29 E. Ohio St. (Wabash Ave.) | 312-321-1000

## Pizzeria Due ❶ *Pizza*

**River North** | 619 N. Wabash Ave. (bet. Ohio & Ontario Sts.) | 312-943-2400
www.unos.com

Among "Chicago's top tourist destinations", this "historic" duo of "deep-dish" "icons" ("not the chain Uno, the original") is beloved for its "buttery, crunchy crust" and "generous portions of meat, cheese and sauce" ("prepare for a reptilian stupor" that's "worth every groan"); "servers struggle to do their best" at the "crowded" and perhaps "shopworn" sire, so some head to the "quieter" sequel for the "same pizza", and while loyalists insist they've "upheld the tradition", others lament they've "lost a little pizzazz over the years."

## P.J. Clarke's *American*

17 | 14 | 17 | $27

**Streeterville** | Embassy Suites Hotel | 302 E. Illinois St. (Columbus Dr.) | 312-670-7500
**Gold Coast** | 1204 N. State Pkwy. (Division St.) | 312-664-1650
www.pjclarkeschicago.com

No relation to New York, these "old-school" "watering holes" with "lively bar scenes" and a "neighborhood hangout feel" boast the

American "comfort-food" "basics", including "classic burgers", meatloaf, "big salads", "great Bloody Marys and nice sandwiches" at "reasonable prices" in settings that are "more pub than restaurant" (with patios).

**Pomegranate** *Mediterranean/Mideastern* ▽ 18 | 11 | 15 | $13

**Evanston** | 1633 Orrington Ave. (bet. Church & Davis Sts.) | 847-475-6002

"Fresh, fast Middle Eastern" meals including "salads, pitas and entrees" "at a good price" have raters "returning again and again" to this red-walled Evanston "counter-service" BYO for a "quick bite" – and "they deliver, a big bonus."

**Pompei Bakery** *Italian* 19 | 14 | 16 | $16

**Streeterville** | 212 E. Ohio St. (bet. State St. & Wabash Ave.) | 312-482-9900

**Lakeview** | 2955 N. Sheffield Ave. (bet. Oakdale & Wellington Aves.) | 773-325-1900

**Little Italy** | 1531 W. Taylor St. (bet. Ashland Ave. & Laflin St.) | 312-421-5179

**Schaumburg** | 1261 E. Higgins Rd. (bet. Meacham Rd. & National Pkwy.) | 847-619-5001

**Oakbrook Terrace** | 17 W. 744 22nd St. (bet. Butterfield Rd. & Summit Ave.) | 630-620-0600
www.pompeibakery.com

A "wide selection" of "solid", "quick-service Italian specialties" like "strudel pizza", "pasta in good-size portions and tasty salad specials" are a "value for a quick lunch or dinner" at this "cafeteria-style" series; service varies and it's "not fine dining, but you can bring the whole family and not break the bank", so most are "glad it's in the neighborhood."

**☑ Potbelly Sandwich Works** *Sandwiches* 19 | 13 | 17 | $10

**Loop** | One Illinois Ctr. | 111 E. Wacker Dr. (Michigan Ave.) | 312-861-0013 ☒

**Loop** | Insurance Exchange | 175 W. Jackson Blvd. (bet. Financial Pl. & Wells St.) | 312-588-1150 ☒

**Loop** | 190 N. State St. (Lake St.) | 312-683-1234

**Loop** | 303 W. Madison St. (Franklin St.) | 312-346-1234 ☒

**Loop** | 55 W. Monroe St. (bet. Clark & Dearborn Sts.) | 312-577-0070 ☒

**River North** | 508 N. Clark St. (bet. Grand Ave. & Illinois St.) | 312-644-9131

**River North** | Shops at North Bridge | 520 N. Michigan Ave., 4th fl. (Grand Ave.) | 312-644-1008

**Lakeview** | 3424 N. Southport Ave. (bet. Newport Ave. & Roscoe St.) | 773-289-1807

**Lincoln Park** | 1422 W. Webster Ave. (Clybourn Ave.) | 773-755-1234

**Lincoln Park** | 2264 N. Lincoln Ave. (bet. Belden & Webster Aves.) | 773-528-1405
www.potbelly.com
Additional locations throughout the Chicago area

"For a quick, economical lunch", they keep the "cattle line" "moving" at this "multitude" of "reliable" relatives serving "unique" "toasted sandwiches" that Dagwoods deem "better than fast-food burgers" "at a very competitive price" (it's Milwaukee's Best Buy); "location doesn't matter", the goods "are always hot and fresh" and noshers note "live music adds to the experience" (it varies by location) so that even those who name it "nothing special" concede it's "better than other chains."

### Praga Ⓜ American/Eclectic
-|-|-| M

**Lombard** | 229 W. St. Charles Rd. (bet. Elizabeth & Lincoln Sts.) | 630-495-0470

Lombard locals laud this NewAmerican–Eclectic "gem" "for an enjoyable evening" over "tasty, authentic" dishes combined with a "diverse wine list" "that would cost much more in the city"; "helpful service" and "outdoor summer seating" "under umbrellas" add to the reasons "you can't beat it for the price."

### 🆕 Prairie Fire American
-|-|-| M

**West Loop** | 215 N. Clinton St. (Lake St.) | 312-382-8300 | www.prairiefirechicago.com

The power team behind North Suburban Prairie Grass Cafe migrates back downtown (chef-owners Sarah Stegner and George Bumbaris starred for years at the late, great Ritz-Carlton Dining Room), bringing its New American comfort food to the West Loop (some PGC signatures, some new dishes); the landmark building, formerly Powerhouse, is warmly lit and handsomely appointed in dark wood and earth tones with a modernized Prairie School vibe, plus there's weekend brunch, seasonal outdoor seating and a dine-at bar with house cocktails, a separate, lighter menu and plasma TVs.

### Prairie Grass Cafe American
22 | 19 | 21 | $37

**Northbrook** | 601 Skokie Blvd. (bet. Dundee & Lake Cook Rds.) | 847-205-4433 | www.prairiegrasscafe.com

"Celebrity chefs" Sarah Stegner and George Bumbaris "come down to earth" in Northbrook by serving "straightforward" American comfort food "with élan" and the "best local ingredients" – including "homestyle desserts" and "Sunday brunch" – supported by a "fine list of beers, wines and specialty drinks" in a "casual", "modern Arts and Crafts dining room"; some say "service could improve", but given the "accessible prices" and "downtown quality", most give a thumbs-up for "lunch or dinner, family or date night"; N.B. Prairie Fire opened in the West Loop post-Survey.

### 🆕 Prasino American/Vegetarian
-|-|-| M

**La Grange** | 93 S. La Grange Rd. (Cossitt Ave.) | 708-469-7058 | www.eatgreenlivewell.com

Green-minded, gourmet fare finds a home at this La Grange New American offering a midpriced, all-day menu with plenty of vegetarian and vegan options, plus an organic drink list; the contemporary, eco-chic setting is rendered in reclaimed materials, from the bare wood tables to the light fixtures, and there's a bar dispensing coffee, juice and smoothies; N.B. a second location is planned for St. Charles.

| | FOOD | DECOR | SERVICE | COST |
|---|---|---|---|---|

## Prosecco �‍ *Italian*  |  24 | 23 | 23 | $57

**River North** | 710 N. Wells St. (bet. Huron & Superior Sts.) | 312-951-9500 | www.ristoranteprosecco.com

Bubbly boosters say this "sophisticated" River Norther cooks up regional dishes "with a little twist" while pouring from an "extensive" exclusively Italian wine list, all delivered by an "accommodating", "professional" staff in a "warm, comfortable, Venetian-style" setting that includes a "huge bar"; it's "not cheap", but the fare is "satisfying" and "reliable", and most agree it's an "enjoyable" "experience overall" for a "romantic" "date" or "dinner with friends."

## Province �‍ *American*  |  23 | 22 | 22 | $48

**West Loop** | 161 N. Jefferson St. (bet. Lake & Randolph Sts.) | 312-669-9900 | www.provincerestaurant.com

Chef Randy Zweiban's "great instincts" combine with "locally sourced ingredients" for a "lovely", "inventive" "seasonal" New American menu with Latin and Spanish "accents" offered in "various plate sizes" at this "green" West Looper in a LEED-certified building; the "smart, sleek" dining room is decorated with "natural branches", the "cocktails are fabulous" and there's an "interesting wine list", and though a faction of faultfinders say there's "more style than substance", most find the staff "knowledgeable."

## ☒ Publican, The *American*  |  25 | 20 | 22 | $47

**West Loop** | 837 W. Fulton Mkt. (Green St.) | 312-733-9555 | www.thepublicanrestaurant.com

Those who "do swine and brew totally dig" this "unique" West Loop "pork paradise" "from the team that brought us avec and Blackbird", an "offal good place" that "caters to the well-heeled hipster" willing to "get out of the comfort zone and try something new" from a "wonderfully innovative" New American pub menu paired with an "extensive" "beer selection like no other"; be prepared for a "loud atmosphere" with "European flair" in the farmhouse-style setting with "communal tables" (or "swinging-door pens" "for more privacy"), and know that the "knowledgeable staff" is "overwhelmed at times."

## Puck's at the MCA Ⓜ *American*  |  20 | 21 | 18 | $33

**Streeterville** | Museum of Contemporary Art | 220 E. Chicago Ave. (Mies Van Der Rohe Way) | 312-397-4034 | www.mcachicago.org

"For lunch when mind and feet give out" in Streeterville's Museum of Contemporary Art, Wolfgang Puck's "informal" "respite" delivers "better-than-average" midpriced New American fare ("there's nothing like the Chinois chicken salad") and a Sunday "brunch buffet" that's "over the top" in a "pretty" space with a "delightful outdoor terrace" showcasing "beautiful city and lake views"; N.B. museum admission is not required to dine.

## ☒ Pump Room, The *American*  |  22 | 25 | 23 | $67

**Gold Coast** | Ambassador East Hotel | 1301 N. State Pkwy. (Goethe St.) | 312-266-0360 | www.pumproom.com

Traditionalists "regale in the atmosphere" of this Gold Coast "piece of Chicago history" "from another era" (1938) ensconced in the

|  | FOOD | DECOR | SERVICE | COST |

Ambassador East and adorned with pictures "of the notables" who have "occupied booth No. 1"; while surveyors split on whether it's New American "fine dining" or "hotel" fare, loyalists say this "posh" "legend" with service to match "just keeps ticking", perhaps without the "flair" "of days gone by", but "still worth a visit" and "every cent" – if only for "a drink at the bar and a spin on the tiny dance floor"; N.B. there's live entertainment Wednesday–Saturday.

### 🆕 Purple Pig, The ❶ *Mediterranean* — | — | — | M

**River North** | 500 N. Michigan Ave. (Illinois St.) | 312-464-1744 | www.thepurplepigchicago.com

Talent from Heaven on Seven and Mia Francesca have teamed up for this River North Med offering midpriced sharing plates heavy on the pig parts, plus a wine list with numerous selections by the glass, quartino or half-bottle; the sleek space features communal high-tops, a white marble bar and outdoor seating overlooking the Mag Mile, while design highlights include reclaimed wood floors, wine barrels and illuminated menu descriptions; N.B. food is served until midnight (1 AM on weekends).

### Quartino ❶ *Italian* 21 | 18 | 21 | $32

**River North** | 626 N. State St. (Ontario St.) | 312-698-5000 | www.quartinochicago.com

"A lovely assortment" of "small-plate Italian dishes", "authentic pizzas" and "addictive housemade salumi" for "sharing" are served up at this "loud, happening", moderately priced River North trattoria that's usually "packed solid"; tables "are very close, so be prepared to get friendly" and when it's "mayhem" service gives some "agita", but "outstanding" "cheap" "wine by the carafe" helps as does "outdoor seating" – plus it's one of the "best late-night options" in the area (1 AM nightly); P.S. "definitely try the housemade limoncello."

### Quince Ⓜ *American* 23 | 23 | 24 | $53

**Evanston** | Homestead Hotel | 1625 Hinman Ave. (Davis St.) | 847-570-8400 | www.quincerestaurant.net

Despite "chef turnovers", this "exceptionally pleasant" New American "hidden in a residential" Evanston hotel issues "innovative preparations" of pricey New American cuisine "with flair" and an "admirable wine list" ferried by an "accommodating staff" (that's earned a boost in scores); the "warm, relaxing" setting includes a "handsome porch", and while a few left "disappointed", most want to "go back."

### Raj Darbar *Indian* ▽ 18 | 13 | 18 | $29

**Lincoln Park** | 2660 N. Halsted St. (Wrightwood Ave.) | 773-348-1010 | www.rajdarbar.com

Lincoln Park's "go-to" for "decent Indian food" at a "decent value" including "delicious tikka masala" and "biryani" (plus an "excellent Sunday lunch buffet"), this subcontinental longtimer also offers "attentive" service from a "well-meaning" staff and is a "favorite" "for delivery" with a wide geographic range.

|  | FOOD | DECOR | SERVICE | COST |
|---|---|---|---|---|

### Ras Dashen *Ethiopian* ∇ 23 | 18 | 22 | $30

**Edgewater** | 5846 N. Broadway St. (bet. Ardmore & Rosedale Aves.) |
773-506-9601 | www.rasdashenchicago.com

Ethiopian fare including "terrific fish" "ranges from very mild to
quite spicy", so there's "something for everyone" at this flatware-
free, "lovely, authentic-feeling" Edgewater eatery; "service can be
hit-or-miss on a crowded night", but it's "friendly" and the Friday
"live music" is "not too loud for conversation"; N.B. a beer list includes some regional selections, and there's also outdoor seating.

### RA Sushi *Japanese* 19 | 18 | 16 | $35

**Gold Coast** | 1139 N. State St. (Elm St.) | 312-274-0011
**Glenview** | 2601 Aviator Ln. (Patriot Blvd.) | 847-510-1100
**Lombard** | Shops on Butterfield | 310 Yorktown Ctr. (Highland Ave.) |
630-627-6800
www.rasushi.com

"Decent sushi" in "creative combos" and a selection of Japanese hot
dishes are the draw at this midpriced city and suburban chain; surveyors call out the "happy-hour deals", "sake selection" and other
drinks, though "service is spotty", and those who mark it "mediocre"
maintain it's "not bad, but you won't hear a 'ra' from me either."

### RB Grille *Steak* - | - | - | M

**River North** | Rock Bottom Brewery | 1 W. Grand Ave. (State St.) |
312-755-0189 | www.rbgrille.com

The River North location of the Rock Bottom Brewery chain grows a
'grille' with this more upscale (but still affordable) steak-and-
seafood concept set in a refined, warm-brown space done up with
wood paneling, shimmering drapery and candles; N.B. the brewery's beer list is offered on tap, along with a large wine list with
plenty of by-the-glass options.

### Real Tenochtitlán Ⓜ *Mexican* ∇ 20 | 15 | 19 | $36

**Logan Square** | 2451 N. Milwaukee Ave. (bet. Richmond St. &
Sacramento Ave.) | 773-227-1050 | www.realtenochtitlan.com

Supporters say "if you can swallow the name, you'll love" the "luscious moles and other Mexican specialties" at Geno Bahena's "high-
end" yet moderately priced "out-of-the-way" Logan Square BYO
where "service aims to please" in a colorful, rustic setting; what a
few call "pedestrian" fare "with a few sophisticated exceptions",
others dub "tasty and satisfying."

### NEW Red Brick *Eclectic/Mediterranean* - | - | - | I

**Lakeview** | 1938 W. Irving Park Rd. (bet. Damen & Wolcott Aves.) |
773-904-8540 | www.redbrickchicago.com

Casual Mediterranean and Eclectic comfort foods feed Lakeview locals at this low-cost neighborhood spot serving everything from
falafel to meatball sandwiches to chili to steaks; the low-key environs are done up with yellow brick walls adorned with framed photos and vintage ads, and seating options include red leather
banquettes and a fireplace-equipped front lounge; N.B. the bar
boasts 10 plasma screens tuned to the games.

| | FOOD | DECOR | SERVICE | COST |
|---|---|---|---|---|

### Red Light *Asian*     23 | 23 | 21 | $46

**West Loop** | 820 W. Randolph St. (Green St.) | 312-733-8880 | www.redlight-chicago.com

"Taste sensations abound" in "experienced chef" Jackie Shen's "innovative", "upscale" "Asian-inspired cuisine" (and "her famous chocolate-bag dessert") at this "hip", "dynamic" Market District mainstay that's "been around" since 1996; "reliable service" works co-owner Jerry Kleiner's "over-the-top" room featuring a "Buddha centerpiece" and "possibly the coolest bathrooms in Chicago" (and there's perhaps "the best mango martini in town" too), causing commenters to quip "it's called Red Light for a reason - you have to stop" here.

### Reel Club *Seafood*     23 | 21 | 22 | $42

**Oak Brook** | Oakbrook Center Mall | 272 Oakbrook Ctr. (Rte. 83) | 630-368-9400 | www.leye.com

Higher food and service scores support surveyors who say LEYE's Oak Brook mall fishery "has improved so much since it opened", with a "professional" staff delivering a variety of "delicious" "options for seafood lovers" (though "nothing too fancy") and an "interesting wine list" in contemporary digs; some say tabs are "reasonable", others "a bit overpriced", but most are reeled in for a "date", "weekend afternoon" or "after a day of shopping"; P.S. "in summer the outdoor seating" adds to the "happy" experience.

### NEW RendezVous Bistro *French*     - | - | - | M

**Lincoln Square** | 2656 W. Lawrence Ave. (bet. Talman & Washtenaw Aves.) | 773-865-7466 | www.lerendezvousbistro.com

A textbook-traditional bistro menu and BYO with no corkage combine at this cozy, moderately priced rendezvous housed in an unassuming Lincoln Square storefront; the comfortable room features blue banquettes, walls decorated with French advertising posters, vintage-inspired chandeliers and rooster knickknacks.

### Retro Bistro ⊠ *French*     23 | 18 | 23 | $41

**Mt. Prospect** | Mount Prospect Commons | 1746 W. Golf Rd. (Busse Rd.) | 847-439-2424 | www.retrobistro.com

Conjuring "memories of eating in France", this "friendly", "low-key" "shining star" in a "dumpy" Mount Prospect "strip mall" is "always reliable" for "excellent bistro" fare at a "wonderful value" (the prix fixe deals "cannot be beat"); fans "love the wine selection" and the "friendly, cozy bar" - plus "they're glad to have you as a customer."

### NEW Revolution Brewing *Pub Food*     - | - | - | M

**Logan Square** | 2323 N. Milwaukee Ave. (Belden Ave.) | 773-227-2739 | www.revbrew.com

This hip Logan Square brewpub brings midpriced beer-friendly fare (burgers, salads, pizza) to a striking rehabbed historic building with tin ceilings, repurposed wood and vintage bourbon barrels (with light fixtures fashioned from the rusted hoops), a fireplace and an open kitchen; the big bar boasts 16 handles (10 house), 50-plus bottled beers and more than 25 American bourbons.

| | FOOD | DECOR | SERVICE | COST |
|---|---|---|---|---|

### Reza's  *Mediterranean/Mideastern*    | 18 | 14 | 18 | $28 |

**River North** | 432 W. Ontario St. (Orleans St.) | 312-664-4500
**Andersonville** | 5255 N. Clark St. (Berwyn Ave.) | 773-561-1898 ◑
**Oak Brook** | 40 N. Tower Rd. (Butterfield Rd.) | 630-424-9900
www.rezasrestaurant.com

"Plentiful" (some say "gigantic") portions and "huge" brunch and lunch buffets – not to mention "tasty, authentic Persian" options – keep this Middle Eastern–Med trio "busy"; though most pundits appreciate the "laid-back" setting and "bountiful" choices – regulars advise for such an "affordable" tab "do not expect ambiance or pampered service" and you might even "bring your meat tenderizer."

### Rhapsody  *American*    | 20 | 21 | 21 | $50 |

**Loop** | Symphony Ctr. | 65 E. Adams St. (bet. Michigan & Wabash Aves.) | 312-786-9911 | www.rhapsodychicago.com

With its "emphasis on local ingredients", this "quiet" "pre-concert" "find" is favored for "creative" New American fare, a "convenient" Loop location adjacent to Symphony Center and "pleasant service"; while many "meaningful conversations" are sparked over the "fabulous" wine selection plus there's a "friendly bar" and "garden" patio that "doubles your enjoyment", thrifty types figure "it would be overpriced somewhere else."

### NEW Ria ⑤ Ⓜ *American*    | – | – | – | E |

**Gold Coast** | Elysian | 11 E. Walton St. (bet. Rush & State Sts.) | 312-880-4400 | www.riarestaurantchicago.com

The Gold Coast's Elysian is home to this opulent white-tablecloth destination offering visually striking American culinary creations with an emphasis on seafood and global flavors; there's also an encyclopedic wine list, and a champagne cart that rolls through the posh, sparkling space decorated with cushy banquettes, silk walls, silver leather chairs and a modern wall sculpture representing a school of fish.

### Ribs 'n' Bibs ◑ *BBQ*    | 21 | 7 | 17 | $22 |

**Hyde Park** | 5300 S. Dorchester Ave. (53rd St.) | 773-493-0400

Dishing out "authentic" barbecue, this rustic Hyde Park carryout with limited indoor and outdoor seating sidesteps "pizzazz" to concentrate on its "great sauce" and "tender", "meaty ribs and tips"; it's considered "a must" for "U of C students after an evening of study", though regulars recommend leaving extra time, given "how lo-o-o-ng it takes" to get the goods.

### ☑ Riccardo Trattoria *Italian*    | 27 | 19 | 23 | $46 |

**Lincoln Park** | 2119 N. Clark St. (bet. Dickens & Webster Aves.) | 773-549-0038 | www.riccardotrattoria.com

Dining at this "understated" Lincoln Park trattoria – the top-rated Italian in this Survey – "truly and genuinely" "brings back trips to Italy" say insiders, who prefer to steer the "masses" away from their "tiny gem" offering "fantastic" "classic" and "seasonal" dishes delivered by a "personable", "on-point staff"; a "delightful", simple setting with wood tables further evokes the "unpretentious" "spirit of Tuscany" for a "bargain" of a "special" experience that fans long to repeat "again and again."

**Ringo**  *Japanese*                                    - | - | - | M

**Lincoln Park** | 2507 N. Lincoln Ave. (bet. Fullerton Pkwy. & Wrightwood Ave.) | 773-248-5788 | www.ringosushi.com

"Don't tell anybody about the [frequent] all-you-can-eat sushi" promotion beg those hooked on this "dependable", "friendly" Japanese, a "more-affordable option in Lincoln Park" where the decor may be "lacking" but the "cheap" rolls – especially the signature "firecracker" – are "particularly tasty"; though the place is "unmemorable" to a few, any shortcomings can be remedied by "ordering out more often than dining in."

**Rise**  *Japanese*                                    21 | 20 | 17 | $39

**Wrigleyville** | 3401 N. Southport Ave. (Roscoe St.) | 773-525-3535 | www.risesushi.com

Adherents "look for every excuse to return" to this midpriced Wrigleyville sib to Shine Morida and Sushi Taiyo that serves "creative sushi" in a "modern" setting with "floor-to-ceiling windows"; the Japanese fare "rises to the occasion" when dining with "girlfriends or for a date night" with "beautiful rolls and people" adding visual appeal, and though service swings from "friendly" to "snarky", it all "fits" the Southport "scene."

**Risqué Café**  *BBQ*                                    - | - | - | M

**Lakeview** | 3419 N. Clark St. (bet. Newport Ave. & Roscoe St.) | 773-525-7711 | www.risquechicago.com

Though it's "not for families", this "entertaining" "tongue-in-cheek" Lakeview "joint" – from the owner of the late Fixture and Meritage – is a "good-ol' barbecue" destination say smoke-seekers who troll the "impressive" "binder full" of beer, single-malt scotch and whiskey amid "blood-red walls" "covered with pinups"; whether considered a perk or deterrent, edgy B-movies and vintage "softcore porn" on the TV help pass the time while waiting for the grub, which gets mixed reviews.

**Ristorante al Teatro**  Ⓜ *Italian/Mediterranean*      - | - | - | M

**Pilsen** | Thalia Hall | 1227 W. 18th St. (Allport St.) | 312-784-9100 | www.alteatro.us

"Trying hard and succeeding", this "simply addictive" Italian-Med set in Pilsen's historic Thalia Hall is a "pleasant surprise" with a midpriced menu that includes 20 kinds of pizza, "delicious" housemade gelato and coffee roasted on-site; the "lovely space" features columns, murals and vintage photos, plus a downstairs wine cellar with a water wall, and the "friendly staff" contributes to the "neighborhood feel"; P.S. Sunday brunch is an "amazing value."

**ristorante we**  *Italian*                             ▽ 20 | 17 | 19 | $43

**Loop** | W Chicago City Ctr. | 172 W. Adams St. (LaSalle St.) | 312-917-5608 | www.ristorantewe.com

"Centrally located" near "art and theater", this pricey Northern Italian steakhouse in the "cool" W Chicago City Center is a "surprisingly not crowded" option in the Loop for a "good dinner" or a "memorable breakfast" "topped off with cappuccino"; the contemporary digs feature black tabletops and red upholstery, and there's a DJ Monday–Friday.

### Riva  *Seafood*  | 20 | 22 | 20 | $54 |

**Streeterville** | Navy Pier | 700 E. Grand Ave. (Lake Shore Dr.) | 312-644-7482 | www.stefanirestaurants.com

"Request a table by the window" at this "elegant" Streeterville seafooder to best appreciate the "beautiful" "skyline" and "shimmering" "lake views"; though it's "expensive" and perhaps not for the "typical Navy Pier tourist", it's an oasis of "calm" for those heading to the "Shakespeare Theater" or attending a "business conference", though service is sometimes "not up to par."

### R.J. Grunts  *American*  | 19 | 16 | 19 | $23 |

**Lincoln Park** | 2056 N. Lincoln Park W. (bet. Armitage & Dickens Aves.) | 773-929-5363 | www.leye.com

"Melman's original" "Lettuce" restaurant in Lincoln Park "still serves up the '70s in warmth and style" along with American "cheap eats" delivered by a "friendly staff" in a "down-to-earth" "dive" setting – albeit a "packed" one – adorned with photos of employees; those who "need a fix" hit the "salad bar" ("it was the first in Chicago and remains one of the best") or order it alongside burgers or Sunday brunch and chow down to a "throwback soundtrack" while "loving that things never change here."

### ⊠ RL  *American*  | 23 | 26 | 23 | $53 |

**Gold Coast** | 115 E. Chicago Ave. (Michigan Ave.) | 312-475-1100 | www.rlrestaurant.com

Shoppers "doing the Mag Mile" pepper the "elegant clientele" at this "classy" Gold Coaster that exudes a "members-only" feel with its "chichi" crowd and "graciously served" – if "exorbitantly" priced – "classic" American fare; located "next to his flagship store", it's just "what you would expect from Ralph Lauren" with a setting "decked out in leather" and a "fireplace in the bar" that appeals whether "you're a millionaire or just want to feel like one"; P.S. a seat in the "sidewalk cafe is a must in the summer."

### Robinson's No. 1 Ribs  *BBQ*  | 21 | 8 | 14 | $22 |

**Loop** | Union Station | 225 S. Canal St. (bet. Adams St. & Jackson Blvd.) | 312-258-8477 | www.rib1.com ⊄

**Lincoln Park** | 655 W. Armitage Ave. (Orchard St.) | 312-337-1399 | www.ribs1.com Ⓜ

**Oak Park** | 940 W. Madison St. (Clinton St.) | 708-383-8452 | www.rib1.com

"Distinctive sauce" slathers "lip-smackingly delicious", "meaty" ribs at this affordable city and suburban "Chicago tradition" for "top-notch barbecue"; since "the atmosphere isn't much" and service "could be better", many prefer "takeout", but always come "back for more" – including "peach cobbler"; N.B. there's a dog-friendly patio in Lincoln Park.

|  | FOOD | DECOR | SERVICE | COST |
|---|---|---|---|---|

### Rockit Bar & Grill ◐ *American*  | 19 | 17 | 17 | $29 |

**River North** | 22 W. Hubbard St. (bet. Dearborn & State Sts.) | 312-645-6000

**Wrigleyville** | 3700 N. Clark St. (Waveland Ave.) | 773-645-4400
www.rockitbarandgrill.com

A "young, hip crowd" chows down on "high-end" "bar food" from a menu printed on "dollar-bin vintage vinyl" at this "trendy" mid-priced River North American with a Wrigleyville sib; while the signature "Kobe burger" and "truffle fries" are "all that", the atmosphere is "laid-back" and the service "prompt", the less-impressed simply "focus on the drinks"; P.S. there's a build-your-own "Bloody Mary cart" during weekend brunch.

### Roditys ◑ *Greek*  | 21 | 16 | 19 | $30 |

**Greektown** | 222 S. Halsted St. (bet. Adams St. & Jackson Blvd.) | 312-454-0800 | www.roditys.com

"Close the menu" and "trust" the waiters, who are "part of the ambiance" at this "family"-friendly Greektown "standard" dispensing "saganaki", "moussaka", "lamb in alternate preparations" and other "well-done" Hellenic fare; the "comfortable" setting might not be "quite as polished" as at higher-end spots, but the "convenient" location and "reasonable prices" make up for that..

### 𝗡𝗘𝗪 Rolis Restaurant *Mexican*  | - | - | - | I |

**Uptown** | 5004 N. Sheridan Rd. (Argyle St.) | 773-728-6200

The new owners of Uptown's former Riques may have changed the name, but they've kept the same fresh, affordable BYO Mexican concept – think classic entrees and combination plates, tortas (sandwiches), seafood, omelets and other egg dishes; the colorful, casual setting offers well-spaced tables on a painted concrete floor with deep-blue and sunny-yellow walls.

### Rollapalooza 🅼 *Japanese*  | - | - | - | I |

**Lakeview** | 3344 N. Halsted St. (bet. Buckingham Pl. & Roscoe St.) | 773-281-6400

Cravings for "creative rolls" are satisfied at this colorful Boystown neighborhood sushi spot, where the "variety" of "offerings" "won't disappoint"; coupled with service by "nice people", it's determined a "value" for both dining in and "takeout."

### 𝗡𝗘𝗪 Rootstock  | ∇ 24 | 22 | 23 | $29 |
### Wine & Beer Bar ◐🅈 *American*

**Humboldt Park** | 954 N. California Ave. (Augusta Blvd.) | 773-292-1616 | www.rootstockbar.com

"Way cool" if "out of the way", this Humboldt Park "neighborhood joint" from Webster's Wine Bar vets offers "craft beers", a compact but "well-done wine list" and "excellent" midpriced New American small plates, charcuterie and cheeses; the funky digs include secondhand furniture, and when it comes to "pairing recommendations", the "welcoming, attentive" "hipster" staff is "spot on"; P.S. seasonal patio seating and late-night hours are a "real treat" too.

| | FOOD | DECOR | SERVICE | COST |
|---|---|---|---|---|

## RoPa Restaurant & Wine Bar Ⓜ *Mediterranean*

| - | - | - | M |

**Rogers Park** | 1146 W. Pratt Blvd. (Sheridan Rd.) | 773-508-0002 | www.roparestaurant.com

Named for the Rogers Park neighborhood where it resides, this mid-priced Mediterranean charmer with "high ceilings" and "big windows" in a "lovely" wood-and-tile dining room fills a "dire need" say option-strapped locals, serving "surprisingly good" salads, pasta, seafood and steaks; when service is "a bit slow", ordering a wine flight can pass the time; P.S. there's live piano on Wednesdays.

## RoSal's Italian Kitchen Ⓩ *Italian*

| 26 | 18 | 23 | $32 |

**Little Italy** | 1154 W. Taylor St. (Racine Ave.) | 312-243-2357 | www.rosals.com

Go ahead – "use the loaf of bread" to "chase the sauce" at this "simple" but "phenomenal" Little Italy Sicilian where "personable" servers and "authentic", "reasonably priced" "homemade Italian favorites" in "huge portions" make up for the "no-frills" setting; just keep in mind that it's akin to "eating at a friend's house", meaning the kitchen's delivery may be "slow"; P.S. there's a *"Big Night"*-themed menu the last Tuesday of the month.

## Rose Angelis Ⓜ *Italian*

| 24 | 20 | 22 | $32 |

**Lincoln Park** | 1314 W. Wrightwood Ave. (bet. Racine & Southport Aves.) | 773-296-0081 | www.roseangelis.com

Ravenous regulars "go hungry" to this "quaint", "financially affordable" Italian "institution" in Lincoln Park that's a popular pick for "first dates" and dinner with "friends" or "family"; "its strengths" – including "giant portions" of "rustic" fare and the "best patio imaginable" – are enough to keep tables in "high demand", especially with its no-reservations policy, though disheartened diners are "still not sure why people wait hours on weekends."

## Ⓩ Rosebud, The *Italian*

| 22 | 19 | 20 | $41 |

**Little Italy** | 1500 W. Taylor St. (Laflin St.) | 312-942-1117

## Ⓩ Rosebud Italian Specialties & Pizzeria *Italian*
## (fka Rosebud Burger & Comfort Foods)

**Naperville** | 48 W. Chicago Ave. (Washington St.) | 630-548-9800

## Ⓩ Rosebud of Highland Park *Italian*

**Highland Park** | 1850 Second St. (Central Ave.) | 847-926-4800

## Ⓩ Rosebud of Schaumburg *Italian*

**Schaumburg** | 1370 Bank Dr. (Meacham Rd.) | 847-240-1414

## Ⓩ Rosebud on Rush *Italian*

**Gold Coast** | 720 N. Rush St. (Superior St.) | 312-266-6444

## Ⓩ Rosebud Theater District Ⓩ *Italian*

**Loop** | 3 First National Plaza | 70 W. Madison St. (bet. Clark & Dearborn Sts.) | 312-332-9500
www.rosebudrestaurants.com

Red sauce-seekers head for the "original" Taylor Street "cornerstone" and its "old-school" Italian cousins in the city and suburbs for "classics" in "large portions" at "reasonable prices"; dissenters who steer clear claiming "incredibly loud" confines, "bland", "generic" preparations and "surly" service are outweighted by fans who "can't eat there enough."

### Rosebud Prime  *Steak*  25 | 22 | 24 | $57

**Loop** | 1 S. Dearborn St. (Madison St.) | 312-384-1900

### Rosebud Steakhouse  *Steak*

**Streeterville** | 192 E. Walton St. (Mies van Der Rohe Way) | 312-397-1000

www.rosebudrestaurants.com

Loop and Streeterville "movers and shakers" are "packed like sardines" into these "classy", "energetic" "business-lunch" and "pre-theater" beef "fixtures" that are rated the "best of the 'Buds" by surveyors; an "impeccable" staff knows the "steak and chop–driven menu" inside out and it's predictably "expensive", but you might want to bring "earplugs on weekends."

### Rosebud Trattoria  *Italian*  22 | 17 | 22 | $42

**River North** | 445 N. Dearborn St. (Illinois St.) | 312-832-7700 | www.rosebudrestaurants.com

Part of the Rosebud *famiglia*, this "casual" River North offshoot serves "hearty" Italian classics such as meatballs "like mama used to make" as well as Roman-style thin-crust pies, daily fish selections and regional specialties on a seasonally changing menu; a "decent wine list", soft-colored decor with wood accents and "cheerful" service help keep things pleasant, even when it's "packed cheek to jowl."

### Roti Mediterranean Grill  *Mediterranean*  21 | 13 | 17 | $14

**NEW** **Loop** | 310 W. Adams St. (bet. Franklin St. & Lower Wacker Dr.) | 312-236-3500 ⑤

**River West** | 10 S. Riverside Plaza (bet. Madison & Monroe Sts.) | 312-775-7000 ⑤

**NEW** **Northbrook** | 984 Willow Rd. (Three Lakes Dr.) | 847-418-2400

**NEW** **Vernon Hills** | 1240 E. Route 45 (bet. Hickory Ave. & Shady Ln.) | 847-883-8800

www.rotiusa.com

"Healthy", "delicious choices" of "quick", "counter-service" Mediterranean fare including hummus, falafel and kebabs are served "cafeteria-style" at this chain catering to Loop lunch-breakers and their suburban counterparts; considering the "good value" and "quality", surveyors warn "expect to compete for a chair" for a pay-off that's "refreshingly enjoyable."

### Roy's  *Hawaiian*  25 | 23 | 23 | $53

**River North** | 720 N. State St. (Superior St.) | 312-787-7599 | www.roysrestaurant.com

"Visit the islands" without leaving town at this "transcendent" River North catch, a "stylish", tropically decorated link in the Hawaiian chain where the "fusion" fare – including "butterfish that melts in your mouth" – hooks its share of fanatics; it's just "like every other Roy's" down to an "attentive yet unobtrusive staff", and if cost-crunchers carp that it's "expensive", the "prix fixe is a deal."

|  | FOOD | DECOR | SERVICE | COST |
|---|---|---|---|---|

## Ruby of Siam  *Thai*

23 | 14 | 20 | $18

**Evanston** | 1125 Emerson St. (Ridge Ave.) | 847-492-1008
**Skokie** | Skokie Fashion Sq. | 9420 Skokie Blvd. (Gross Point Rd.) |
847-675-7008
www.rubyofsiam.com

With possibly the "biggest Thai menu in town", this North Shore BYO
duo turns out "outstanding" Siamese "standards" – plus "dishes not
often seen" – for patrons who don't mind less-than-stellar decor and
service considering the "affordable", "high-quality" fare; P.S. the
"lunch buffet is a buy" and a convenient "way to introduce novices
to the pleasures" of the cuisine.

## Rumba  🈂️Ⓜ️  *Nuevo Latino*

▽ 23 | 24 | 25 | $48

**River North** | 351 W. Hubbard St. (bet. N. Kingsbury & N. Orleans Sts.) |
312-222-1226 | www.rumba351.com

Salsa "dancing on the weekends" (the "floor gets packed") and
"people-watching" add to the "lively" vibe at this River North supper
club that also dishes up Nuevo Latino plates; the setting – floor-to-
ceiling red velvet curtains, overstuffed booths – is as "excellent" as the
drinks, which include a signature punch and classic mojito, but the
initiated warn that "service goes downhill" when the decibels rise.

## Russell's Barbecue  *BBQ*

19 | 9 | 14 | $16

**Rolling Meadows** | 2885 Algonquin Rd. (bet. Carriageway &
Newport Drs.) | 847-259-5710
**Elmwood Park** | 1621 N. Thatcher Ave. (North Ave.) | 708-453-7065
www.russellsbarbecue.com

Opened in 1930, this Elmwood Park "landmark" dishes out barbecue "for the ages" say devotees who chow down on the beef and
"pork sandwiches" and other "low-cost", "family-friendly" fare
served on "paper plates"; though it "never changes" (including the
"simple decor") and doubters are "bewildered by all the fuss", nostalgists contend the original "classic" and its Rolling Meadows mate
remain "venerable" choices for "ribs and a beer."

## Russian Tea Time  *Russian*

22 | 22 | 22 | $40

**Loop** | 77 E. Adams St. (bet. Michigan & Wabash Aves.) |
312-360-0000 | www.russianteatime.com

"Borscht" boosters flock to this "atmospheric" (some say "weird,
dark") mahogany-paneled Loop spot serving "authentic", "filling"
Russian cuisine, afternoon tea and "vodka flights" that "sneak up on
you"; naysayers think it needs "new energy" and is "a little overpriced", but pluses include its "convenient location near the Art
Institute" and "pleasant service" that adds to the "civility."

## 🆕 Rustico Grill  *Mexican*

- | - | - | M

**Logan Square** | 2515 N. California Ave. (Altgeld St.) | 773-235-0002 |
www.rusticogrill.com

Enthusiasts are lured by the "incredibly complex moles", tequilas
and mezcals dispensed by this "creative" midpriced Mexican
kitchen with communal seating in Logan Square; while much of its
modern, lodgelike design – glass atrium garden, seasonal dining

area – is attributable to its predecessor, Rustik, few could miss the "attention to detail" that's giving the cuisine a new look.

## ☑ Ruth's Chris Steak House  *Steak*    25 | 20 | 23 | $62

**River North** | 431 N. Dearborn St. (Hubbard St.) | 312-321-2725
**Northbrook** | Renaissance Hotel | 933 Skokie Blvd. (Dundee Rd.) | 847-498-6889
**South Barrington** | Arboretum Mall | 100 W. Higgins Rd. (Rte. 59) | 847-551-3730
www.ruthschris.com

"Prime steaks sizzling in butter" keep herds of carnivores coming to this "big-box" chophouse chain (born in the bayou) with River North and suburban locations, where the "delicious, unique" beef presentation includes a "hot platter"; the "men's club atmosphere" and service that's "their trademark" make it suitable for a special "occasion", with the tabs to match.

## Sabatino's ⏺ *Italian*    24 | 17 | 24 | $33

**Northwest Side** | 4441 W. Irving Park Rd. (bet. Cicero & Pulaski Aves.) | 773-283-8331 | www.sabatinoschicago.com

"You keep waiting for the Rat Pack to stroll in" at this "cavernous" Northwest Side "flashback" decked out in dimly lit "'70s decor" and serving "large portions" of "flaming" "tableside" dishes along with its "old-fashioned", "red-gravy Italian" fare (plus "value"-minded "specials"); though it isn't "hard on the pocketbook", the "Midwest-style service" is "wonderful" and "it's impossible to leave hungry."

## 🆕 Sable Kitchen & Bar  *American*    – | – | – | M

**River North** | Hotel Palomar | 505 N. State St. (Illinois St.) | 312-755-9704 | www.sablechicago.com

At this swanky gastro-lounge in River North's new Kimpton boutique hotel, chef Heather Terhune (ex Atwood Cafe) crafts small, medium and large plates of midpriced, locavore-friendly New American fare, plus brick-oven flatbreads, accompanied by an ambitious cocktail program; the updated 'supper club' setting features cushy leather booths, a big bar, a fireplace and a seasonal patio.

## 🆕 Sabor Saveur  *French/Mexican*    – | – | – | M

**Ukrainian Village** | 2013 W. Division St. (Damen Ave.) | 773-235-7310 | www.saborsaveur.com

"Adventuresome" French-Mexican cuisine is on the menu "full of treats" (including "delicious" hazelnut-sauced lobster enchiladas) cooked up in the open kitchen of this midpriced Ukrainian Village hybrid; the painted white-brick dining room features "white tablecloths", candles in ornate holders and a gallerylike feel, while in the rear a curvaceous "more casual" communal area accommodates "larger parties"; P.S. it's "BYO at the moment."

## Sage Grille ⓂＡ *American*    21 | 21 | 20 | $49

**Highwood** | 260 Green Bay Rd. (Highwood Ave.) | 847-433-7005 | www.sagegrille.com

Offering a "welcome alternative in Highwood", this New American bistro with "something for everyone" is built for "casual" dining but

| | FOOD | DECOR | SERVICE | COST |
|---|---|---|---|---|

"sophisticated" enough for a "night on the town"; a "lovely" dining room, "competent staff" and "carefully chosen wine list" buffer slightly "pricey" tabs, and "live music is a plus" with jazz on Fridays.

### Sai Café  *Japanese*

| 25 | 16 | 20 | $41 |
|---|---|---|---|

**Lincoln Park** | 2010 N. Sheffield Ave. (Armitage Ave.) | 773-472-8080 | www.saicafe.com

"Solid sushi" from "friendly", "skilled chefs" draws devotees to this "reliable" Lincoln Park Japanese "neighborhood place" where "portions are large" and diners feel "welcome"; though some find it a little "expensive" with a "limited" wine and sake list, three differently decorated rooms lure everyone from "singles" to "seniors" to "families."

### Saloon Steakhouse, The  *Steak*

| 23 | 20 | 22 | $56 |
|---|---|---|---|

**Streeterville** | Seneca Hotel | 200 E. Chestnut St.
(Mies Van Der Rohe Way) | 312-280-5454 | www.saloonsteakhouse.com

An "alternative to the see-and-be-seen" options, this "busy" Streeterville steakhouse "well-hidden" in the Seneca Hotel serves "great food without the 'tude", "tourists" or "uptightness"; the "neighborhood" clientele calls it a "value" for its "jumbo martinis", "insanely sized portions" and "outstanding rib-eyes" as much as the "retro"-meets-"metro" setting, "attentive, knowledgeable" service and the ability to "hear your own conversation."

### Salpicón  *Mexican*

| 26 | 20 | 23 | $49 |
|---|---|---|---|

**Old Town** | 1252 N. Wells St. (bet. Goethe & Scott Sts.) | 312-988-7811 | www.salpicon.com

Amigos attest this "smolderingly sublime", "upscale" Old Towner offers "genius" "modern Mexican creations" (such as "finger-licking-good quail") from Priscila Satkoff along with an "outstanding" tequila selection and a wine list that's "one of the best around"; while a "lively" colorful space that's "relatively small and challenged" leaves some "begging for more comfortable seating", "super-personal service" adds incentive to "look for excuses to return"; a post-Survey remodeling is not reflected in the Decor score.

### Salsa 17  *Mexican*

| 22 | 21 | 21 | $29 |
|---|---|---|---|

### (fka Fuego Mexican Grill & Margarita Bar)

**Arlington Heights** | 17 W. Campbell St. (bet. Dunton & Vail Aves.) | 847-590-1122 | www.fuegomexicangrill.com

"Upscale compared to most" "neighborhood Mexican" cantinas, this renamed Arlington Heights spot offers an "extensive menu" of moderately priced "inventive dishes" ("don't miss the moles"), "guacamole made fresh tableside" and "great margaritas"; it's "fun" "for couples or family" but even amigos find the "noise level" "overwhelming" on "mariachi band nights."

### Sam & Harry's Steakhouse  *Steak*

| - | - | - | E |
|---|---|---|---|

**Schaumburg** | Renaissance Schaumburg Hotel & Convention Ctr. | 1551 N. Thoreau Dr. (Meacham Rd.) | 847-303-4050 | www.samandharrys.com

"Sweet", "succulent" crab legs and aged prime Delmonico and other steaks net regulars and conventioneers at this national chain location that's "a bit hidden" in the Renaissance Schaumburg Hotel; generally "attentive service" and "impressive decor" including white linens and candlelight are pluses, though some call the "quality"-to-"money" ratio "just ok."

### San Gabriel Mexican Cafe  *Mexican*   17 | 15 | 14 | $31

**Bannockburn** | Bannockburn Green Shopping Ctr. | 2535 Waukegan Rd. (Half Day Rd.) | 847-940-0200 | www.sangabcafe.com

"Excellent" "tableside-made guacamole", an extensive tequila selection and "margaritas with fresh-squeezed lime juice" attract spice-lovers to this upscale, midpriced Bannockburn hacienda in a "strip mall" – one of the few options for "Mexican in Lake County"; though a few shrug there's "nothing memorable" about the menu, the decor is "authentic" and there's "outdoor seating in the summer too."

### Sanook  *Japanese/Thai*   - | - | - | M

**North Center/St. Ben's** | 2845 W. Irving Park Rd. (Mozart St.) | 773-463-7299 | www.sanookchicago.com

There's a clubby vibe to this contemporary, midpriced Pan-Asian BYO in North Center, where faraway landscapes are projected on walls and a large menu of "competently prepared Thai dishes" and inventive sushi reel in a crowd; those who are "unimpressed" find the blue-and-white setting "sterile" and the service "lacking."

### San Soo Gab San  ● *Korean*   ▽ 21 | 12 | 14 | $31

**Northwest Side** | 5247 N. Western Ave. (Foster Ave.) | 773-334-1589

When late-night kalbi cravings hit, surveyors navigate to the Northwest Side and this midpriced "Korean barbecue joint" in Lincoln Square, where the tables are filled with "little [side] dishes"; sure, it helps to "know Korean" and the "smoky" scent leaves diners ready to "shower afterwards", but that's a small price to pay for such "consistently" "delicious" grub – even "at 2 AM."

### Santorini  ● *Greek/Seafood*   21 | 20 | 20 | $37

**Greektown** | 800 W. Adams St. (Halsted St.) | 312-829-8820 | www.santorinichicago.com

Shouts of *"opa!"* punctuate this "inviting" Halsted Street "taverna" that "excels at seafood" – including "terrific chargrilled octopus" – and other "reasonably priced" fare offered with "gracious service"; loyalists swear it was "transplanted straight from the Aegean" and is "a cut above most Greektown places", particularly when in the "cozy bar" or by the "warm fireplace in winter", plus it's a "hit with a group"; P.S. "valet parking" is complimentary.

### Sapore di Napoli  Ⓜ *Pizza*   ▽ 20 | 9 | 16 | $23

**Lakeview** | 1406 W. Belmont Ave. (Southport Ave.) | 773-935-1212 | www.saporedinapoli.net

"An alternative to Chicago deep-dish", the "Neapolitan pizzas" at this kid-friendly Lakeview BYO – "thin-crust", "wood-fired" pies topped with the "freshest of ingredients" – are a "great getaway" from their heftier competitors; whether dining in (yes, they accept reservations) or doing takeout, a "selection of gelato", open kitchen and thrifty tabs are added reasons to frequent the small, casual, earth-toned storefront.

### Sapori Trattoria *Italian* 23 | 18 | 23 | $36

**Lincoln Park** | 2701 N. Halsted St. (Schubert Ave.) | 773-832-9999 | www.saporitrattoria.net

"Families" and other locals flock to this Lincoln Park "neighborhood trattoria" where the "simple", "consistent" midpriced Italian fare includes handmade pasta and desserts that "shine"; regulars know to "make a reservation" and request "outdoor seating in summer", as it's sometimes "impossible to talk" in the "cozy interior" with "warm brick and low lighting"; a "helpful staff", "reasonably priced wines" and "frequent diner's discounts" sweeten the deal.

### Sarkis Cafe ⊅ *Diner* ▽ 15 | 5 | 13 | $14

**Evanston** | 2632 Gross Point Rd. (Crawford St.) | 847-328-9703

"Colorful local characters" and "Northwestern kids" "with hangovers" wolf down breakfasts (especially omelets) and other cheap diner fare – including a famed, cheesy sausage sandwich dubbed the "disaster" – from Evanston's quintessential, if "small", "greasy spoon" with a name that pays homage to its "unique" original owner; though detractors assure the "fixture" is "stuck in '70s mode", cognoscenti concur if you're willing to "accept this place for what it is", it's generally "enjoyable."

### NEW Sarks in the Park *Sandwiches* - | - | - | I

**Lincoln Park** | 444 W. Fullerton Pkwy. (Clark St.) | 773-404-9000 | www.sarksinthepark.com

Lincoln Parkers "no longer have to drive to the suburbs", heading instead to this "popular" nook (a sibling of the Evanston original) for AM eats including omelets and breakfast sandwiches with homemade sausage on French bread; it's a "knockout location for outdoor eating", though the "tiny" space and "complacent service" strike some as "nothing to write home about"; N.B. hours are expanded in summer.

### Sayat Nova *Armenian* 23 | 19 | 21 | $28

**Streeterville** | 157 E. Ohio St. (bet. Michigan Ave. & St. Clair St.) | 312-644-9159 | www.sayatnovachicago.com

"Wonderful aromas" greet devotees of this "friendly", "decades"-old Streeterville Armenian adorned with cut-out lanterns and "hidden" just "steps off Michigan Avenue"; even the "outstanding lamb" dishes "won't break the bank" – although a "parking space" may cost "twice the price" of a meal; N.B. a DJ spins Thursday and Saturday nights.

### ☑ Schwa ⊠Ⓜ *American* 29 | 15 | 25 | $105

**Wicker Park** | 1466 N. Ashland Ave. (Le Moyne St.) | 773-252-1466 | www.schwarestaurant.com

Zealots call Michael Carlson a "god among men" for his "fascinating" New American cuisine with "bright, surprising flavors" and a "side of wit"; the prix fixe menu is "served by the chefs", adding to an "unforgettable" experience that unfolds in a "relaxed", "small" Wicker

Park BYO storefront; though it's "not inexpensive", fans contend it offers a "wonderful value", and if a few gripe that this "quirky" place comes off as "too complicated for its good", the fact that you must "persevere" to "secure a reservation" proves they're outvoted.

### Scoozi! *Italian*                                    19 | 20 | 20 | $36

**River North** | 410 W. Huron St. (bet. Kingsbury & Orleans Sts.) |
312-943-5900 | www.leye.com

"After all these years", this "consistent" River North Lettuce Entertain You Italian "standby" is still "buzzing with laughter" and crowds – complete with "squirmy kids" – in its art deco setting; service is "enthusiastic" and the thin-crust, brick-oven pizza and homemade gnocchi have fans, though dissenters suggest the midpriced "Americanized" fare and scene aren't "intended to be taken seriously."

### ☒ Seasons *American*                              27 | 25 | 27 | $83

**Gold Coast** | Four Seasons Hotel | 120 E. Delaware Pl., 7th fl.
(bet. Michigan Ave. & Rush St.) | 312-649-2349 | www.fourseasons.com

Acolytes aver the "formal" experience "never fails" at this "swelle-gant" Gold Coast hotel eatery, where "fabulous" dining on chef Kevin Hickey's "innovative" seasonal New American cuisine merits the "big splurge"; even if the "room looks like every other Four Seasons", the view from the seventh floor combined with a "comfortable", "quiet" setting and "phenomenal" service make for a "perfect evening"; P.S. Sunday "brunch is wonderful."

### Seasons 52 *American*                            – | – | – | M

**Schaumburg** | 1770 E. Higgins Rd. | 847-517-5252

A national 'fresh grill' chain with a calorie-counting concept – no dish over 475 calories, including custom flatbreads and mini desserts – comes to Northwest Suburban Schaumburg serving midpriced New American lunch and dinner crafted with local ingredients, with 60 wines by the glass and specialty martinis from the bar; the hand-some, upscale environment with warm wood and rustic stone elements features a fireplace and piano bar.

### Sepia *American*                                  24 | 24 | 24 | $56

**West Loop** | 123 N. Jefferson St. (bet. Randolph & Washington Sts.) |
312-441-1920 | www.sepiachicago.com

"Interesting", "not too-clever" New American fare by NoMI vet Andrew Zimmerman – much of it "locavore" "riffs on classic dishes" – plus "fantastic" cocktails draw devotees to this "pricey", "beautiful", "modern" yet "warm" "Michelle Obama favorite" in the West Loop; "muted lighting" sparks "tête-à-têtes" (when it's not "monstrously noisy") and the "cordial" service can get "harried at times", but mostly it's "wonderful in every possible way."

### 1776 ☒ *American*                                22 | 18 | 22 | $40

**Crystal Lake** | 397 W. Virginia St./Rte. 14 (bet. Dole & McHenry Aves.) |
815-356-1776 | www.1776restaurant.com

Loyalists proclaim they're "treated like family" by the "informed staff" – including "owner Andy [Andresky], a font of wine advice" for the 600-bottle list – at this "reliable" "favorite in Crystal Lake" that dishes out "fair portions" of "inventive" New American cuisine including "wonderful game"; the setting is "comfortable", but the resistance reckons it's "getting old" and the sometimes "pricey" fare is not all "it should be"; still, "way out" in the Northwest Suburbs, "it's the best you'll find."

### ☑ Shanghai Terrace ☒ *Asian*    25 | 28 | 27 | $66

**River North** | Peninsula Hotel | 108 E. Superior St., 5th fl. (bet. Michigan Ave. & Rush St.) | 312-573-6744 | www.chicago.peninsula.com

A "stunning", '30s-style Asian supper club setting sets the stage at this expensive, "elegant" and "tranquil" respite in the Peninsula Hotel in River North, where acolytes claim they've had some of the "best Chinese meals outside of China"; "wonderful" Michigan Avenue views from the "outdoor terrace" in summer add to the appeal, as does "knowledgeable" service, though the less-smitten are "disappointed" that the former "chef is gone"; N.B. hours vary by season.

### ☑ Shaw's Crab House *Seafood*    24 | 21 | 23 | $50

**River North** | 21 E. Hubbard St. (bet. State St. & Wabash Ave.) | 312-527-2722
**Schaumburg** | 1900 E. Higgins Rd. (Rte. 53) | 847-517-2722
www.shawscrabhouse.com

"Like an old friend", this "justly crowded" River North "fish house" "favorite" (with a Schaumburg sibling) from Lettuce Entertain You "always delivers" a "dependable" experience featuring "hand-shucked" bivalves, "huge king crab legs" and global, sustainably focused seafood served in the oyster bar and "throwback-chic" dining room; the "service can't be beat", but this "trip to the ocean-side" "ain't cheap" – unless you just come for a "designer martini" and "great jazz"; N.B. both locations offer a popular brunch buffet on Sunday.

### Shikago ☒ *Asian*    ▽ 18 | 16 | 18 | $39

**Loop** | 190 S. LaSalle St. (Adams St.) | 312-781-7300 | www.shikagorestaurant.com

Patrons of this "hidden" Asian spot amid the Loop's "financial district" "action" say Alan Shikami's low-lit setting – adorned with modern art and tables made from reclaimed 100-year-old trees – makes a "good alternative" for a "personal or business lunch" or dinner; service is "fast, if need be", though the midpriced izakaya-style menu of ramen, sushi and sizzle plates strikes some as "nothing special"; N.B. private functions can be held in the Philip Johnson-designed library on the building's 39th floor.

### Shine Morida *Chinese/Japanese*    - | - | - | M

**Lincoln Park** | 756 W. Webster Ave. (Halsted St.) | 773-296-0101 | www.shinemorida.com

In Lincoln Park down the street from its original digs, this "dependable" Chinese–Japanese "combo" with two dining rooms – one dim and relaxed, the other a brighter sushi bar – remains a "cut above" your average "neighborhood" spot; it suits "any occasion" by appealing to "raw-fish-fearing friends" and fin fans alike thanks to its varied menu, "welcoming" staff and "hot" entrees in "huge portions for the price."

## Shui Wah  *Chinese*
∇ 24 | 4 | 13 | $18

**Chinatown** | 2162 S. Archer Ave. (Cermak Rd.) | 312-225-8811

"Everyone knows how good it is" confirm cognoscenti of this budget-loving Chinatowner and its "excellent selection" of "no-frills dim sum" offered from breakfast through lunchtime (it's open for dinner too); salt-and-pepper squid, Hong Kong–style dumplings and such are ordered "off a list" rather than "carted around" the small, carpeted room – just "be prepared to wait" for a table.

## Shula's Steakhouse  *Steak*
21 | 20 | 20 | $62

**Streeterville** | Sheraton Chicago Hotel & Towers | 301 E. North Water St. (Columbus Dr.) | 312-670-0788

**Itasca** | Westin Chicago NW | 400 Park Blvd. (Thorndale Ave.) | 630-775-1499

www.donshula.com

Cheerleaders of this "memorabilia"-laden steak chain promise "even Bears fans" feel at home at the Streeterville and Itasca outposts decorated in an undefeated 1972 Dolphins theme; diners who'd opt to "read a football rather than throw one" (the menu's printed on a pigskin) praise "large" cuts of beef, "comfortable booths" "roomy" enough for a "lineman" and service with "great humor", though some feel they "drop the ball" with the price.

## NEW Siboney Cuban Cuisine  *Cuban*
- | - | - | I

**Bucktown** | 2165 N. Western Ave. (bet. Palmer St. & Shakespeare Ave.) | 773-904-7210 | www.siboneychicago.com

"Intensely flavorful" ropa vieja lures surveyors to Bucktown's "pretty" Cuban storefront with its bright, mural-decorated exterior; once inside the casual-chic, wood-trimmed dining room with moody lighting, vintage tin ceiling and slow-spinning tropical fans, expect "outstanding" service and "reasonable prices", with Latin jazz Thursday–Sunday helping smooth out any missteps.

## ☑ Signature Room  *American*
18 | 26 | 19 | $54

**Streeterville** | John Hancock Ctr. | 875 N. Michigan Ave., 95th fl. (bet. Chestnut St. & Delaware Pl.) | 312-787-9596 | www.signatureroom.com

"When out-of-towners are in tow", surveyors "skip the Hancock Observatory" and head for this 95th-floor Streeterville American where the "view on a clear day" is so "priceless" that "marriage proposals arrive daily"; an "impressive" Sunday brunch and Saturday lunch buffet (an "unbelievable deal") are further incentives to overlook sometimes "erratic service", "dated" decor and "unpredictable" fare; P.S. don't forget to "check out" the vista "from the ladies' room."

## Sikia  Ⓜ *African*
- | - | - | M

**Far South Side** | Washburne Culinary Institute | 740 W. 63rd St. (Halsted St.) | 773-602-5200 | www.ccc.edu/sikia

This on-campus African restaurant is a "diamond in the rough", operated for dinner Thursday through Saturday by "students" at

Englewood's Washburne Culinary Institute; the "vibrant" BYOB –
adorned with "interesting artwork" and "artifacts" – leaves most
diners "surprised" by fare such as "wonderful tagines" delivered by
a "hospitable staff" at moderate prices; N.B. Sunday brunch and live
entertainment on weekends are added Incentives.

### Silver Seafood ● *Chinese/Seafood*　　23 | 10 | 16 | $23

**Uptown** | 4829 N. Broadway St. (Lawrence Ave.) | 773-784-0668
For "excellent" Cantonese "north of Chinatown", surveyors stop by
this affordable Uptown "family-style" storefront with a "large",
"varied" menu emphasizing "fresh", "first-rate" seafood; adventure-
seekers recommend "jumping off the deep end" to order from the
more "authentic" specialties but warn "language can be an issue",
as can the lack of service and "shabby surroundings"; N.B. only beer,
wine and sake are served.

### Simply It Ⓜ *Vietnamese*　　22 | 11 | 18 | $22

**Lincoln Park** | 2269 N. Lincoln Ave. (Belden Ave.) | 773-248-0884 |
www.simplyitrestaurant.com
"The name says it all" at this "super-hospitable" Vietnamese "gem"
in Lincoln Park from a former owner of the "late, lamented Pasteur",
where the "killer value" at lunch and "BYO policy" help make for an
"easy-on-the-wallet" "best-kept secret"; "outstanding" pho and
"clay pot preparations" are some of the reasons greedy types say it
"deserves some attention" but "not too much."

### ☒ Sixteen *American*　　22 | 27 | 22 | $100

**River North** | Trump International Hotel & Tower | 401 N. Wabash Ave.
(Kinzie St.) | 312-588-8030 | www.trumpchicagohotel.com
A "voyeur's view of the city" distinguishes Trump International Hotel &
Tower's "stunning" River Norther, where 30-ft. "floor-to-ceiling windows" and a "striking" Swarovski-crystal chandelier are a backdrop for
"delicious" New American fare that's "creative" but not "gimmicky";
"polite", "professional service" and a deep wine list complete an
"over-the-top" package enjoyed "best on an expense account."

### Smith & Wollensky *Steak*　　23 | 22 | 23 | $63

**River North** | 318 N. State St. (Upper Wacker Dr.) | 312-670-9900 |
www.smithandwollensky.com
Steakhouse stalwarts recommend bringing "an extra stomach",
"your wallet and someone else's" plus "your cardiologist on speed
dial" to this "nostalgic", clubby River Norther with a "riverside" location offering "fantastic views" – especially from the "patio"; while
some detractors assert it "isn't as memorable" as the NYC original,
the majority of the "well-heeled crowd" (including businessmen)
appreciates the "knowledgeable staff" and "fine cuts of beef."

### ☒ Smoke Daddy *BBQ*　　24 | 14 | 18 | $25

**Wicker Park** | 1804 W. Division St. (Wood St.) | 773-772-6656 |
www.thesmokedaddy.com
"Real-deal Q", "slow-grilled and oh-so-smoky" attracts "neighborhood" ribs lovers to this "crowded" Wicker Park "joint" with a retro

vibe – and on most nights, "live music" to "keep you entertained" during the "wait time"; with an "offbeat staff" and "funky setting" featuring jazz and other "memorabilia" plus "interesting beers" and "cheap" tabs, cravers ask "how can you go wrong?"

### ☑ Smoque BBQ Ⓜ *BBQ*                 26 | 10 | 18 | $19

**Northwest Side** | 3800 N. Pulaski Rd. (Grace St.) | 773-545-7427 | www.smoquebbq.com

An "unexpected gem in an unexpected spot", this Northwest Side BYO is where "brisket lovers" "don't wear good clothes" to dive into "messy" but "terrific" barbecue ribs and other "beyond belief" smoked meat; despite "efficient" "counter service", fans "rub elbows with neighbors" at "cramped" tables when lucky – and endure "lines out the door" when not – but most agree this "decently priced" "real thing" is "worth it"; P.S. "save room for the sides" including "amazing mac 'n' cheese."

### socca *French/Italian*                 22 | 18 | 20 | $42

**Lakeview** | 3301 N. Clark St. (Aldine Ave.) | 773-248-1155 | www.soccachicago.com

"Fools" can go on "waiting an eternity" "down the street" say regulars of this "little gem" in Lakeview dishing up "reasonably priced", "upper-end" Italian-French "must tries" in "laid-back", bistro-style surroundings; service is "attentive", and when the dining room gets "conversationally challenged", the "lovely outdoor seating" is a "delightful" fair-weather alternative.

### sola *American*                 25 | 21 | 22 | $45

**Lakeview** | 3868 N. Lincoln Ave. (Byron St.) | 773-327-3868 | www.sola-restaurant.com

Chef-owner Carol Wallack turns out "consistently" "wonderful" New American dishes with a "seasonal" "Hawaiian-Asian" influence in "surprisingly casual" Lakeview digs; the "innovative" fish dishes "amaze" (you'd "trade your firstborn" for a taste), but this "refined" "neighborhood" "heavyweight" also serves a "superb" weekend brunch loaded with "twists" on "breakfast classics"; though most find the service "solid", some admit "if the place is busy", it "can be slow."

### Sol de Mexico *Mexican*                 25 | 19 | 23 | $34

**Northwest Side** | 3018 N. Cicero Ave. (bet. Nelson St. & Wellington Ave.) | 773-282-4119 | www.soldemexicochicago.com

Experience "mole to the max" urge compadres of this "cozy" mid-priced regional Mexican "joint" on the Northwest Side that fans reckon would be "booked solid" if not for its "location" along a "desolate stretch of Cicero"; those deeming it "worth the drive" to the colorful digs are "still talking about" the "glorious" lamb in Oaxacan black mole, "impressive" tequila list and "charming staff."

### 🆕 Southern, The 🗲 *Southern*                 - | - | - | M

**Bucktown** | 1840 W. North Ave. (Honore St.) | 773-342-1840 | www.thesouthernchicago.com

The former Chaise Lounge is reborn as this more casual, late-night Bucktown Southerner with creative and classic bar food, plates and

FOOD | DECOR | SERVICE | COST

sides accompanied by beers and cocktails with a drawl (including punches by the carafe); high-tops with steel stools, reclaimed wood banquettes and safety lighting lend a raw, stylized look to the first floor, while the second-floor roof-deck houses two cozy draped cabanas along with lounge-style seating.

### South Gate Cafe  *American*   20 | 18 | 21 | $38

**Lake Forest** | 655 Forest Ave. (Deerpath Rd.) | 847-234-8800 | www.southgatecafe.com

"You won't find a better" patio "in summertime" promise patrons who remain "delighted" by this "longtime" Lake Forest midpriced American set in a century-old building; though service may sometimes be "slow", enthusiasts enjoy the "constantly changing" seasonal "eclectic" menu, especially for "lunch in the garden room."

### Southport Grocery & Café  *Sandwiches*   22 | 14 | 17 | $18

**Lakeview** | 3552 N. Southport Ave. (bet. Addison & Eddy Sts.) | 773-665-0100 | www.southportgrocery.com

The "wait" "on weekends" for brunch is "brutal" but "worth it" vouch veterans of this "crowded" Lakeview grocer and affordable New American cafe that "satisfies your sweet tooth" with "cupcake pancakes" and mascarpone- and preserve-filled "adult pop tarts"; the "fresh and healthy" lunch options and sandwiches are "awesome" too, so that complaints that it's "too small" and service can be "slow" are drowned out by fans' "stomach growling."

### South Water Kitchen  *American*   16 | 16 | 18 | $33

**Loop** | Hotel Monaco | 225 N. Wabash Ave. (Lake St.) | 312-236-9300 | www.southwaterkitchen.com

Feeling like a "hideaway" "surrounded" by "tourist-laden joints", this "solid" Loop American adjacent to the Hotel Monaco dishes up "varied" regional "home cooking" that's "priced right"; the "cozy, casual" setting is "welcoming on cold winter days and nights", and while snipers snip that "nothing stands out", proponents note that it's "convenient" to theaters and works for "Downtown lunch or after-work drinks."

### Spacca Napoli Pizzeria  M *Pizza*   23 | 18 | 21 | $27

**Ravenswood** | 1769 W. Sunnyside Ave. (bet. Hermitage & Ravenswood Aves.) | 773-878-2420 | www.spaccanapolipizzeria.com

Groupies of this "authentic" Neapolitan pizzeria in Ravenswood gush about its "'scary great" pies with "heavenly crusts" that are "never overwhelmed" by their "supporting cast" of "fresh ingredients" – provided "you don't mind waiting" "for a table"; the "convivial" atmosphere adds to the appeal for most with "friendly service" that's "like visiting your Italian grandma", though a few find the fare "a bit pricey"; N.B. the Decor score does not reflect a post-Survey expansion.

### Z Spiaggia  *Italian*   27 | 27 | 27 | $93

**Gold Coast** | One Magnificent Mile Bldg. | 980 N. Michigan Ave., 2nd fl. (Oak St.) | 312-280-2750 | www.spiaggiarestaurant.com

"It may be cheaper to fly to Rome" than to dine at Tony Mantuano's Gold Coast "destination", but surveyors succumb to the "breathtak-

| | FOOD | DECOR | SERVICE | COST |
|---|---|---|---|---|

ing" cheese selection, "delicate, handmade pastas", "velvety sauces" and entrees that "sing your name" matched by a "superb", "extensive Italian wine list"; the "quiet", "elegant", "multilevel" dining room offering "exquisite views of the lake" – alone "an experience" – has "attentive" yet "unobtrusive" service, but "as astounding as it is", some favor the less "formal" "cafe next door"; N.B. jackets are required.

### Spoon Thai  *Thai*                                23 | 14 | 19 | $21

**Lincoln Square** | 4608 N. Western Ave. (Wilson Ave.) | 773-769-1173 | www.spoonthai.com

Fanatics call this budget-friendly "authentic" Lincoln Square BYO "not your average Thai" – especially if you're "adventurous" enough to "order off" the translated "no-longer-secret" menu ("try the Isaan sausage"); while some "stick to the specials and authentic items", others go for the "usual choices"; still, the "simple" setting and service aren't quite as "lovely" as the "delicious" fare.

### ☒ Spring ☒ *American/Seafood*                     27 | 24 | 26 | $59

**Wicker Park** | 2039 W. North Ave. (Damen Ave.) | 773-395-7100 | www.springrestaurant.net

Acolytes attest "it's criminal that they make you choose" since all the fare is "superb" at Shawn McClain's "serene, spare" Asian-tinged New American seafooder in a converted Wicker Park bathhouse, where the fish is so "divine" "there's no reason to get anything else", though the "creative" menu proves "all-around satisfying" with "fabulous cocktails" and an "awesome" "wine list to match"; the "elegant" minimalist setting "allows for privacy" and the service is "outstanding", adding up to an "absolutely wonderful", "unique experience" surveyors call "reasonably priced" for the "quality."

### Spring World  *Chinese*                           - | - | - | M

**Chinatown** | 2109 S. China Pl. (Wells St.) | 312-326-9966

"One of the hidden" Chinatown "gems", this Yunnan "quiet storefront" preps "wonderful", spicy dishes (anything with "special mushrooms" is "to die for"); though it may be "a bit pricier" than its neighbors, the "unusual" fare helps justify the expense, earning it cult status.

### NEW Sprout ☒☒ *American/French*                   28 | 22 | 24 | $82

**Lincoln Park** | 1417 W. Fullerton Ave. (bet. Janssen & Southport Aves.) | 773-348-0706 | www.sproutrestaurant.com

Dale Levitski's "mysterious", "cryptic" prix fixe menu "surprises", delivering "real excitement" and "complex flavors" at this "inspired", "high-end" "seasonal" French-American bistro in Lincoln Park; low lighting, red-velvet banquettes and French doors that open to an enclosed patio lend the "attractive" space a "welcoming" feeling; wines, beers and libations – like the earthy name – lean organic.

### Stained Glass Wine Bar Bistro  *American*         23 | 19 | 22 | $46

**Evanston** | 1735 Benson Ave. (bet. Church & Clark Sts.) | 847-864-8600 | www.thestainedglass.com

"Ever-changing" flights and a "strong" wine list lend credibility to this "intimate" exposed-brick "Evanston staple" with a "serious", slightly pricey American menu that samplers deem built for "grazing" (but there are entrees too); while often "crowded", this storefront remains a "favorite" among "novices and wine snobs" alike, though service ranges from "spotty" to "friendly" and "knowledgeable."

### Stanley's Kitchen & Tap  *American*     18 | 15 | 14 | $19
**Lincoln Park** | 1970 N. Lincoln Ave. (Armitage Ave.) | 312-642-0007

### Stanley's on Racine  *American*
**West Loop** | 324 S. Racine Ave. (bet. Jackson Blvd. & Van Buren St.) | 312-433-0007
www.stanleyskitchenandtap.com

"Down-home" and "laid-back", this American duo with Lincoln Park and West Loop outposts dishes up "quality" "comfort food" that's "the next-best thing" to "carbo-loading" at "grandma's house" – providing granny enjoys "a little hair of the dog"; the "cheap" regular menu includes "unbeatable fried chicken and mac 'n' cheese", and "weekend brunch" is a guaranteed "hangover cure", just don't be in a rush because the "staff is slow."

### Star of Siam  *Thai*     20 | 17 | 19 | $21
**River North** | 11 E. Illinois St. (State St.) | 312-670-0100 | www.starofsiamchicago.com

Among the most "established" Thai eateries in town (opened in 1984), this "inexpensive" mainstay with "faux floor seating" plus "regular tables" "never disappoints" its followers, who find it a "cozy", "dependable" spot for "big servings" in River North; purists opine "it's probably not very authentic", but with "quick", "friendly service", it's a viable "lunch option."

### NEW State and Lake  *American*     21 | 20 | 22 | $38
**Loop** | theWit Hotel | 201 N. State St. (Lake St.) | 312-239-9400 | www.stateandlakechicago.com

Named after its location, theWit hotel's ground-floor "hot spot" in the Loop is a "delight" with its "cool", curvaceous bar lined with seltzer bottles and "pleasant" earthy-hued dining room for "creative" "reasonably priced" New American fare; cognoscenti call it "convenient" and "quick" for lunch or dinner with a staff that's "eager to please."

### Steve's Deli  *Deli*     17 | 13 | 16 | $18
**River North** | 354 W. Hubbard St. (bet. Kingsbury & Orleans Sts.) | 312-467-6868 | www.stevesdeli.com

"Delicious" deli fare hits River North by way of this casually decorated Michigan transplant that serves "huge" sandwiches (corned beef, brisket, chopped liver), salads and hearty soups; those with quibbles find it "a bit overpriced" and "cannot understand the popularity."

### Stir Crazy  *Asian*     19 | 17 | 18 | $24
**Northbrook** | Northbrook Court Shopping Ctr. | 1186 Northbrook Ct. (Lake Cook Rd.) | 847-562-4800
**Schaumburg** | Woodfield Mall | 5 Woodfield Mall (Frontage & Golf Rds.) | 847-330-1200

*(continued)*

*(continued)*

## Stir Crazy

**Oak Brook** | Oakbrook Center Mall | 105 Oakbrook Ctr. (Rte. 83) |
630-575-0155
**Warrenville** | 28252 Diehl Rd. (Windfield Rd.) | 630-393-4700
www.stircrazy.com

"If your meal isn't good, you have yourself to blame" given that most choose to "assemble ingredients" for their stir-fries at these economical, "ever popular" Asian woks that "cater to families" with "suburban palates"; those who accept it "for what it is" and are willing to get "creative" or order off the menu find it "worthwhile."

## SugarToad *American*                      19 | 19 | 19 | $53

**Naperville** | Hotel Arista | 2139 CityGate Ln. (bet. Ferry Rd. & I-88) |
630-579-7840 | www.sugartoad.com
In a dining room designed by Dirk Lohan, grandson of Mies van der Rohe, this New American "hidden in" Naperville's Hotel Arista serves farm-focused regional cuisine; though fans call it a "rare jewel", others come with "high expectations", only to have them "dashed" by "overpriced" meals and iffy service.

## Sullivan's Steakhouse *Steak*              22 | 21 | 20 | $57

**River North** | 415 N. Dearborn St. (Hubbard St.) | 312-527-3510
**Lincolnshire** | 250 Marriott Dr. (Milwaukee Ave.) | 847-883-0311
**Naperville** | 244 S. Main St. (bet. Jackson & Jefferson Aves.) |
630-305-0230
www.sullivansteakhouse.com
Beef eaters declare this "clubby" 1940s-inspired threesome ("part of a national chain") "worth the price" of admission for a "faithful steakhouse experience"; though some think others "in town are better" and decry spotty service, a "bustling bar", signature martinis and live jazz "add value."

## Sunda *Asian*                             23 | 24 | 20 | $55

**River North** | 110 W. Illinois St. (bet. Clark & LaSalle Sts.) |
312-644-0500 | www.sundachicago.com
The "prettiest people" "fight the crowds" for a table at this "hip", "happening" River North "knockout" from the Rockit Bar & Grill team with a "contemporary" setting and a "unique take" on Asian fusion fare that's "long on style"; the initiated urge bring "friends so you can try everything" including the "amazing duck buns", "interesting sushi" and "handcrafted cocktails"; add in a "courteous", "knowledgeable" staff" and "what's not to like" – except perhaps the "high" prices.

## ☒ Superdawg Drive-In *Burgers/Hot Dogs*   21 | 15 | 18 | $11

**Northwest Side** | 6363 N. Milwaukee Ave. (Devon Ave.) |
773-763-0660 ●🍴
**Southwest Side** | Midway Int'l Airport | 5700 S. Cicero Ave. (55th St.) |
773-948-6300
**NEW** Wheeling | 333 S. Milwaukee Ave. (Mors Ave.) | 847-459-1900
www.superdawg.com
"Return to your adolescent years" at Chicago's No. 1 Bang for the Buck, a "kitschy" "car-hopping" Northwest Side "drive-in" "icon"

(with Wheeling and airport outposts) where the "dawgs" come "stuffed" into a "cute box" and deliver an "elevated" "spin" on the Chicago hot dog (even if the "relish is a little too green"); though "cravers" concede "the car steers itself here" for "easy-on-the-budget" "burgers, fries" and "thick shakes" too, the "freaky blinking-eyed mascots" on the roof "are reason enough to go."

### Sura ◐ *Thai* ▽ 20 | 19 | 16 | $24

**Lakeview** | 3124 N. Broadway (Briar Pl.) | 773-248-7872 | www.surachicago.com

"It's like eating inside of an iPod" declare fans of this "hip", futuristic Lakeview Thai with clear, hemispheric seats hanging from the ceiling; popular with the after-work crowd, it features a menu that's built "for sharing", so everyone can "try several items"; insiders also note that everything is "value"-minded befitting a "local" crowd.

### Sushi Ai *Japanese* - | - | - | M

**Palatine** | 710 W. Euclid Ave. (Parkside Dr.) | 847-221-5100

"Downtown caliber sushi" lures fish fanciers to this Japanese in a Palatine "strip mall", where "fresh", "artfully prepared" signature rolls (e.g. the Dirty Old Man) offer "unexpected pleasure" at moderate prices; "comfortable booths and tables" and "attentive" but "not overbearing" service are enhanced by conversation starters on walls adorned with '50s-era records and bold, modern art.

### Sushi Naniwa *Japanese* 23 | 15 | 23 | $38

**River North** | 607 N. Wells St. (bet. Ohio & Ontario Sts.) | 312-255-8555 | www.sushinaniwa.com

Supporters call this "fantastic" River North Japanese a "low-key version" of its sibling, Bob San, minus the "frills, bells, whistles" and "long waits"; fortunately, the "reasonably priced" selection of "high-quality", "super-fresh" "slabs of sushi" and "solid" "cooked" dishes make up for the "unassuming" "straightforward" setting, as does service that's taken a ratings jump; P.S. the "patio is great for summer."

### SushiSamba rio ◐ *Japanese/S American* 21 | 24 | 19 | $51

**River North** | 504 N. Wells St. (bet. Grand Ave. & Illinois St.) | 312-595-2300 | www.sushisamba.com

"Hold on to your hats" for an "East meets South" experience at River North's "sexy", "clubby" hub for Brazilian-Peruvian-Japanese cuisine; the "attractive", "over-the-top" dining room lures "celebs" and others who "go to be seen" and are willing to "pay for" the "ambiance", which comes complete with an "aural assault" and "péppy servers"; P.S. the "cool" year-round rooftop deck is a "killer" perch for cocktails.

### NEW Sushi Taiyo *Japanese* - | - | - | M

**River North** | Sheraton Four Points Hotel | 58 E. Ontario St. (bet. Rush St. & Wabash Ave.) | 312-440-1717

"Fabulous" sushi and Pan-Asian creations via the Rise and Shine crew are served in a "small", "cool space" featuring funky bamboo ceiling art at this midpriced River North Japanese "just off Michigan

Avenue"; though some suggest there's nothing "to rave about", the few surveyors who've sampled it promise "guaranteed quality" and a menu "similar" to its siblings; N.B. second-floor Izakaya Hapa serves Asian bar bites and sake-infused cocktails Thursday–Saturday.

### ☑ sushi wabi *Japanese*                    27 | 18 | 20 | $44

**West Loop** | 842 W. Randolph St. (bet. Green & Peoria Sts.) | 312-563-1224 | www.sushiwabi.com

"Sushi snobs" regard this modern West Loop Japanese as "one of the best" spots to "belly up" for "inventive" maki ("it's like buttah"); just "plan to spend a few bucks", and keep in mind that "service lacks often" and tables in the "industrial"-looking setting afford little "privacy from your neighbors" – most notably during "prime time" when it's "crowded" and "high-energy (translate: loud)."

### Sushi X *Japanese*                    21 | 13 | 18 | $33

**River West** | 1136 W. Chicago Ave. (bet. May St. & Racine Ave.) | 312-491-9232 | www.sushi-x.net

Stark, modern details give way to "inventive" rolls at this "consistent", moderately priced River West sushi bar where fin fanatics find the BYO policy a "huge bonus"; some deem the "dining room" "pretty dreadful", but "takeout and delivery are terrific" and portions are "generous."

### Swordfish *Japanese*                    ▽ 27 | 21 | 24 | $44

**Batavia** | 207 N. Randall Rd. (McKee St.) | 630-406-6463 | www.swordfishsushi.com

"Put on your blinders" and "you'll never know" you're in "the boonies" attest admirers of the "outstanding" "fresh" sushi served at this contemporary far West Suburban Japanese (a sibling to Wildfish) that's "nestled in a strip mall"; trendy rolls, creative hot dishes and "excellent drinks" add to the "downtown" feel, as does the service and slightly pricey tabs.

### Szechwan North *Chinese*                    19 | 12 | 16 | $25

**Glenview** | 2857 Pfingsten Rd. (Willow Rd.) | 847-272-0007 | www.szechwannorth.com

Glenview locals look to this "master of Sichuan cooking" for affordable "traditional dishes" made with "quality ingredients" and "care", contending it's "one of the better" "in the 'burbs"; those who had "forgotten" about it are "pleasantly surprised" when they go back, saying they "wish" it were "closer."

### TABLE fifty-two *American/Southern*                    24 | 23 | 23 | $60

**Gold Coast** | 52 W. Elm St. (bet. Clark & Dearborn Sts.) | 312-573-4000 | www.tablefifty-two.com

For "knockout" "soul food north of the Mason-Dixon line", surveyors jump aboard the "biscuit bandwagon" at this "upscale" Gold Coast American belonging to Oprah's onetime chef, Art Smith; enthusiasts dub the "beautiful" "homestyle" setting – plus "hummingbird cake" and "fried chicken" that leave you "feeling fat" – an "interesting take" on the Southern experience, and though a few say it's "overhyped and overpriced", most find the service "lovely."

| | FOOD | DECOR | SERVICE | COST |
|---|---|---|---|---|

### NEW Taco Fuego ● *Mexican* — | — | — | I

**Lakeview** | 1648 W. Belmont Ave. (bet. Ashland Ave. & Paulina St.) | 773-935-9472 | www.tacofuego.com

Quick, casual, el cheapo Mexican comestibles – including lots of tacos, quesadillas and burritos (watch out for the foot-long 'monster') – plus classic plates like fajitas and even breakfast fare are on offer at this little, no-frills Lakeview taqueria; dishes come liberally laced with über-hot habanero peppers, and there are seven fresh salsa varieties to choose from, so you'll likely want some liquid relief in the form of horchata, jamaica and sodas.

### ☑ Takashi Ⓜ *American/French* 26 | 20 | 23 | $62

**Bucktown** | 1952 N. Damen Ave. (Armitage Ave.) | 773-772-6170 | www.takashichicago.com

"Vibrant" flavors launch seemingly "simple" dishes to "culinary stardom" at Ambria vet Takashi Yagihashi's Japanese-tinged French-American "gem" in Bucktown that's akin to "eating in someone's" "understated, classy" house, albeit one with an "interesting" wine and sake list; service, generally viewed as "attentive" "without being intrusive", and "less than astronomical prices" result in near "uniformly positive experiences"; P.S. "check out the hip upstairs dining room" "if there's a table available."

### ☑ Tallgrass Ⓜ *French* 28 | 23 | 24 | $74

**Lockport** | 1006 S. State St. (10th St.) | 815-838-5566 | www.tallgrassrestaurant.com

It's "well worth the drive from Downtown" gush groupies of this "relaxed", "romantic" French in a "beautiful" vintage building, where "decades of culinary experience" "shows" in the modern prix fixe-only menu; it's "still a value" after all these years, with a "knowledgeable" staff and "fantastic" wine list that's "extremely fairly" priced sealing its status as a "special night out" in the Southwest Suburbs; P.S. jackets are suggested.

### Tamales *Mexican* 20 | 16 | 21 | $27
### (fka Hot Tamales)

**Highland Park** | 493 Central Ave. (St. Johns Ave.) | 847-433-4070 | www.tamalesrestaurant.com

"Unique" dishes "make it hard to choose" when dining at this brightly colored North Shore Mexican that's known for its "unconventional tamales" and "phenomenal duck tacos" plus "personalized service"; those familiar with the "small", "crowded" setting promise it's "worth the wait" – "especially in summer" when outdoor seating becomes available and even more so when you have an "amazing margarita" in hand.

### Tamarind *Asian* 23 | 19 | 20 | $28

**South Loop** | 614 S. Wabash Ave. (Harrison St.) | 312-379-0970 | www.tamarindsushi.com

An "extensive" selection of midpriced Pan-Asian dishes from "solid" sushi to design-"your-own stir-fry" plus "lots of" noodle dishes means this bamboo-walled South Looper has something for "almost everyone"; service is generally "efficient", and there's a summer patio; N.B. Wednesday nights cater to singles ('come alone, dine together') from 7:30 to 10 PM.

### Tango *Argentinean*　　　　　▽ 22 | 16 | 20 | $33

**Naperville** | 5 W. Jackson Ave. (Washington St.) | 630-848-1818 | www.tangogrill.com

You'll want to dollop the "chimichurri" "on anything" plus "sop it up with the bread" say habitués of this "enjoyable" midpriced Argentinean in Downtown Naperville where you can "go the tapas route" and "share everything" or tackle the signature 26-inch steak; it's a "regular stop" for some, who cite "value" and "solid service" as draws.

### Tango Sur *Argentinean/Steak*　　24 | 16 | 19 | $32

**Lakeview** | 3763 N. Southport Ave. (Grace St.) | 773-477-5466

Meat mavens meet at this "beloved" BYO Argentine that serves "wonderfully" prepared, "quality beef" to "expats" and "Lakeview twentysomethings"; a "loud" setting and "ridiculously long waits" that "do not abate late" can be "frustrating", but "eye-candy waiters" and "huge" portions offering "incredible value" "are worth it"; N.B. its newer, more romantic sib, Folklore, is a relatively mellower late-night alternative.

### Tank Sushi *Japanese*　　　　23 | 19 | 18 | $39

**Lincoln Square** | 4514 N. Lincoln Ave. (Sunnyside Ave.) | 773-769-2600 | www.tanksushi.com

Zealots assure the sushi and rolls really are "all that" at this midpriced Lincoln Square Japanese that offers "creative" "combinations" in a "lively", contemporary setting complete with a "thwump-thwump soundtrack"; "friendly" service adds to the allure, and penny-pinchers applaud the "best-kept secret in town" – "half price" maki during lunch Monday–Friday and on weekends from 1–6 PM.

### Tanoshii *Japanese*　　　　　 - | - | - | E

**Andersonville** | 5547 N. Clark St. (Gregory St.) | 773-878-6886

Loyalists laud this "one-of-a-kind" Japanese "neighborhood institution" located "off the beaten path" in Andersonville as an "excellent" option for sushi including "some winners you can't find anywhere else"; "regulars" "go with friends" to try as many "concoctions as possible" or ask the chef to "custom design" maki to suit their "cravings", assuring that "dinner will surely please, even if the check doesn't."

### Tapas Barcelona *Spanish*　　　21 | 18 | 18 | $29

**Evanston** | Northshore Hotel Retirement Home | 1615 Chicago Ave. (bet. Church & Davis Sts.) | 847-866-9900 | www.tapasbarcelona.com

"Delicious" tapas lure an "amiable crowd" of "families, couples and Northwestern students" to this "casual" Evanston Spaniard that has been a "favorite" "for years" and delivers "super value"; though service "can be slow", sangria and a "selection of sherries" help to pass the time, and while the "colorful" indoors can get "noisy", sitting on the "pleasant" patio affords a "wonderful" "alfresco" experience "in summer."

### Tapas Gitana ☑ Spanish
**24 | 18 | 22 | $34**

**Northfield** | Northfield Village Ctr. | 310 Happ Rd. (bet. Willow Rd. & Winnetka Ave.) | 847-784-9300 | www.tapasgitana.com

For a "fine" "variety of cold and hot" tapas plus "killer paella" patrons "keep coming back" to this romantic "gem" "tucked away" in the North Shore where a "cordial", "attentive" staff, occasional "live music" and "reasonable prices" help "take it over the top"; P.S. sit on the "lovely", "large patio" "when the weather is nice."

### Tapas Las Ramblas Spanish
**∇ 23 | 20 | 19 | $28**

**Andersonville** | 5101 N. Clark St. (Carmen Ave.) | 773-769-9700 | www.tapaslasramblas.com

Andersonvillers grab a "group of friends" for a "slice of sunny Barcelona" at this "convivial" "better-than-neighborhood" "tapas joint" with a "bright, colorful", lantern-lit dining room and windows that swing open on breezy days; most find the "broad selection" of "reasonably priced" "small plates" a "pleasant surprise" and the service "fair" but "friendly."

### Tarantino's ☑ Italian
**22 | 20 | 22 | $39**

**Lincoln Park** | 1112 W. Armitage Ave. (Seminary Ave.) | 773-871-2929 | www.tarantinos.com

There may not be "a lot of hype" surrounding this midpriced Lincoln Park trattoria, but it's nonetheless a "favorite" cozy "comfort zone" for "neighborhood Italian" including "solid pasta"; admirers warn "you'll be tempted to order" "three times more than you can eat" because dishes "never fail to satisfy", while a "friendly staff" helps to keep it "consistently enjoyable."

### Tasting Room, The ◑☒ American
**20 | 21 | 21 | $34**

**West Loop** | 1415 W. Randolph St. (Ogden Ave.) | 312-942-1313 | www.thetastingroomchicago.com

"Wine and cheese lovers" rendezvous over "interesting", "smaller-sized" New American dishes and entrees at this "quiet" West Loop "date spot" with some of the "best views of Chicago" from its "second-floor" lounge; cohorts concur there's "plenty to keep you interested" – starting with the "extensive" vino selection explained by a "knowledgeable staff" – and moderate tabs won't break the bank.

### Tavern at the Park ☒ American
**20 | 19 | 20 | $42**

**Loop** | 130 E. Randolph St. (Michigan Ave.) | 312-552-0070 | www.tavernatthepark.com

Its "choice location" overlooking Millennium Park lends a "lovely setting" to this bi-level New American, while its "convenient" Loop address and "varied menu" make it popular with a mix of "tourists", "business" types and theatergoers; adventurers admit there's "nothing exotic" in the mix, and adversaries note "spotty service" adding "you pay for the view whether you get it or not"; luckily, there's seasonal patio seating, and rooftop dining is in the works.

### Tavern on Rush ● *Steak* | 21 | 20 | 20 | $49 |

**Gold Coast** | 1031 N. Rush St. (Bellevue Pl.) | 312-664-9600 | www.tavernonrush.com

"People-watching" from a "second-floor window" is highly recommended at this "Viagra triangle" steakhouse that's "always jammed" with "politicos", "pretty people" and "pickup" artists working the "happening" Gold Coast "scene"; "perfect drinks" and solid meat dishes are additional come-ons, even though some "suspect expense accounts abound" and there's "too much attitude" from the staff; still, "nothing's better than a patio seat in summer."

### Taxim *Greek* | 22 | 17 | 20 | $45 |

**Wicker Park** | 1558 N. Milwaukee Ave. (Damen Ave.) | 773-252-1558 | www.taximchicago.com

"Don't expect broken plates and *'opas!'*" at this Wicker Park Greek where "lovely", "modern" fare is delivered with "helpful service" in an "elegant" setting with copper-top tables, hanging lanterns and exposed brick; the "interesting" "seasonal offerings" made with "fresh ingredients" are a "unique" alternative to "flaming cheese", yet are "not absurdly expensive"; N.B. there's also a sidewalk cafe and deck with city view.

### Tempo ●♻ *Diner* | 20 | 13 | 17 | $20 |

**Gold Coast** | 6 E. Chestnut St. (State St.) | 312-943-4373 | www.tempocafechicago.com

"Honest breakfasts" (some say "late-night lifesavers") and other diner fare is dished out 24/7 at this "pretense"-free, "cash-only" Gold Coast spot offering "delicious omelets" so big they "spill" off the plate; the "old-fashioned"-meets-contemporary setting isn't "long on ambiance" but service is "efficient" and "easygoing", and though "the wait on weekends is a drag" most contend it's "worth it."

### Terragusto *Italian* | 25 | 16 | 20 | $48 |

**Lincoln Park** | 340 W. Armitage Ave. (Orleans St.) | 773-281-7200
**Roscoe Village** | 1851 W. Addison St. (bet. Ravenswood & Wolcott Aves.) | 773-248-2777 Ⓜ
www.terragustocafe.com

"Focus on the fresh, housemade pastas" to enter "carb-loading paradise" promise patrons of these "cozy" *fratelli* that dish out "simple", "organic" Italian fare including "extraordinary", "robust" sauces; "tiny" Roscoe Village is BYO while Lincoln Park's quarters are "tight", but on the plus side, "friendly, informed" service takes the edge off "pricey" tabs.

### NEW Terzo Piano *Italian* | 21 | 23 | 20 | $36 |

**Loop** | Art Institute of Chicago | 159 E. Monroe St. (bet. Columbus Dr. & Michigan Ave.) | 312-443-8650 | www.terzopianochicago.com

"Giant windows" look out from a "spectacular", "minimalist" "white" setting "worthy" of its location in the Modern Wing of the Art Institute at Tony Mantuano's "artful" Spiaggia sibling serving "high-end" Italian dishes by day (and dinners Thursday only); while some find it "a bit pricey for lunch" and dub the decor the "most luxurious high-school cafeteria ever", service is "fine" enough and the "views of Millennium Park" (especially from the terrace) are "stunning"; N.B. to dine without paying museum admission enter via the park's bridge.

### Texas de Brazil Churrascaria *Brazilian*  | 22 | 21 | 22 | $55 |

**River North** | 51 E. Ohio St. (bet. N. Rush St. & N. Wabash Ave.) | 312-670-1006
**Schaumburg** | Woodfield Mall | 5 Woodfield Mall (Frontage & Golf Rds.) | 847-413-1600
www.texasdebrazil.com

Sages suggest avoiding the "exceptional" salad bars to focus on "meat and more meat" at these "Brazilian-style" "all-you-can-eat" churrascarias in River North and Schaumburg where it's "socially acceptable" to "stuff yourself"; gaucho waiters "could double as a NASCAR pit crew" as they circulate the "gorgeous rooms" with red walls, leading "über-meat" fanciers to conclude it's "worth" the "splurge"; P.S. the city location features aerial "wine angels", who fetch bottles from a showy, two-story cellar.

### Thai Classic *Thai*  | 23 | 16 | 20 | $22 |

**Lakeview** | 3332 N. Clark St. (Buckingham St.) | 773-404-2000 | www.thaiclassicrestaurant.com

"Flavorful and aromatic traditional dishes" are the hallmark of this affordable, casual Lakeview "favorite", a long-standing Thai BYO with a "quiet", "lovely" setting and service that's "right on"; the "generous" buffet, offered at lunchtime on Saturdays and Sundays, gets accolades for its "many options" that "all taste fresh"; P.S. the kitchen is "not afraid to crank up the spice level" when asked.

### Thai Pastry *Thai*  | 23 | 10 | 16 | $21 |

**Uptown** | 4925 N. Broadway St. (bet. Ainslie & Argyle Sts.) | 773-784-5399
**Harwood Heights** | 7350 W. Lawrence Ave. (Odell Ave.) | 708-867-8840
www.thaipastry.com

Devotees say this "funky little coffee shop–style" Uptown Thai (with a Suburban Northwest sibling) has "awesome" "authentic" fare plus a "notable" bakery; the "beautifully presented" dishes – including some "unusual" alternatives to "standard-issue" options – come with usually "rapid-fire service" and a "check so small you'll shake your head"; P.S. the "lunch specials are a steal."

### Thai Urban Kitchen ⊠ *Asian*  | 16 | 14 | 15 | $26 |

**Loop** | Ogilvie Transportation Ctr. | 500 W. Madison St. (Canal St.) | 312-575-0266 | www.thaiurbankitchen.com

Ogilvie train station's "tasty little oasis", this midpriced Sura sibling seduces more than commuters with a Pan-Asian–Japanese "mix" served in "chic" "modern" quarters with oversize windows and "attractive" globe lighting; for "lunch"-time Loop workers and the "pre-opera" crowd, the waterfall thankfully soothes when service gets "confused."

|  | FOOD | DECOR | SERVICE | COST |
|--|------|-------|---------|------|

### Thalia Spice  *Asian*   | 19 | 16 | 18 | $36 |

**River West** | 833 W. Chicago Ave. (Green St.) | 312-226-6020 | www.thaliaspice.com

"Surprisingly" "eclectic" and "original" Pan-Asian fare in an "inviting", "out-of-the-way" River West setting runs the gamut from Thai to "sushi, curry" and "attractive" "fusion" plates – all in "small servings" at moderate prices; the "friendly" "helpful" staff adds to the "warm atmosphere" in which surveyors note you can "have a conversation with your date."

### NEW  33 Club  *American*   | 20 | 25 | 20 | $45 |

**Old Town** | 1419 N. Wells St. (bet. Burton Pl. & Schiller St.) | 312-664-1419 | www.33clubchicago.com

"Stunning" decor dazzles at this "cavernous", "noisy" Old Town New American "'it' place" from Jerry Kleiner (Carnivale, Opera) that boasts "beautiful" "velvet touches", "plenty of color" and a "sweeping staircase" recalling "the Titanic"; if the "decent" service is not quite as "impressive" and the "standard" fare is somewhat "expensive" (though "portions are enormous"), admirers advise you "come for the vibe" and "people-watching" – plus the "lively bar and outdoor cafe"; N.B. the Food score does not reflect a recent chef change.

### Three Happiness ❶ *Chinese*   | 21 | 11 | 14 | $22 |

**Chinatown** | 209 W. Cermak Rd. (Wentworth Ave.) | 312-842-1964

You've "got to love those carts" say fans of this "popular" Chinatown fixture for affordable dim sum and "don't-miss eggrolls" plus dishes that are "never shown to tourists"; though it's open 24 hours weekends and almost around-the-clock weekdays, there are still waits (and they're "worth it"); N.B. there's no connection to nearby New Three Happiness.

### 312 Chicago  *Italian*   | 21 | 21 | 21 | $42 |

**Loop** | Hotel Allegro | 136 N. LaSalle St. (Randolph St.) | 312-696-2420 | www.312chicago.com

Dialed in as a "solid choice" for a "classy" "business breakfast or lunch" and an "upscale after-work" and "pre-theater" stop (the "efficient", "accommodating" staff helps diners "make the curtain"), this Loop lair adjacent to the Hotel Allegro serves "fresh, seasonally focused" Italian fare; a renovation of the "comfortable, clubby" space boosted the Decor score, but "it gets noisy", so for some the "convenient location" is the main draw; P.S. the "prix fixe is quite a bargain."

### Tiffin  *Indian*   | 21 | 18 | 21 | $29 |

**West Rogers Park** | 2536 W. Devon Ave. (Maplewood Ave.) | 773-338-2143 | www.tiffinrestaurant.com

"More upscale than" its "surrounding Devon Avenue" neighbors, this midpriced Indian in West Rogers Park gets props for "delicious" mainstays such as "tikka" and "tandoori" plus "amazingly complex vegetarian dishes"; hotheads note even "their mild is impressively spicy" and are sure to ask the "hovering" staff for extra "tasty naan" to "soak up the sauce"; P.S. the "lunch buffet" offers lots of "variety" at a "good price."

### Tin Fish *Seafood*

23 | 18 | 20 | $40

**Tinley Park** | Cornerstone Ctr. | 18201 S. Harlem Ave. (183rd St.) | 708-532-0200 | www.tinfishrestaurant.com

"Pick your fish", "your preparation" and "accompaniment" and enjoy the "unique" experience offered at this "solid" midpriced Tinley Park seafooder where tin finned creatures hang from the ceiling; the "beautifully prepared" "fresh" fare, "good" "selection of wines" and helpful staff add to a "visit" surveyors call "worth the drive."

### Toast *American*

22 | 16 | 19 | $19

**Lincoln Park** | 746 W. Webster Ave. (Halsted St.) | 773-935-5600
**Bucktown** | 2046 N. Damen Ave. (bet. Dickens & McLean Aves.) | 773-772-5600
www.toast-chicago.com

"Original breakfast creations" fanatics call "so good they cause hallucinations" are on the menu at this "funky" Bucktown and Lincoln Park pair where diners brave "daunting lines" to indulge; lunch items are also available, prices are "pretty reasonable" and the "efficient" but "not necessarily friendly" service gets the job done, even during the madcap "weekend brunch"; N.B. closed at dinner.

### Tocco Ⓜ *Italian*

12 | 15 | 10 | $33

**Bucktown** | 1266 N. Milwaukee Ave. (Paulina St.) | 773-687-8895 | www.toccochicago.com

"Impress your date" at this "upscale" but "cozy" midpriced Bucktown wine bar, an ultramod hot-pink, black-and-white sibling to the former FoLLia that serves "robust" fare including pizzas and "basic" pastas; service ranges from "attentive" to a "helping of attitude", and though some aren't "running back" others say it's "worth a visit."

### Topaz Café *American*

▽ 23 | 22 | 23 | $41

**Burr Ridge** | 780 Village Center Dr. (County Line Rd.) | 630-654-1616 | www.topazcafe.com

Southwest Suburbanites are "thrilled" to have this "sleek", slightly pricey Burr Ridge sibling to Westmont's Amber Cafe around as a "regular" haunt for "impressive" New American fare "perfectly prepared" with "many seasonal" ingredients; the urban space – with an open kitchen, stylish lounge and patio – is "inviting" once you get past the "not particularly exciting" mall-centered address and the experience is enhanced by "professional service."

### Topo Gigio Ristorante *Italian*

23 | 18 | 20 | $38

**Old Town** | 1516 N. Wells St. (North Ave.) | 312-266-9355 | www.topogigiochicago.com

"Charming" and "accommodating", this midpriced Old Town "neighborhood standby" turns out "traditional" Italian fare that's "consistently respectable if not exciting" with "something for everyone" from "kids" to "cougars" (though some just "go for the bar scene"); its "outside patio" is a prime summer perch for "people-watching" adding to the reasons regulars say it's on the "topo my list."

| | FOOD | DECOR | SERVICE | COST |
|---|---|---|---|---|

## ⚡ Topolobampo ☒Ⓜ *Mexican* | 28 | 24 | 26 | $68

**River North** | 445 N. Clark St. (bet. Hubbard & Illinois Sts.) |
312-661-1434 | www.rickbayless.com

"Converts" call Rick Bayless' "modern", "refined" River North standout
"the best" "gourmet Mexican" "in the country", declaring the
"remarkable" "regional" flavors "expensive but worth it"; the art-
adorned, "white-tablecloth" setting – plus the "fine wine service" and
a "skilled", "professional" staff – makes patrons "forget" preconcep-
tions about "south-of-the-border" cuisine (just be sure to reserve
"long in advance"); P.S. "value"-hunters might try the chef's "casual
Frontera Grill" next door or grab a torta from nearby XOCO.

## Trader Vic's *Polynesian* | 17 | 21 | 19 | $46

**Gold Coast** | Newberry Plaza | 1030 N. State St. (Maple St.) |
312-642-6500 | www.tradervicschicago.com

"Nostalgic kitsch" "beyond belief" attracts "tourists" and locals to this
spendy Gold Coast link in the Polynesian chain with "decent" pupu
platters, "umbrella drinks" (including the original "mai tai") and
endless "campy" tiki trappings; while not everyone "writes home
about" the fare or service, and some say it's a "shadow of its former,
grander days", few argue it's anything but a "genuine good time."

## Tramonto's
## Steak & Seafood *Seafood/Steak* | 24 | 25 | 22 | $63

**Wheeling** | Westin Chicago North Shore | 601 N. Milwaukee Ave.
(Lake Cook Rd.) | 847-777-6575 | www.westin.com

Namesake chef Rick Tramonto has departed these North Shore digs
now owned by Westin hotels, but the steak and seafood menu and
extensive wine cellar holding "some wonderful bargains" remain,
delivered with "professional service" in a "stylish dining room" with
a waterfall wall; however, "for the price", some diners squawk that
the "choppy" "concept" "doesn't live up to expectations."

## Trattoria D.O.C. *Italian/Pizza* | 19 | 16 | 19 | $33

**Evanston** | 706 Main St. (Custer Ave.) | 847-475-1111 |
www.trattoria-doc.com

"City folks" meet their "North Suburban friends" at this "solid",
"family-friendly" Neapolitan pizza place in Evanston that offers
"fantastic" "wood-fired" pies along with pasta and other Italian
fare plus wine at "everyday affordable" prices; despite a few
grumbles about "inconsistent" service, most agree it's "fine if you're
in the area."

## Trattoria Gianni Ⓜ *Italian* | ▽ 26 | 19 | 24 | $38

**Lincoln Park** | 1711 N. Halsted St. (bet. North Ave. & Willow St.) |
312-266-1976 | www.trattoriagianni.com

"Convenient" "before or after a show at the Steppenwolf or Royal
George" theaters, this fireplace-lit Lincoln Parker is a fixture for
"fresh", "authentic" Italian favorites coupled with "always accommodating" service and a "wonderfully edited selection of wines";
partisans promise it's "worth" visiting – even if you don't "live in the
neighborhood"; N.B. ask for a seat on the patio when it's warm.

| | FOOD | DECOR | SERVICE | COST |
|---|---|---|---|---|

### Trattoria Isabella  *Italian*    ▽ 26 | 26 | 24 | $35

**West Loop** | 217 N. Jefferson St. (bet. Fulton & Lake Sts.) | 312-207-1900 | www.trattoriaisabellachicago.com

"Generous" portions of red-sauce Italian "standards" (housemade pasta, "brick-oven pizza") bring "bliss" to *amici* of this "affordable" West Looper in a "comfortable", wood-trimmed setting; service that's "on the mark" helps make it "recommended for families too"; P.S. the "outdoor patio and bar with a flat-screen TV is a gem."

### Trattoria No. 10  ⑤ *Italian*    24 | 21 | 23 | $43

**Loop** | 10 N. Dearborn St. (Madison St.) | 312-984-1718 | www.trattoriaten.com

Subterranean digs belie the "wonderful" experience at this "quiet", "consistent" Loop "Italiano" known for its "winning" "homemade ravioli" and "attentive" service in a "charming atmosphere" complete with arches and murals; a "must for theatergoers", "business lunches" and "romantic dates", it offers "good value" for something so "refined"; P.S. the "after-work buffet is spectacular."

### Trattoria Roma  *Italian*    21 | 13 | 19 | $38

**Old Town** | 1535 N. Wells St. (bet. North Ave. & Schiller St.) | 312-664-7907 | www.trattoriaroma.com

There's a reason this "neighborhoody" Old Town Italian is "packed with locals" – the "no-nonsense" moderately priced menu of pasta, pizza, fish and other dishes offers a "can't-miss" meal; though it's "compact" and "service is sometimes slow when it's busy", "people don't mind" as it's "warm" and "user-friendly"; N.B. the Decor score doesn't reflect the post-Survey expansion of the bar.

### Trattoria Trullo  *Italian*    23 | 19 | 21 | $44

**Lincoln Square** | 4767 N. Lincoln Ave. (Lawrence Ave.) | 773-506-0093

"Puglian" fare is "truly a treat" at this Lincoln Square kitchen where "real Italians" go in search of "quality" cooking from the "convivial" chef-owner; a "neighborhood feel", "value" prices and a "friendly", "informed staff" help "make the experience."

### Trattoria 225  *Italian*    - | - | - | M

**Oak Park** | 225 Harrison St. (Harvey Ave.) | 708-358-8555 | www.trattoria225.com

Situated in Oak Park's Arts District, this spacious, "family-friendly" "neighborhood place" with exposed-brick walls, local artwork and a concrete bar supplies moderately priced "creative", "wood-grilled" seasonal Italian fare ("pizza is the star") delivered by an "earnest" staff; the majority appreciates having a "nice glass of wine" as the younger set looks over the "kids' menu"; N.B. there was a post-Survey change in ownership.

### Tre Kronor  *Scandinavian*    23 | 17 | 22 | $23

**Northwest Side** | 3258 W. Foster Ave. (bet. Sawyer & Spaulding Aves.) | 773-267-9888 | www.trekronorestaurant.com

Expats are in "herring heaven" at this "spare" Northwest Side Scandinavian serving "excellent renditions" of "affordable" "com-

FOOD | DECOR | SERVICE | COST

fort food" "all day" from Swedish pancakes and quiche to "outstanding fish" – "especially anything with salmon"; a "Sunday brunch tradition", the "homey" "storefront" BYO is also a "winner" come Christmastime when the "amazing" "julbord" smorgasbord makes "memories" that last "all year."

### ☑ Tru ☒ *French*                    28 | 27 | 28 | $130

**Streeterville** | 676 N. St. Clair St. (bet. Erie & Huron Sts.) | 312-202-0001 | www.trurestaurant.com

Streeterville's jacket-required, "world-class" New French from Rick Tramonto and Gale Gand stays "true to its reputation" with "flawless" "super-luxury" tastings and famed, "expense account"–required "crystal steps of caviar"; while perhaps "a little stuffy", this "adult-only" go-to for "anniversaries" and "special occasions" is capped by a "wonderful wine selection", "serene", art-adorned dining room and "extraordinary" service that resembles "heaven on earth"; N.B. M Burger, also from the Lettuce group, just opened next door.

### Tsuki ⓜ *Japanese*                    23 | 20 | 18 | $42

**Lincoln Park** | 1441-45 W. Fullerton Ave. (Janssen Ave.) | 773-883-8722 | www.tsuki.us

"Amazing, fresh sushi" served in a "modern" setting makes this pricey Lincoln Park Japanese suitable for "groups" and "dates" – especially given its solid "sake" selection; service that can be "slow" is compensated for by multiple spaces including a "lounge" and "garden" "patio", leading voters to believe "this place has it all."

### Tub Tim Thai ☒ *Thai*                    ▽ 24 | 14 | 20 | $21

**Skokie** | 4927 Oakton St. (Niles Ave.) | 847-675-8424 | www.tubtimthai.com

They "do everything a little bit better" than their peers say fans of this Downtown Skokie storefront Thai that impresses even those who take multiple "trips to Thailand"; praise goes to the "complex", "reasonably priced" menu of both "unique" and familiar offerings, "beautiful presentations", "gracious hospitality" and "rotating, original" local artwork in the "cozy" surroundings; but a fickle few find it's "not worth all the acclaim it gets."

### Tufano's Vernon Park Tap ⓜ⇗ *Italian*         20 | 13 | 20 | $26

**University Village** | 1073 W. Vernon Park Pl. (Carpenter St.) | 312-733-3393

You'll think you've "walked straight into a mob movie" at this "down-to-earth" University Village Italian, where the "blackboard menu" features "honest", "family-style" dishes with "huge flavors" (go for the "lemon chicken to die for"); but the "charismatic" staff and generous portions at this 1930s vintage "standby" don't sway the handful of detractors put off by the "long waits"; N.B. cash only.

### Turquoise *Turkish*                    23 | 18 | 21 | $34

**Roscoe Village** | 2147 W. Roscoe St. (bet. Hamilton Ave. & Leavitt St.) | 773-549-3523 | www.turquoisedining.com

For "unbelievable", "authentic" Turkish fare with "flair", boosters beat a path to this "inviting", moderately priced Roscoe Village "treasure" serving "gorgeous home-baked bread" and "outstanding" lamb in an "elegant but not ornate" white-tablecloth setting (there's sidewalk seating also); just "be patient in summer during the busy weekend crush."

### Tuscany *Italian*

22 | 19 | 21 | $39

**Little Italy** | 1014 W. Taylor St. (Morgan St.) | 312-829-1990
**Wheeling** | 550 S. Milwaukee Ave. (Manchester Dr.) |
847-465-9988
**Oak Brook** | 1415 W. 22nd St. (Rte. 83) | 630-990-1993 🅢
www.stefanirestaurants.com

Wake up and "smell the garlic" at Phil Stefani's Tuscan offspring, where the "classics" "do not fail", the service "never feels rushed" and the "old-world ambiance", though varied from one location to the next, seems "intimate"; go-to spots for "business meals", dates and "family events", they generally afford a "tasty" trip, unless you're among the minority that regards this "carb" extravaganza as an "uninspired" "chain operation."

### Tweet ⊄ *American*

22 | 18 | 20 | $18

**Uptown** | 5020 N. Sheridan Rd. (Argyle St.) | 773-728-5576 |
www.tweet.biz

"Locals" can't get enough of Uptown's "fun, bright", inexpensive neighborhood New American that serves "one of the best" brunches in Chicago, plus "caloric" breakfasts and daytime eats, including a "terrific Reuben" sandwich, crab cakes and organic burgers "worth" the "forever wait"; "smile your way through" by ordering a Bloody Mary from the "charming" staff – they're "welcoming to all"; N.B. "be sure to bring cash."

### Twin Anchors *BBQ*

23 | 14 | 20 | $29

**Old Town** | 1655 N. Sedgwick St. (bet. Eugenie St. & North Ave.) |
312-266-1616 | www.twinanchorsribs.com

This "pure Chicago" "institution" in Old Town has achieved "landmark status" for its "dripping, sock-it-to-me ribs" ("gotta get 'em 'zesty'"), its "funky", "old-school" digs and its "jeans and a T-shirt" crowd that, at one time, included Sinatra; still, notwithstanding this restaurant's role "in the movie *Return to Me*", a contingent of 'cue cravers complains about "waits" and "perfunctory service", crying it "rests on its laurels"; P.S. reservations aren't taken so "go early" or carry out.

### Twist *Eclectic*

21 | 17 | 21 | $30

**Lakeview** | 3412 N. Sheffield Ave. (bet. Newport Ave. & Roscoe St.) |
773-388-2727 | www.twistinchicago.com

Its "creative" small plates may suffer from an "identity crisis" ("not really Spanish, not really Latin"), but this Eclectic spot is "a good alternative" to the "bar scene" "around Wrigleyville"; those who deem the "inventive" bites, like the "bacon-wrapped dates", "outstanding" believe the "lively", "close quarters" are "so worth the squeeze", but others say the "average dishes" push them toward "better places for tapas in Chicago"; N.B. no reservations.

## Twisted Spoke ❶ *Pub Food*

18 | 16 | 16 | $20

**Near West** | 501 N. Ogden Ave. (Grand Ave.) | 312-666-1500 | www.twistedspoke.com

Regulars "get revved up" over this "funky", "family-friendly" Near West pseudo "biker bar" with one of the "best outdoor" patios "in the city" and decor of "metal tables" and motorcycle parts; the "hospitable", "heavily tattooed servers" appear to "care" about the "solid" "American bar food", "delicious" burgers, "killer Bloody Marys" and "wide beer and liquor selection" they sling, but "despite attempts to be edgy" – every Saturday post-midnight they turn on the "old-school porn" for a 'Smut and Eggs' event – it's all "pretty tame."

## Udupi Palace *Indian*

23 | 11 | 16 | $19

**West Rogers Park** | 2543 W. Devon Ave. (bet. Maplewood Ave. & Rockwell St.) | 773-338-2152

**Schaumburg** | Market Sq. | 730 E. Schaumburg Rd. (Plum Grove Rd.) | 847-884-9510

www.udupipalace.com

The "wide selection" of "painfully spicy", primarily Southern Indian dishes "clears sinus passages" at this "simple" Rogers Park BYO with a "reliable" Schaumburg sibling; "adventurous" diners tout the "piping hot" preps, including "to-die-for" dosas and "consistently exceptional" "for the dollar" vegetarian fare, though hotheads gripe about "bland" eats and servers who seem to do little more than "try."

## Uncle John's BBQ ⌧⇏ *BBQ*

– | – | – | I

**Far South Side** | 337 E. 69th St. (Calumet Ave.) | 773-892-1233

Finger-lickers fawn over this no-frills South Side cash and "carryout-only" BBQ "winner", pronouncing the "heavenly", "hot links" and "terrific" "tips" – bestowed from behind a glass-enclosed counter – "truly authentic"; the "deeply smoky" "goodness" extends to sauce you'll want to "sip through a straw", so dress the part because it "almost never lasts the car ride home."

## Uncle Julio's Hacienda *Tex-Mex*

18 | 16 | 17 | $25

**Old Town** | 855 W. North Ave. (Clybourn Ave.) | 312-266-4222 | www.unclejulios.com

Fajita fans go *loco* over the "fresh-made tortillas" and other "tasty" Tex-Mex – accompanied by "swirled" libations – at this Old Town hub that's a "solid" choice for families, "friends and parties"; even if faultfinders say the "Americanized" fare in a "big box", "cheesy", "warehouse" setting "isn't the best on the block", others "love it."

## Uncommon Ground *Coffeehouse*

22 | 19 | 20 | $27

**Edgewater** | 1401 W. Devon Ave. (Glenwood Ave.) | 773-465-9801

**Lakeview** | 3800 N. Clark St. (Grace St.) | 773-929-3680

www.uncommonground.com

"Down-to-earth diners" dig the "earthy" Eclectic "comfort" fare featuring "locally sourced ingredients" (some from the "rooftop garden") at this "laid-back" Lakeview coffee shop, bar and performance venue with an Edgewater counterpart in a former speakeasy; popular for brunch, it's a "great place to meet friends anytime", but tight-wads "avoid it for dinner" saying it's too "costly" then.

### Union Pizzeria  *Pizza*
23 | 19 | 19 | $26

**Evanston** | 1245 Chicago Ave. (bet. Dempster & Hamilton Sts.) | 847-475-2400 | www.unionpizza.com

A "young, hip crowd" that includes lots of "Northwestern students" converges over "crisp" "wood-fired pies", "fabulous small-bite appetizers" and large, affordable beer and wine lists at this Evanston pizzeria from the folks behind Campagnola; though the "cool scene", "family-friendly" vibe and "funky", "modern decor", including wood-beam-and-ductwork ceilings, are pluses, potential pitfalls include what some call "small portions", "high prices" and "lacka-daisical" service; N.B. it also houses the performance venue SPACE.

### urbanbelly  Ⓜ *Asian*
24 | 14 | 15 | $23

**Logan Square** | 3053 N. California Ave. (bet. Barry Ave. & Nelson St.) | 773-583-0500 | www.urbanbellychicago.com

Bill Kim's "stunning" "labor of love" in a Logan Square "strip mall" achieves cult status courtesy of "quirky", "operatic" Asian fusion noodles and dumplings that "defy traditional logic"; the "hip" counter-only service, the "communal seating" in a space "with all the panache of a shed" and the BYO policy only leave surveyors more "smitten" with this "real bargain"; the main problems are "crowds" and not knowing "what to order" when "everything looks fabulous."

### Veerasway  Ⓜ *Indian*
21 | 20 | 19 | $41

**West Loop** | 844 W. Randolph St. (bet. Green & Peoria Sts.) | 312-491-0844 | www.veerasway.com

Offering a "moderately priced", "creatively reimagined" "twist on Indian" street food, with small plates and staples that "beat the sari off" Devon Street competitors, this West Loop storefront with a communal table and an on-display tandoor oven attracts a "lively", trendy crowd; thankfully, "warm" service helps soften the blow for the few who order one of the "complete misses" from a menu that also has plenty of "big hits"; P.S. watch out for the "inventive" and "delicious" – but "deceptively alcoholic" – cocktails.

### Venus Greek-Cypriot Cuisine  *Greek*
– | – | – | M

**Greektown** | 820 W. Jackson Blvd. (bet. Green & Halsted Sts.) | 312-714-1001 | www.venuschicago.com

Diners in the mood for something "a little different from [tradi-tional] Greek" head to this well-priced Cypriot "gem" in Greektown where the "wonderful" menu includes both typical Hellenic fare and some "unusual" dishes (the meze is an "outstanding way to sample a full array"); the staff is "attentive" and "friendly", plus there's live piano on Fridays and Greek music on Saturdays.

### Vermilion  *Indian/Nuevo Latino*
22 | 22 | 21 | $50

**River North** | 10 W. Hubbard St. (bet. Dearborn & State Sts.) | 312-527-4060 | www.thevermilionrestaurant.com

"New taste sensations" abound at this "inventive", "Indian-meets-Latin" "hybrid" in River North, where the expensive, high "sensory" "thrill" takes place in a "sexy", "vibrant" dining room punctuated with images from hot fashion photog Farrokh Chothia; while service generally is "spot-on", a handful of "frustrated" diners dis the "odd" combos and "weird" flavors; N.B. there's an offshoot, At Vermilion, in Manhattan.

### Via Carducci  *Italian*     23 | 18 | 21 | $36

**Lincoln Park** | 1419 W. Fullerton Ave. (bet. Janssen & Southport Aves.) | 773-665-1981

### Via Carducci La Sorella  *Italian*

**Wicker Park** | 1928 W. Division St. (Winchester Ave.) | 773-252-2246
www.viacarducci-lasorella.com

"Loyal customers" champion this reasonably priced Lincoln Park Southern Italian – and its Wicker Park mate – for "never failing to deliver" "homey" if "ubiquitous" "favorites", including "outstanding" thin-crust pizza and "out-of-this-world" gnocchi in a "quaint", "romantic" "cafe" setting; "personal" service aside, however, a few bellyachers balk over what they call a "lack of flavor."

### Viand Bar & Kitchen  *American*     22 | 18 | 23 | $33

**Streeterville** | 155 E. Ontario St. (Michigan Ave.) | 312-255-8505 | www.viandchicago.com

Chef Steve Chiappetti knows how to do "simple food" right say proponents of this moderately priced Streeterville New American with an "attentive", "friendly staff" in a setting with art deco touches adjacent to the Marriott Courtyard; though the comfort food is "interesting" but "a bit heavy" to some, the "awesome French toast" strikes a note at breakfast, and the quarters are "cozy in winter and delightful outside in summer."

### Viceroy of India  *Indian*     21 | 18 | 18 | $26

**Northwest Side** | 2520 W. Devon Ave. (bet. Campbell & Maplewood Aves.) | 773-743-4100

**Lombard** | 233 E. Roosevelt Rd. (Highland Ave.) | 630-627-4411
www.viceroyofindia.com

A "wide selection" of moderately priced, "authentic" Indian dishes, including "consistently excellent" curries, is the hallmark of this "upscale" "pioneer" with locations on the Northwest Side and in Lombard; while the "great lunch buffet" pleases bargain-hunters and vegetarians, detractors say the "drab interior" makes you "feel like you're eating in a self-serve cafeteria."

### Victory's Banner  *Eclectic/Vegetarian*     ▽ 24 | 16 | 22 | $17

**Roscoe Village** | 2100 W. Roscoe St. (Hoyne Ave.) | 773-665-0227 | www.victorysbanner.com

"Sensational" vegetarian and vegan fare lures tree-huggers to this "small", "bright", affordable Roscoe Village breakfast, lunch and brunch "find" that's "packed" on weekends; the "who-needs-meat-anyway" vibe and "sweet, attentive service" – not to mention the "recommended" French toast – attracts legions of disciples, but others say the "spiritual", even "cult"-like, atmosphere can be "kind [of] creepy."

|  | FOOD | DECOR | SERVICE | COST |
|---|---|---|---|---|

### ☑ Vie ⌸ *American* — 27 | 25 | 28 | $68

**Western Springs** | 4471 Lawn Ave. (Burlington Ave.) | 708-246-2082 | www.vierestaurant.com

Locavores "drive from the city" and beyond to Paul Virant's "deservedly respected" New American "haven" in Western Springs, where "magical" dishes are crafted using "simple", "sustainable" ingredients (including house-"pickled garnishes" and "great charcuterie"); the "lovely" 1940s-era, French-inspired interior, the "wonderful" service and the high prices – though "lower than Downtown" – place it in the "special-occasion category", but admirers could "eat [here] every day"; N.B. a portion of proceeds from a monthly Sunday family dinner goes to charity.

### Viet Bistro & Lounge *Vietnamese* — ▽ 25 | 23 | 24 | $33

**Rogers Park** | 1346 W. Devon Ave. (bet. Glenwood & Wayne Aves.) | 773-465-5720 | www.vietbistrochi.blogspot.com

"Even the fussiest of eaters" finds something to love about Dan Nguyen's loungey, "conversation-friendly" Rogers Park follow-up to his shuttered Pasteur, be it the "exceptional" Vietnamese menu, the service that "makes you feel comfortable" or the "casual" but "elegant" setting with high-backed, tamarind-toned banquettes; prices may be "a bit high" compared to competitors, but most admit the "quality merits the upcharge."

### Village, The ● *Italian* — 21 | 21 | 20 | $36

**Loop** | Italian Vill. | 71 W. Monroe St., 2nd fl. (bet. Clark & Dearborn Sts.) | 312-332-7005 | www.italianvillage-chicago.com

This "romantic" 83-year-old Loop "standby" – one of the Capitanini family's Italian Village trio at the same location – "looks the same" as ever with its twinkly "little lights" and "private booths"; a "favorite" with "pre-theater"-goers and "tourists" who find "familiar" comfort in the "reasonably priced", "reliable" pastas, extensive wine list and "professional" staff, it's merely "mediocre" to modernists, who quip it "tastes like" it's been around since 1927.

### Vinci ☒ *Italian* — 21 | 19 | 23 | $43

**Lincoln Park** | 1732 N. Halsted St. (Willow St.) | 312-266-1199 | www.vincichicago.com

Those who "stumble upon" Paul LoDuca's "unparalleled" Lincoln Park "*cucina*" – located "across from [the] Steppenwolf" Theatre – "linger" in a "relaxed atmosphere" over "amazing", "homemade" Tuscan cuisine, including "delicate" pasta and a "do-not-miss" grilled portobello and polenta appetizer; because the "respectable" classics are brought to table by "friendly servers" at "more than reasonable prices", the majority considers it a "winner."

### NEW Vintage 338 ⌸☒ *European* — - | - | - | M

**Lincoln Park** | 338 W. Armitage Ave. (bet. Orleans & Sedgwick Sts.) | 773-525-0521 | www.vintage338.com

A compact Euro wine list and tapas-style 'Southern European' small-plates selection of cheese and charcuterie, plus spreads, salads and sandwiches with artisanal ingredients lure Lincoln Parkers to this comfortably elegant, midpriced wine bar done in neutrals and dark wood with sparkling light fixtures, vintage mirrors and seasonal patio.

## Vito & Nick's ⊅ *Pizza*  25 | 12 | 18 | $17

**Far South Side** | 8433 S. Pulaski Rd. (84th Pl.) | 773-735-2050 | www.vitoandnick.com

This "respected" South Side pizzeria has tossed out cracker-"thin crust" "at its best" amid carpeted walls and "sultry" blue lighting for more than 30 years; the "personable" staff "runs on no one's schedule but their own", so you may have to "flag your waitress down" to get your pie – luckily "it's worth the wait"; P.S. the "army who eat here daily can't be wrong."

## Vivere ●⊠ *Italian*  22 | 21 | 22 | $53

**Loop** | Italian Vill. | 71 W. Monroe St. (bet. Clark & Dearborn Sts.) | 312-332-4040 | www.vivere-chicago.com

Christened "the best" of the Italian Village trio, this "romantic-yet-bustling", "modern" Italian with a "fabulous" wine list and "super-cool" "Jordan Mozer eye-candy" room is a "convenient" "pre-theater choice" in the Loop; while "formal and costly" compared to its kin, it "deserves a bit more respect" say its fans, but foes frown over "spotty" service that leads to waits so long "your clothes might go out of style"; P.S. be sure to "make reservations."

## Vivo *Italian*  24 | 20 | 20 | $39

**West Loop** | 838 W. Randolph St. (bet. Green & Peoria Sts.) | 312-733-3379 | www.vivo-chicago.com

A "cozy but luxurious" "date spot" for Southern Italian fare along Randolph Street's Restaurant Row, this longtime West Loop trattoria inspires the pasta-loving populace with both "inventive" and traditional preparations; while claustrophobes cringe over "crammed together" tables, the "nice wine list" and "sizable portions" make up for it; P.S. "for a special occasion", ask for the "adorable" "elevator shaft table" perched "above the main floor."

## Volare *Italian*  24 | 17 | 21 | $40

**Streeterville** | 201 E. Grand Ave. (St. Clair St.) | 312-410-9900
**Oakbrook Terrace** | 1919 S. Meyers Rd. (22nd St.) | 630-495-0200
www.volarerestaurant.com

You'll feel like *la famiglia* at this "quaint" Streeterville Venetian with an equally "lively", wood-trimmed Oakbrook Terrace sib, where the "fairly priced", "hearty portions" of "real Italian" fare (try the osso buco) are "incredible" and the staff "bends over backwards"; the close, "crowded" tables and bad acoustics, however, mean the "fracas" reaches "deafening" levels.

## Volo Restaurant & Wine Bar ⊠ *American*  - | - | - | M

**Roscoe Village** | 2008 W. Roscoe St. (Damen Ave.) | 773-348-4600 | www.volorestaurant.com

Oenophiles wish this New American "taste of California" in Roscoe Village would stay "undiscovered", but the "outstanding" small plates and "excellent" wines (most available by the glass or flight)

keep it buzzing; what's more, the "exceptional" patio and "romantic booths" are "perfect for a date."

### Wakamono  *Japanese*  | 22 | 19 | 15 | $32 |

**Lakeview** | 3317 N. Broadway St. (Buckingham Pl.) | 773-296-6800 | www.wakamonosushi.com

"Amazing" fish at "value prices" hooks "happy campers" at this Lakeview Japanese with "inventive" rolls, "delicious" sashimi and plenty of cooked selections; you can BYO or order one of the "excellent drinks" – both a consolation for the "painfully slow service" that leads to "long waits on weekends"; N.B. there's sidewalk seating.

### Wave  *Mediterranean*  | ∇ 13 | 21 | 13 | $58 |

**Streeterville** | W Chicago Lakeshore | 644 N. Lake Shore Dr. (Ontario St.) | 312-255-4460 | www.waverestaurant.com

"Beautiful decor" and a "great view of the lake" set the tone at this "trendy" Mediterranean small-plates concept off the lobby of Streeterville's W hotel; fans find the "pretty" fare is exactly what "you'd expect", yet grouches grump that the "quality" and "attitude" is enough to make them "wave goodbye"; P.S. desserts are a "steal", and a "long, interesting drink menu" adds happy-hour appeal.

### Weber Grill  *BBQ*  | 20 | 18 | 19 | $36 |

**River North** | Hilton Garden Inn | 539 N. State St. (Grand Ave.) | 312-467-9696

**Schaumburg** | 1010 N. Meacham Rd. (American Ln.) | 847-413-0800

**Lombard** | 2331 Fountain Square Dr. (Meyers Rd.) | 630-953-8880

www.webergrillrestaurant.com

It's like a "year-round barbecue" in your backyard say sizzle-seekers of this trio of midpriced "meat-lovers' paradises" in River North and the 'burbs, where "industrial-size" Webers fire up the burgers, pork ribs, beef brisket and Parmesan-crusted tilapia; while the "decor won't win you over" and it can get "overrun with tourists", "convention attendees" and those who "can tolerate long waits", it "beats standing outside to grill in winter."

### Webster Wine Bar ● *Eclectic*  | 20 | 18 | 20 | $30 |

**Lincoln Park** | 1480 W. Webster Ave. (bet. Ashland Ave. & Clybourn St.) | 773-868-0608 | www.websterwinebar.com

Whether "you're an expert or not", the "oddball" but "amazing" vinos – many poured "by the glass" – at this "candlelit" Lincoln Park wine bar "boggle the mind", especially when teamed with "terrific cheeses" and Eclectic small plates; though "off the beaten track", it's a prime perch for "dates", "pre-movie drinks" or powwows with colleagues, and all benefit from the "ridiculously knowledgeable", "friendly" staff and "fair prices."

### West Town Tavern ⌧ *American*  | 24 | 21 | 21 | $43 |

**West Town** | 1329 W. Chicago Ave. (Throop St.) | 312-666-6175 | www.westtowntavern.com

"So cozy [you'll] want to bring your blankie", this "consistent" New American charmer located in West Town gets "accolades" for "delicious comfort food", including "traditional" ("but not boring") fried chicken and "exceptional" pot roast; "whether you graze" or "order a full meal", it's a "standout" thanks to "reasonable" prices, a "simple" yet "amazing" wine list and "darn nice", "knowledgeable" service.

### White Fence Farm ⓜ *American* | 22 | 18 | 21 | $22 |

Romeoville | 1376 Joliet Rd. (Bolingbrook Dr.) | 630-739-1720 | www.whitefencefarm.com

The "mouth-watering" Traditional American fare from this "South Suburban icon" is "as good as it ever was" attest fanatics of the "fantastic", "juicy" fried chicken, "really special" corn fritters and "great hushpuppies"; with seating in "lots of different" "old-fashioned" rooms filled with "kitschy decor", it's all "worth the drive" to "the boonies"; P.S. check out the "auto museum and farm animals" at the on-site petting zoo.

### ⓩ Wiener's Circle, The ●⊄ *Hot Dogs* | 21 | 5 | 14 | $9 |

Lincoln Park | 2622 N. Clark St. (Wrightwood Ave.) | 773-477-7444

"Go after the bars close", "yell out your order" and add "a couple of expletives" for "the full experience" at Lincoln Park's "sassy" "side show" where the "staff commentary is almost as good" as the char-dogs (some of the "best" in the city); the "wild scene" "never gets old" say its "foul-mouthed fans", but sober sorts bristle at the service and decor, saying "go somewhere else if you aren't completely inebriated."

### ⓩ Wildfire *Steak* | 23 | 21 | 21 | $43 |

River North | 159 W. Erie St. (bet. LaSalle Blvd. & Wells St.) | 312-787-9000

Lincolnshire | 235 Parkway Dr. (Milwaukee Ave.) | 847-279-7900

Glenview | 1300 Patriot Blvd. (Lake Ave.) | 847-657-6363

Schaumburg | 1250 E. Higgins Rd. (National Pkwy.) | 847-995-0100

Oak Brook | Oakbrook Center Mall | 232 Oakbrook Ctr. (Rte. 83) | 630-586-9000

www.wildfirerestaurant.com

"Consistent" from "location to location", these "always packed" River North and suburban steakhouses from the Lettuce Entertain You group have a "broad", if pricey, menu of "superb" wood-grilled meat ("love the trio of filets"), "solid sides" and "excellent seafood" – all in "huge portions"; still, the sometimes "mediocre service", "unpleasantly noisy" environs and "clubby", "1940s"-ish decor make it feel a bit "like a chain" for some; P.S. "reservations are a must."

### Wildfish *Japanese* | 21 | 17 | 17 | $37 |

Deerfield | Deerfield Commons Shopping Ctr. | 730 Waukegan Rd. (bet. Deerfield Rd. & Osterman Ave.) | 847-317-9453

Arlington Heights | Arlington Town Sq. | 60 S. Arlington Heights Rd. (bet. Northwest Hwy. & Sigwalt St.) | 847-870-8260

www.wildfishsushi.com

Sushi fans are "impressed" with the "innovative", "artistically presented" "specialty rolls" and "wide selection of sake" at this loungey Deerfield and Arlington Heights Japanese duo where "Chicago quality" begets "Chicago prices"; still, a minority is brought down by service that ranges from "enthusiastic" to "comically bad."

|  | FOOD | DECOR | SERVICE | COST |
|---|---|---|---|---|

### Wishbone  *Southern*    21 | 16 | 20 | $21

**Roscoe Village** | 3300 N. Lincoln Ave. (School St.) | 773-549-2663
**West Loop** | 1001 W. Washington Blvd. (Morgan St.) | 312-850-2663
**Berwyn** | 6611 Roosevelt Rd. (bet. Clarence & East Aves.) |
708-749-1295  M
www.wishbonechicago.com

Find "inexpensive" Southern "comfort" at this "down-home" threesome where the meals (including some Cajun choices) are "nothing fancy" but are nonetheless a "slice of heaven" – especially the grits, biscuits and other "classic" breakfast selections; they "don't miss a beat on the plate", but the "bustling" dining rooms can get "crowded", so "come early" and don't be put off by the "laid-back", "perfunctory" service.

### Woo Lae Oak  *Korean*    20 | 21 | 17 | $39

**Rolling Meadows** | 3201 Algonquin Rd. (Newport Dr.) | 847-870-9910 |
www.woolaeoakchicago.com

Kimchi cravers are "shocked" to find "such a large, high-end" Korean barbecue in Rolling Meadows, "highly recommending" this "formal" eatery with "wonderful" decor and "solid" grill-your-own grub; those not on an "expense account" opt for the weekday "lunch special" – and don't be "in a rush" because service "can be slow."

### NEW  XOCO  🅢 M  *Mexican*    25 | 16 | 18 | $20

**River North** | 449 N. Clark St. (Illinois St.) | 312-334-3688 |
www.xocochicago.com

Master Chef Rick Bayless' LEED-certified "counter-service"-meets-"haute"-style River North Mexican cultivates *pasión* among "street food" enthusiasts, who brave the "cosmic" waits for "outstanding" tortas ("especially any with pork"), "giant bowls of caldos", "addictive churros" and cacao bean-to-cup hot chocolate; "what it lacks in comfort" – an "odd" ordering protocol, "cramped", communal seating – is forgiven once the "awe-inspiring" eats arrive, hot from a wood-burning oven.

### Yard House  *American*    18 | 17 | 18 | $28

**Glenview** | The Glen | 1880 Tower Dr. (Patriot Blvd.) | 847-729-9273 |
www.yardhouse.com

"It's all about the beer" (over 130 by draft) at this family-friendly North Suburban outpost of a national chain; fans say it sometimes "transcends the typical" with its "modernized" American pub grub, famed suds by the half-"yard" and "perfect" setting "for happy hours or to watch a game", but "don't go there if you want to talk" because the "noise level is horrendous"; N.B. there's a gluten-free menu.

### Yolk  *American*    22 | 17 | 20 | $17

**NEW  River North** | 747 N. Wells St. (bet. Chicago Ave. & Superior St.) |
312-787-2277
**South Loop** | 1120 S. Michigan Ave. (11th St.) | 312-789-9655
www.yolk-online.com

The South Loop original "is so good that they opened another" outpost of this "yolk"-hued, "phenomenal breakfast" (and BYO lunch) nook in River North, where the same "alluring aroma" of "bacon waffles", pancakes and omelets prompts you to order a "gigantic portion"; the lines can seem "endless" and the acoustics "terrible", but the majority finds the affordable offerings "worth the wait."

## Yoshi's Café 🅼 *French/Japanese*    25 | 19 | 25 | $51

**Lakeview** | 3257 N. Halsted St. (Aldine Ave.) | 773-248-6160 | www.yoshiscafe.com

Yoshi Katsumura's "quaint little" Lakeview haunt is "still good after many, many years" insists the "eclectic crowd" that appreciates its "warm" "welcome", "elegantly remodeled" space and "no-shortcuts" approach to "unpretentious" and "unique" Japanese/French-influenced fare; just remember, "you get what you pay for" here, so "be prepared to spend."

## Zak's Place 🅂 *American*    - | - | - | E

**Hinsdale** | 112 S. Washington St. (bet. 1st & 2nd Sts.) | 630-323-9257 | www.zaksplace.com

"Comfortable" and "down-to-earth", this Hinsdale "gem" named for a beloved pet offers "serious", "seasonal" New American fare and a 300-bottle wine list in a setting with exposed brick, cherry wood and copper trim; proponents tell of bar bites that are "uniformly delicious" and servers who "could sell ice to Eskimos", though the downer is prices that can be "astounding."

## Zapatista *Mexican*    20 | 20 | 17 | $30

**South Loop** | 1307 S. Wabash Ave. (13th St.) | 312-435-1307
**Northbrook** | 992 Willow Rd. (Old Willow Rd.) | 847-559-0939
www.zapatistamexicangrill.com

"Holy guacamole" effuse amigos over this "airy", "upscale" South Loop Mexican (and its newer Northbrook sib) that caters to a "young crowd" "jonesing for a 'rita", "Americanized" fajita, tableside guac and "anything with pork" ("these guys know how to treat a pig"); though the service is "erratic" and the noise level will leave you "conversationally challenged", at least you can head for the "fabulous" sidewalk patio in warm weather.

## Zealous 🅂🅼 *American*    25 | 24 | 22 | $67

**River North** | 419 W. Superior St. (Sedgewick St.) | 312-475-9112 | www.zealousrestaurant.com

"Genius" chef-owner Michael Taus remains "at the top of his game", creating "inventive flavor combinations" that "blow you away" at his "plush" New American in River North; sophisticates savor the "soothing", "bamboo"-trimmed setting and "well-stocked wine cellar", but fault-finders point to the "high price point" and "inconsistent service."

## ZED 451 *Eclectic*    21 | 24 | 22 | $54

**River North** | 739 N. Clark St. (Superior St.) | 312-266-6691 | www.zed451.com

"Gorge yourself" at this Eclectic River North "churrascaria with a twist" – it's the "hippest" "all-you-can-eat ever" and "not for the weak of appetite"; an "imaginative", seasonal salad bar, "wonderful service", "beautiful", "high-style" dining room and "stellar rooftop" terrace draw the "young and trendy", but wallet-watchers warn that you pay a high price for the "scene", so it's a good thing you won't have to "eat for a week after."

### Zhivago Ⓜ *American/Continental*  `16` `16` `17` `$31`

**Skokie** | 9925 Gross Point Rd. (bet. Kedvale & Keeler Aves.) | 847-982-1400 | www.zhivagochicago.com

Surveyors seesaw on this "serviceable" North Shore Continental that offers up Russian and Eastern European "favorites"; while those with an "affinity" for goulash, beef stroganoff and schnitzel appreciate the hearty cooking and find the kitted-out "banquet hall setting" with dramatic gilding, murals and drapery "unique", others call it "mediocre" overall, noting that "crowds around 5:30" "tell you a lot"; P.S. live music heats up the dance floor on Fridays and Saturdays.

### Zia's Trattoria *Italian*  `24` `18` `21` `$35`

**Edison Park** | 6699 N. Northwest Hwy. (Oliphant Ave.) | 773-775-0808 | www.ziaschicago.com

"Dressed-up" "soccer moms" and families endure the "long waits" and "cramped surroundings" of this "accessible" Edison Park "discovery" in order to enjoy "deftly executed", "huge portions" of "hearty" Italian fare, from the "better-than-expected appetizers" to the "delicious" carb-heavy entrees coupled with a "serviceable wine list"; but a few fusspots frown that the "friendly" staff delivers "spotty" service and the room gets pretty "noisy."

### Zocalo *Mexican*  `20` `18` `19` `$34`

**River North** | 358 W. Ontario St. (Orleans St.) | 312-302-9977 | www.zocalochicago.com

"Upscale" "modern" Mexican fare delivered by "solid" servers at "reasonable prices" draws diners to this "loftlike" River Norther where you've "gotta have the trio of guacamole", guajillo-tinged barbacoa and a margarita; presuming you "order right", "you won't be disappointed" say scribes, who further recommend "sipping tequila" in the "exposed-brick space" or on the sidewalk in summer; N.B. Sunday and Tuesday prix fixe dinners further cajole the chile-charmed.

Menus, photos, voting and more – free at ZAGAT.com

# CHICAGO
# INDEXES

## LOCATION MAPS

# Cuisines

Includes names, locations and Food ratings.

## AFRICAN

| | |
|---|---|
| NEW Bolat \| **Lakeview** | - |
| Icosium Kafe \| **Andersonville** | 19 |
| Sikia \| **Far S Side** | - |

## AMERICAN

| | |
|---|---|
| Abigail's \| **Highland Pk** | 24 |
| Adelle's \| **Wheaton** | 25 |
| Z Alinea \| **Lincoln Pk** | 29 |
| Amber Cafe \| **Westmont** | 22 |
| American Girl \| **Streeterville** | 16 |
| Ann Sather \| **multi.** | 21 |
| Atwater's \| **Geneva** | 20 |
| Atwood Cafe \| **Loop** | 22 |
| Z Avenues \| **River N** | 26 |
| NEW Bakin' & Eggs \| **Lakeview** | 19 |
| Bandera \| **Streeterville** | 22 |
| Bank Lane \| **Lake Forest** | 23 |
| Bar Louie \| **multi.** | 16 |
| Bijan's \| **River N** | 19 |
| Billy Goat \| **multi.** | 17 |
| Bin 36/Wine \| **multi.** | 21 |
| Z Blackbird \| **W Loop** | 27 |
| Bluebird \| **Bucktown** | 20 |
| Blue 13 \| **River N** | 24 |
| BOKA \| **Lincoln Pk** | 25 |
| Bongo Room \| **multi.** | 24 |
| Z Bonsoirée \| **Logan Sq** | 26 |
| Boston Blackies \| **multi.** | 19 |
| Branch 27 \| **W Town** | 17 |
| Breakfast Club \| **Near W** | 20 |
| Briejo \| **Oak Pk** | 14 |
| Bristol \| **Bucktown** | 23 |
| Broadway Cellars \| **Edgewater** | 21 |
| NEW Browntrout \| **North Ctr/St. Ben's** | 24 |
| Cab's Wine Bar \| **Glen Ellyn** | 24 |
| Café Absinthe \| **Bucktown** | 23 |
| Café 103 \| **Far S Side** | - |
| Café Selmarie \| **Lincoln Sq** | 23 |
| NEW Ceres' Table \| **Uptown** | - |
| Chalkboard \| **Lakeview** | 22 |
| Z Charlie Trotter's \| **Lincoln Pk** | 27 |
| Z Cheesecake Factory \| **multi.** | 19 |
| Chef's Station \| **Evanston** | 24 |
| Chicago Firehouse \| **S Loop** | 20 |
| Cité \| **Streeterville** | 20 |
| NEW CityGate \| **Naperville** | - |
| Clubhouse \| **Oak Brook** | 21 |
| NEW Corner 41 \| **North Ctr/St. Ben's** | - |

| | |
|---|---|
| Courtright's \| **Willow Spgs** | 25 |
| Z Crofton on Wells \| **River N** | 26 |
| Custom House \| **Printer's Row** | 25 |
| Dan McGee \| **Frankfort** | - |
| Z David Burke Prime \| **River N** | 25 |
| Deleece Grill \| **Lakeview** | 20 |
| Depot Diner \| **Far W** | - |
| Distinctive Cork \| **Naperville** | 21 |
| NEW DMK Burger \| **Lakeview** | 22 |
| Drake Bros.' \| **Gold Coast** | - |
| Drawing Room \| **Gold Coast** | 23 |
| Duchamp \| **Bucktown** | 17 |
| NEW Duckfat \| **Forest Pk** | - |
| Ed Debevic's \| **multi.** | 15 |
| NEW Elate \| **River N** | 21 |
| Entourage \| **Schaumburg** | 20 |
| NEW Epic \| **River N** | - |
| erwin cafe \| **Lakeview** | 23 |
| Z Eve \| **Gold Coast** | 22 |
| Feast \| **multi.** | 19 |
| Fiddlehead \| **Lincoln Sq** | 20 |
| Fifty/50 \| **Wicker Pk** | 21 |
| 545 North \| **Libertyville** | 20 |
| Flo \| **W Town** | 22 |
| Fred's \| **Gold Coast** | 19 |
| Z Gage \| **Loop** | 22 |
| Gale St. Inn \| **multi.** | 22 |
| NEW Gemini Bistro \| **Lincoln Pk** | 21 |
| NEW Gilt Bar \| **River N** | - |
| Z Glenn's Diner \| **Ravenswood** | 24 |
| Glen Prairie \| **Glen Ellyn** | 23 |
| Goose Island \| **multi.** | 17 |
| Gordon Biersch \| **Bolingbrook** | 16 |
| Grace O'Malley's \| **S Loop** | 18 |
| graham elliot \| **River N** | 24 |
| Grill on Alley \| **Streeterville** | 21 |
| Hackney's \| **multi.** | 18 |
| Hamburger Mary's \| **Andersonville** | 17 |
| NEW Happ Inn \| **Northfield** | 17 |
| Hard Rock \| **River N** | 12 |
| HB Home Bistro \| **Lakeview** | 25 |
| NEW Hearty \| **Wrigleyville** | - |
| Hemmingway's \| **Oak Pk** | 21 |
| Hot Chocolate \| **Bucktown** | 24 |
| HUB 51 \| **River N** | 21 |
| Ina's \| **W Loop** | 23 |
| Inovasi \| **Lake Bluff** | - |
| Jack's on Halsted \| **Lakeview** | 21 |
| J. Alexander's \| **multi.** | 20 |

Menus, photos, voting and more – free at ZAGAT.com

| | |
|---|---|
| NEW Jam \| **Ukrainian Vill** | 21 |
| Jane's \| **Bucktown** | 22 |
| Jilly's Cafe \| **Evanston** | 21 |
| Joey's Brickhouse \| **Lakeview** | 20 |
| John's Place \| **multi.** | 18 |
| NEW Karyn's on Green \| **Greektown** | – |
| Z Keefer's \| **River N** | 25 |
| NEW Kith & Kin \| **Lincoln Pk** | – |
| NEW (k)new \| **Logan Sq** | – |
| Kroll's \| **S Loop** | 19 |
| Z Kuma's \| **Logan Sq** | 26 |
| Landmark \| **Lincoln Pk** | 20 |
| Lawry's \| **River N** | 24 |
| LB Bistro \| **Streeterville** | – |
| NEW Leo's Coney Island \| **Wrigleyville** | – |
| Lockwood \| **Loop** | 19 |
| NEW Longman & Eagle \| **Logan Sq** | – |
| Lou Mitchell's \| **multi.** | 23 |
| Z Lovells \| **Lake Forest** | 23 |
| LuxBar \| **Gold Coast** | 20 |
| L. Woods Tap \| **Lincolnwood** | 20 |
| Magnolia Cafe \| **Ravenswood** | 22 |
| Z Margie's Candies \| **multi.** | 22 |
| Market \| **W Loop** | 18 |
| Markethouse \| **Streeterville** | 21 |
| May St. Market \| **W Loop** | 24 |
| Medici on 57th \| **Hyde Pk** | 17 |
| M. Henry \| **Andersonville** | 25 |
| Mike Ditka's \| **multi.** | 22 |
| Milk & Honey \| **Wicker Pk** | 23 |
| Miller's Pub \| **Loop** | 17 |
| Mirabell \| **NW Side** | 21 |
| Mity Nice Grill \| **Streeterville** | 17 |
| Z mk \| **Near North** | 27 |
| Montarra \| **Algonquin** | 24 |
| Moody's Pub \| **Edgewater** | 19 |
| Z Naha \| **River N** | 27 |
| Next Door \| **Northbrook** | 23 |
| Niche \| **Geneva** | 28 |
| NEW Nightwood \| **Pilsen** | 23 |
| Nookies \| **multi.** | 20 |
| Z North Pond \| **Lincoln Pk** | 25 |
| Oak Tree \| **Gold Coast** | 17 |
| Old Oak Tap \| **Ukrainian Vill** | 20 |
| NEW Old Town Social \| **Old Town** | 18 |
| One North \| **Loop** | 15 |
| Z one sixtyblue \| **W Loop** | 26 |
| Z Original/Walker Pancake \| **multi.** | 24 |
| Otom \| **W Loop** | 22 |
| Over Easy \| **Ravenswood** | 27 |

| | |
|---|---|
| Palette Bistro \| **Lakeview** | – |
| Paramount Room \| **Near W** | 24 |
| Parkers' \| **Downers Grove** | 23 |
| Park 52 \| **Hyde Pk** | 19 |
| Park Grill \| **Loop** | 20 |
| NEW Park Place \| **NW Side** | – |
| Parrot Cage \| **Far S Side** | – |
| Perennial \| **Lincoln Pk** | 24 |
| Petterino's \| **Loop** | 19 |
| Pinstripes \| **multi.** | 17 |
| NEW Pitchfork \| **North Ctr/St. Ben's** | – |
| P.J. Clarke's \| **multi.** | 17 |
| Praga \| **Lombard** | – |
| NEW Prairie Fire \| **W Loop** | – |
| Prairie Grass \| **Northbrook** | 22 |
| NEW Prasino \| **La Grange** | – |
| Province \| **W Loop** | 23 |
| Z Publican \| **W Loop** | 25 |
| Puck's at MCA \| **Streeterville** | 20 |
| Z Pump Room \| **Gold Coast** | 22 |
| Quince \| **Evanston** | 23 |
| Rhapsody \| **Loop** | 20 |
| NEW Ria \| **Gold Coast** | – |
| R.J. Grunts \| **Lincoln Pk** | 19 |
| Z RL \| **Gold Coast** | 23 |
| Rockit B&G \| **multi.** | 19 |
| NEW Rootstock \| **Humboldt Pk** | 24 |
| NEW Sable \| **River N** | – |
| Sage Grille \| **Highwood** | 21 |
| Sarkis Cafe \| **Evanston** | 15 |
| NEW Sarks/Park \| **Lincoln Pk** | – |
| Z Schwa \| **Wicker Pk** | 29 |
| Z Seasons \| **Gold Coast** | 27 |
| Seasons 52 \| **Schaumburg** | – |
| Sepia \| **W Loop** | 24 |
| 1776 \| **Crystal Lake** | 22 |
| Z Signature Room \| **Streeterville** | 18 |
| Z Sixteen \| **River N** | 22 |
| sola \| **Lakeview** | 25 |
| South Gate \| **Lake Forest** | 20 |
| Southport \| **Lakeview** | 22 |
| South Water \| **Loop** | 16 |
| Z Spring \| **Wicker Pk** | 27 |
| NEW Sprout \| **Lincoln Pk** | 28 |
| Stained Glass \| **Evanston** | 23 |
| Stanley's \| **multi.** | 18 |
| NEW State and Lake \| **Loop** | 21 |
| SugarToad \| **Naperville** | 19 |
| TABLE 52 \| **Gold Coast** | 24 |
| Z Takashi \| **Bucktown** | 26 |
| Tasting Room \| **W Loop** | 20 |
| Tavern/Park \| **Loop** | 20 |
| Tavern/Rush \| **Gold Coast** | 21 |

**CHICAGO**

**CUISINES**

| | |
|---|---|
| NEW 33 Club \| **Old Town** | 20 |
| Toast \| **multi.** | 22 |
| Topaz Café \| **Burr Ridge** | 23 |
| Tweet \| **Uptown** | 22 |
| Twisted Spoke \| **Near W** | 18 |
| Viand Bar \| **Streeterville** | 22 |
| Z Vie \| **W Springs** | 27 |
| Volo \| **Roscoe Vill** | - |
| Weber Grill \| **multi.** | 20 |
| West Town \| **W Town** | 24 |
| White Fence \| **Romeoville** | 22 |
| Z Wildfire \| **multi.** | 23 |
| Yard House \| **Glenview** | 18 |
| Yolk \| **multi.** | 22 |
| Zak's Place \| **Hinsdale** | - |
| Zealous \| **River N** | 25 |
| Zhivago \| **Skokie** | 16 |

## ARGENTINEAN

| | |
|---|---|
| NEW Folklore \| **Ukrainian Vill** | - |
| Tango \| **Naperville** | 22 |
| Tango Sur \| **Lakeview** | 24 |

## ARMENIAN

| | |
|---|---|
| Sayat Nova \| **Streeterville** | 23 |

## ASIAN

| | |
|---|---|
| aja \| **River N** | - |
| NEW Belly Shack \| **Humboldt Pk** | 23 |
| Big Bowl \| **multi.** | 20 |
| NEW Bonsai Café \| **Evanston** | - |
| China Grill \| **Loop** | 22 |
| Flat Top Grill \| **multi.** | 20 |
| NEW Han 202 \| **Near S Side** | 25 |
| Hot Woks \| **multi.** | 23 |
| NEW Italiasia \| **River N** | - |
| Karma \| **Mundelein** | 23 |
| Koi \| **Evanston** | 21 |
| Opera \| **S Loop** | 20 |
| pingpong \| **Lakeview** | 20 |
| Red Light \| **W Loop** | 23 |
| Z Shanghai Terrace \| **River N** | 25 |
| Shikago \| **Loop** | 18 |
| Stir Crazy \| **multi.** | 19 |
| Sunda \| **River N** | 23 |
| Thalia Spice \| **River W** | 19 |
| Trader Vic's \| **Gold Coast** | 17 |

## AUSTRIAN

| | |
|---|---|
| Julius Meinl \| **multi.** | 21 |

## BARBECUE

| | |
|---|---|
| Carson's Ribs \| **multi.** | 22 |
| Fat Willy's \| **Logan Sq** | 23 |
| Hecky's \| **Evanston** | 20 |
| Honey 1 BBQ \| **Bucktown** | 20 |
| Lem's BBQ \| **Far S Side** | 25 |
| L. Woods Tap \| **Lincolnwood** | 20 |
| NEW Main St. Smokehouse \| **Libertyville** | - |
| Merle's Smokehouse \| **Evanston** | 19 |
| NEW Piggery \| **Lakeview** | - |
| NEW Pitchfork \| **North Ctr/St. Ben's** | - |
| Ribs 'n' Bibs \| **Hyde Pk** | 21 |
| Risqué Café \| **Lakeview** | - |
| Robinson's Ribs \| **multi.** | 21 |
| Russell's BBQ \| **multi.** | 19 |
| Z Smoke Daddy \| **Wicker Pk** | 24 |
| Z Smoque BBQ \| **NW Side** | 26 |
| Twin Anchors \| **Old Town** | 23 |
| Uncle John's \| **Far S Side** | - |
| Weber Grill \| **multi.** | 20 |

## BELGIAN

| | |
|---|---|
| Hopleaf \| **Andersonville** | 23 |

## BRAZILIAN

| | |
|---|---|
| Al Primo Canto \| **multi.** | 24 |
| Brazzaz \| **River N** | 22 |
| Fogo de Chão \| **River N** | 24 |
| Texas de Brazil \| **multi.** | 22 |

## BURGERS

| | |
|---|---|
| Billy Goat \| **multi.** | 17 |
| Boston Blackies \| **multi.** | 19 |
| Counter \| **Lincoln Pk** | 20 |
| NEW DMK Burger \| **Lakeview** | 22 |
| Ed Debevic's \| **multi.** | 15 |
| NEW Edzo's \| **Evanston** | - |
| Epic Burger \| **Loop** | 22 |
| Five Guys \| **multi.** | 20 |
| fRedhots \| **Glenview** | 21 |
| Hackney's \| **multi.** | 18 |
| Hamburger Mary's \| **Andersonville** | 17 |
| Hop Häus \| **multi.** | 19 |
| NEW J. Wellington's \| **Wicker Pk** | - |
| Z Kuma's \| **Logan Sq** | 26 |
| NEW Lucky Monk \| **S Barrington** | - |
| NEW M Burger \| **Streeterville** | - |
| P.J. Clarke's \| **multi.** | 17 |
| Z Superdawg \| **multi.** | 21 |
| Twisted Spoke \| **Near W** | 18 |
| Z Wiener's Circle \| **Lincoln Pk** | 21 |

## CAJUN

| | |
|---|---|
| Davis St. Fish \| **Evanston** | 19 |
| Dixie Kitchen \| **multi.** | 19 |
| Z Heaven on Seven \| **multi.** | 23 |
| Z Pappadeaux \| **multi.** | 21 |
| Wishbone \| **multi.** | 21 |

Menus, photos, voting and more - free at ZAGAT.com

## CENTRAL AMERICAN

NEW Conoce/Panama | **Logan Sq** | _-_

## CHINESE

(* dim sum specialist)

| | |
|---|---|
| Ben Pao | **River N** | 21 |
| Chens | **Wrigleyville** | 22 |
| Dee's | **Lincoln Pk** | 19 |
| Double Li | **Chinatown** | _-_ |
| Emperor's Choice | **Chinatown** | 23 |
| Evergreen | **Chinatown** | 23 |
| Fornetto Mei | **Gold Coast** | 20 |
| Hai Yen | **multi.** | 21 |
| Happy Chef* | **Chinatown** | 23 |
| House of Fortune | **Chinatown** | 23 |
| NEW Lan's Bistro | **Old Town** | _-_ |
| Z Lao | **multi.** | 24 |
| Lee Wing Wah | **Chinatown** | _-_ |
| LuLu's* | **Evanston** | 21 |
| Mandarin Kitchen | **Chinatown** | _-_ |
| Moon Palace | **Chinatown** | 22 |
| P.F. Chang's | **multi.** | 20 |
| Z Phoenix* | **Chinatown** | 23 |
| Pine Yard | **Evanston** | 18 |
| Shine Morida | **Lincoln Pk** | _-_ |
| Shui Wah* | **Chinatown** | 24 |
| Silver Seafood | **Uptown** | 23 |
| Spring World | **Chinatown** | _-_ |
| Szechwan North | **Glenview** | 19 |
| Three Happiness* | **Chinatown** | 21 |

## COFFEEHOUSES

| | |
|---|---|
| Café Selmarie | **Lincoln Sq** | 23 |
| Julius Meinl | **multi.** | 21 |
| Uncommon Ground | **multi.** | 22 |

## COFFEE SHOPS/ DINERS

| | |
|---|---|
| NEW Bakin' & Eggs | **Lakeview** | 19 |
| Chicago Diner | **Lakeview** | 22 |
| Depot Diner | **Far W** | _-_ |
| Ed Debevic's | **multi.** | 15 |
| Eleven City | **S Loop** | 19 |
| Z Glenn's Diner | **Ravenswood** | 24 |
| Lou Mitchell's | **multi.** | 23 |
| Manny's | **multi.** | 23 |
| Milk & Honey | **Wicker Pk** | 23 |
| Nookies | **multi.** | 20 |
| Orange | **multi.** | 20 |
| Z Original/Walker Pancake | **multi.** | 24 |
| Sarkis Cafe | **Evanston** | 15 |
| Tempo | **Gold Coast** | 20 |

## COLOMBIAN

| | |
|---|---|
| La Fonda | **Andersonville** | _-_ |
| Las Tablas | **multi.** | 20 |

## CONTINENTAL

| | |
|---|---|
| Café la Cave | **Des Plaines** | 21 |
| Châtaigne | **Near North** | _-_ |
| Le P'tit Paris | **Streeterville** | 20 |
| Zhivago | **Skokie** | 16 |

## COSTA RICAN

Irazu | **Bucktown** | 22

## CREOLE

| | |
|---|---|
| Z Heaven on Seven | **multi.** | 23 |
| Z Pappadeaux | **multi.** | 21 |

## CRÊPES

| | |
|---|---|
| NEW Crêpe Crave | **Wicker Pk** | _-_ |
| Crêpes Cafe | **Loop** | _-_ |
| NEW Crêpe Town | **Lakeview** | _-_ |
| L'Eiffel | **S Barrington** | 21 |

## CUBAN

| | |
|---|---|
| Cafe 28 | **North Ctr/St. Ben's** | 26 |
| Habana Libre | **W Town** | 22 |
| NEW 90 Miles | **multi.** | 22 |
| NEW Siboney | **Bucktown** | _-_ |

## CZECH

Czech Plaza | **Berwyn** | 22

## DELIS

| | |
|---|---|
| Bagel | **multi.** | 19 |
| Eleven City | **S Loop** | 19 |
| Manny's | **multi.** | 23 |
| Perry's Deli | **multi.** | 26 |
| Steve's Deli | **River N** | 17 |

## ECLECTIC

| | |
|---|---|
| Briejo | **Oak Pk** | 14 |
| Café 103 | **Far S Side** | _-_ |
| NEW Cellar/Stained Glass | **Evanston** | 21 |
| Châtaigne | **Near North** | _-_ |
| NEW Cuna | **Lakeview** | _-_ |
| Deleece | **Lakeview** | 19 |
| Flatwater | **River N** | 16 |
| Flight | **Glenview** | 17 |
| foodlife | **Streeterville** | 19 |
| Grand Lux | **River N** | 20 |
| NEW Han 202 | **Near S Side** | 25 |
| Heartland Cafe | **Rogers Pk** | 16 |
| HUB 51 | **River N** | 21 |
| NEW Isacco | **St. Charles** | _-_ |
| Jane's | **Bucktown** | 22 |
| Kit Kat | **Lakeview** | 16 |

| | |
|---|---|
| Kitsch'n/K-Cafe \| **multi.** | 19 |
| **NEW** (k)new \| **Logan Sq** | – |
| **Z** Lula Cafe \| **Logan Sq** | 26 |
| MANA Food \| **Wicker Pk** | 27 |
| **NEW** Mezé \| **W Loop** | – |
| **Z** Moto \| **W Loop** | 27 |
| Mundial \| **Pilsen** | – |
| Nosh \| **Geneva** | 24 |
| Orange \| **multi.** | 20 |
| **NEW** Park Place \| **NW Side** | – |
| Praga \| **Lombard** | – |
| **NEW** Red Brick \| **Lakeview** | – |
| Twist \| **Lakeview** | 21 |
| Uncommon Ground \| **Lakeview** | 22 |
| Victory's Banner \| **Roscoe Vill** | 24 |
| Webster Wine \| **Lincoln Pk** | 20 |
| ZED 451 \| **River N** | 21 |

## ETHIOPIAN

| | |
|---|---|
| **Z** Ethiopian Diamond \| **Edgewater** | 23 |
| Ras Dashen \| **Edgewater** | 23 |

## EUROPEAN

| | |
|---|---|
| **NEW** Balsan \| **Gold Coast** | – |
| **NEW** Little Bucharest \| **NW Side** | – |
| **NEW** LOKaL \| **Bucktown** | – |
| **NEW** Vintage 338 \| **Lincoln Pk** | – |

## FILIPINO

| | |
|---|---|
| Coobah \| **Lakeview** | 17 |
| Isla Filipino \| **Lincoln Sq** | – |

## FONDUE

| | |
|---|---|
| Geja's Cafe \| **Lincoln Pk** | 21 |
| Melting Pot \| **multi.** | 19 |

## FRENCH

| | |
|---|---|
| Atwater's \| **Geneva** | 20 |
| **Z** Bonsoirée \| **Logan Sq** | 26 |
| Café/Architectes \| **Gold Coast** | 24 |
| Cafe Matou \| **Bucktown** | 23 |
| **Z** Carlos' \| **Highland Pk** | 27 |
| Dining Rm./Kendall \| **Near W** | 23 |
| Dorado \| **Lincoln Sq** | 23 |
| **Z** Everest \| **Loop** | 27 |
| Froggy's \| **Highwood** | 22 |
| **Z** Gabriel's \| **Highwood** | 25 |
| Jacky's on Prairie \| **Evanston** | 21 |
| Jilly's Cafe \| **Evanston** | 21 |
| la petite folie \| **Hyde Pk** | 24 |
| Le P'tit Paris \| **Streeterville** | 20 |
| **Z** Les Nomades \| **Streeterville** | 29 |
| **Z** Le Titi/Paris \| **Arlington Hts** | 26 |
| Le Vichyssois \| **Lakemoor** | 26 |

| | |
|---|---|
| **NEW** LM \| **Lincoln Sq** | 22 |
| Mexique \| **W Town** | 25 |
| **Z** Michael \| **Winnetka** | 28 |
| **Z** NoMI \| **Gold Coast** | 27 |
| **Z** Oceanique \| **Evanston** | 27 |
| **NEW** Sabor Saveur \| **Ukrainian Vill** | – |
| **NEW** Sprout \| **Lincoln Pk** | 28 |
| **Z** Takashi \| **Bucktown** | 26 |
| **Z** Tallgrass \| **Lockport** | 28 |
| **Z** Tru \| **Streeterville** | 28 |
| Yoshi's Café \| **Lakeview** | 25 |

## FRENCH (BISTRO)

| | |
|---|---|
| **Z** Barrington Country \| **Barrington** | 25 |
| **NEW** Bistro Bordeaux \| **Evanston** | – |
| **Z** Bistro Campagne \| **Lincoln Sq** | 25 |
| Bistro 110 \| **Gold Coast** | 21 |
| Bistrot Margot \| **Old Town** | 20 |
| Bistrot Zinc \| **Gold Coast** | 21 |
| Café Bernard \| **Lincoln Pk** | 19 |
| Cafe Central \| **Highland Pk** | 24 |
| Cafe Pyrenees \| **Libertyville** | 21 |
| **NEW** Café Touché \| **NW Side** | 25 |
| Chez Joël \| **Little Italy** | 24 |
| Cyrano's Bistrot \| **River N** | 22 |
| D & J Bistro \| **Lake Zurich** | 24 |
| Hemmingway's \| **Oak Pk** | 21 |
| Kiki's \| **Near North** | 25 |
| Koda \| **Far S Side** | – |
| La Crêperie \| **Lakeview** | 21 |
| La Sardine \| **W Loop** | 24 |
| La Tache \| **Andersonville** | 22 |
| LB Bistro \| **Streeterville** | – |
| Le Bouchon \| **Bucktown** | 24 |
| L'Eiffel \| **S Barrington** | 21 |
| Maijean \| **Clarendon Hills** | 28 |
| Marché \| **W Loop** | 23 |
| Miramar Bistro \| **Highwood** | 17 |
| Mon Ami Gabi \| **multi.** | 22 |
| Pierrot Gourmet \| **River N** | 20 |
| **NEW** RendezVous \| **Lincoln Sq** | – |
| Retro Bistro \| **Mt. Prospect** | 23 |
| socca \| **Lakeview** | 22 |

## FRENCH (BRASSERIE)

| | |
|---|---|
| Brasserie Jo \| **River N** | 22 |
| **NEW** deca \| **Streeterville** | – |

## GERMAN

| | |
|---|---|
| Berghoff \| **multi.** | 18 |
| Edelweiss \| **Norridge** | 19 |
| Mirabell \| **NW Side** | 21 |

## GREEK

| | |
|---|---|
| Artopolis \| **Greektown** | 22 |
| Athena \| **Greektown** | 21 |
| Costa's \| **Oakbrook Terr** | 22 |
| Greek Islands \| **multi.** | 21 |
| **NEW** Melanthios \| **Lakeview** | – |
| Mythos \| **Lakeview** | 23 |
| OPA Estiatorio \| **Vernon Hills** | 25 |
| Parthenon \| **Greektown** | 21 |
| Pegasus \| **multi.** | 20 |
| Roditys \| **Greektown** | 21 |
| Santorini \| **Greektown** | 21 |
| Taxim \| **Wicker Pk** | 22 |
| Venus \| **Greektown** | – |

## HAWAII REGIONAL

| | |
|---|---|
| Roy's \| **River N** | 25 |

## HOT DOGS

| | |
|---|---|
| **Z** Al's #1 Beef \| **multi.** | 23 |
| **NEW** Edzo's \| **Evanston** | – |
| **NEW** Felony Franks \| **W Loop** | – |
| **NEW** Franks 'N' Dawgs \| **Lincoln Pk** | – |
| fRedhots \| **Glenview** | 21 |
| Gold Coast \| **multi.** | 19 |
| **Z** Hot Doug's \| **NW Side** | 27 |
| **NEW** Leo's Coney Island \| **Wrigleyville** | – |
| **Z** Superdawg \| **multi.** | 21 |
| **Z** Wiener's Circle \| **Lincoln Pk** | 21 |

## INDIAN

| | |
|---|---|
| Chicago Curry \| **S Loop** | 25 |
| Curry Hut \| **Highwood** | 20 |
| Essence/India \| **Lincoln Sq** | 21 |
| Gaylord Indian \| **multi.** | 22 |
| Hema's Kitchen \| **multi.** | 22 |
| **Z** India House \| **multi.** | 25 |
| Indian Garden \| **multi.** | 21 |
| Jaipur \| **W Loop** | – |
| Klay Oven \| **multi.** | 20 |
| Marigold \| **Uptown** | 23 |
| Mt. Everest \| **Evanston** | 22 |
| Raj Darbar \| **Lincoln Pk** | 18 |
| Tiffin \| **W Rogers Pk** | 21 |
| Udupi Palace \| **multi.** | 23 |
| Veerasway \| **W Loop** | 21 |
| Vermilion \| **River N** | 22 |
| Viceroy of India \| **multi.** | 21 |

## INDONESIAN

| | |
|---|---|
| **NEW** Angin Mamiri \| **W Rogers Pk** | – |

## IRISH

| | |
|---|---|
| Chief O'Neill's \| **NW Side** | 18 |
| Grace O'Malley's \| **S Loop** | 18 |
| Irish Oak \| **Wrigleyville** | 19 |
| Mrs. Murphy \| **North Ctr/St. Ben's** | 22 |

## ITALIAN

(N=Northern; S=Southern)

| | |
|---|---|
| **NEW** Accanto \| **Logan Sq** | – |
| **NEW** Aldino's \| **Little Italy** | – |
| Al Primo Canto \| **multi.** | 24 |
| Angelina \| S \| **Lakeview** | 21 |
| Anna Maria \| **Ravenswood** | 24 |
| Anteprima \| **Andersonville** | 25 |
| Antica Pizza \| **Andersonville** | 23 |
| Antico Posto \| **Oak Brook** | 22 |
| **Z** a tavola \| N \| **Ukrainian Vill** | 26 |
| Aurelio's Pizza \| **multi.** | 23 |
| Bacchanalia \| **SW Side** | 24 |
| Bacino's \| **multi.** | 22 |
| Basil Leaf \| N \| **Lincoln Pk** | 18 |
| Bella Notte \| S \| **W Loop** | 21 |
| **NEW** Benny's \| **River N** | – |
| Bice \| **Streeterville** | 21 |
| Brio \| **Lombard** | 22 |
| Bruna's \| **SW Side** | 26 |
| Buona Terra \| N \| **Logan Sq** | 24 |
| Café Bionda \| **S Loop** | 22 |
| **Z** Café Spiaggia \| **Gold Coast** | 25 |
| Campagnola \| **Evanston** | 25 |
| Carlos & Carlos \| N \| **Arlington Hts** | 24 |
| Carlucci \| N \| **Downers Grove** | 19 |
| Carlucci \| N \| **Rosemont** | 20 |
| Carmine's \| **Gold Coast** | 22 |
| **NEW** Ciao Napoli \| **Logan Sq** | – |
| **NEW** Cibo Matto \| **Loop** | 24 |
| Club Lucky \| S \| **Bucktown** | 19 |
| **Z** Coco Pazzo \| N \| **River N** | 25 |
| Coco Pazzo Café \| N \| **Streeterville** | 22 |
| Cucina Paradiso \| **Oak Pk** | 20 |
| Dave's Italian \| S \| **Evanston** | 17 |
| Del Rio \| **Highwood** | 20 |
| Dinotto \| **Old Town** | 19 |
| Di Pescara \| **Northbrook** | 19 |
| Edwardo's Pizza \| **multi.** | 20 |
| EJ's Place \| N \| **Skokie** | 22 |
| Erie Cafe \| **River N** | 22 |
| Filippo's \| **Lincoln Pk** | 24 |
| Fiorentino's \| S \| **Lakeview** | 22 |
| Fontana Grill \| **Uptown** | – |
| Fornetto Mei \| **Gold Coast** | 20 |
| Francesca's \| **multi.** | 22 |
| Francesco's \| **Northbrook** | 24 |

| | |
|---|---|
| Frankie's Scaloppine \| **Gold Coast** | 18 |
| Frasca Pizza \| **Lakeview** | 20 |
| 🆉 Gabriel's \| **Highwood** | 25 |
| Gaetano's \| **Forest Pk** | 24 |
| Gioco \| N \| **S Loop** | 25 |
| Gruppo/Amici \| N \| **Rogers Pk** | 16 |
| Harry Caray's \| **multi.** | 20 |
| Il Mulino \| **Gold Coast** | 25 |
| 🆕 Il Poggiolo \| **Hinsdale** | 19 |
| 🆕 Isacco \| **St. Charles** | - |
| 🆕 Italiasia \| **River N** | - |
| La Bocca/Verità \| **Lincoln Sq** | 22 |
| La Cantina \| N \| **Loop** | 21 |
| 🆉 La Gondola \| **Lakeview** | 24 |
| La Madia \| **River N** | 23 |
| La Scarola \| **River W** | 24 |
| Leonardo's \| N \| **Andersonville** | - |
| Macello \| **W Loop** | - |
| 🆉 mado \| **Bucktown** | 25 |
| 🆉 Maggiano's \| **multi.** | 20 |
| Merlo \| N \| **multi.** | 24 |
| 🆉 Mia Francesca \| **Lakeview** | 26 |
| Natalino's \| **W Town** | 23 |
| 🆕 Nella Pizza \| **Lincoln Pk** | 22 |
| Next Door \| **Northbrook** | 23 |
| 🆕 Orvieto Pizza \| **Lincoln Pk** | - |
| Osteria/Pizzeria Via Stato \| S \| **River N** | 23 |
| Pane Caldo \| N \| **Gold Coast** | 23 |
| Pasta Palazzo \| **Lincoln Pk** | 22 |
| 🆕 Pelago \| **Streeterville** | 26 |
| Philly G's \| **Vernon Hills** | 21 |
| Phil Stefani's \| **River N** | 24 |
| Piazza Bella \| **Roscoe Vill** | 21 |
| Piccolo Sogno \| **Near W** | 24 |
| Pinstripes \| **multi.** | 17 |
| Pizza Capri \| **multi.** | 20 |
| Pizza D.O.C. \| **Lincoln Sq** | 23 |
| Pompei Bakery \| **multi.** | 19 |
| Prosecco \| **River N** | 24 |
| Quartino \| **River N** | 21 |
| 🆉 Riccardo \| N \| **Lincoln Pk** | 27 |
| Rist. al Teatro \| **Pilsen** | - |
| rist. we \| N \| **Loop** | 20 |
| RoSal's \| S \| **Little Italy** | 26 |
| Rose Angelis \| **Lincoln Pk** | 24 |
| 🆉 Rosebud \| **multi.** | 22 |
| Rosebud Trattoria \| **River N** | 22 |
| Sabatino's \| **NW Side** | 24 |
| Sapore/Napoli \| **Lakeview** | 20 |
| Sapori Trattoria \| **Lincoln Pk** | 23 |
| Scoozi! \| **River N** | 19 |
| socca \| **Lakeview** | 22 |

| | |
|---|---|
| Spacca Napoli \| **Ravenswood** | 23 |
| 🆉 Spiaggia \| **Gold Coast** | 27 |
| Tarantino's \| **Lincoln Pk** | 22 |
| Terragusto \| **multi.** | 25 |
| 🆕 Terzo Piano \| **Loop** | 21 |
| 312 Chicago \| **Loop** | 21 |
| Tocco \| **Bucktown** | 12 |
| Topo Gigio \| **Old Town** | 23 |
| Trattoria D.O.C. \| **Evanston** | 19 |
| Trattoria Gianni \| **Lincoln Pk** | 26 |
| Trattoria Isabella \| **W Loop** | 26 |
| Trattoria No. 10 \| **Loop** | 24 |
| Trattoria Roma \| **Old Town** | 21 |
| Trattoria Trullo \| S \| **Lincoln Sq** | 23 |
| Trattoria 225 \| **Oak Pk** | - |
| Tufano's Tap \| S \| **University Vill** | 20 |
| Tuscany \| N \| **multi.** | 22 |
| Via Carducci \| S \| **multi.** | 23 |
| Village \| **Loop** | 21 |
| Vinci \| **Lincoln Pk** | 21 |
| Vito & Nick's \| **Far S Side** | 25 |
| Vivere \| **Loop** | 22 |
| Vivo \| **W Loop** | 24 |
| Volare \| **multi.** | 24 |
| Zia's Trattoria \| **Edison Pk** | 24 |

## JAPANESE

(* sushi specialist)

| | |
|---|---|
| Agami* \| **Uptown** | 24 |
| Ai Sushi* \| **River N** | 24 |
| Akai Hana* \| **Wilmette** | 21 |
| Aria* \| **Loop** | 24 |
| Benihana \| **multi.** | 18 |
| 🆕 Blue Ocean* \| **Ravenswood** | 23 |
| Bob San* \| **Wicker Pk** | 24 |
| Butterfly* \| **multi.** | 22 |
| Chens* \| **Wrigleyville** | 22 |
| Coast Sushi/South Coast* \| **multi.** | 24 |
| Dee's* \| **Lincoln Pk** | 19 |
| Hachi's Kitchen* \| **Logan Sq** | - |
| 🆕 Hana* \| **Rogers Pk** | - |
| Indie Cafe* \| **Edgewater** | 24 |
| Itto Sushi* \| **Lincoln Pk** | 24 |
| 🆉 Japonais* \| **River N** | 24 |
| Kamehachi* \| **multi.** | 21 |
| Kansaku* \| **Evanston** | 22 |
| 🆕 Katakana & Koko* \| **Logan Sq** | - |
| 🆉 Katsu* \| **NW Side** | 27 |
| 🆕 Kin* \| **River W** | - |
| Kuni's* \| **Evanston** | 24 |
| 🆕 Macku Sushi* \| **Lincoln Pk** | - |
| Makisu Sushi* \| **Skokie** | - |
| 🆕 Masu Izakaya \| **Lincoln Pk** | - |

| | |
|---|---|
| Meiji* \| **W Loop** | 25 |
| Mirai Sushi* \| **Wicker Pk** | 25 |
| Mizu Yakitori* \| **Old Town** | 24 |
| NEW Nagoya \| **Naperville** | - |
| Niu \| **Streeterville** | 19 |
| NEW Oba* \| **Des Plaines** | - |
| Oysy* \| **multi.** | 20 |
| RA Sushi* \| **multi.** | 19 |
| Ringo* \| **Lincoln Pk** | - |
| Rise* \| **Wrigleyville** | 21 |
| Rollapalooza* \| **Lakeview** | - |
| Sai Café* \| **Lincoln Pk** | 25 |
| Sanook \| **North Ctr/St. Ben's** | - |
| Shine Morida* \| **Lincoln Pk** | - |
| Sushi Ai* \| **Palatine** | - |
| Sushi Naniwa* \| **River N** | 23 |
| SushiSamba* \| **River N** | 21 |
| NEW Sushi Taiyo* \| **River N** | - |
| Z sushi wabi* \| **W Loop** | 27 |
| Sushi X* \| **River W** | 21 |
| Swordfish* \| **Batavia** | 27 |
| Tamarind* \| **S Loop** | 23 |
| Tank Sushi* \| **Lincoln Sq** | 23 |
| Tanoshii* \| **Andersonville** | - |
| Thai Urban* \| **Loop** | 16 |
| Tsuki* \| **Lincoln Pk** | 23 |
| Wakamono* \| **Lakeview** | 22 |
| Wildfish* \| **multi.** | 21 |
| Yoshi's Café \| **Lakeview** | 25 |

## JEWISH

| | |
|---|---|
| Bagel \| **multi.** | 19 |
| Manny's \| **multi.** | 23 |

## KOREAN

(* barbecue specialist)

| | |
|---|---|
| Amitabul \| **NW Side** | 21 |
| Jin Ju \| **Andersonville** | 23 |
| San Soo Gab San* \| **NW Side** | 21 |
| Woo Lae Oak* \| **Rolling Meadows** | 20 |

## KOSHER/
## KOSHER-STYLE

| | |
|---|---|
| NEW Manghal \| **Evanston** | - |
| NEW Morgan Harbor \| **Rogers Pk** | - |

## LEBANESE

| | |
|---|---|
| Kan Zaman \| **River N** | - |
| Maza \| **Lincoln Pk** | 21 |

## MEDITERRANEAN

| | |
|---|---|
| Andies \| **multi.** | 18 |
| Artopolis \| **Greektown** | 22 |
| Z avec \| **W Loop** | 26 |
| Café/Architectes \| **Gold Coast** | 24 |
| NEW CityGate \| **Naperville** | - |

| | |
|---|---|
| NEW Corner 41 \| **North Ctr/St. Ben's** | - |
| NEW Laurel \| **Naperville** | - |
| Z mado \| **Bucktown** | 25 |
| NEW Manghal \| **Evanston** | - |
| Nia \| **W Loop** | - |
| Z Pita Inn \| **multi.** | 24 |
| Pomegranate \| **Evanston** | 18 |
| NEW Purple Pig \| **River N** | - |
| NEW Red Brick \| **Lakeview** | - |
| Reza's \| **multi.** | 18 |
| Rist. al Teatro \| **Pilsen** | - |
| RoPa \| **Rogers Pk** | - |
| Roti \| **multi.** | 21 |
| Venus \| **Greektown** | - |
| Wave \| **Streeterville** | 13 |

## MEXICAN

| | |
|---|---|
| Adobo \| **multi.** | 21 |
| NEW Big Star \| **Wicker Pk** | 23 |
| Cafe 28 \| **North Ctr/St. Ben's** | 26 |
| NEW Chilam Balam \| **Lakeview** | 25 |
| NEW Co-Si-Na \| **Andersonville** | - |
| de cero \| **W Loop** | 21 |
| NEW Decolores \| **Pilsen** | - |
| Don Juan's \| **Edison Pk** | 20 |
| Dorado \| **Lincoln Sq** | 23 |
| NEW Dos Diablos \| **River N** | - |
| Estrella Negra \| **Logan Sq** | - |
| Fonda del Mar \| **North Ctr/St. Ben's** | 25 |
| NEW Fonda Isabel \| **Lombard** | - |
| La Cocina/Frida \| **multi.** | 20 |
| Z Frontera Grill \| **River N** | 27 |
| Fuego \| **Logan Sq** | 24 |
| La Casa/Isaac \| **Highland Pk** | 20 |
| NEW La Ciudad \| **Uptown** | - |
| La Fonda/Gusto \| **Wicker Pk** | - |
| Las Palmas \| **multi.** | 21 |
| Los Moles \| **Lakeview** | - |
| Lupita's \| **Evanston** | 21 |
| Maiz \| **Humboldt Pk** | 23 |
| NEW Mercadito \| **River N** | 22 |
| Mexique \| **W Town** | 25 |
| Mixteco Grill \| **Lakeview** | 25 |
| Real Tenochtitlán \| **Logan Sq** | 20 |
| NEW Rolis \| **Uptown** | - |
| NEW Rustico Grill \| **Logan Sq** | - |
| NEW Sabor Saveur \| **Ukrainian Vill** | - |
| Salpicón \| **Old Town** | 26 |
| Salsa 17 \| **Arlington Hts** | 22 |
| San Gabriel \| **Bannockburn** | 17 |
| Sol de Mexico \| **NW Side** | 25 |
| NEW Taco Fuego \| **Lakeview** | - |

Tamales | **Highland Pk** 20
☑ Topolobampo | **River N** 28
**NEW** XOCO | **River N** 25
Zapatista | **multi.** 20
Zocalo | **River N** 20

## MIDDLE EASTERN

Aladdin's Eatery | **Lincoln Pk** 18
Alhambra | **W Loop** 16
Andies | **multi.** 18
Chickpea | **W Town** 22
Old Jerusalem | **Old Town** 19
☑ Pita Inn | **multi.** 24
Pomegranate | **Evanston** 18

## MOROCCAN

Andalous | **Lakeview** 22

## NEPALESE

Chicago Curry | **S Loop** 25
Curry Hut | **Highwood** 20
Mt. Everest | **Evanston** 22

## NOODLE SHOPS

Joy Yee | **multi.** 20
Mandarin Kitchen | **Chinatown** -
Penny's Noodle | **multi.** 20
urbanbelly | **Logan Sq** 24

## NUEVO LATINO

**NEW** Belly Shack | **Humboldt Pk** 23
☑ Carnivale | **Loop** 23
Coobah | **Lakeview** 17
Depot Nuevo | **Wilmette** 18
Estrella Negra | **Logan Sq** -
**NEW** Havana | **River N** -
Maya Del Sol | **Oak Pk** 23
☑ Nacional 27 | **River N** 23
Rumba | **River N** 23
Vermilion | **River N** 22

## PERSIAN

Noon-O-Kabab | **NW Side** 25
Reza's | **multi.** 18

## PIZZA

Antica Pizza | **Andersonville** 23
Art of Pizza | **Lakeview** 22
Aurelio's Pizza | **multi.** 23
Bacino's | **multi.** 22
Bricks | **multi.** 22
Chicago Pizza | **Lincoln Pk** 23
**NEW** Ciao Napoli | **Logan Sq** -
Coalfire Pizza | **W Loop** 23
Crust | **Wicker Pk** 19

Edwardo's Pizza | **multi.** 20
**NEW** Fame da Lupo | **Uptown** -
**NEW** Flo & Santos | **S Loop** -
Frankie's Scaloppine | **Gold Coast** 18
Frasca Pizza | **Lakeview** 20
☑ Giordano's | **multi.** 23
Great Lake | **Andersonville** 23
Gruppo/Amici | **Rogers Pk** 16
☑ La Gondola | **Lakeview** 24
La Madia | **River N** 23
☑ Lou Malnati's | **multi.** 24
**NEW** Lucky Monk | **S Barrington** -
**NEW** Nella Pizza | **Lincoln Pk** 22
☑ Original Gino's | **multi.** 22
**NEW** Orvieto Pizza | **Lincoln Pk** -
Parkers' | **Downers Grove** 23
Piece | **Wicker Pk** 23
Pizza Capri | **multi.** 20
Pizza D.O.C. | **Lincoln Sq** 23
Pizzeria Uno/Due | **River N** 22
**NEW** Pizzeria Serio | **Roscoe Vill** -
Osteria/Pizzeria Via Stato | **River N** 23
Pompei Bakery | **multi.** 19
Sapore/Napoli | **Lakeview** 20
Spacca Napoli | **Ravenswood** 23
Trattoria D.O.C. | **Evanston** 19
Union Pizza | **Evanston** 23
Vito & Nick's | **Far S Side** 25

## POLISH

**NEW** Flo & Santos | **S Loop** -

## POLYNESIAN

Trader Vic's | **Gold Coast** 17

## PUB FOOD

Bar Louie | **multi.** 16
Billy Goat | **multi.** 17
Boston Blackies | **multi.** 19
Chief O'Neill's | **NW Side** 18
Duke of Perth | **Lakeview** 20
**NEW** Flo & Santos | **S Loop** -
**NEW** Fountainhead | **Ravenswood** -
Goose Island | **multi.** 17
Gordon Biersch | **Bolingbrook** 16
Grace O'Malley's | **S Loop** 18
Irish Oak | **Wrigleyville** 19
Jury's | **North Ctr/St. Ben's** 18
**NEW** Lucky Monk | **S Barrington** -
Moody's Pub | **Edgewater** 19
Mrs. Murphy | **North Ctr/St. Ben's** 22
Old Oak Tap | **Ukrainian Vill** 20
☑ Publican | **W Loop** 25

| | |
|---|---|
| **NEW** Revolution Brewing \| **Logan Sq** | ⎯ |
| Twin Anchors \| **Old Town** | 23 |

## RUSSIAN

| | |
|---|---|
| Russian Tea \| **Loop** | 22 |

## SANDWICHES

| | |
|---|---|
| ☑ Al's #1 Beef \| **multi.** | 23 |
| Bagel \| **multi.** | 19 |
| Berghoff \| **multi.** | 18 |
| Birchwood \| **Bucktown** | 23 |
| ☑ Hannah's Bretzel \| **Loop** | 23 |
| Jerry's \| **multi.** | 22 |
| ☑ Mr. Beef \| **River N** | 24 |
| ☑ Potbelly \| **multi.** | 19 |
| **NEW** Sarks/Park \| **Lincoln Pk** | ⎯ |
| Southport \| **Lakeview** | 22 |

## SCANDINAVIAN

| | |
|---|---|
| Tre Kronor \| **NW Side** | 23 |

## SCOTTISH

| | |
|---|---|
| Duke of Perth \| **Lakeview** | 20 |

## SEAFOOD

| | |
|---|---|
| ☑ Bob Chinn's \| **Wheeling** | 23 |
| Cape Cod Room \| **Streeterville** | 22 |
| ☑ Catch 35 \| **multi.** | 24 |
| Chinn's Fishery \| **Lisle** | 25 |
| C-House \| **Streeterville** | 21 |
| Davis St. Fish \| **Evanston** | 19 |
| Devon Seafood \| **River N** | 21 |
| Di Pescara \| **Northbrook** | 19 |
| Emperor's Choice \| **Chinatown** | 23 |
| Fonda del Mar \| **North Ctr/St. Ben's** | 25 |
| Fulton's \| **River N** | 19 |
| ☑ Glenn's Diner \| **Ravenswood** | 24 |
| Half Shell \| **Lakeview** | 24 |
| Holy Mackerel! \| **Lombard** | 21 |
| ☑ Hugo's \| **multi.** | 24 |
| ☑ Joe's Sea/Steak \| **River N** | 26 |
| ☑ Keefer's \| **River N** | 25 |
| La Cantina \| **Loop** | 21 |
| Lee Wing Wah \| **Chinatown** | ⎯ |
| Lobby \| **River N** | 28 |
| ☑ L2O \| **Lincoln Pk** | 27 |
| McCormick/Schmick's \| **multi.** | 21 |
| Mitchell's \| **Glenview** | 21 |
| **NEW** Morgan Harbor \| **Rogers Pk** | ⎯ |
| **NEW** Nagoya \| **Naperville** | ⎯ |
| Nick's Fishmarket \| **Rosemont** | 23 |
| ☑ N9ne Steak \| **Loop** | 24 |
| ☑ Oceanique \| **Evanston** | 27 |

| | |
|---|---|
| ☑ Pappadeaux \| **multi.** | 21 |
| **NEW** Pelago \| **Streeterville** | 26 |
| Pete Miller \| **multi.** | 22 |
| Reel Club \| **Oak Brook** | 23 |
| Riva \| **Streeterville** | 20 |
| Sam & Harry's \| **Schaumburg** | ⎯ |
| Santorini \| **Greektown** | 21 |
| ☑ Shaw's Crab \| **multi.** | 24 |
| Silver Seafood \| **Uptown** | 23 |
| ☑ Spring \| **Wicker Pk** | 27 |
| Tin Fish \| **Tinley Park** | 23 |
| Tramonto's \| **Wheeling** | 24 |

## SERBIAN

| | |
|---|---|
| **NEW** Klopa Grill \| **Lincoln Sq** | ⎯ |

## SMALL PLATES

(See also Spanish tapas specialist)

| | |
|---|---|
| ☑ avec \| Med. \| **W Loop** | 26 |
| Bluebird \| Amer. \| **Bucktown** | 20 |
| BOKA \| Amer. \| **Lincoln Pk** | 25 |
| **NEW** Bolat \| Eclectic \| **Lakeview** | ⎯ |
| **NEW** Browntrout \| Amer. \| **North Ctr/St. Ben's** | 24 |
| **NEW** Cellar/Stained Glass \| Eclectic \| **Evanston** | 21 |
| C-House \| Seafood \| **Streeterville** | 21 |
| Distinctive Cork \| Amer. \| **Naperville** | 21 |
| Flight \| Eclectic \| **Glenview** | 17 |
| ☑ Green Zebra \| Veg. \| **W Town** | 26 |
| Maza \| Lebanese \| **Lincoln Pk** | 21 |
| **NEW** Mezé \| Eclectic \| **W Loop** | ⎯ |
| Nia \| Med. \| **W Loop** | ⎯ |
| **NEW** Purple Pig \| Med. \| **River N** | ⎯ |
| Quartino \| Italian \| **River N** | 21 |
| **NEW** Rootstock \| Amer. \| **Humboldt Pk** | 24 |
| **NEW** Sable \| Amer. \| **River N** | ⎯ |
| Tango \| Argent. \| **Naperville** | 22 |
| Taxim \| Greek \| **Wicker Pk** | 22 |
| **NEW** Vintage 338 \| Euro. \| **Lincoln Pk** | ⎯ |
| Volo \| Amer. \| **Roscoe Vill** | ⎯ |
| Wave \| Med. \| **Streeterville** | 13 |
| Webster Wine \| Eclectic \| **Lincoln Pk** | 20 |

## SOUL FOOD

| | |
|---|---|
| Army & Lou's \| **Far S Side** | 26 |
| **NEW** Dee's Place \| **Wicker Pk** | ⎯ |

## SOUTH AMERICAN

| | |
|---|---|
| SushiSamba \| **River N** | 21 |

## SOUTHERN

| | |
|---|---|
| Army & Lou's \| **Far S Side** | 26 |
| Big Jones \| **Andersonville** | 21 |
| **NEW** Dee's Place \| **Wicker Pk** | – |
| Dixie Kitchen \| **multi.** | 19 |
| Fat Willy's \| **Logan Sq** | 23 |
| **NEW** Southern \| **Bucktown** | – |
| TABLE 52 \| **Gold Coast** | 24 |
| Wishbone \| **multi.** | 21 |

## SOUTHWESTERN

| | |
|---|---|
| Bandera \| **Streeterville** | 22 |
| Flo \| **W Town** | 22 |
| Jack Rabbit \| **Lincoln Sq** | – |

## SPANISH

(* tapas specialist)

| | |
|---|---|
| Azucar* \| **Logan Sq** | 22 |
| Cafe Ba-Ba-Reeba!* \| **Lincoln Pk** | 22 |
| Café Iberico* \| **River N** | 22 |
| **NEW** Cafe Marbella* \| **Jefferson Pk** | – |
| Z Emilio's Tapas* \| **multi.** | 24 |
| 1492* \| **River N** | 21 |
| La Tasca* \| **Arlington Hts** | 24 |
| Z Mercat \| **S Loop** | 26 |
| Mesón Sabika* \| **multi.** | 23 |
| **NEW** Pasha \| **W Loop** | – |
| Tapas Barcelona* \| **Evanston** | 21 |
| Tapas Gitana* \| **Northfield** | 24 |
| Tapas Las Ramblas* \| **Andersonville** | 23 |
| Twist* \| **Lakeview** | 21 |

## STEAKHOUSES

| | |
|---|---|
| Benihana \| **multi.** | 18 |
| **NEW** Benny's \| **River N** | – |
| Brazzaz \| **River N** | 22 |
| Z Capital Grille \| **multi.** | 25 |
| Carmichael's \| **W Loop** | 22 |
| Z Chicago Chop \| **River N** | 25 |
| Z David Burke Prime \| **River N** | 25 |
| Deleece Grill \| **Lakeview** | 20 |
| EJ's Place \| **Skokie** | 22 |
| Entourage \| **Schaumburg** | 20 |
| Erie Cafe \| **River N** | 22 |
| Fleming's \| **multi.** | 23 |
| Fogo de Chão \| **River N** | 24 |
| **NEW** Folklore \| **Ukrainian Vill** | – |
| Fulton's \| **River N** | 19 |
| Z Gene & Georgetti \| **River N** | 24 |
| Z Gibsons \| **multi.** | 26 |
| Grill on Alley \| **Streeterville** | 21 |
| Grillroom \| **Loop** | 15 |
| Harry Caray's \| **multi.** | 20 |

| | |
|---|---|
| Z Joe's Sea/Steak \| **River N** | 26 |
| Z Keefer's \| **River N** | 25 |
| Kinzie Chophouse \| **River N** | 22 |
| Las Tablas \| **multi.** | 20 |
| Lawry's \| **River N** | 24 |
| **NEW** Melanthios \| **Lakeview** | – |
| Mike Ditka's \| **multi.** | 22 |
| Montarra \| **Algonquin** | 24 |
| Z Morton's \| **multi.** | 26 |
| Myron & Phil Steak \| **Lincolnwood** | 21 |
| Z N9ne Steak \| **Loop** | 24 |
| Palm \| **Loop** | 24 |
| Pete Miller \| **multi.** | 22 |
| Phil Stefani's \| **River N** | 24 |
| RB Grille \| **River N** | – |
| rist. we \| **Loop** | 20 |
| Rosebud Prime/Steak \| **multi.** | 25 |
| Z Ruth's Chris \| **multi.** | 25 |
| Saloon Steak \| **Streeterville** | 23 |
| Sam & Harry's \| **Schaumburg** | – |
| Shula's Steak \| **multi.** | 21 |
| Smith & Wollensky \| **River N** | 23 |
| Sullivan's Steak \| **multi.** | 22 |
| Tango \| **Naperville** | 22 |
| Tango Sur \| **Lakeview** | 24 |
| Tavern/Rush \| **Gold Coast** | 21 |
| Texas de Brazil \| **Schaumburg** | 22 |
| Tramonto's \| **Wheeling** | 24 |
| Z Wildfire \| **multi.** | 23 |
| ZED 451 \| **River N** | 21 |

## SWEDISH

| | |
|---|---|
| Ann Sather \| **multi.** | 21 |

## TEX-MEX

| | |
|---|---|
| **NEW** Dos Diablos \| **River N** | – |
| Uncle Julio's \| **Old Town** | 18 |

## THAI

| | |
|---|---|
| Z Arun's \| **NW Side** | 28 |
| Butterfly \| **multi.** | 22 |
| **NEW** Duck Walk \| **multi.** | 19 |
| Indie Cafe \| **Edgewater** | 24 |
| **NEW** Kin \| **River W** | – |
| **NEW** Pho & I \| **Lakeview** | – |
| Ruby of Siam \| **multi.** | 23 |
| Sanook \| **North Ctr/St. Ben's** | – |
| Spoon Thai \| **Lincoln Sq** | 23 |
| Star of Siam \| **River N** | 20 |
| Sura \| **Lakeview** | 20 |
| Thai Classic \| **Lakeview** | 23 |
| Thai Pastry \| **multi.** | 23 |
| Thai Urban \| **Loop** | 16 |
| Tub Tim Thai \| **Skokie** | 24 |

Menus, photos, voting and more – free at ZAGAT.com

## TURKISH

| | | |
|---|---|---|
| A La Turka | **Lakeview** | 20 |
| NEW Istanbul | **Lakeview** | - |
| Turquoise | **Roscoe Vill** | 23 |

## VEGETARIAN

(^ vegan)

| | | |
|---|---|---|
| Aladdin's Eatery | **Lincoln Pk** | 18 |
| Amitabul* | **NW Side** | 21 |
| Andies | **multi.** | 18 |
| Blind Faith* | **Evanston** | 21 |
| Chicago Diner | **Lakeview** | 22 |
| Z Ethiopian Diamond | **Edgewater** | 23 |
| Z Green Zebra | **W Town** | 26 |
| Heartland Cafe | **Rogers Pk** | 16 |
| Hema's Kitchen | **multi.** | 22 |
| Karyn's* | **multi.** | 20 |

| | | |
|---|---|---|
| NEW Karyn's on Green* | **Greektown** | - |
| NEW Loving Hut* | **Edgewater** | - |
| MANA Food | **Wicker Pk** | 27 |
| NEW Prasino | **La Grange** | - |
| Tiffin | **W Rogers Pk** | 21 |
| Udupi Palace | **multi.** | 23 |
| Victory's Banner | **Roscoe Vill** | 24 |

## VIETNAMESE

| | | |
|---|---|---|
| Hai Yen | **multi.** | 21 |
| Z Le Colonial | **Gold Coast** | 24 |
| NEW Pho & I | **Lakeview** | - |
| Pho 777 | **Uptown** | 21 |
| Phò Xe Tång | **Uptown** | 26 |
| Simply It | **Lincoln Pk** | 22 |
| Viet Bistro | **Rogers Pk** | 25 |

CHICAGO

CUISINES

# Locations

Includes names, cuisines, Food ratings and, for locations that are mapped, top list with map coordinates.

## City North

### ANDERSONVILLE/EDGEWATER

| | |
|---|---|
| Andies | *Med./Mideast* | 18 |
| Ann Sather | *Amer./Swedish* | 21 |
| Anteprima | *Italian* | 25 |
| Antica Pizza | *Pizza* | 23 |
| Big Jones | *Southern* | 21 |
| Broadway Cellars | *Amer.* | 21 |
| **NEW** Co-Si-Na | *Mex.* | - |
| **Z** Ethiopian Diamond | *Ethiopian* | 23 |
| Francesca's | *Italian* | 22 |
| Great Lake | *Pizza* | 23 |
| Hamburger Mary's | *Burgers* | 17 |
| Hopleaf | *Belgian* | 23 |
| Icosium Kafe | *African* | 19 |
| Indie Cafe | *Japanese/Thai* | 24 |
| Jin Ju | *Korean* | 23 |
| La Cocina/Frida | *Mex.* | 20 |
| La Fonda | *Colombian* | - |
| La Tache | *French* | 22 |
| Leonardo's | *Italian* | - |
| **NEW** Loving Hut | *Veg./Vegan* | - |
| M. Henry | *Amer.* | 25 |
| Moody's Pub | *Pub* | 19 |
| Ras Dashen | *Ethiopian* | 23 |
| Reza's | *Med./Mideast.* | 18 |
| Tanoshii | *Japanese* | - |
| Tapas Las Ramblas | *Spanish* | 23 |
| Uncommon Ground | *Eclectic/Coffee* | 22 |

### GOLD COAST

(See map on page 213)

**TOP FOOD**

| | | |
|---|---|---|
| NoMI | *French* | **I3** | 27 |
| Spiaggia | *Italian* | **G4** | 27 |
| Seasons | *Amer.* | **H3** | 27 |
| Morton's | *Steak* | **G2** | 26 |
| Gibsons | *Steak* | **G2** | 26 |
| Café Spiaggia | *Italian* | **G4** | 25 |
| Il Mulino | *Italian* | **F2** | 25 |
| Le Colonial | *Viet.* | **H2** | 24 |
| Merlo | *Italian* | **G2** | 24 |
| Hugo's | *Seafood* | **G2** | 24 |

**LISTING**

| | |
|---|---|
| **NEW** Balsan | *Euro.* | - |
| Big Bowl | *Asian* | 20 |
| Bistro 110 | *French* | 21 |
| Bistrot Zinc | *French* | 21 |
| Café/Architectes | *French/Med.* | 24 |
| **Z** Café Spiaggia | *Italian* | 25 |
| Carmine's | *Italian* | 22 |
| Drake Bros.' | *American* | - |
| Drawing Room | *Amer.* | 23 |
| Edwardo's Pizza | *Pizza* | 20 |
| **Z** Eve | *Amer.* | 22 |
| Feast | *Amer.* | 19 |
| Fornetto Mei | *Chinese/Italian* | 20 |
| Frankie's Scaloppine | *Italian/Pizza* | 18 |
| Fred's | *Amer.* | 19 |
| Gaylord Indian | *Indian* | 22 |
| **Z** Gibsons | *Steak* | 26 |
| **Z** Hugo's | *Seafood* | 24 |
| Il Mulino | *Italian* | 25 |
| **Z** Le Colonial | *Viet.* | 24 |
| LuxBar | *Amer.* | 20 |
| McCormick/Schmick's | *Seafood* | 21 |
| Merlo | *Italian* | 24 |
| Mike Ditka's | *Steak* | 22 |
| **Z** Morton's | *Steak* | 26 |
| **Z** NoMI | *French* | 27 |
| Oak Tree | *Amer.* | 17 |
| Pane Caldo | *Italian* | 23 |
| P.J. Clarke's | *Amer.* | 17 |
| **Z** Pump Room | *Amer.* | 22 |
| RA Sushi | *Japanese* | 19 |
| **NEW** Ria | *Amer.* | - |
| **Z** RL | *Amer.* | 23 |
| **Z** Rosebud | *Italian* | 22 |
| **Z** Seasons | *Amer.* | 27 |
| **Z** Spiaggia | *Italian* | 27 |
| TABLE 52 | *Amer./Southern* | 24 |
| Tavern/Rush | *Steak* | 21 |
| Tempo | *Diner* | 20 |
| Trader Vic's | *Polynesian* | 17 |

### LAKEVIEW/WRIGLEYVILLE

| | |
|---|---|
| A La Turka | *Turkish* | 20 |
| Andalous | *Moroccan* | 22 |
| Angelina | *Italian* | 21 |
| Ann Sather | *Amer./Swedish* | 21 |
| Art of Pizza | *Pizza* | 22 |
| Bagel | *Deli* | 19 |
| **NEW** Bakin' & Eggs | *Amer.* | 19 |
| Bar Louie | *Pub* | 16 |

Menus, photos, voting and more – free at ZAGAT.com

| | |
|---|---|
| NEW Bolat | *African* | — |
| Chalkboard | *Amer.* | 22 |
| Chens | *Chinese/Japanese* | 22 |
| Chicago Diner | *Diner* | 22 |
| NEW Chilam Balam | *Mex.* | 25 |
| Coobah | *Filipino/Nuevo Latino* | 17 |
| NEW Crêpe Town | *Crêpes* | — |
| NEW Cuna | *Eclectic* | — |
| Deleece | *Eclectic* | 19 |
| Deleece Grill | *Amer.* | 20 |
| NEW DMK Burger | *Burgers* | 22 |
| NEW Duck Walk | *Thai* | 19 |
| Duke of Perth | *Scottish* | 20 |
| erwin cafe | *Amer.* | 23 |
| Fiorentino's | *Italian* | 22 |
| Flat Top Grill | *Asian* | 20 |
| Frasca Pizza | *Pizza* | 20 |
| La Cocina/Frida | *Mex.* | 20 |
| Z Giordano's | *Pizza* | 23 |
| Goose Island | *Pub* | 17 |
| Half Shell | *Seafood* | 24 |
| HB Home Bistro | *Amer.* | 25 |
| NEW Hearty | *Amer.* | — |
| Irish Oak | *Pub* | 19 |
| NEW Istanbul | *Turkish* | — |
| Jack's on Halsted | *Amer.* | 21 |
| Joey's Brickhouse | *Amer.* | 20 |
| Julius Meinl | *Austrian* | 21 |
| Kit Kat | *Eclectic* | 16 |
| La Crêperie | *Crêpes/French* | 21 |
| Z La Gondola | *Italian* | 24 |
| Las Tablas | *Colombian/Steak* | 20 |
| NEW Leo's Coney Island | *Hot Dogs* | — |
| Los Moles | *Mex.* | — |
| NEW Melanthios | *Greek/Steak* | — |
| Z Mia Francesca | *Italian* | 26 |
| Mixteco Grill | *Mex.* | 25 |
| Mythos | *Greek* | 23 |
| NEW 90 Miles | *Cuban* | 22 |
| Nookies | *Diner* | 20 |
| Orange | *Eclectic* | 20 |
| Palette Bistro | *Amer.* | — |
| Penny's Noodle | *Asian* | 20 |
| NEW Pho & I | *Thai/Viet.* | — |
| NEW Piggery | *BBQ* | — |
| pingpong | *Asian* | 20 |
| Pizza Capri | *Pizza* | 20 |
| Pompei Bakery | *Italian* | 19 |
| Z Potbelly | *Sandwiches* | 19 |
| NEW Red Brick | *Eclectic/Med.* | — |
| Rise | *Japanese* | 21 |
| Risqué Café | *BBQ* | — |
| Rockit B&G | *Amer.* | 19 |

| | |
|---|---|
| Rollapalooza | *Japanese* | — |
| Sapore/Napoli | *Pizza* | 20 |
| socca | *French/Italian* | 22 |
| sola | *Amer.* | 25 |
| Southport | *Sandwiches* | 22 |
| Sura | *Thai* | 20 |
| NEW Taco Fuego | *Mex.* | — |
| Tango Sur | *Argent./Steak* | 24 |
| Thai Classic | *Thai* | 23 |
| Twist | *Eclectic* | 21 |
| Uncommon Ground | *Eclectic/Coffee* | 22 |
| Wakamono | *Japanese* | 22 |
| Yoshi's Café | *French/Japanese* | 25 |

## LINCOLN PARK

(See map on page 214)

### TOP FOOD

| | |
|---|---|
| Alinea | *Amer.* | **I7** | 29 |
| L2O | *Seafood* | **E10** | 27 |
| Charlie Trotter's | *Amer.* | **G6** | 27 |
| Riccardo | *Italian* | **F10** | 27 |
| BOKA | *Amer.* | **I7** | 25 |
| North Pond | *Amer.* | **B10** | 25 |
| Terragusto | *Italian* | **G10** | 25 |
| Sai Café | *Japanese* | **G5** | 25 |
| Rose Angelis | *Italian* | **B3** | 24 |
| Merlo | *Italian* | **B5** | **G7** | 24 |
| Itto Sushi | *Japanese* | **B6** | 24 |
| Perennial | *Amer.* | **H11** | 24 |
| Lou Malnati's | *Pizza* | **B5** | 24 |
| Original/Walker Pancake | *Amer.* | **F10** | 24 |
| Chicago Pizza | *Pizza* | **F10** | 23 |

### LISTING

| | |
|---|---|
| Aladdin's Eatery | *Mideast.* | 18 |
| Z Alinea | *Amer.* | 29 |
| Z Al's #1 Beef | *Sandwiches* | 23 |
| Bacino's | *Italian* | 22 |
| Basil Leaf | *Italian* | 18 |
| BOKA | *Amer.* | 25 |
| Boston Blackies | *Burgers* | 19 |
| Bricks | *Pizza* | 22 |
| Cafe Ba-Ba-Reeba! | *Spanish* | 22 |
| Café Bernard | *French* | 19 |
| Z Charlie Trotter's | *Amer.* | 27 |
| Chicago Pizza | *Pizza* | 23 |
| Counter | *Burgers* | 20 |
| Dee's | *Asian* | 19 |
| NEW Duck Walk | *Thai* | 19 |
| Edwardo's Pizza | *Pizza* | 20 |
| Filippo's | *Italian* | 24 |
| Five Guys | *Burgers* | 20 |
| NEW Franks 'N' Dawgs | *Hot Dogs* | — |

| | |
|---|---|
| Geja's Cafe | *Fondue* | 21 |
| **NEW** Gemini Bistro | *Amer.* | 21 |
| Goose Island | *Pub* | 17 |
| Hai Yen | *Chinese/Viet.* | 21 |
| Hema's Kitchen | *Indian* | 22 |
| Itto Sushi | *Japanese* | 24 |
| J. Alexander's | *Amer.* | 20 |
| John's Place | *Amer.* | 18 |
| Karyn's | *Veg.* | 20 |
| **NEW** Kith & Kin | *Amer.* | - |
| Landmark | *Amer.* | 20 |
| **Z** Lou Malnati's | *Pizza* | 24 |
| **Z** L2O | *Seafood* | 27 |
| **NEW** Macku Sushi | *Japanese* | - |
| **NEW** Masu Izakaya | *Japanese* | - |
| Maza | *Mideast.* | 21 |
| Merlo | *Italian* | 24 |
| Mon Ami Gabi | *French* | 22 |
| **NEW** Nella Pizza | *Pizza* | 22 |
| Nookies | *Diner* | 20 |
| **Z** North Pond | *Amer.* | 25 |
| Orange | *Eclectic* | 20 |
| **Z** Original Gino's | *Pizza* | 22 |
| **Z** Original/Walker Pancake | *Amer.* | 24 |
| **NEW** Orvieto Pizza | *Pizza* | - |
| Pasta Palazzo | *Italian* | 22 |
| Penny's Noodle | *Asian* | 20 |
| Perennial | *Amer.* | 24 |
| Pizza Capri | *Pizza* | 20 |
| **Z** Potbelly | *Sandwiches* | 19 |
| Raj Darbar | *Indian* | 18 |
| **Z** Riccardo | *Italian* | 27 |
| Ringo | *Japanese* | - |
| R.J. Grunts | *Amer.* | 19 |
| Robinson's Ribs | *BBQ* | 21 |
| Rose Angelis | *Italian* | 24 |
| Sai Café | *Japanese* | 25 |
| Sapori Trattoria | *Italian* | 23 |
| **NEW** Sarks/Park | *Sandwiches* | - |
| Shine Morida | *Chinese/Japanese* | - |
| Simply It | *Viet.* | 22 |
| **NEW** Sprout | *Amer./French* | 28 |
| Stanley's | *Amer.* | 18 |
| Tarantino's | *Italian* | 22 |
| Terragusto | *Italian* | 25 |
| Toast | *Amer.* | 22 |
| Trattoria Gianni | *Italian* | 26 |
| Tsuki | *Japanese* | 23 |
| Via Carducci | *Italian* | 23 |
| Vinci | *Italian* | 21 |
| **NEW** Vintage 338 | *Euro.* | - |
| Webster Wine | *Eclectic* | 20 |
| **Z** Wiener's Circle | *Hot Dogs* | 21 |

## LINCOLN SQUARE/ UPTOWN

| | |
|---|---|
| Agami | *Japanese* | 24 |
| **Z** Bistro Campagne | *French* | 25 |
| Café Selmarie | *Amer.* | 23 |
| **NEW** Ceres' Table | *Amer.* | - |
| Dorado | *French/Mex.* | 23 |
| Essence/India | *Indian* | 21 |
| **NEW** Fame da Lupo | *Pizza* | - |
| Fiddlehead | *Amer.* | 20 |
| Fontana Grill | *Italian* | - |
| Hai Yen | *Chinese/Viet.* | 21 |
| Isla Filipino | *Filipino* | - |
| Jack Rabbit | *SW* | - |
| Julius Meinl | *Austrian* | 21 |
| **NEW** Klopa Grill | *Serbian* | - |
| La Bocca/Verità | *Italian* | 22 |
| **NEW** La Ciudad | *Mex.* | - |
| **NEW** LM | *French* | 22 |
| Marigold | *Indian* | 23 |
| Pho 777 | *Viet.* | 21 |
| Phò Xe Tång | *Viet.* | 26 |
| Pizza D.O.C. | *Pizza* | 23 |
| **NEW** RendezVous | *French* | - |
| **NEW** Rolis | *Mex.* | - |
| Silver Seafood | *Chinese/Seafood* | 23 |
| Spoon Thai | *Thai* | 23 |
| Tank Sushi | *Japanese* | 23 |
| Thai Pastry | *Thai* | 23 |
| Trattoria Trullo | *Italian* | 23 |
| Tweet | *Amer.* | 22 |

## NEAR NORTH

| | |
|---|---|
| Châtaigne | *Continental/Eclectic* | - |
| Fleming's | *Steak* | 23 |
| Kiki's | *French* | 25 |
| **Z** mk | *Amer.* | 27 |

## NORTH CENTER/ ST. BEN'S

| | |
|---|---|
| **NEW** Browntrout | *American* | 24 |
| Cafe 28 | *Cuban/Mex.* | 26 |
| **NEW** Corner 41 | *Amer.* | - |
| Fonda del Mar | *Mex./Seafood* | 25 |
| Jury's | *Pub* | 18 |
| Mrs. Murphy | *Pub* | 22 |
| **NEW** Pitchfork | *BBQ* | - |
| Sanook | *Japanese/Thai* | - |

## OLD TOWN

| | |
|---|---|
| Adobo | *Mex.* | 21 |
| Bistrot Margot | *French* | 20 |
| Dinotto | *Italian* | 19 |
| Flat Top Grill | *Asian* | 20 |
| Kamehachi | *Japanese* | 21 |
| **NEW** Lan's Bistro | *Chinese* | - |

| | |
|---|---|
| Mizu Yakitori | *Japanese* | 24 |
| Nookies | *Diner* | 20 |
| Old Jerusalem | *Mideast.* | 19 |
| **NEW** Old Town Social | *Amer.* | 18 |
| Salpicón | *Mex.* | 26 |
| **NEW** 33 Club | *Amer.* | 20 |
| Topo Gigio | *Italian* | 23 |
| Trattoria Roma | *Italian* | 21 |
| Twin Anchors | *BBQ* | 23 |
| Uncle Julio's | *Tex-Mex* | 18 |

## ROGERS PARK/ WEST ROGERS PARK

| | |
|---|---|
| **NEW** Angin Mamiri | *Indonesian* | - |
| Five Guys | *Burgers* | 20 |
| Gruppo/Amici | *Pizza* | 16 |
| **NEW** Hana | *Japanese* | - |
| Heartland Cafe | *Eclectic/Veg.* | 16 |
| Hema's Kitchen | *Indian* | 22 |
| Hop Häus | *Burgers* | 19 |
| Indian Garden | *Indian* | 21 |
| **NEW** Morgan Harbor | *Kosher/Seafood* | - |
| RoPa | *Med.* | - |
| Tiffin | *Indian* | 21 |
| Udupi Palace | *Indian* | 23 |
| Viet Bistro | *Viet.* | 25 |

## Downtown

### LOOP

| | |
|---|---|
| Aria | *Asian* | 24 |
| Atwood Cafe | *Amer.* | 22 |
| Aurelio's Pizza | *Pizza* | 23 |
| Bacino's | *Italian* | 22 |
| Berghoff | *German* | 18 |
| Billy Goat | *Amer.* | 17 |
| Boston Blackies | *Burgers* | 19 |
| **Z** Carnivale | *Nuevo Latino* | 23 |
| **Z** Catch 35 | *Seafood* | 24 |
| China Grill | *Asian* | 22 |
| **NEW** Cibo Matto | *Italian* | 24 |
| Crêpes Cafe | *Crêpes* | - |
| Epic Burger | *Burgers* | 22 |
| **Z** Everest | *French* | 27 |
| Flat Top Grill | *Asian* | 20 |
| **Z** Gage | *Amer.* | 22 |
| **Z** Giordano's | *Pizza* | 23 |
| Gold Coast | *Hot Dogs* | 19 |
| Grillroom | *Steak* | 15 |
| **Z** Hannah's Bretzel | *Sandwiches* | 23 |
| **Z** Heaven on Seven | *Cajun/Creole* | 23 |
| Hot Woks | *Asian* | 23 |
| La Cantina | *Italian/Seafood* | 21 |
| Lockwood | *Amer.* | 19 |

| | |
|---|---|
| Lou Mitchell's | *Diner* | 23 |
| McCormick/Schmick's | *Seafood* | 21 |
| Miller's Pub | *Amer.* | 17 |
| **Z** Morton's | *Steak* | 26 |
| **Z** N9ne Steak | *Seafood/Steak* | 24 |
| One North | *Amer.* | 15 |
| Palm | *Steak* | 24 |
| Park Grill | *Amer.* | 20 |
| Perry's Deli | *Deli* | 26 |
| Petterino's | *Amer.* | 19 |
| **Z** Potbelly | *Sandwiches* | 19 |
| Rhapsody | *Amer.* | 20 |
| rist. we | *Italian* | 20 |
| Robinson's Ribs | *BBQ* | 21 |
| **Z** Rosebud | *Italian* | 22 |
| Rosebud Prime/Steak | *Steak* | 25 |
| Roti | *Med.* | 21 |
| Russian Tea | *Russian* | 22 |
| Shikago | *Asian* | 18 |
| South Water | *Amer.* | 16 |
| **NEW** State and Lake | *Amer.* | 21 |
| Tavern/Park | *Amer.* | 20 |
| **NEW** Terzo Piano | *Italian* | 21 |
| Thai Urban | *Asian* | 16 |
| 312 Chicago | *Italian* | 21 |
| Trattoria No. 10 | *Italian* | 24 |
| Village | *Italian* | 21 |
| Vivere | *Italian* | 22 |

### RIVER NORTH

(See map on page 212)

**TOP FOOD**

| | |
|---|---|
| Topolobampo | *Mex.* | **D6** | 28 |
| Naha | *Amer.* | **D6** | 27 |
| Frontera Grill | *Mex.* | **D6** | 27 |
| Joe's Sea/Steak | *Seafood/Steak* | **C8** | 26 |
| Avenues | *Amer.* | **A8** | 26 |
| Crofton on Wells | *Amer.* | **C5** | 26 |
| Zealous | *Amer.* | **A4** | 25 |
| Shanghai Terrace | *Asian* | **A8** | 25 |
| XOCO | *Mex.* | **D6** | 25 |
| Coco Pazzo | *Italian* | **D5** | 25 |
| David Burke Prime | *Steak* | **C8** | 25 |
| Keefer's | *Amer.* | **D7** | 25 |
| Chicago Chop | *Steak* | **B7** | 25 |
| Ruth's Chris | *Steak* | **D7** | 25 |
| Roy's | *Hawaiian* | **A7** | 25 |

**LISTING**

| | |
|---|---|
| Ai Sushi | *Japanese* | 24 |
| aja | *Asian* | - |
| Al Primo Canto | *Brazilian/Italian* | 24 |
| **Z** Al's #1 Beef | *Sandwiches* | 23 |
| **Z** Avenues | *Amer.* | 26 |

| | |
|---|---|
| Bar Louie \| *Pub* | 16 |
| NEW Benny's \| *Italian/Steak* | - |
| Ben Pao \| *Chinese* | 21 |
| Big Bowl \| *Asian* | 20 |
| Bijan's \| *Amer.* | 19 |
| Billy Goat \| *Amer.* | 17 |
| Bin 36/Wine \| *Amer.* | 21 |
| Blue 13 \| *Amer.* | 24 |
| Brasserie Jo \| *French* | 22 |
| Brazzaz \| *Brazilian/Steak* | 22 |
| Café Iberico \| *Spanish* | 22 |
| Carson's Ribs \| *BBQ* | 22 |
| Z Chicago Chop \| *Steak* | 25 |
| Z Coco Pazzo \| *Italian* | 25 |
| Z Crofton on Wells \| *Amer.* | 26 |
| Cyrano's Bistrot \| *French* | 22 |
| Z David Burke Prime \| *Steak* | 25 |
| Devon Seafood \| *Seafood* | 21 |
| NEW Dos Diablos \| *Tex-Mex* | - |
| Ed Debevic's \| *Diner* | 15 |
| NEW Elate \| *Amer.* | 21 |
| NEW Epic \| *Amer.* | - |
| Erie Cafe \| *Italian/Steak* | 22 |
| Flatwater \| *Eclectic* | 16 |
| Fogo de Chão \| *Brazilian/Steak* | 24 |
| 1492 \| *Spanish* | 21 |
| Z Frontera Grill \| *Mex.* | 27 |
| Fulton's \| *Seafood/Steak* | 19 |
| Z Gene & Georgetti \| *Steak* | 24 |
| NEW Gilt Bar \| *Amer.* | - |
| Z Giordano's \| *Pizza* | 23 |
| graham elliot \| *Amer.* | 24 |
| Grand Lux \| *Eclectic* | 20 |
| Hard Rock \| *Amer.* | 12 |
| Harry Caray's \| *Italian/Steak* | 20 |
| NEW Havana \| *Nuevo Latino* | - |
| Z Heaven on Seven \| *Cajun/Creole* | 23 |
| Hop Häus \| *Burgers* | 19 |
| HUB 51 \| *Amer./Eclectic* | 21 |
| Z India House \| *Indian* | 25 |
| NEW Italiasia \| *Asian/Italian* | - |
| Z Japonais \| *Japanese* | 24 |
| Z Joe's Sea/Steak \| *Seafood/Steak* | 26 |
| Kan Zaman \| *Lebanese* | - |
| Karyn's \| *Vegan* | 20 |
| Z Keefer's \| *Amer.* | 25 |
| Kinzie Chophouse \| *Steak* | 22 |
| Kitsch'n/K-Cafe \| *Eclectic* | 19 |
| Klay Oven \| *Indian* | 20 |
| La Madia \| *Italian/Pizza* | 23 |
| Lawry's \| *Amer./Steak* | 24 |
| Lobby \| *Euro./Seafood* | 28 |
| Z Lou Malnati's \| *Pizza* | 24 |
| Z Maggiano's \| *Italian* | 20 |
| Melting Pot \| *Fondue* | 19 |
| NEW Mercadito \| *Mex.* | 22 |
| Z Mr. Beef \| *Sandwiches* | 24 |
| Z Nacional 27 \| *Nuevo Latino* | 23 |
| Z Naha \| *Amer.* | 27 |
| Orange \| *Eclectic* | 20 |
| Z Original Gino's \| *Pizza* | 22 |
| Osteria/Pizzeria Via Stato \| *Italian* | 23 |
| Oysy \| *Japanese* | 20 |
| P.F. Chang's \| *Chinese* | 20 |
| Phil Stefani's \| *Italian/Steak* | 24 |
| Pierrot Gourmet \| *French* | 20 |
| Pizzeria Uno/Due \| *Pizza* | 22 |
| Z Potbelly \| *Sandwiches* | 19 |
| Prosecco \| *Italian* | 24 |
| NEW Purple Pig \| *Med.* | - |
| Quartino \| *Italian* | 21 |
| RB Grille \| *Steak* | - |
| Reza's \| *Med./Mideast.* | 18 |
| Rockit B&G \| *Amer.* | 19 |
| Rosebud Trattoria \| *Italian* | 22 |
| Roy's \| *Hawaiian* | 25 |
| Rumba \| *Nuevo Latino* | 23 |
| Z Ruth's Chris \| *Steak* | 25 |
| NEW Sable \| *Amer.* | - |
| Scoozi! \| *Italian* | 19 |
| Z Shanghai Terrace \| *Asian* | 25 |
| Z Shaw's Crab \| *Seafood* | 24 |
| Z Sixteen \| *Amer.* | 22 |
| Smith & Wollensky \| *Steak* | 23 |
| Star of Siam \| *Thai* | 20 |
| Steve's Deli \| *Deli* | 17 |
| Sullivan's Steak \| *Steak* | 22 |
| Sunda \| *Asian* | 23 |
| Sushi Naniwa \| *Japanese* | 23 |
| SushiSamba \| *Japanese/S Amer.* | 21 |
| NEW Sushi Taiyo \| *Japanese* | - |
| Texas de Brazil \| *Brazilian* | 22 |
| Z Topolobampo \| *Mex.* | 28 |
| Vermilion \| *Indian/Nuevo Latino* | 22 |
| Weber Grill \| *BBQ* | 20 |
| Z Wildfire \| *Steak* | 23 |
| NEW XOCO \| *Mex.* | 25 |
| Yolk \| *Amer.* | 22 |
| Zealous \| *Amer.* | 25 |
| ZED 451 \| *Eclectic* | 21 |
| Zocalo \| *Mex.* | 20 |

## STREETERVILLE

| | |
|---|---|
| American Girl \| *Amer.* | 16 |
| Bandera \| *Amer.* | 22 |

| | |
|---|---|
| Bice | *Italian* | 21 |
| Billy Goat | *Amer.* | 17 |
| Boston Blackies | *Burgers* | 19 |
| Cape Cod Room | *Seafood* | 22 |
| ☑ Capital Grille | *Steak* | 25 |
| ☑ Cheesecake Factory | *Amer.* | 19 |
| C-House | *Seafood* | 21 |
| Cité | *Amer.* | 20 |
| Coco Pazzo Café | *Italian* | 22 |
| NEW deca | *French* | - |
| ☑ Emilio's Tapas | *Spanish* | 24 |
| foodlife | *Eclectic* | 19 |
| Francesca's | *Italian* | 22 |
| Grill on Alley | *Amer.* | 21 |
| Indian Garden | *Indian* | 21 |
| Kamehachi | *Japanese* | 21 |
| LB Bistro | *Amer.* | - |
| Le P'tit Paris | *Continental/French* | 20 |
| ☑ Les Nomades | *French* | 29 |
| Markethouse | *Amer.* | 21 |
| NEW M Burger | *Burgers* | - |
| Mity Nice Grill | *Amer.* | 17 |
| Niu | *Asian* | 19 |
| ☑ Original Gino's | *Pizza* | 22 |
| ☑ Original/Walker Pancake | *Amer.* | 24 |
| NEW Pelago | *Italian* | 26 |
| P.J. Clarke's | *Amer.* | 17 |
| Pompei Bakery | *Italian* | 19 |
| Puck's at MCA | *Amer.* | 20 |
| Riva | *Seafood* | 20 |
| Rosebud Prime/Steak | *Steak* | 25 |
| Saloon Steak | *Steak* | 23 |
| Sayat Nova | *Armenian* | 23 |
| Shula's Steak | *Steak* | 21 |
| ☑ Signature Room | *Amer.* | 18 |
| ☑ Tru | *French* | 28 |
| Viand Bar | *Amer.* | 22 |
| Volare | *Italian* | 24 |
| Wave | *Med.* | 13 |

## City Northwest

### BUCKTOWN

(See map on page 216)

**TOP FOOD**

| | | |
|---|---|---|
| Takashi | *Amer./French* | **E5** | 26 |
| mado | *Italian/Med.* | **G4** | 25 |
| Coast Sushi/South Coast | *Japanese* | **D5** | 24 |
| Hot Chocolate | *Amer.* | **G5** | 24 |
| Le Bouchon | *French* | **E5** | 24 |

**LISTING**

| | | |
|---|---|---|
| Birchwood | *Sandwiches* | 23 |
| Bluebird | *Amer.* | 20 |

| | |
|---|---|
| Bricks | *Pizza* | 22 |
| Bristol | *Amer.* | 23 |
| Café Absinthe | *Amer.* | 23 |
| Cafe Matou | *French* | 23 |
| Club Lucky | *Italian* | 19 |
| Coast Sushi/South Coast | *Japanese* | 24 |
| Duchamp | *Amer.* | 17 |
| Feast | *Amer.* | 19 |
| Honey 1 BBQ | *BBQ* | 20 |
| Hot Chocolate | *Amer.* | 24 |
| Irazu | *Costa Rican* | 22 |
| Jane's | *Amer./Eclectic* | 22 |
| Las Palmas | *Mex.* | 21 |
| Le Bouchon | *French* | 24 |
| NEW LOKaL | *Euro.* | - |
| ☑ mado | *Italian/Med.* | 25 |
| ☑ Margie's Candies | *Amer.* | 22 |
| NEW Siboney | *Cuban* | - |
| NEW Southern | *Southern* | - |
| ☑ Takashi | *Amer./French* | 26 |
| Toast | *Amer.* | 22 |
| Tocco | *Italian* | 12 |

### EDISON PARK/ O'HARE AREA

| | |
|---|---|
| Berghoff | *German* | 18 |
| Big Bowl | *Asian* | 20 |
| Billy Goat | *Amer.* | 17 |
| Café la Cave | *Continental* | 21 |
| ☑ Capital Grille | *Steak* | 25 |
| Carlucci | *Italian* | 20 |
| ☑ Cheesecake Factory | *Amer.* | 19 |
| Don Juan's | *Mex.* | 20 |
| Fleming's | *Steak* | 23 |
| ☑ Gibsons | *Steak* | 26 |
| ☑ Giordano's | *Pizza* | 23 |
| Gold Coast | *Hot Dogs* | 19 |
| Harry Caray's | *Italian/Steak* | 20 |
| Lou Mitchell's | *Diner* | 23 |
| ☑ Morton's | *Steak* | 26 |
| Nick's Fishmarket | *Seafood* | 23 |
| NEW Oba | *Japanese* | - |
| ☑ Original Gino's | *Pizza* | 22 |
| ☑ Original/Walker Pancake | *Amer.* | 24 |
| Sullivan's Steak | *Steak* | 22 |
| ☑ Wildfire | *Steak* | 23 |
| Zia's Trattoria | *Italian* | 24 |

### HUMBOLDT PARK

| | |
|---|---|
| NEW Belly Shack | *Asian* | 23 |
| Maiz | *Mex.* | 23 |
| NEW Rootstock | *Amer.* | 24 |

## LOGAN SQUARE

**NEW** Accanto | *Italian* – |
Azucar | *Spanish* 22 |
**Z** Bonsoirée | *Amer./French* 26 |
Buona Terra | *Italian* 24 |
**NEW** Ciao Napoli | *Pizza* – |
**NEW** Conoce/Panama | *Central Amer.* – |
Estrella Negra | *Mex./Nuevo Latino* – |
Fat Willy's | *BBQ/Southern* 23 |
Fuego | *Mex.* 24 |
Hachi's Kitchen | *Japanese* – |
**NEW** Katakana & Koko | *Japanese* – |
**NEW** (k)new | *Amer./Eclectic* – |
**Z** Kuma's | *Amer.* 26 |
**NEW** Longman & Eagle | *Amer.* – |
**Z** Lula Cafe | *Eclectic* 26 |
**NEW** 90 Miles | *Cuban* 22 |
Real Tenochtitlán | *Mex.* 20 |
**NEW** Revolution Brewing | *Pub* – |
**NEW** Rustico Grill | *Mex.* – |
urbanbelly | *Asian* 24 |

## NORTHWEST SIDE/ RAVENSWOOD

Al Primo Canto | *Brazilian/Italian* 24 |
Amitabul | *Korean* 21 |
Andies | *Med./Mideast* 18 |
Anna Maria | *Italian* 24 |
**Z** Arun's | *Thai* 28 |
**NEW** Blue Ocean | *Japanese* 23 |
**NEW** Cafe Marbella | *Spanish* – |
**NEW** Café Touché | *French* 25 |
Chief O'Neill's | *Pub* 18 |
**NEW** Fountainhead | *Pub* – |
Gale St. Inn | *Amer.* 22 |
**Z** Giordano's | *Pizza* 23 |
**Z** Glenn's Diner | *Diner* 24 |
**Z** Hot Doug's | *Hot Dogs* 27 |
Hot Woks | *Asian* 23 |
**Z** Katsu | *Japanese* 27 |
Las Tablas | *Colombian/Steak* 20 |
**NEW** Little Bucharest | *Euro.* – |
Magnolia Cafe | *Amer.* 22 |
**Z** Margie's Candies | *Amer.* 22 |
Mirabell | *Amer./German* 21 |
Noon-O-Kabab | *Persian* 25 |
Over Easy | *Amer.* 27 |
**NEW** Park Place | *Amer./Eclectic* – |
Sabatino's | *Italian* 24 |
San Soo Gab San | *Korean* 21 |
**Z** Smoque BBQ | *BBQ* 26 |
Sol de Mexico | *Mex.* 25 |

Spacca Napoli | *Pizza* 23 |
**Z** Superdawg | *Burgers/Hot Dogs* 21 |
Tre Kronor | *Scan.* 23 |
Viceroy of India | *Indian* 21 |

## ROSCOE VILLAGE

John's Place | *Amer.* 18 |
Kitsch'n/K-Cafe | *Eclectic* 19 |
Orange | *Eclectic* 20 |
Piazza Bella | *Italian* 21 |
**NEW** Pizzeria Serio | *Pizza* – |
Terragusto | *Italian* 25 |
Turquoise | *Turkish* 23 |
Victory's Banner | *Eclectic/Veg.* 24 |
Volo | *Amer.* – |
Wishbone | *Southern* 21 |

## WICKER PARK

(See map on page 216)

### TOP FOOD

Schwa | *Amer.* | **I8** 29 |
Spring | *Amer./Seafood* | **H4** 27 |
Mirai Sushi | *Japanese* | **K4** 25 |
Smoke Daddy | *BBQ* | **K6** 24 |
Bongo Room | *Amer.* | **I5** 24 |

### LISTING

Adobo | *Mex.* 21 |
**NEW** Big Star | *Mex.* 23 |
Bin 36/Wine | *Amer.* 21 |
Bob San | *Japanese* 24 |
Bongo Room | *Amer.* 24 |
**NEW** Crêpe Crave | *Crêpes* – |
Crust | *Pizza* 19 |
**NEW** Dee's Place | *Soul/Southern* – |
Fifty/50 | *Amer.* 21 |
Francesca's | *Italian* 22 |
Jerry's | *Sandwiches* 22 |
**NEW** J. Wellington's | *Burgers* – |
La Fonda/Gusto | *Mex.* – |
MANA Food | *Eclectic/Veg.* 27 |
Milk & Honey | *Amer.* 23 |
Mirai Sushi | *Japanese* 25 |
Penny's Noodle | *Asian* 20 |
Piece | *Pizza* 23 |
**Z** Schwa | *Amer.* 29 |
**Z** Smoke Daddy | *BBQ* 24 |
**Z** Spring | *Amer./Seafood* 27 |
Taxim | *Greek* 22 |
Via Carducci | *Italian* 23 |

## City South

## CHINATOWN

**Z** Al's #1 Beef | *Sandwiches* 23 |
Double Li | *Chinese* – |

| | |
|---|---|
| Emperor's Choice | *Chinese* | 23 |
| Evergreen | *Chinese* | 23 |
| Happy Chef | *Chinese* | 23 |
| House of Fortune | *Chinese* | 23 |
| Joy Yee | *Asian* | 20 |
| ☑ Lao | *Chinese* | 24 |
| Lee Wing Wah | *Chinese* | - |
| Mandarin Kitchen | *Chinese* | - |
| Moon Palace | *Chinese* | 22 |
| ☑ Phoenix | *Chinese* | 23 |
| Shui Wah | *Chinese* | 24 |
| Spring World | *Chinese* | - |
| Three Happiness | *Chinese* | 21 |

## FAR SOUTH SIDE

| | |
|---|---|
| Army & Lou's | *Southern* | 26 |
| Café 103 | *Amer./Eclectic* | - |
| Koda | *French* | - |
| Lem's BBQ | *BBQ* | 25 |
| Parrot Cage | *Amer.* | - |
| Sikia | *African* | - |
| Uncle John's | *BBQ* | - |
| Vito & Nick's | *Pizza* | 25 |

## HYDE PARK/ KENWOOD

| | |
|---|---|
| Bar Louie | *Pub* | 16 |
| Edwardo's Pizza | *Pizza* | 20 |
| ☑ Giordano's | *Pizza* | 23 |
| la petite folie | *French* | 24 |
| Medici on 57th | *Amer.* | 17 |
| ☑ Original/Walker Pancake | *Amer.* | 24 |
| Park 52 | *Amer.* | 19 |
| Pizza Capri | *Pizza* | 20 |
| Ribs 'n' Bibs | *BBQ* | 21 |

## NEAR SOUTH SIDE

| | |
|---|---|
| NEW Han 202 | *Asian/Eclectic* | 25 |

## PILSEN

| | |
|---|---|
| NEW Decolores | *Mex.* | - |
| Mundial | *Eclectic* | - |
| NEW Nightwood | *Amer.* | 23 |
| Rist. al Teatro | *Italian/Med.* | - |

## PRINTER'S ROW

| | |
|---|---|
| Bar Louie | *Pub* | 16 |
| Custom House | *Amer.* | 25 |
| Hackney's | *Burgers* | 18 |

## SOUTH LOOP

| | |
|---|---|
| Bongo Room | *Amer.* | 24 |
| Café Bionda | *Italian* | 22 |
| Chicago Curry | *Indian/Nepalese* | 25 |
| Chicago Firehouse | *Amer.* | 20 |

| | |
|---|---|
| Coast Sushi/South Coast | *Japanese* | 24 |
| Edwardo's Pizza | *Pizza* | 20 |
| Eleven City | *Diner* | 19 |
| NEW Flo & Santos | *Pizza/Pub Food* | - |
| Gioco | *Italian* | 25 |
| Grace O'Malley's | *Pub* | 18 |
| Joy Yee | *Asian* | 20 |
| Kroll's | *Amer.* | 19 |
| Manny's | *Deli* | 23 |
| ☑ Mercat | *Spanish* | 26 |
| Mesón Sabika | *Spanish* | 23 |
| Opera | *Asian* | 20 |
| Oysy | *Japanese* | 20 |
| Tamarind | *Asian* | 23 |
| Yolk | *Amer.* | 22 |
| Zapatista | *Mex.* | 20 |

## SOUTHWEST SIDE

| | |
|---|---|
| Bacchanalia | *Italian* | 24 |
| Bruna's | *Italian* | 26 |
| ☑ Giordano's | *Pizza* | 23 |
| Gold Coast | *Hot Dogs* | 19 |
| Harry Caray's | *Italian/Steak* | 20 |
| ☑ Lou Malnati's | *Pizza* | 24 |
| Manny's | *Deli* | 23 |
| Pegasus | *Greek* | 20 |
| ☑ Superdawg | *Burgers/Hot Dogs* | 21 |

## City West

### FAR WEST

| | |
|---|---|
| Depot Diner | *Diner* | - |

### GREEKTOWN

| | |
|---|---|
| Artopolis | *Greek/Med.* | 22 |
| Athena | *Greek* | 21 |
| ☑ Giordano's | *Pizza* | 23 |
| Greek Islands | *Greek* | 21 |
| NEW Karyn's on Green | *Amer./Vegan* | - |
| Parthenon | *Greek* | 21 |
| Pegasus | *Greek* | 20 |
| Roditys | *Greek* | 21 |
| Santorini | *Greek/Seafood* | 21 |
| Venus | *Greek* | - |

### LITTLE ITALY/ UNIVERSITY VILLAGE

| | |
|---|---|
| NEW Aldino's | *Italian* | - |
| ☑ Al's #1 Beef | *Sandwiches* | 23 |
| Bar Louie | *Pub* | 16 |
| Chez Joël | *French* | 24 |
| Francesca's | *Italian* | 22 |
| Perry's Deli | *Deli* | 26 |

| | |
|---|---|
| Pompei Bakery | *Italian* | 19 |
| RoSal's | *Italian* | 26 |
| ☑ Rosebud | *Italian* | 22 |
| Tufano's Tap | *Italian* | 20 |
| Tuscany | *Italian* | 22 |

## NEAR WEST

| | |
|---|---|
| Breakfast Club | *Amer.* | 20 |
| Dining Rm./Kendall | *French* | 23 |
| Orange | *Eclectic* | 20 |
| Paramount Room | *Amer.* | 24 |
| Piccolo Sogno | *Italian* | 24 |
| Twisted Spoke | *Pub* | 18 |

## RIVER WEST

| | |
|---|---|
| NEW Kin | *Japanese/Thai* | - |
| La Scarola | *Italian* | 24 |
| Roti | *Med.* | 21 |
| Sushi X | *Japanese* | 21 |
| Thalia Spice | *Asian* | 19 |

## UKRAINIAN VILLAGE

| | |
|---|---|
| ☑ a tavola | *Italian* | 26 |
| NEW Folklore | *Argent./Steak* | - |
| NEW Jam | *Amer.* | 21 |
| Old Oak Tap | *Pub* | 20 |
| NEW Sabor Saveur | *French/Mex.* | - |

## WEST LOOP

| | |
|---|---|
| Alhambra | *Mideast.* | 16 |
| ☑ avec | *Med.* | 26 |
| Bacino's | *Italian* | 22 |
| Bar Louie | *Pub* | 16 |
| Bella Notte | *Italian* | 21 |
| Billy Goat | *Amer.* | 17 |
| ☑ Blackbird | *Amer.* | 27 |
| Butterfly | *Japanese/Thai* | 22 |
| Carmichael's | *Steak* | 22 |
| Coalfire Pizza | *Pizza* | 23 |
| de cero | *Mex.* | 21 |
| NEW Felony Franks | *Hot Dogs* | - |
| Flat Top Grill | *Asian* | 20 |
| Ina's | *Amer.* | 23 |
| Jaipur | *Indian* | - |
| Jerry's | *Sandwiches* | 22 |
| La Sardine | *French* | 24 |
| Macello | *Italian* | - |
| Marché | *French* | 23 |
| Market | *Amer.* | 18 |
| May St. Market | *Amer.* | 24 |
| Meiji | *Japanese* | 25 |
| NEW Mezé | *Eclectic* | - |
| ☑ Moto | *Eclectic* | 27 |
| Nia | *Med.* | - |
| ☑ one sixtyblue | *Amer.* | 26 |

| | |
|---|---|
| Otom | *Amer.* | 22 |
| NEW Pasha | *Spanish* | - |
| NEW Prairie Fire | *Amer.* | - |
| Province | *Amer.* | 23 |
| ☑ Publican | *Amer.* | 25 |
| Red Light | *Asian* | 23 |
| Sepia | *Amer.* | 24 |
| Stanley's | *Amer.* | 18 |
| ☑ sushi wabi | *Japanese* | 27 |
| Tasting Room | *Amer.* | 20 |
| Trattoria Isabella | *Italian* | 26 |
| Veerasway | *Indian* | 21 |
| Vivo | *Italian* | 24 |
| Wishbone | *Southern* | 21 |

## WEST TOWN

| | |
|---|---|
| Branch 27 | *Amer.* | 17 |
| Butterfly | *Japanese/Thai* | 22 |
| Chickpea | *Mideast.* | 22 |
| Flo | *Amer.* | 22 |
| ☑ Green Zebra | *Veg.* | 26 |
| Habana Libre | *Cuban* | 22 |
| Mexique | *Mex.* | 25 |
| Natalino's | *Italian* | 23 |
| West Town | *Amer.* | 24 |

# Suburbs

## SUBURBAN NORTH

| | |
|---|---|
| Abigail's | *Amer.* | 24 |
| Akai Hana | *Japanese* | 21 |
| ☑ Al's #1 Beef | *Sandwiches* | 23 |
| Bagel | *Deli* | 19 |
| Bank Lane | *Amer.* | 23 |
| Bar Louie | *Pub* | 16 |
| Benihana | *Japanese/Steak* | 18 |
| NEW Bistro Bordeaux | *French* | - |
| Blind Faith | *Veg.* | 21 |
| ☑ Bob Chinn's | *Seafood* | 23 |
| NEW Bonsai Café | *Asian* | - |
| Boston Blackies | *Burgers* | 19 |
| Cafe Central | *French* | 24 |
| Cafe Pyrenees | *French* | 21 |
| Campagnola | *Italian* | 25 |
| ☑ Carlos' | *French* | 27 |
| Carson's Ribs | *BBQ* | 22 |
| NEW Cellar/Stained Glass | *Eclectic* | 21 |
| ☑ Cheesecake Factory | *Amer.* | 19 |
| Chef's Station | *Amer.* | 24 |
| Curry Hut | *Indian/Nepalese* | 20 |
| Dave's Italian | *Italian* | 17 |
| Davis St. Fish | *Seafood* | 19 |
| Del Rio | *Italian* | 20 |
| Depot Nuevo | *Nuevo Latino* | 18 |

| | |
|---|---|
| Di Pescara | *Italian/Seafood* | 19 |
| Dixie Kitchen | *Cajun/Southern* | 19 |
| Edwardo's Pizza | *Pizza* | 20 |
| NEW Edzo's | *Burgers* | - |
| EJ's Place | *Italian/Steak* | 22 |
| 545 North | *Amer.* | 20 |
| Flat Top Grill | *Asian* | 20 |
| Flight | *Eclectic* | 17 |
| Francesca's | *Italian* | 22 |
| Francesco's | *Italian* | 24 |
| fRedhots | *Hot Dogs* | 21 |
| Froggy's | *French* | 22 |
| Z Gabriel's | *French/Italian* | 25 |
| Gale St. Inn | *Amer.* | 22 |
| Hackney's | *Burgers* | 18 |
| NEW Happ Inn | *Amer.* | 17 |
| Hecky's | *BBQ* | 20 |
| Jacky's on Prairie | *French* | 21 |
| J. Alexander's | *Amer.* | 20 |
| Jilly's Cafe | *Amer./French* | 21 |
| Joy Yee | *Asian* | 20 |
| Kamehachi | *Japanese* | 21 |
| Kansaku | *Japanese* | 22 |
| Karma | *Asian* | 23 |
| Koi | *Asian* | 21 |
| Kuni's | *Japanese* | 24 |
| La Casa/Isaac | *Mex.* | 20 |
| Z Lou Malnati's | *Pizza* | 24 |
| Z Lovells | *Amer.* | 23 |
| LuLu's | *Asian* | 21 |
| Lupita's | *Mex.* | 21 |
| L. Woods Tap | *Amer./BBQ* | 20 |
| Z Maggiano's | *Italian* | 20 |
| NEW Main St. Smokehouse | *BBQ* | - |
| Makisu Sushi | *Japanese* | - |
| NEW Manghal | *Med./Kosher* | - |
| McCormick/Schmick's | *Seafood* | 21 |
| Merle's Smokehouse | *BBQ* | 19 |
| Z Michael | *French* | 28 |
| Miramar Bistro | *French* | 17 |
| Mitchell's | *Seafood* | 21 |
| Z Morton's | *Steak* | 26 |
| Mt. Everest | *Indian* | 22 |
| Myron & Phil Steak | *Steak* | 21 |
| Next Door | *Amer./Italian* | 23 |
| Z Oceanique | *French/Seafood* | 27 |
| OPA Estiatorio | *Greek* | 25 |
| Orange | *Eclectic* | 20 |
| Z Original Gino's | *Pizza* | 22 |
| Z Original/Walker Pancake | *Amer.* | 24 |
| Oysy | *Japanese* | 20 |
| Penny's Noodle | *Asian* | 20 |
| Pete Miller | *Seafood/Steak* | 22 |
| P.F. Chang's | *Chinese* | 20 |
| Philly G's | *Italian* | 21 |
| Pine Yard | *Chinese* | 18 |
| Pinstripes | *Amer./Italian* | 17 |
| Z Pita Inn | *Med./Mideast.* | 24 |
| Pomegranate | *Med./Mideast.* | 18 |
| Prairie Grass | *Amer.* | 22 |
| Quince | *Amer.* | 23 |
| RA Sushi | *Japanese* | 19 |
| Z Rosebud | *Italian* | 22 |
| Roti | *Med.* | 21 |
| Ruby of Siam | *Thai* | 23 |
| Z Ruth's Chris | *Steak* | 25 |
| Sage Grille | *Amer.* | 21 |
| San Gabriel | *Mex.* | 17 |
| Sarkis Cafe | *Diner* | 15 |
| South Gate | *Amer.* | 20 |
| Stained Glass | *Amer.* | 23 |
| Stir Crazy | *Asian* | 19 |
| Z Superdawg | *Burgers/Hot Dogs* | 21 |
| Szechwan North | *Chinese* | 19 |
| Tamales | *Mex.* | 20 |
| Tapas Barcelona | *Spanish* | 21 |
| Tapas Gitana | *Spanish* | 24 |
| Tramonto's | *Seafood/Steak* | 24 |
| Trattoria D.O.C. | *Italian/Pizza* | 19 |
| Tub Tim Thai | *Thai* | 24 |
| Tuscany | *Italian* | 22 |
| Union Pizza | *Pizza* | 23 |
| Z Wildfire | *Steak* | 23 |
| Wildfish | *Japanese* | 21 |
| Yard House | *Amer.* | 18 |
| Zapatista | *Mex.* | 20 |
| Zhivago | *Amer./Continental* | 16 |

## SUBURBAN NW

| | |
|---|---|
| Z Al's #1 Beef | *Sandwiches* | 23 |
| Aurelio's Pizza | *Pizza* | 23 |
| Z Barrington Country | *French* | 25 |
| Benihana | *Japanese/Steak* | 18 |
| Big Bowl | *Asian* | 20 |
| Boston Blackies | *Burgers* | 19 |
| Carlos & Carlos | *Italian* | 24 |
| Z Cheesecake Factory | *Amer.* | 19 |
| D & J Bistro | *French* | 24 |
| Edelweiss | *German* | 19 |
| Entourage | *Amer.* | 20 |
| Francesca's | *Italian* | 22 |
| Gaylord Indian | *Indian* | 22 |
| Hackney's | *Burgers* | 18 |
| Z India House | *Indian* | 25 |
| Indian Garden | *Indian* | 21 |
| Inovasi | *Amer.* | - |
| Las Palmas | *Mex.* | 21 |

| | | |
|---|---|---|
| La Tasca | *Spanish* | 24 |
| L'Eiffel | *Crêpes/French* | 21 |
| **Z** Le Titi/Paris | *French* | 26 |
| Le Vichyssois | *French* | 26 |
| **Z** Lou Malnati's | *Pizza* | 24 |
| **NEW** Lucky Monk | *Pizza/Pub* | - |
| **Z** Maggiano's | *Italian* | 20 |
| McCormick/Schmick's | *Seafood* | 21 |
| Melting Pot | *Fondue* | 19 |
| Montarra | *Amer.* | 24 |
| **Z** Morton's | *Steak* | 26 |
| **Z** Original Gino's | *Pizza* | 22 |
| **Z** Original/Walker Pancake | *Amer.* | 24 |
| **Z** Pappadeaux | *Seafood* | 21 |
| P.F. Chang's | *Chinese* | 20 |
| Pinstripes | *Amer./Italian* | 17 |
| Pompei Bakery | *Italian* | 19 |
| Retro Bistro | *French* | 23 |
| Rosebud | *Italian* | 22 |
| Russell's BBQ | *BBQ* | 19 |
| **Z** Ruth's Chris | *Steak* | 25 |
| Salsa 17 | *Mex.* | 22 |
| Sam & Harry's | *Steak* | - |
| Seasons 52 | *Amer.* | - |
| 1776 | *Amer.* | 22 |
| **Z** Shaw's Crab | *Seafood* | 24 |
| Shula's Steak | *Steak* | 21 |
| Stir Crazy | *Asian* | 19 |
| Sushi Ai | *Japanese* | - |
| Texas de Brazil | *Brazilian* | 22 |
| Thai Pastry | *Thai* | 23 |
| Udupi Palace | *Indian* | 23 |
| Weber Grill | *BBQ* | 20 |
| White Fence | *Amer.* | 22 |
| **Z** Wildfire | *Steak* | 23 |
| Wildfish | *Japanese* | 21 |
| Woo Lae Oak | *Korean* | 20 |

## SUBURBAN SOUTH

| | | |
|---|---|---|
| **Z** Al's #1 Beef | *Sandwiches* | 23 |
| Aurelio's Pizza | *Pizza* | 23 |
| Dixie Kitchen | *Cajun/Southern* | 19 |
| **Z** Original/Walker Pancake | *Amer.* | 24 |

## SUBURBAN SW

| | | |
|---|---|---|
| **Z** Al's #1 Beef | *Sandwiches* | 23 |
| Aurelio's Pizza | *Pizza* | 23 |
| Bar Louie | *Pub* | 16 |
| Courtright's | *Amer.* | 25 |
| Dan McGee | *Amer.* | - |
| Hackney's | *Burgers* | 18 |
| **Z** Original Gino's | *Pizza* | 22 |
| P.F. Chang's | *Chinese* | 20 |

| | | |
|---|---|---|
| **Z** Tallgrass | *French* | 28 |
| Tin Fish | *Seafood* | 23 |
| Topaz Café | *Amer.* | 23 |

## SUBURBAN WEST

| | | |
|---|---|---|
| Adelle's | *Amer.* | 25 |
| **Z** Al's #1 Beef | *Sandwiches* | 23 |
| Amber Cafe | *Amer.* | 22 |
| Antico Posto | *Italian* | 22 |
| Atwater's | *Amer./French* | 20 |
| Aurelio's Pizza | *Pizza* | 23 |
| Bacino's | *Italian* | 22 |
| Bar Louie | *Pub* | 16 |
| Benihana | *Japanese/Steak* | 18 |
| Boston Blackies | *Burgers* | 19 |
| Briejo | *Amer./Eclectic* | 14 |
| Brio | *Italian* | 22 |
| Cab's Wine Bar | *Amer.* | 24 |
| **Z** Capital Grille | *Steak* | 25 |
| Carlucci | *Italian* | 19 |
| **Z** Catch 35 | *Seafood* | 24 |
| **Z** Cheesecake Factory | *Amer.* | 19 |
| Chinn's Fishery | *Seafood* | 25 |
| **NEW** CityGate | *Amer./Med.* | - |
| Clubhouse | *Amer.* | 21 |
| Costa's | *Greek* | 22 |
| Cucina Paradiso | *Italian* | 20 |
| Czech Plaza | *Czech* | 22 |
| Distinctive Cork | *Amer.* | 21 |
| **NEW** Duckfat | *Amer.* | - |
| Ed Debevic's | *Diner* | 15 |
| Edwardo's Pizza | *Pizza* | 20 |
| **Z** Emilio's Tapas | *Spanish* | 24 |
| Five Guys | *Burgers* | 20 |
| Flat Top Grill | *Asian* | 20 |
| **NEW** Fonda Isabel | *Mex.* | - |
| Francesca's | *Italian* | 22 |
| Gaetano's | *Italian* | 24 |
| Glen Prairie | *Amer.* | 23 |
| Gordon Biersch | *Pub* | 16 |
| Greek Islands | *Greek* | 21 |
| Harry Caray's | *Italian/Steak* | 20 |
| **Z** Heaven on Seven | *Cajun/Creole* | 23 |
| Hemmingway's | *Amer./French* | 21 |
| Holy Mackerel! | *Seafood* | 21 |
| **Z** Hugo's | *Seafood* | 24 |
| **NEW** Il Poggiolo | *Italian* | 19 |
| **Z** India House | *Indian* | 25 |
| **NEW** Isacco | *Italian/Eclectic* | - |
| J. Alexander's | *Amer.* | 20 |
| Joy Yee | *Asian* | 20 |
| Klay Oven | *Indian* | 20 |
| **Z** Lao | *Chinese* | 24 |

CHICAGO

LOCATIONS

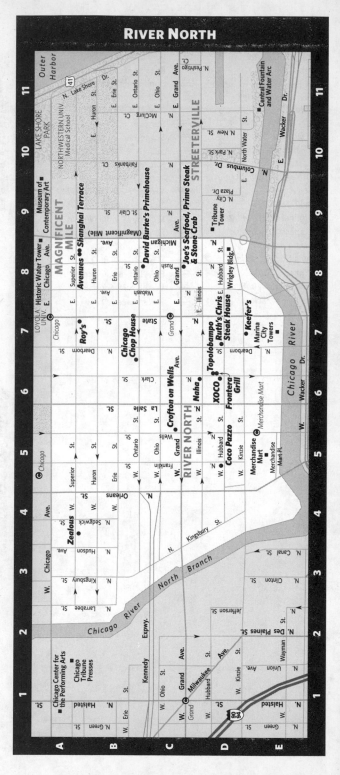

# RIVER NORTH

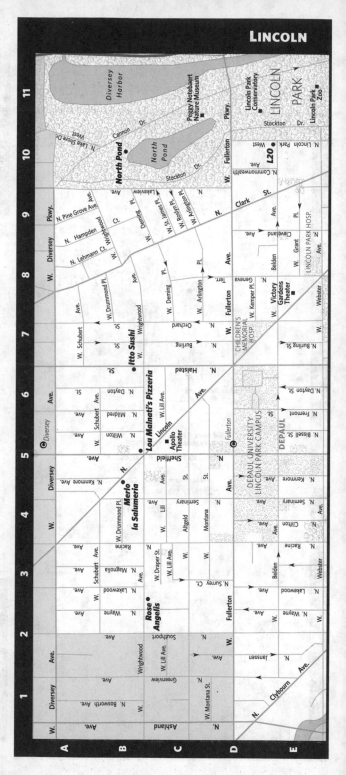

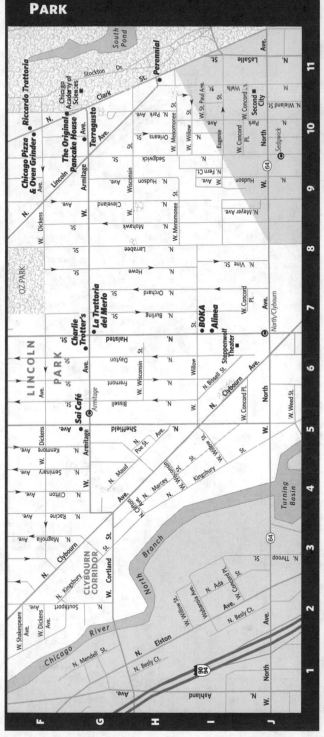

South Pond

Stockton Dr.

LaSalle St.

N.

11

Clark St.

Chicago Academy of Sciences

**Perennial**

W. St. Paul Ave.

N. Wieland St.

N. Wells

St.

W. Concord

**Second City**

Riccardo Trattoria

N.

N. Park Ave.

W. Menomonee St.

W. Willow

Eugenie St.

Park

W. Concord Pl.

**North**

Sedgwick

10

Chicago Pizza & Oven Grinder

**The Original Pancake House**

Lincoln Ave.

**Terragusto**

Sedgwick St.

N. Orleans St.

St.

W. Eugenie

N. Fern Ct.

N.

(64)

Ave.

Armitage Ave.

N. Wisconsin

N. Hudson

N. Meyer Ave.

N. Hudson

W.

9

N. Dickens St.

W. Cleveland Ave.

N. Mohawk

N. Menomonee St.

8

OZ PARK

St.

St.

N. Larrabee St.

N. Howe St.

N. Vine St.

W. Concord Pl.

7

**La Trattoria del Merlo**

N. Orchard St.

N. Burling St.

**BOKA**

**Alinea**

North/Clybourn

**Charlie Trotter's**

Halsted St.

N.

LINCOLN PARK

Armitage Ave.

Ave.

St.

N. Dayton

N. Wisconsin St.

N. Willow

**Steppenwolf Theater**

N. Bissell St.

N. Clybourn

Ave.

6

**Sai Café**

St.

N. Fremont

N. Bissell

W. Concord Pl.

**North**

W. Weed St.

5

Armitage

Sheffield Ave.

N.

N. Poe St.

N. Willow St.

W. Willow St.

Dickens Ave.

N. Kenmore Ave.

N. Seminary Ave.

N. Clifton Ave.

N. Racine Ave.

Ave.

N. Maud

N. Marcey St.

N. Clifton Ave.

W. Wisconsin

Kingsbury

Turning Basin

4

W. Magnolia Ave.

N. Clybourn

St.

River

Branch

(64)

3

W. Shakespeare Ave.

W. Dickens Ave.

Southport

N. Kingsbury

**CLYBOURN CORRIDOR**

W. Cortland St.

North

N. Throop St.

W. Willow St.

Wabansia Ave.

N. Ada

W. Concord Pl.

St.

2

Chicago River

N. Mendell St.

N. Elston

N. Besly Ct.

Ave.

1

90 94

North Ave.

N. Ashland

W.

F   G   H   I   J

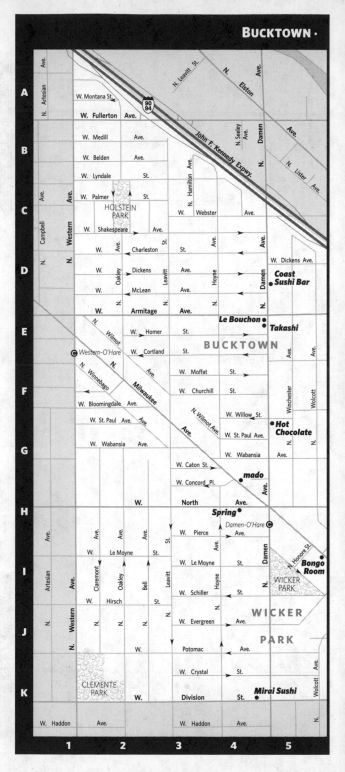

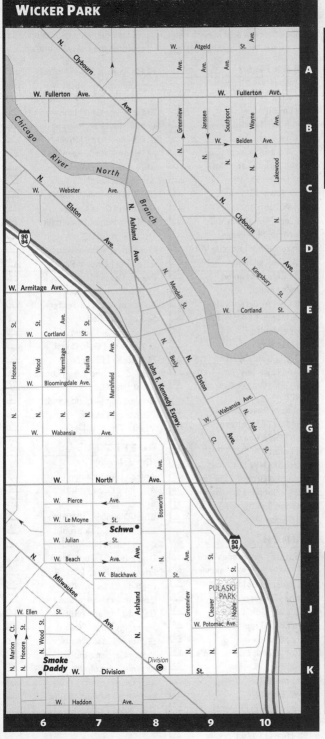

# WICKER PARK

# Special Features

Listings cover the best in each category and include names, locations and Food ratings. Multi-location restaurants' features may vary by branch.

## BREAKFAST

(See also Hotel Dining)

| | |
|---|---|
| Ann Sather | **multi.** | 21 |
| Bagel | **multi.** | 19 |
| Bongo Room | **multi.** | 24 |
| Breakfast Club | **Near W** | 20 |
| Café Selmarie | **Lincoln Sq** | 23 |
| Chicago Diner | **Lakeview** | 22 |
| Depot Diner | **Far W** | – |
| Flo | **W Town** | 22 |
| Ina's | **W Loop** | 23 |
| NEW Jam | **Ukrainian Vill** | 21 |
| Julius Meinl | **Lakeview** | 21 |
| Kitsch'n/K-Cafe | **Roscoe Vill** | 19 |
| Lou Mitchell's | **multi.** | 23 |
| Z Lula Cafe | **Logan Sq** | 26 |
| Manny's | **multi.** | 23 |
| M. Henry | **Andersonville** | 25 |
| Milk & Honey | **Wicker Pk** | 23 |
| Nookies | **multi.** | 20 |
| Nosh | **Geneva** | 24 |
| Oak Tree | **Gold Coast** | 17 |
| Orange | **Lakeview** | 20 |
| Z Original/Walker Pancake | **multi.** | 24 |
| Over Easy | **Ravenswood** | 27 |
| Z Phoenix | **Chinatown** | 23 |
| Tempo | **Gold Coast** | 20 |
| Toast | **multi.** | 22 |
| Tre Kronor | **NW Side** | 23 |
| Uncommon Ground | **Lakeview** | 22 |
| Victory's Banner | **Roscoe Vill** | 24 |
| Wishbone | **multi.** | 21 |
| Yolk | **S Loop** | 22 |

## BRUNCH

| | |
|---|---|
| Ann Sather | **Andersonville** | 21 |
| NEW Bakin' & Eggs | **Lakeview** | 19 |
| NEW Balsan | **Gold Coast** | – |
| Big Jones | **Andersonville** | 21 |
| Bistro 110 | **Gold Coast** | 21 |
| Bongo Room | **multi.** | 24 |
| Bristol | **Bucktown** | 23 |
| Cafe 28 | **North Ctr/St. Ben's** | 26 |
| erwin cafe | **Lakeview** | 23 |
| Feast | **multi.** | 19 |
| Flo | **W Town** | 22 |
| Z Frontera Grill | **River N** | 27 |
| Z Gage | **Loop** | 22 |
| NEW Hearty | **Wrigleyville** | – |

| | |
|---|---|
| Z Heaven on Seven | **multi.** | 23 |
| Hot Chocolate | **Bucktown** | 24 |
| Kitsch'n/K-Cafe | **Roscoe Vill** | 19 |
| NEW Klopa Grill | **Lincoln Sq** | – |
| Lobby | **River N** | 28 |
| NEW Mercadito | **River N** | 22 |
| M. Henry | **Andersonville** | 25 |
| Milk & Honey | **Wicker Pk** | 23 |
| Niche | **Geneva** | 28 |
| NEW Nightwood | **Pilsen** | 23 |
| Z NoMI | **Gold Coast** | 27 |
| Z North Pond | **Lincoln Pk** | 25 |
| Orange | **multi.** | 20 |
| Over Easy | **Ravenswood** | 27 |
| Perennial | **Lincoln Pk** | 24 |
| Prairie Grass | **Northbrook** | 22 |
| Z Publican | **W Loop** | 25 |
| Puck's at MCA | **Streeterville** | 20 |
| Z RL | **Gold Coast** | 23 |
| Salpicón | **Old Town** | 26 |
| Z Seasons | **Gold Coast** | 27 |
| Z Sixteen | **River N** | 22 |
| NEW State and Lake | **Loop** | 21 |
| Toast | **multi.** | 22 |
| Uncommon Ground | **multi.** | 22 |
| Wishbone | **multi.** | 21 |
| Yoshi's Café | **Lakeview** | 25 |

## BUFFET

(Check availability)

| | |
|---|---|
| Andies | **Andersonville** | 18 |
| Aurelio's Pizza | **multi.** | 23 |
| Chicago Curry | **S Loop** | 25 |
| Chief O'Neill's | **NW Side** | 18 |
| Clubhouse | **Oak Brook** | 21 |
| Curry Hut | **Highwood** | 20 |
| Drake Bros.' | **Gold Coast** | – |
| Edwardo's Pizza | **Oak Pk** | 20 |
| Fogo de Chão | **River N** | 24 |
| Gale St. Inn | **Jefferson Pk** | 22 |
| Gaylord Indian | **multi.** | 22 |
| Hemmingway's | **Oak Pk** | 21 |
| Z India House | **multi.** | 25 |
| Indian Garden | **multi.** | 21 |
| Karyn's | **Lincoln Pk** | 20 |
| Klay Oven | **multi.** | 20 |
| La Fonda | **Andersonville** | – |
| Las Tablas | **Lakeview** | 20 |
| Lobby | **River N** | 28 |

Menus, photos, voting and more – free at ZAGAT.com

| | |
|---|---|
| Mandarin Kitchen \| **Chinatown** | -‚ |
| Mesón Sabika \| **multi.** | 23 |
| Miramar Bistro \| **Highwood** | 17 |
| Mt. Everest \| **Evanston** | 22 |
| Z NoMI \| **Gold Coast** | 27 |
| Z Pappadeaux \| **Arlington Hts** | 21 |
| Pizza D.O.C. \| **Lincoln Sq** | 23 |
| Puck's at MCA \| **Streeterville** | 20 |
| Reza's \| **multi.** | 18 |
| Ringo \| **Lincoln Pk** | -‚ |
| R.J. Grunts \| **Lincoln Pk** | 19 |
| Robinson's Ribs \| **Oak Pk** | 21 |
| Ruby of Siam \| **multi.** | 23 |
| Z Seasons \| **Gold Coast** | 27 |
| Z Shaw's Crab \| **multi.** | 24 |
| Z Signature Room \| **Streeterville** | 18 |
| Z Sixteen \| **River N** | 22 |
| Stanley's \| **multi.** | 18 |
| Tango \| **Naperville** | 22 |
| Thai Classic \| **Lakeview** | 23 |
| Tiffin \| **W Rogers Pk** | 21 |
| Udupi Palace \| **Schaumburg** | 23 |
| Viceroy of India \| **multi.** | 21 |
| ZED 451 \| **River N** | 21 |

## BUSINESS DINING

| | |
|---|---|
| Abigail's \| **Highland Pk** | 24 |
| Ai Sushi \| **River N** | 24 |
| aja \| **River N** | -‚ |
| Z Alinea \| **Lincoln Pk** | 29 |
| Aria \| **Loop** | 24 |
| Atwood Cafe \| **Loop** | 22 |
| Z Avenues \| **River N** | 26 |
| NEW Balsan \| **Gold Coast** | -‚ |
| NEW Benny's \| **River N** | -‚ |
| Bice \| **Streeterville** | 21 |
| Z Blackbird \| **W Loop** | 27 |
| Brasserie Jo \| **River N** | 22 |
| Brazzaz \| **River N** | 22 |
| Café/Architectes \| **Gold Coast** | 24 |
| Z Capital Grille \| **Streeterville** | 25 |
| Carlucci \| **Downers Grove** | 19 |
| Carlucci \| **Rosemont** | 20 |
| Carmichael's \| **W Loop** | 22 |
| Z Catch 35 \| **Loop** | 24 |
| Z Charlie Trotter's \| **Lincoln Pk** | 27 |
| Z Chicago Chop \| **River N** | 25 |
| C-House \| **Streeterville** | 21 |
| NEW Cibo Matto \| **Loop** | 24 |
| NEW CityGate \| **Naperville** | -‚ |
| Z Coco Pazzo \| **River N** | 25 |
| Z Crofton on Wells \| **River N** | 26 |
| Custom House \| **Printer's Row** | 25 |
| Z David Burke Prime \| **River N** | 25 |

| | |
|---|---|
| NEW deca \| **Streeterville** | -‚ |
| Devon Seafood \| **River N** | 21 |
| NEW Elate \| **River N** | 21 |
| NEW Epic \| **River N** | -‚ |
| Erie Cafe \| **River N** | 22 |
| Z Eve \| **Gold Coast** | 22 |
| Z Everest \| **Loop** | 27 |
| Fleming's \| **Lincolnshire** | 23 |
| Fogo de Chão \| **River N** | 24 |
| Fred's \| **Gold Coast** | 19 |
| Fulton's \| **River N** | 19 |
| Z Gage \| **Loop** | 22 |
| Z Gene & Georgetti \| **River N** | 24 |
| Z Gibsons \| **multi.** | 26 |
| Glen Prairie \| **Glen Ellyn** | 23 |
| Grill on Alley \| **Streeterville** | 21 |
| Grillroom \| **Loop** | 15 |
| Harry Caray's \| **multi.** | 20 |
| Il Mulino \| **Gold Coast** | 25 |
| Inovasi \| **Lake Bluff** | -‚ |
| NEW Italiasia \| **River N** | -‚ |
| Jacky's on Prairie \| **Evanston** | 21 |
| Z Japonais \| **River N** | 24 |
| Z Joe's Sea/Steak \| **River N** | 26 |
| Karma \| **Mundelein** | 23 |
| Z Keefer's \| **River N** | 25 |
| Kinzie Chophouse \| **River N** | 22 |
| Lawry's \| **River N** | 24 |
| Z Le Colonial \| **Gold Coast** | 24 |
| Z Les Nomades \| **Streeterville** | 29 |
| Z Le Titi/Paris \| **Arlington Hts** | 26 |
| Lockwood \| **Loop** | 19 |
| Z L2O \| **Lincoln Pk** | 27 |
| McCormick/Schmick's \| **Gold Coast** | 21 |
| Z Michael \| **Winnetka** | 28 |
| Mike Ditka's \| **Gold Coast** | 22 |
| Z mk \| **Near North** | 27 |
| Z Morton's \| **multi.** | 26 |
| Z Naha \| **River N** | 27 |
| Nick's Fishmarket \| **Rosemont** | 23 |
| Z N9ne Steak \| **Loop** | 24 |
| Z NoMI \| **Gold Coast** | 27 |
| Z one sixtyblue \| **W Loop** | 26 |
| Palm \| **Loop** | 24 |
| Park 52 \| **Hyde Pk** | 19 |
| Park Grill \| **Loop** | 20 |
| Perennial \| **Lincoln Pk** | 24 |
| Phil Stefani's \| **River N** | 24 |
| Piccolo Sogno \| **Near W** | 24 |
| NEW Prairie Fire \| **W Loop** | -‚ |
| NEW Prasino \| **La Grange** | -‚ |
| Province \| **W Loop** | 23 |
| Quince \| **Evanston** | 23 |

| | |
|---|---|
| RB Grille \| **River N** | — |
| Rhapsody \| **Loop** | 20 |
| **NEW** Ria \| **Gold Coast** | — |
| **Z** RL \| **Gold Coast** | 23 |
| Roy's \| **River N** | 25 |
| **Z** Ruth's Chris \| **multi.** | 25 |
| **NEW** Sable \| **River N** | — |
| Saloon Steak \| **Streeterville** | 23 |
| Sam & Harry's \| **Schaumburg** | — |
| **Z** Seasons \| **Gold Coast** | 27 |
| Sepia \| **W Loop** | 24 |
| **Z** Shaw's Crab \| **multi.** | 24 |
| **Z** Sixteen \| **River N** | 22 |
| Smith & Wollensky \| **River N** | 23 |
| **Z** Spiaggia \| **Gold Coast** | 27 |
| **NEW** State and Lake \| **Loop** | 21 |
| SugarToad \| **Naperville** | 19 |
| Sullivan's Steak \| **multi.** | 22 |
| Tavern/Park \| **Loop** | 20 |
| 312 Chicago \| **Loop** | 21 |
| **Z** Topolobampo \| **River N** | 28 |
| Vivere \| **Loop** | 22 |
| Vivo \| **W Loop** | 24 |
| Weber Grill \| **River N** | 20 |
| Zak's Place \| **Hinsdale** | — |

## BYO

| | |
|---|---|
| Amitabul \| **NW Side** | 21 |
| Andalous \| **Lakeview** | 22 |
| Ann Sather \| **multi.** | 21 |
| Antica Pizza \| **Andersonville** | 23 |
| Art of Pizza \| **Lakeview** | 22 |
| Bagel \| **Lakeview** | 19 |
| **NEW** Bakin' & Eggs \| **Lakeview** | 19 |
| **NEW** Belly Shack \| **Humboldt Pk** | 23 |
| Birchwood \| **Bucktown** | 23 |
| **NEW** Bonsai Café \| **Evanston** | — |
| **Z** Bonsoirée \| **Logan Sq** | 26 |
| Butterfly \| **multi.** | 22 |
| **NEW** Cafe Marbella \| **Jefferson Pk** | — |
| Café 103 \| **Far S Side** | — |
| Chickpea \| **W Town** | 22 |
| **NEW** Chilam Balam \| **Lakeview** | 25 |
| Coast Sushi/South Coast \| **Bucktown** | 24 |
| **NEW** Conoce/Panama \| **Logan Sq** | — |
| **NEW** Co-Si-Na \| **Andersonville** | — |
| **NEW** Crêpe Crave \| **Wicker Pk** | — |
| Crêpes Cafe \| **Loop** | — |
| **NEW** Crêpe Town \| **Lakeview** | — |
| **NEW** Decolores \| **Pilsen** | — |
| Depot Diner \| **Far W** | — |
| Dorado \| **Lincoln Sq** | 23 |

| | |
|---|---|
| Double Li \| **Chinatown** | — |
| **NEW** Duck Walk \| **multi.** | 19 |
| Edwardo's Pizza \| **Hyde Pk** | 20 |
| Estrella Negra \| **Logan Sq** | — |
| **NEW** Fame da Lupo \| **Uptown** | — |
| **NEW** Franks 'N' Dawgs \| **Lincoln Pk** | — |
| **Z** Giordano's \| **multi.** | 23 |
| Great Lake \| **Andersonville** | 23 |
| Habana Libre \| **W Town** | 22 |
| **NEW** Han 202 \| **Near S Side** | 25 |
| HB Home Bistro \| **Lakeview** | 25 |
| Hecky's \| **Evanston** | 20 |
| Hema's Kitchen \| **multi.** | 22 |
| Honey 1 BBQ \| **Bucktown** | 20 |
| Hot Woks \| **NW Side** | 23 |
| Icosium Kafe \| **Andersonville** | 19 |
| Indie Cafe \| **Edgewater** | 24 |
| Irazu \| **Bucktown** | 22 |
| Isla Filipino \| **Lincoln Sq** | — |
| **NEW** Istanbul \| **Lakeview** | — |
| **NEW** Jam \| **Ukrainian Vill** | 21 |
| Jerry's \| **W Loop** | 22 |
| Joy Yee \| **multi.** | 20 |
| **NEW** J. Wellington's \| **Wicker Pk** | — |
| Kan Zaman \| **River N** | — |
| Karyn's \| **Lincoln Pk** | 20 |
| **NEW** Kin \| **River W** | — |
| **NEW** Klopa Grill \| **Lincoln Sq** | — |
| **NEW** (k)new \| **Logan Sq** | — |
| **NEW** La Ciudad \| **Uptown** | — |
| **NEW** Lan's Bistro \| **Old Town** | — |
| **Z** Lao \| **Chinatown** | 24 |
| **Z** mado \| **Bucktown** | 25 |
| Medici on 57th \| **Hyde Pk** | 17 |
| Melting Pot \| **River N** | 19 |
| M. Henry \| **Andersonville** | 25 |
| Mixteco Grill \| **Lakeview** | 25 |
| **NEW** Morgan Harbor \| **Rogers Pk** | — |
| Mythos \| **Lakeview** | 23 |
| **NEW** 90 Miles \| **multi.** | 22 |
| Nookies \| **multi.** | 20 |
| Old Jerusalem \| **Old Town** | 19 |
| Orange \| **multi.** | 20 |
| **Z** Original Gino's \| **Lincoln Pk** | 22 |
| Over Easy \| **Ravenswood** | 27 |
| Penny's Noodle \| **multi.** | 20 |
| **NEW** Pho & I \| **Lakeview** | — |
| Pho 777 \| **Uptown** | 21 |
| Phò Xe Tång \| **Uptown** | 26 |
| Pizza Capri \| **Lincoln Pk** | 20 |
| Pomegranate \| **Evanston** | 18 |
| Pompei Bakery \| **Streeterville** | 19 |
| Real Tenochtitlán \| **Logan Sq** | 20 |

NEW RendezVous | **Lincoln Sq** `-`
Robinson's Ribs | **multi.** `21`
NEW Rolis | **Uptown** `-`
Rollapalooza | **Lakeview** `-`
Ruby of Siam | **Skokie** `23`
NEW Sabor Saveur | **Ukrainian Vill** `-`
Sanook | **North Ctr/St. Ben's** `-`
Sapore/Napoli | **Lakeview** `20`
Z Schwa | **Wicker Pk** `29`
Sikia | **Far S Side** `-`
Simply It | **Lincoln Pk** `22`
Z Smoque BBQ | **NW Side** `26`
Spoon Thai | **Lincoln Sq** `23`
Spring World | **Chinatown** `-`
Sushi X | **River W** `21`
Tango Sur | **Lakeview** `24`
Tanoshii | **Andersonville** `-`
Terragusto | **Roscoe Vill** `25`
Thai Classic | **Lakeview** `23`
Thai Pastry | **multi.** `23`
Tre Kronor | **NW Side** `23`
Udupi Palace | **multi.** `23`
urbanbelly | **Logan Sq** `24`
Yolk | **multi.** `22`

## CELEBRITY CHEFS

Domenico Acampora
  NEW Accanto | **Logan Sq** `-`
Grant Achatz
  Z Alinea | **Lincoln Pk** `29`
Geno Bahena
  Real Tenochtitlán | **Logan Sq** `20`
Jimmy Bannos Jr.
  NEW Purple Pig | **River N** `-`
Rick Bayless
  Z Frontera Grill | **River N** `27`
  Z Topolobampo | **River N** `28`
  NEW XOCO | **River N** `25`
Graham Elliot Bowles
  graham elliot | **River N** `24`
Laurent Branlard
  LB Bistro | **Streeterville** `-`
George Bumbaris & Sarah Stegner
  NEW Prairie Fire | **W Loop** `-`
  Prairie Grass | **Northbrook** `22`
Homaro Cantu
  Z Moto | **W Loop** `27`
Michael Carlson
  Z Schwa | **Wicker Pk** `29`
Suzy Crofton
  Z Crofton on Wells | **River N** `26`
Jose Garces
  Z Mercat | **S Loop** `26`

Susan Goss
  West Town | **W Town** `24`
Laurent Gras
  Z L2O | **Lincoln Pk** `27`
Koren Grieveson
  Z avec | **W Loop** `26`
John Hogan
  Z Keefer's | **River N** `25`
Jean Joho
  Brasserie Jo | **River N** `22`
  Z Everest | **Loop** `27`
Paul Kahan
  NEW Big Star | **Wicker Pk** `23`
  Z Publican | **W Loop** `25`
Michael Taus
  Duchamp | **Bucktown** `17`
  Zealous | **River N** `25`
Yoshi Katsumura
  Yoshi's Café | **Lakeview** `25`
Michael Kornick
  NEW DMK Burger | **Lakeview** `22`
  Z mk | **Near North** `27`
Michael Lachowitz
  Z Michael | **Winnetka** `28`
Dale Levitski
  NEW Sprout | **Lincoln Pk** `28`
Michael Maddox
  Z Le Titi/Paris | **Arlington Hts** `26`
Tony Mantuano
  Z Spiaggia | **Gold Coast** `27`
  NEW Terzo Piano | **Loop** `21`
Shawn McClain
  Z Green Zebra | **W Town** `26`
  Z Spring | **Wicker Pk** `27`
Michael McDonald
  Z one sixtyblue | **W Loop** `26`
Jason McLeod
  NEW Ria | **Gold Coast** `-`
Frank Mnuk
  NEW Bistro Bordeaux | **Evanston** `-`
Carrie Nahabedian
  Z Naha | **River N** `27`
Martial Noguier
  Café/Architectes | **Gold Coast** `24`
Tony Priolo
  Piccolo Sogno | **Near W** `24`
Arun Sampanthavivat
  Z Arun's | **NW Side** `28`
Marcus Samuelsson
  C-House | **Streeterville** `21`
Giuseppe Scurato
  NEW Ceres' Table | **Uptown** `-`

| | |
|---|---|
| **Mindy Segal** | |
| Hot Chocolate \| **Bucktown** | 24 |
| **Mike Sheerin** | |
| ☑ Blackbird \| **W Loop** | 27 |
| **Jackie Shen** | |
| Red Light \| **W Loop** | 23 |
| **Bruce Sherman** | |
| ☑ North Pond \| **Lincoln Pk** | 25 |
| **Art Smith** | |
| TABLE 52 \| **Gold Coast** | 24 |
| **Dan Smith** | |
| NEW Hearty \| **Wrigleyville** | - |
| **Brendan Sodikoff** | |
| NEW Gilt Bar \| **River N** | - |
| **Todd Stein** | |
| NEW Cibo Matto \| **Loop** | 24 |
| **Giuseppe Tentori** | |
| BOKA \| **Lincoln Pk** | 25 |
| **Charlie Trotter** | |
| ☑ Charlie Trotter's \| **Lincoln Pk** | 27 |
| **Paul Virant** | |
| ☑ Vie \| **W Springs** | 27 |
| **Stephen Wambach** | |
| NEW Epic \| **River N** | - |
| **Takashi Yagihashi** | |
| ☑ Takashi \| **Bucktown** | 26 |
| **Randy Zweiban** | |
| Province \| **W Loop** | 23 |

## CHILD-FRIENDLY

(Alternatives to the usual fast-food places; * children's menu available)

| | |
|---|---|
| American Girl \| **Streeterville** | 16 |
| Ann Sather* \| **multi.** | 21 |
| Antico Posto* \| **Oak Brook** | 22 |
| Artopolis \| **Greektown** | 22 |
| Bandera* \| **Streeterville** | 22 |
| Benihana* \| **multi.** | 18 |
| Berghoff \| **O'Hare Area** | 18 |
| Big Bowl* \| **multi.** | 20 |
| ☑ Bob Chinn's* \| **Wheeling** | 23 |
| Breakfast Club \| **Near W** | 20 |
| Café Selmarie* \| **Lincoln Sq** | 23 |
| Carson's Ribs* \| **River N** | 22 |
| ☑ Cheesecake Factory* \| **multi.** | 19 |
| Chicago Pizza \| **Lincoln Pk** | 23 |
| Dave's Italian \| **Evanston** | 17 |
| Davis St. Fish* \| **Evanston** | 19 |
| Depot Diner \| **Far W** | - |
| Ed Debevic's* \| **River N** | 15 |
| Edwardo's Pizza* \| **multi.** | 20 |
| Flat Top Grill \| **multi.** | 20 |
| foodlife \| **Streeterville** | 19 |
| Gold Coast \| **Loop** | 19 |
| Hackney's* \| **multi.** | 18 |

| | |
|---|---|
| Hard Rock* \| **River N** | 12 |
| Harry Caray's* \| **multi.** | 20 |
| ☑ Heaven on Seven* \| **multi.** | 23 |
| ☑ Hot Doug's \| **NW Side** | 27 |
| Ina's \| **W Loop** | 23 |
| John's Place* \| **Lincoln Pk** | 18 |
| Joy Yee \| **multi.** | 20 |
| Kansaku \| **Evanston** | 22 |
| Kitsch'n/K-Cafe* \| **Roscoe Vill** | 19 |
| Lawry's* \| **River N** | 24 |
| NEW Leo's Coney Island* \| **Wrigleyville** | - |
| ☑ Lou Malnati's* \| **multi.** | 24 |
| Lou Mitchell's* \| **multi.** | 23 |
| LuLu's \| **Evanston** | 21 |
| ☑ Maggiano's* \| **multi.** | 20 |
| Manny's* \| **SW Side** | 23 |
| ☑ Margie's Candies* \| **Bucktown** | 22 |
| Mity Nice Grill* \| **Streeterville** | 17 |
| Oak Tree \| **Gold Coast** | 17 |
| OPA Estiatorio* \| **Vernon Hills** | 25 |
| Orange* \| **Lakeview** | 20 |
| ☑ Original Gino's* \| **multi.** | 22 |
| ☑ Original/Walker Pancake* \| **multi.** | 24 |
| Pegasus \| **SW Side** | 20 |
| P.F. Chang's \| **River N** | 20 |
| Pizza Capri* \| **multi.** | 20 |
| Pizza D.O.C. \| **Lincoln Sq** | 23 |
| Pizzeria Uno/Due* \| **River N** | 22 |
| ☑ Potbelly \| **multi.** | 19 |
| R.J. Grunts* \| **Lincoln Pk** | 19 |
| Robinson's Ribs* \| **multi.** | 21 |
| Russell's BBQ* \| **Elmwood Pk** | 19 |
| Sapore/Napoli \| **Lakeview** | 20 |
| Sapori Trattoria \| **Lincoln Pk** | 23 |
| Scoozi!* \| **River N** | 19 |
| ☑ Smoque BBQ* \| **NW Side** | 26 |
| Stanley's* \| **Lincoln Pk** | 18 |
| Stir Crazy* \| **multi.** | 19 |
| Tempo \| **Gold Coast** | 20 |
| Toast* \| **multi.** | 22 |
| Trattoria D.O.C. \| **Evanston** | 19 |
| Tufano's Tap \| **University Vill** | 20 |
| Twin Anchors* \| **Old Town** | 23 |
| Uncle Julio's* \| **Old Town** | 18 |
| Uncommon Ground* \| **Lakeview** | 22 |
| White Fence* \| **Romeoville** | 22 |
| Wishbone* \| **multi.** | 21 |

## DANCING

| | |
|---|---|
| Alhambra \| **W Loop** | 16 |
| Gale St. Inn \| **Mundelein** | 22 |
| ☑ Nacional 27 \| **River N** | 23 |

| | |
|---|---|
| **NEW** Pasha \| **W Loop** | -▏ |
| **Z** Pump Room \| **Gold Coast** | 22▏ |
| Rosebud Trattoria \| **River N** | 22▏ |
| Rumba \| **River N** | 23▏ |
| Sayat Nova \| **Streeterville** | 23▏ |

## DELIVERY/TAKEOUT

(D=delivery, T=takeout)

| | |
|---|---|
| Adobo \| T \| **multi.** | 21▏ |
| Akai Hana \| D, T \| **Wilmette** | 21▏ |
| Aladdin's Eatery \| D, T \| **Lincoln Pk** | 18▏ |
| A La Turka \| T \| **Lakeview** | 20▏ |
| Andies \| D, T \| **Andersonville** | 18▏ |
| Athena \| T \| **Greektown** | 21▏ |
| Bella Notte \| D, T \| **W Loop** | 21▏ |
| Benihana \| T \| **multi.** | 18▏ |
| Berghoff \| T \| **multi.** | 18▏ |
| Bijan's \| T \| **River N** | 19▏ |
| **Z** Bob Chinn's \| T \| **Wheeling** | 23▏ |
| Cafe Ba-Ba-Reeba! \| T \| **Lincoln Pk** | 22▏ |
| **Z** Café Spiaggia \| T \| **Gold Coast** | 25▏ |
| Coco Pazzo Café \| T \| **Streeterville** | 22▏ |
| **Z** Crofton on Wells \| T \| **River N** | 26▏ |
| D & J Bistro \| T \| **Lake Zurich** | 24▏ |
| Davis St. Fish \| T \| **Evanston** | 19▏ |
| Don Juan's \| T \| **Edison Pk** | 20▏ |
| **Z** Emilio's Tapas \| T \| **multi.** | 24▏ |
| erwin cafe \| T \| **Lakeview** | 23▏ |
| Filippo's \| T \| **Lincoln Pk** | 24▏ |
| foodlife \| D, T \| **Streeterville** | 19▏ |
| Francesca's \| D, T \| **multi.** | 22▏ |
| Gale St. Inn \| D, T \| **multi.** | 22▏ |
| **Z** Gene & Georgetti \| T \| **River N** | 24▏ |
| **Z** Gibsons \| T \| **multi.** | 26▏ |
| Gioco \| T \| **S Loop** | 25▏ |
| **Z** Heaven on Seven \| D, T \| **multi.** | 23▏ |
| Hema's Kitchen \| D, T \| **Lincoln Pk** | 22▏ |
| **Z** Japonais \| T \| **River N** | 24▏ |
| **Z** Joe's Sea/Steak \| T \| **River N** | 26▏ |
| **Z** Keefer's \| T \| **River N** | 25▏ |
| La Sardine \| T \| **W Loop** | 24▏ |
| La Scarola \| T \| **River W** | 24▏ |
| La Tasca \| T \| **Arlington Hts** | 24▏ |
| **Z** Le Colonial \| D, T \| **Gold Coast** | 24▏ |
| **Z** Lula Cafe \| T \| **Logan Sq** | 26▏ |
| L. Woods Tap \| T \| **Lincolnwood** | 20▏ |
| **Z** Maggiano's \| T \| **multi.** | 20▏ |
| Mesón Sabika \| T \| **Naperville** | 23▏ |
| **Z** Mia Francesca \| T \| **Lakeview** | 26▏ |
| Mirai Sushi \| T \| **Wicker Pk** | 25▏ |
| Mon Ami Gabi \| T \| **multi.** | 22▏ |
| Old Jerusalem \| D, T \| **Old Town** | 19▏ |
| Opera \| T \| **S Loop** | 20▏ |
| Orange \| T \| **Lakeview** | 20▏ |

| | |
|---|---|
| Parthenon \| T \| **Greektown** | 21▏ |
| Pierrot Gourmet \| T \| **River N** | 20▏ |
| **Z** Potbelly \| D, T \| **multi.** | 19▏ |
| Red Light \| T \| **W Loop** | 23▏ |
| R.J. Grunts \| T \| **Lincoln Pk** | 19▏ |
| RoSal's \| T \| **Little Italy** | 26▏ |
| **Z** Rosebud \| D, T \| **multi.** | 22▏ |
| Saloon Steak \| D, T \| **Streeterville** | 23▏ |
| San Soo Gab San \| D, T \| **NW Side** | 21▏ |
| Scoozi! \| T \| **River N** | 19▏ |
| **Z** Shaw's Crab \| D, T \| **multi.** | 24▏ |
| Smith & Wollensky \| T \| **River N** | 23▏ |
| Sullivan's Steak \| T \| **River N** | 22▏ |
| Sushi Naniwa \| D, T \| **River N** | 23▏ |
| **Z** sushi wabi \| D, T \| **W Loop** | 27▏ |
| Swordfish \| T \| **Batavia** | 27▏ |
| Tapas Gitana \| T \| **Northfield** | 24▏ |
| Tarantino's \| T \| **Lincoln Pk** | 22▏ |
| Trattoria Roma \| T \| **Old Town** | 21▏ |
| Twin Anchors \| T \| **Old Town** | 23▏ |
| Village \| D, T \| **Loop** | 21▏ |
| Volare \| D, T \| **Streeterville** | 24▏ |
| Yoshi's Café \| T \| **Lakeview** | 25▏ |

## DINING ALONE

(Other than hotels and places
with counter service)

| | |
|---|---|
| Amitabul \| **NW Side** | 21▏ |
| Ann Sather \| **multi.** | 21▏ |
| Bar Louie \| **multi.** | 16▏ |
| Bin 36/Wine \| **River N** | 21▏ |
| Blind Faith \| **Evanston** | 21▏ |
| Breakfast Club \| **Near W** | 20▏ |
| Chicago Diner \| **Lakeview** | 22▏ |
| Eleven City \| **S Loop** | 19▏ |
| Flat Top Grill \| **multi.** | 20▏ |
| foodlife \| **Streeterville** | 19▏ |
| Gold Coast \| **Loop** | 19▏ |
| Heartland Cafe \| **Rogers Pk** | 16▏ |
| **Z** Hot Doug's \| **NW Side** | 27▏ |
| Indie Cafe \| **Edgewater** | 24▏ |
| Kinzie Chophouse \| **River N** | 22▏ |
| Koi \| **Evanston** | 21▏ |
| Kroll's \| **S Loop** | 19▏ |
| **NEW** Lucky Monk \| **S Barrington** | -▏ |
| **Z** Lula Cafe \| **Logan Sq** | 26▏ |
| Maiz \| **Humboldt Pk** | 23▏ |
| Manny's \| **S Loop** | 23▏ |
| Meiji \| **W Loop** | 25▏ |
| Moody's Pub \| **Edgewater** | 19▏ |
| Mrs. Murphy \| **North Ctr/St. Ben's** | 22▏ |
| Nookies \| **multi.** | 20▏ |
| Oak Tree \| **Gold Coast** | 17▏ |
| Penny's Noodle \| **multi.** | 20▏ |

Puck's at MCA | **Streeterville** 20

Reza's | **multi.** 18

**NEW** Taco Fuego | **Lakeview** -

Toast | **multi.** 22

Tsuki | **Lincoln Pk** 23

Tweet | **Uptown** 22

Viand Bar | **Streeterville** 22

Z Wiener's Circle | **Lincoln Pk** 21

## ENTERTAINMENT

(Call for days and times
of performances)

A La Turka | belly dancing | **Lakeview** 20

Z Catch 35 | piano | **Loop** 24

Z Chicago Chop | piano | **River N** 25

Chief O'Neill's | Irish | **NW Side** 18

Costa's | piano | **Oakbrook Terr** 22

Cyrano's Bistrot | cabaret | **River N** 22

Edelweiss | German | **Norridge** 19

Geja's Cafe | flamenco/guitar | **Lincoln Pk** 21

Hackney's | piano | **Wheeling** 18

Irish Oak | rock | **Wrigleyville** 19

Kit Kat | celebrity impersonators | **Lakeview** 16

Lobby | jazz | **River N** 28

Mesón Sabika | flamenco | **Naperville** 23

Myron & Phil Steak | karaoke/piano | **Lincolnwood** 21

Z Nacional 27 | DJ | **River N** 23

Parkers' | jazz/piano | **Downers Grove** 23

Philly G's | piano | **Vernon Hills** 21

Z Pump Room | live music | **Gold Coast** 22

Rumba | jazz | **River N** 23

Sabatino's | piano | **NW Side** 24

Sayat Nova | DJ | **Streeterville** 23

Z Shaw's Crab | blues/jazz | **multi.** 24

Z Signature Room | jazz | **Streeterville** 18

Z Smoke Daddy | varies | **Wicker Pk** 24

Sullivan's Steak | jazz | **multi.** 22

Tapas Gitana | guitar | **Northfield** 24

Uncommon Ground | varies | **Lakeview** 22

## FIREPLACES

Adelle's | **Wheaton** 25

Ai Sushi | **River N** 24

Andies | **Andersonville** 18

Ann Sather | **Lakeview** 21

Athena | **Greektown** 21

Atwater's | **Geneva** 20

Bacino's | **Loop** 22

Bistrot Margot | **Old Town** 20

Bluebird | **Bucktown** 20

Boston Blackies | **Arlington Hts** 19

Brio | **Lombard** 22

Café la Cave | **Des Plaines** 21

Carlucci | **Downers Grove** 19

Carson's Ribs | **Deerfield** 22

Chens | **Wrigleyville** 22

Chicago Firehouse | **S Loop** 20

Chief O'Neill's | **NW Side** 18

Clubhouse | **Oak Brook** 21

Costa's | **Oakbrook Terr** 22

Courtright's | **Willow Spgs** 25

Dee's | **Lincoln Pk** 19

Deleece Grill | **Lakeview** 20

Devon Seafood | **River N** 21

Edelweiss | **Norridge** 19

EJ's Place | **Skokie** 22

Entourage | **Schaumburg** 20

Erie Cafe | **River N** 22

1492 | **River N** 21

Francesca's | **multi.** 22

Froggy's | **Highwood** 22

Gale St. Inn | **Mundelein** 22

Z Gene & Georgetti | **River N** 24

Z Gibsons | **multi.** 26

Greek Islands | **multi.** 21

Hackney's | **Lake Zurich** 18

Half Shell | **Lakeview** 24

Hecky's | **Evanston** 20

Il Mulino | **Gold Coast** 25

Inovasi | **Lake Bluff** -

Z Japonais | **River N** 24

Jerry's | **Wicker Pk** 22

John's Place | **Lincoln Pk** 18

Z Keefer's | **River N** 25

Koi | **Evanston** 21

La Madia | **River N** 23

Z Les Nomades | **Streeterville** 29

Le Vichyssois | **Lakemoor** 26

Z Lovells | **Lake Forest** 23

Maijean | **Clarendon Hills** 28

McCormick/Schmick's | **Gold Coast** 21

Melting Pot | **Schaumburg** 19

Milk & Honey | **Wicker Pk** 23

Moody's Pub | **Edgewater** 19

Mrs. Murphy | **North Ctr/St. Ben's** 22

Z North Pond | **Lincoln Pk** 25

Old Oak Tap | **Ukrainian Vill** 20

Z Original/Walker Pancake | **Lake Zurich** 24

| | |
|---|---|
| Otom \| **W Loop** | 22 |
| Oysy \| **S Loop** | 20 |
| Parkers' \| **Downers Grove** | 23 |
| Park Grill \| **Loop** | 20 |
| **NEW** Pelago \| **Streeterville** | 26 |
| Penny's Noodle \| **multi.** | 20 |
| Perennial \| **Lincoln Pk** | 24 |
| Prairie Grass \| **Northbrook** | 22 |
| **Z** Pump Room \| **Gold Coast** | 22 |
| Quartino \| **River N** | 21 |
| Quince \| **Evanston** | 23 |
| **NEW** Red Brick \| **Lakeview** | - |
| Reza's \| **River N** | 18 |
| Ribs 'n' Bibs \| **Hyde Pk** | 21 |
| **Z** RL \| **Gold Coast** | 23 |
| Robinson's Ribs \| **Lincoln Pk** | 21 |
| Rockit B&G \| **Wrigleyville** | 19 |
| Russell's BBQ \| **Rolling Meadows** | 19 |
| **Z** Ruth's Chris \| **Northbrook** | 25 |
| Sage Grille \| **Highwood** | 21 |
| Sai Café \| **Lincoln Pk** | 25 |
| Santorini \| **Greektown** | 21 |
| sola \| **Lakeview** | 25 |
| Sullivan's Steak \| **Lincolnshire** | 22 |
| Sunda \| **River N** | 23 |
| Swordfish \| **Batavia** | 27 |
| **Z** Tallgrass \| **Lockport** | 28 |
| Tavern/Park \| **Loop** | 20 |
| **NEW** 33 Club \| **Old Town** | 20 |
| Trattoria Gianni \| **Lincoln Pk** | 26 |
| Tsuki \| **Lincoln Pk** | 23 |
| Udupi Palace \| **W Rogers Pk** | 23 |
| Uncommon Ground \| **multi.** | 22 |
| **Z** Vie \| **W Springs** | 27 |
| Weber Grill \| **multi.** | 20 |
| Webster Wine \| **Lincoln Pk** | 20 |

## HISTORIC PLACES

(Year opened; * building)

| | |
|---|---|
| 1800 \| Chief O'Neill's* \| **NW Side** | 18 |
| 1800 \| Il Mulino* \| **Gold Coast** | 25 |
| 1847 \| Mesón Sabika* \| **Naperville** | 23 |
| 1865 \| Crofton on Wells* \| **River N** | 26 |
| 1870 \| Depot Nuevo* \| **Wilmette** | 18 |
| 1880 \| West Town* \| **W Town** | 24 |
| 1881 \| Twin Anchors* \| **Old Town** | 23 |
| 1890 \| Pasta Palazzo* \| **Lincoln Pk** | 22 |
| 1890 \| Pizzeria Uno/Due* \| **River N** | 22 |
| 1890 \| Sapori Trattoria* \| **Lincoln Pk** | 23 |
| 1890 \| Webster Wine* \| **Lincoln Pk** | 20 |
| 1897 \| Tallgrass* \| **Lockport** | 28 |
| 1900 \| Antica Pizza* \| **Andersonville** | 23 |

| | |
|---|---|
| 1900 \| Duchamp* \| **Bucktown** | 17 |
| 1900 \| Vivo* \| **W Loop** | 24 |
| 1901 \| Bank Lane* \| **Lake Forest** | 23 |
| 1901 \| South Gate* \| **Lake Forest** | 20 |
| 1905 \| Carnivale* \| **Loop** | 23 |
| 1905 \| Chicago Firehouse* \| **S Loop** | 20 |
| 1912 \| Eleven City* \| **S Loop** | 19 |
| 1920 \| Chef's Station* \| **Evanston** | 24 |
| 1920 \| Drake Bros.' \| **Gold Coast** | - |
| 1921 \| Margie's Candies \| **Bucktown** | 22 |
| 1922 \| Del Rio* \| **Highwood** | 20 |
| 1923 \| Lou Mitchell's \| **Loop** | 23 |
| 1927 \| Francesca's* \| **Edgewater** | 22 |
| 1927 \| Village* \| **Loop** | 21 |
| 1927 \| Vivere* \| **Loop** | 22 |
| 1930 \| Russell's BBQ \| **Elmwood Pk** | 19 |
| 1930 \| Tufano's Tap* \| **University Vill** | 20 |
| 1933 \| Bruna's \| **SW Side** | 26 |
| 1933 \| Cape Cod Room \| **Streeterville** | 22 |
| 1934 \| Billy Goat \| **multi.** | 17 |
| 1935 \| Duckfat* \| **Forest Pk** | - |
| 1935 \| Miller's Pub \| **Loop** | 17 |
| 1938 \| Al's #1 Beef \| **multi.** | 23 |
| 1938 \| Pump Room \| **Gold Coast** | 22 |
| 1939 \| Hackney's \| **multi.** | 18 |
| 1940 \| L2O* \| **Lincoln Pk** | 27 |
| 1941 \| Gene & Georgetti \| **River N** | 24 |
| 1942 \| Manny's \| **S Loop** | 23 |
| 1945 \| Army & Lou's \| **Far S Side** | 26 |
| 1948 \| Superdawg \| **NW Side** | 21 |
| 1954 \| White Fence \| **Romeoville** | 22 |
| 1955 \| La Cantina \| **Loop** | 21 |
| 1955 \| Pizzeria Uno/Due \| **River N** | 22 |
| 1959 \| Aurelio's Pizza \| **multi.** | 23 |
| 1959 \| Moody's Pub \| **Edgewater** | 19 |
| 1960 \| Moon Palace \| **Chinatown** | 22 |
| 1960 \| Original/Walker Pancake \| **Wilmette** | 24 |

## HOTEL DINING

| | |
|---|---|
| Affinia Chicago Hotel | |
|   C-House \| **Streeterville** | 21 |
| Allegro, Hotel | |
|   312 Chicago \| **Loop** | 21 |
| Ambassador East Hotel | |
|   **Z** Pump Room \| **Gold Coast** | 22 |
| Arista, Hotel | |
|   SugarToad \| **Naperville** | 19 |
| Belden-Stratford Hotel | |
|   **Z** L2O \| **Lincoln Pk** | 27 |
|   Mon Ami Gabi \| **Lincoln Pk** | 22 |

Blackstone Hotel
Ζ Mercat | **S Loop** 26

Blake, Hotel
Custom House | **Printer's Row** 25

Burnham, Hotel
Atwood Cafe | **Loop** 22

Crowne Plaza Glen Ellyn
Glen Prairie | **Glen Ellyn** 23

Dana Hotel & Spa
aja | **River N** ─

Doubletree Libertyville
Karma | **Mundelein** 23

Doubletree Magnificent Mile
Markethouse | **Streeterville** 21

Doubletree O'Hare
Ζ Gibsons | **Rosemont** 26

Drake Hotel
Cape Cod Room | **Streeterville** 22
Drake Bros.' | **Gold Coast** ─

Elysian, The
NEW Balsan | **Gold Coast** ─

Elysian
NEW Ria | **Gold Coast** ─

Embassy Suites Hotel
P.J. Clarke's | **Streeterville** 17

Fairmont Chicago Hotel
Aria | **Loop** 24

Felix, Hotel
NEW Elate | **River N** 21

Four Seasons Hotel
Ζ Seasons | **Gold Coast** 27

Hard Rock Hotel
China Grill | **Loop** 22

Herrington Inn
Atwater's | **Geneva** 20

Hilton Garden Inn
Weber Grill | **River N** 20

Holiday Inn Chicago Downtown
Aurelio's Pizza | **Loop** 23

Holiday Inn Chicago Mart Plaza
NEW Italiasia | **River N** ─

Homestead Hotel
Quince | **Evanston** 23

James Chicago Hotel, The
Ζ David Burke Prime | **River N** 25

Monaco, Hotel
South Water | **Loop** 16

Palmer House Hilton
Lockwood | **Loop** 19

Palomar, Hotel
NEW Sable | **River N** ─

Park Hyatt Chicago
Ζ NoMI | **Gold Coast** 27

Park View Hotel
Perennial | **Lincoln Pk** 24

Peninsula Hotel
Ζ Avenues | **River N** 26
Lobby | **River N** 28
Pierrot Gourmet | **River N** 20
Ζ Shanghai Terrace | **River N** 25

Raffaello Hotel
NEW Pelago | **Streeterville** 26

Red Roof Inn
Coco Pazzo Café | **Streeterville** 22

Renaissance North Shore Hotel
Ζ Ruth's Chris | **Northbrook** 25

Renaissance Schaumburg Hotel
Sam & Harry's | **Schaumburg** ─

Ritz-Carlton Hotel
NEW deca | **Streeterville** ─

Seneca Hotel
Francesca's | **Streeterville** 22
Saloon Steak | **Streeterville** 23

Sheraton Chicago Hotel
LB Bistro | **Streeterville** ─
Shula's Steak | **Streeterville** 21

Sheraton Four Points Hotel
NEW Sushi Taiyo | **River N** ─

Sofitel Chicago Water Tower
Café/Architectes | **Gold Coast** 24

Swissôtel
Palm | **Loop** 24

theWit Hotel
NEW Cibo Matto | **Loop** 24
NEW State and Lake | **Loop** 21

Tremont Hotel
Mike Ditka's | **Gold Coast** 22

Trump Int'l Hotel
Ζ Sixteen | **River N** 22

W Chicago City Ctr.
rist. we | **Loop** 20

W Chicago Lakeshore
Wave | **Streeterville** 13

Westin Chicago North Shore
Tramonto's | **Wheeling** 24

Westin Chicago NW
Shula's Steak | **Itasca** 21

Westin Lombard
Holy Mackerel! | **Lombard** 21

Westin Michigan Ave.
Grill on Alley | **Streeterville** 21

Whitehall Hotel, The
Fornetto Mei | **Gold Coast** 20

Write Inn, The
Hemmingway's | **Oak Pk** 21

## JACKET REQUIRED

- ☑ Carlos' | **Highland Pk** — 27
- ☑ Charlie Trotter's | **Lincoln Pk** — 27
- ☑ Les Nomades | **Streeterville** — 29
- ☑ Spiaggia | **Gold Coast** — 27
- ☑ Tru | **Streeterville** — 28

## LATE DINING

(Weekday closing hour)

- Agami | 12 AM | **Uptown** — 24
- ☑ Al's #1 Beef | varies | **multi.** — 23
- Artopolis | 12 AM | **Greektown** — 22
- Athena | 12 AM | **Greektown** — 21
- ☑ avec | 12 AM | **W Loop** — 26
- Bar Louie | varies | **multi.** — 16
- NEW Big Star | 2 AM | **Wicker Pk** — 23
- Bijan's | 3:30 AM | **River N** — 19
- Billy Goat | varies | **River N** — 17
- Bluebird | varies | **Bucktown** — 20
- Blue 13 | 12 AM | **River N** — 24
- Boston Blackies | 12 AM | **Arlington Hts** — 19
- Café Iberico | 11:30 PM | **River N** — 22
- Carmine's | 12 AM | **Gold Coast** — 22
- Coast Sushi/South Coast | 12 AM | **Bucktown** — 24
- NEW Dos Diablos | varies | **River N** — –
- Drawing Room | 4 AM | **Gold Coast** — 23
- Emperor's Choice | 12 AM | **Chinatown** — 23
- Fifty/50 | 1 AM | **Wicker Pk** — 21
- ☑ Gibsons | varies | **multi.** — 26
- ☑ Giordano's | varies | **multi.** — 23
- Gold Coast | varies | **multi.** — 19
- Greek Islands | varies | **Greektown** — 21
- Happy Chef | 2 AM | **Chinatown** — 23
- Hard Rock | 12 AM | **River N** — 12
- Hop Häus | varies | **multi.** — 19
- HUB 51 | 12 AM | **River N** — 21
- ☑ Hugo's | varies | **multi.** — 24
- Itto Sushi | 12 AM | **Lincoln Pk** — 24
- Kamehachi | varies | **Old Town** — 21
- NEW Kith & Kin | 12 AM | **Lincoln Pk** — –
- ☑ Kuma's | 1 AM | **Logan Sq** — 26
- La Cantina | 12 AM | **Loop** — 21
- NEW Lan's Bistro | 12 AM | **Old Town** — –
- ☑ Lao | varies | **multi.** — 24
- NEW Little Bucharest | 2 AM | **NW Side** — –
- NEW Longman & Eagle | 1 AM | **Logan Sq** — –
- ☑ Lou Malnati's | 12 AM | **Naperville** — 24
- Lou Mitchell's | varies | **O'Hare Area** — 23
- LuxBar | 1:30 AM | **Gold Coast** — 20
- ☑ Margie's Candies | varies | **Bucktown** — 22
- Market | 2 AM | **W Loop** — 18
- Melting Pot | varies | **multi.** — 19
- NEW Mercadito | varies | **River N** — 22
- NEW Mezé | 2 AM | **W Loop** — –
- Mike Ditka's | varies | **Oakbrook Terr** — 22
- Miller's Pub | 2 AM | **Loop** — 17
- Moody's Pub | 1 AM | **Edgewater** — 19
- Old Oak Tap | 12 AM | **Ukrainian Vill** — 20
- Parthenon | 12 AM | **Greektown** — 21
- Pegasus | varies | **multi.** — 20
- Pete Miller | varies | **Evanston** — 22
- pingpong | 12 AM | **Lakeview** — 20
- Pizzeria Uno/Due | varies | **River N** — 22
- Quartino | 1 AM | **River N** — 21
- Reza's | varies | **Andersonville** — 18
- Ribs 'n' Bibs | 12 AM | **Hyde Pk** — 21
- Rockit B&G | 1:30 AM | **multi.** — 19
- Roditys | 12 AM | **Greektown** — 21
- NEW Rootstock | 1 AM | **Humboldt Pk** — 24
- NEW Sable | varies | **River N** — –
- San Soo Gab San | 24 hrs. | **NW Side** — 21
- Santorini | 12 AM | **Greektown** — 21
- Silver Seafood | 1 AM | **Uptown** — 23
- ☑ Superdawg | varies | **NW Side** — 21
- SushiSamba | 1 AM | **River N** — 21
- NEW Taco Fuego | 3 AM | **Lakeview** — –
- Tasting Room | 12 AM | **W Loop** — 20
- Tavern/Rush | 12 AM | **Gold Coast** — 21
- Tempo | 24 hrs. | **Gold Coast** — 20
- Three Happiness | 6 AM | **Chinatown** — 21
- Twisted Spoke | 1 AM | **Near W** — 18
- Village | 11:30 PM | **Loop** — 21
- NEW Vintage 338 | varies | **Lincoln Pk** — –
- Vivere | 12 AM | **Loop** — 22
- Webster Wine | 12:30 AM | **Lincoln Pk** — 20
- ☑ Wiener's Circle | 4 AM | **Lincoln Pk** — 21

## MEET FOR A DRINK

(Most top hotels and the following standouts)

- aja | **River N** — –
- Alhambra | **W Loop** — 16

Bandera | **Streeterville** 22

NEW Benny's | **River N** –

Bijan's | **River N** 19

Bin 36/Wine | **multi.** 21

Bistro 110 | **Gold Coast** 21

BOKA | **Lincoln Pk** 25

Brasserie Jo | **River N** 22

Broadway Cellars | **Edgewater** 21

Cab's Wine Bar | **Glen Ellyn** 24

Café/Architectes | **Gold Coast** 24

Z Carnivale | **Loop** 23

Z Catch 35 | **Loop** 24

Chief O'Neill's | **NW Side** 18

China Grill | **Loop** 22

Coobah | **Lakeview** 17

NEW Cuna | **Lakeview** –

NEW deca | **Streeterville** –

Di Pescara | **Northbrook** 19

Distinctive Cork | **Naperville** 21

Drawing Room | **Gold Coast** 23

Entourage | **Schaumburg** 20

NEW Epic | **River N** –

Fleming's | **Lincolnshire** 23

Flight | **Glenview** 17

NEW Fountainhead | **Ravenswood** –

Fred's | **Gold Coast** 19

Z Frontera Grill | **River N** 27

Fuego | **Logan Sq** 24

Fulton's | **River N** 19

Z Gage | **Loop** 22

Z Gibsons | **multi.** 26

Glen Prairie | **Glen Ellyn** 23

Goose Island | **multi.** 17

Gordon Biersch | **Bolingbrook** 16

graham elliot | **River N** 24

Harry Caray's | **multi.** 20

HUB 51 | **River N** 21

NEW Italiasia | **River N** –

Z Japonais | **River N** 24

Z Joe's Sea/Steak | **River N** 26

Z Keefer's | **River N** 25

Landmark | **Lincoln Pk** 20

NEW Longman & Eagle | **Logan Sq** –

NEW Lucky Monk | **S Barrington** –

LuxBar | **Gold Coast** 20

Marché | **W Loop** 23

Market | **W Loop** 18

Markethouse | **Streeterville** 21

NEW Masu Izakaya | **Lincoln Pk** –

McCormick/Schmick's | **Gold Coast** 21

NEW Mercadito | **River N** 22

Mike Ditka's | **Gold Coast** 22

Miramar Bistro | **Highwood** 17

Z mk | **Near North** 27

Moody's Pub | **Edgewater** 19

Z Nacional 27 | **River N** 23

Z N9ne Steak | **Loop** 24

Z NoMI | **Gold Coast** 27

Old Oak Tap | **Ukrainian Vill** 20

NEW Old Town Social | **Old Town** 18

Z one sixtyblue | **W Loop** 26

Osteria/Pizzeria Via Stato | **River N** 23

Park 52 | **Hyde Pk** 19

Perennial | **Lincoln Pk** 24

NEW Prairie Fire | **W Loop** –

Prairie Grass | **Northbrook** 22

Prosecco | **River N** 24

Province | **W Loop** 23

Z Publican | **W Loop** 25

NEW Purple Pig | **River N** –

Quartino | **River N** 21

Red Light | **W Loop** 23

NEW Revolution Brewing | **Logan Sq** –

Rhapsody | **Loop** 20

Z RL | **Gold Coast** 23

Rockit B&G | **River N** 19

Rosebud Prime/Steak | **Streeterville** 25

Rosebud Trattoria | **River N** 22

Rumba | **River N** 23

NEW Sable | **River N** –

Scoozi! | **River N** 19

Sepia | **W Loop** 24

Z Shaw's Crab | **multi.** 24

Shikago | **Loop** 18

Z Signature Room | **Streeterville** 18

Z Sixteen | **River N** 22

Smith & Wollensky | **River N** 23

NEW Southern | **Bucktown** –

South Water | **Loop** 16

Stained Glass | **Evanston** 23

NEW State and Lake | **Loop** 21

SugarToad | **Naperville** 19

Sullivan's Steak | **River N** 22

Sunda | **River N** 23

Sura | **Lakeview** 20

SushiSamba | **River N** 21

Tasting Room | **W Loop** 20

Tavern/Park | **Loop** 20

Tavern/Rush | **Gold Coast** 21

NEW 33 Club | **Old Town** 20

312 Chicago | **Loop** 21

Tocco | **Bucktown** 12

Topaz Café | **Burr Ridge** 23
Trader Vic's | **Gold Coast** 17
Tramonto's | **Wheeling** 24
Trattoria No. 10 | **Loop** 24
Twisted Spoke | **Near W** 18
NEW Vintage 338 | **Lincoln Pk** -
Volo | **Roscoe Vill** -
Wave | **Streeterville** 13
Webster Wine | **Lincoln Pk** 20
Zak's Place | **Hinsdale** -
Zapatista | **S Loop** 20
Zocalo | **River N** 20

## MICROBREWERIES

Goose Island | **multi.** 17
Gordon Biersch | **Bolingbrook** 16
NEW Lucky Monk | **S Barrington** -
Piece | **Wicker Pk** 23
RB Grille | **River N** -

## NOTEWORTHY NEWCOMERS

Accanto | **Logan Sq** -
Aldino's | **Little Italy** -
Angin Mamiri | **W Rogers Pk** -
Bakin' & Eggs | **Lakeview** 19
Balsan | **Gold Coast** -
Belly Shack | **Humboldt Pk** 23
Benny's | **River N** -
Big Star | **Wicker Pk** 23
Bistro Bordeaux | **Evanston** -
Blue Ocean | **Ravenswood** 23
Bolat | **Lakeview** -
Bonsai Café | **Evanston** -
Browntrout | **North Ctr/St. Ben's** 24
Cafe Marbella | **Jefferson Pk** -
Café Touché | **NW Side** 25
Cellar/Stained Glass | **Evanston** 21
Ceres' Table | **Uptown** -
Chilam Balam | **Lakeview** 25
Ciao Napoli | **Logan Sq** -
Cibo Matto | **Loop** 24
CityGate | **Naperville** -
Conoce/Panama | **Logan Sq** -
Corner 41 | **North Ctr/St. Ben's** -
Co-Si-Na | **Andersonville** -
Crêpe Crave | **Wicker Pk** -
Crêpe Town | **Lakeview** -
Cuna | **Lakeview** -
deca | **Streeterville** -
Decolores | **Pilsen** -
Dee's Place | **Wicker Pk** -
DMK Burger | **Lakeview** 22
Dos Diablos | **River N** -

Duckfat | **Forest Pk** -
Duck Walk | **Lincoln Pk** 19
Edzo's | **Evanston** -
Elate | **River N** 21
Epic | **River N** -
Fame da Lupo | **Uptown** -
Felony Franks | **W Loop** -
Flo & Santos | **S Loop** -
Folklore | **Ukrainian Vill** -
Fonda Isabel | **Lombard** -
Fountainhead | **Ravenswood** -
Franks 'N' Dawgs | **Lincoln Pk** -
Gemini Bistro | **Lincoln Pk** 21
Gilt Bar | **River N** -
Hana | **Rogers Pk** -
Han 202 | **Near S Side** 25
Happ Inn | **Northfield** 17
Havana | **River N** -
Hearty | **Wrigleyville** -
Hot Woks | **Loop** 23
Il Poggiolo | **Hinsdale** 19
Isacco | **St. Charles** -
Istanbul | **Lakeview** -
Italiasia | **River N** -
Jacky's on Prairie | **Evanston** 21
Jam | **Ukrainian Vill** 21
J. Wellington's | **Wicker Pk** -
Karyn's on Green | **Greektown** -
Katakana & Koko | **Logan Sq** -
Kin | **River W** -
Kith & Kin | **Lincoln Pk** -
Klopa Grill | **Lincoln Sq** -
(k)new | **Logan Sq** -
La Ciudad | **Uptown** -
Lan's Bistro | **Old Town** -
Laurel | **Naperville** -
Leo's Coney Island | **Wrigleyville** -
Little Bucharest | **NW Side** -
LM | **Lincoln Sq** 22
LOKaL | **Bucktown** -
Longman & Eagle | **Logan Sq** -
Loving Hut | **Edgewater** -
Lucky Monk | **S Barrington** -
Macku Sushi | **Lincoln Pk** -
Main St. Smokehouse | **Libertyville** -
Manghal | **Evanston** -
Masu Izakaya | **Lincoln Pk** -
M Burger | **Streeterville** -
Melanthios | **Lakeview** -
Mercadito | **River N** 22
Mezé | **W Loop** -
Morgan Harbor | **Rogers Pk** -
Nagoya | **Naperville** -
Nella Pizza | **Lincoln Pk** 22

CHICAGO

SPECIAL FEATURES

| | |
|---|---|
| Nightwood \| **Pilsen** | 23 |
| 90 Miles \| **Logan Sq** | 22 |
| Oba \| **Des Plaines** | - |
| Old Town Social \| **Old Town** | 18 |
| Orvieto Pizza \| **Lincoln Pk** | - |
| Park Place \| **NW Side** | - |
| Pasha \| **W Loop** | - |
| Pelago \| **Streeterville** | 26 |
| Pho & I \| **Lakeview** | - |
| Piggery \| **Lakeview** | - |
| Pitchfork \| **North Ctr/St. Ben's** | - |
| Pizzeria Serio \| **Roscoe Vill** | - |
| Prairie Fire \| **W Loop** | - |
| Prasino \| **La Grange** | - |
| Purple Pig \| **River N** | - |
| Red Brick \| **Lakeview** | - |
| RendezVous \| **Lincoln Sq** | - |
| Revolution Brewing \| **Logan Sq** | - |
| Ria \| **Gold Coast** | - |
| Rolis \| **Uptown** | - |
| Rootstock \| **Humboldt Pk** | 24 |
| Roti \| **multi.** | 21 |
| Rustico Grill \| **Logan Sq** | - |
| Sable \| **River N** | - |
| Sabor Saveur \| **Ukrainian Vill** | - |
| Sarks/Park \| **Lincoln Pk** | - |
| Siboney \| **Bucktown** | - |
| Southern \| **Bucktown** | - |
| Sprout \| **Lincoln Pk** | 28 |
| State and Lake \| **Loop** | 21 |
| Sushi Taiyo \| **River N** | - |
| Taco Fuego \| **Lakeview** | - |
| Terzo Piano \| **Loop** | 21 |
| 33 Club \| **Old Town** | 20 |
| Vintage 338 \| **Lincoln Pk** | - |
| XOCO \| **River N** | 25 |

## OUTDOOR DINING

(G=garden; P=patio; S=sidewalk;
T=terrace; W=waterside)

| | |
|---|---|
| Athena \| G \| **Greektown** | 21 |
| Atwater's \| P \| **Geneva** | 20 |
| Bice \| S \| **Streeterville** | 21 |
| 🅉 Bistro Campagne \| G \| **Lincoln Sq** | 25 |
| BOKA \| P \| **Lincoln Pk** | 25 |
| Cafe Ba-Ba-Reeba! \| P \| **Lincoln Pk** | 22 |
| Carmine's \| P \| **Gold Coast** | 22 |
| Chez Joël \| P \| **Little Italy** | 24 |
| Chicago Firehouse \| P \| **S Loop** | 20 |
| Dinotto \| P \| **Old Town** | 19 |
| Duchamp \| P \| **Bucktown** | 17 |
| NEW Elate \| **River N** | 21 |
| Erie Cafe \| T, W \| **River N** | 22 |
| Feast \| G, S \| **multi.** | 19 |

| | |
|---|---|
| Flatwater \| P, W \| **River N** | 16 |
| Fred's \| T \| **Gold Coast** | 19 |
| Fulton's \| P, W \| **River N** | 19 |
| 🅉 Gage \| P \| **Loop** | 22 |
| Hackney's \| G, P, S, T \| **multi.** | 18 |
| 🅉 Japonais \| P \| **River N** | 24 |
| 🅉 Le Colonial \| S, T \| **Gold Coast** | 24 |
| NEW Mercadito \| P \| **River N** | 22 |
| Mesón Sabika \| G, P \| **multi.** | 23 |
| 🅉 Mia Francesca \| P \| **Lakeview** | 26 |
| Miramar Bistro \| S \| **Highwood** | 17 |
| Moody's Pub \| G \| **Edgewater** | 19 |
| 🅉 NoMI \| G \| **Gold Coast** | 27 |
| OPA Estiatorio \| P \| **Vernon Hills** | 25 |
| Park Grill \| P \| **Loop** | 20 |
| Parrot Cage \| P \| **Far S Side** | - |
| Pegasus \| T \| **Greektown** | 20 |
| NEW Pelago \| P \| **Streeterville** | 26 |
| Perennial \| P \| **Lincoln Pk** | 24 |
| Piccolo Sogno \| G \| **Near W** | 24 |
| Puck's at MCA \| P, W \| **Streeterville** | 20 |
| Riva \| P, W \| **Streeterville** | 20 |
| 🅉 RL \| P \| **Gold Coast** | 23 |
| 🅉 Shanghai Terrace \| T \| **River N** | 25 |
| Smith & Wollensky \| G, P, T, W \| **River N** | 23 |
| SushiSamba \| S \| **River N** | 21 |
| Tavern/Park \| P \| **Loop** | 20 |
| Tavern/Rush \| P, S \| **Gold Coast** | 21 |
| NEW Terzo Piano \| P \| **Loop** | 21 |
| Topo Gigio \| G, S \| **Old Town** | 23 |

## PEOPLE-WATCHING

| | |
|---|---|
| Adobo \| **Old Town** | 21 |
| aja \| **River N** | - |
| Alhambra \| **W Loop** | 16 |
| American Girl \| **Streeterville** | 16 |
| 🅉 avec \| **W Loop** | 26 |
| NEW Benny's \| **River N** | - |
| Bice \| **Streeterville** | 21 |
| Bin 36/Wine \| **River N** | 21 |
| Bistro 110 \| **Gold Coast** | 21 |
| 🅉 Blackbird \| **W Loop** | 27 |
| BOKA \| **Lincoln Pk** | 25 |
| Bongo Room \| **Wicker Pk** | 24 |
| Brasserie Jo \| **River N** | 22 |
| Carmine's \| **Gold Coast** | 22 |
| 🅉 Carnivale \| **Loop** | 23 |
| 🅉 Chicago Chop \| **River N** | 25 |
| C-House \| **Streeterville** | 21 |
| Coobah \| **Lakeview** | 17 |
| NEW Cuna \| **Lakeview** | - |
| NEW deca \| **Streeterville** | - |

Menus, photos, voting and more – free at ZAGAT.com

| | |
|---|---|
| NEW DMK Burger \| **Lakeview** | 22 |
| Drawing Room \| **Gold Coast** | 23 |
| Entourage \| **Schaumburg** | 20 |
| NEW Epic \| **River N** | - |
| Fifty/50 \| **Wicker Pk** | 21 |
| Fred's \| **Gold Coast** | 19 |
| Z Gibsons \| **Gold Coast** | 26 |
| graham elliot \| **River N** | 24 |
| Z Green Zebra \| **W Town** | 26 |
| Hamburger Mary's \| **Andersonville** | 17 |
| NEW Happ Inn \| **Northfield** | 17 |
| Harry Caray's \| **River N** | 20 |
| NEW Hearty \| **Wrigleyville** | - |
| HUB 51 \| **River N** | 21 |
| Il Mulino \| **Gold Coast** | 25 |
| Z Japonais \| **River N** | 24 |
| Z Keefer's \| **River N** | 25 |
| Landmark \| **Lincoln Pk** | 20 |
| Z Le Colonial \| **Gold Coast** | 24 |
| LuxBar \| **Gold Coast** | 20 |
| Manny's \| **S Loop** | 23 |
| Marché \| **W Loop** | 23 |
| Market \| **W Loop** | 18 |
| NEW Mercadito \| **River N** | 22 |
| Z Mercat \| **S Loop** | 26 |
| NEW Mezé \| **W Loop** | - |
| Mirai Sushi \| **Wicker Pk** | 25 |
| Miramar Bistro \| **Highwood** | 17 |
| Z mk \| **Near North** | 27 |
| Z Naha \| **River N** | 27 |
| Z N9ne Steak \| **Loop** | 24 |
| Niu \| **Streeterville** | 19 |
| Z NoMI \| **Gold Coast** | 27 |
| NEW Old Town Social \| **Old Town** | 18 |
| Opera \| **S Loop** | 20 |
| Osteria/Pizzeria Via Stato \| **River N** | 23 |
| Park 52 \| **Hyde Pk** | 19 |
| Perennial \| **Lincoln Pk** | 24 |
| Prosecco \| **River N** | 24 |
| Province \| **W Loop** | 23 |
| Z Publican \| **W Loop** | 25 |
| NEW Purple Pig \| **River N** | - |
| Quartino \| **River N** | 21 |
| Z Rosebud \| **multi.** | 22 |
| Rosebud Prime/Steak \| **Streeterville** | 25 |
| NEW Sable \| **River N** | - |
| Scoozi! \| **River N** | 19 |
| Shikago \| **Loop** | 18 |
| Z Sixteen \| **River N** | 22 |
| NEW Southern \| **Bucktown** | - |
| Z Spring \| **Wicker Pk** | 27 |
| NEW State and Lake \| **Loop** | 21 |

| | |
|---|---|
| SugarToad \| **Naperville** | 19 |
| Sunda \| **River N** | 23 |
| Sura \| **Lakeview** | 20 |
| SushiSamba \| **River N** | 21 |
| Tavern/Rush \| **Gold Coast** | 21 |
| NEW Terzo Piano \| **Loop** | 21 |
| NEW 33 Club \| **Old Town** | 20 |
| Tocco \| **Bucktown** | 12 |
| Topaz Café \| **Burr Ridge** | 23 |
| Trader Vic's \| **Gold Coast** | 17 |
| Tramonto's \| **Wheeling** | 24 |
| Wave \| **Streeterville** | 13 |
| Zapatista \| **S Loop** | 20 |
| Zhivago \| **Skokie** | 16 |

## POWER SCENES

| | |
|---|---|
| Z Alinea \| **Lincoln Pk** | 29 |
| Z Avenues \| **River N** | 26 |
| NEW Benny's \| **River N** | - |
| Z Capital Grille \| **Streeterville** | 25 |
| Z Charlie Trotter's \| **Lincoln Pk** | 27 |
| Z Chicago Chop \| **River N** | 25 |
| Z Coco Pazzo \| **River N** | 25 |
| Custom House \| **Printer's Row** | 25 |
| Z David Burke Prime \| **River N** | 25 |
| Entourage \| **Schaumburg** | 20 |
| NEW Epic \| **River N** | - |
| Z Everest \| **Loop** | 27 |
| Fred's \| **Gold Coast** | 19 |
| Fulton's \| **River N** | 19 |
| Z Gene & Georgetti \| **River N** | 24 |
| Z Gibsons \| **multi.** | 26 |
| graham elliot \| **River N** | 24 |
| Z Hugo's \| **Gold Coast** | 24 |
| Il Mulino \| **Gold Coast** | 25 |
| Z Keefer's \| **River N** | 25 |
| Z Les Nomades \| **Streeterville** | 29 |
| Z L2O \| **Lincoln Pk** | 27 |
| Z mk \| **Near North** | 27 |
| Z Morton's \| **multi.** | 26 |
| Z Naha \| **River N** | 27 |
| Z NoMI \| **Gold Coast** | 27 |
| NEW Ria \| **Gold Coast** | - |
| Z RL \| **Gold Coast** | 23 |
| Z Ruth's Chris \| **multi.** | 25 |
| Z Seasons \| **Gold Coast** | 27 |
| Z Sixteen \| **River N** | 22 |
| Smith & Wollensky \| **River N** | 23 |
| Z Spiaggia \| **Gold Coast** | 27 |
| Z Spring \| **Wicker Pk** | 27 |
| NEW State and Lake \| **Loop** | 21 |
| SugarToad \| **Naperville** | 19 |
| Tocco \| **Bucktown** | 12 |
| Z Tru \| **Streeterville** | 28 |

## PRIVATE ROOMS

(Restaurants charge less at off times; call for capacity)

| | |
|---|---|
| Z Alinea \| **Lincoln Pk** | 29 |
| Athena \| **Greektown** | 21 |
| Ben Pao \| **River N** | 21 |
| Brasserie Jo \| **River N** | 22 |
| Z Carnivale \| **Loop** | 23 |
| Z Catch 35 \| **multi.** | 24 |
| Z Charlie Trotter's \| **Lincoln Pk** | 27 |
| Z Chicago Chop \| **River N** | 25 |
| Club Lucky \| **Bucktown** | 19 |
| Costa's \| **Oakbrook Terr** | 22 |
| Edwardo's Pizza \| **multi.** | 20 |
| Z Everest \| **Loop** | 27 |
| Francesca's \| **multi.** | 22 |
| Z Frontera Grill \| **River N** | 27 |
| Z Gabriel's \| **Highwood** | 25 |
| Z Gene & Georgetti \| **River N** | 24 |
| Z Gibsons \| **multi.** | 26 |
| Gioco \| **S Loop** | 25 |
| Goose Island \| **multi.** | 17 |
| Greek Islands \| **multi.** | 21 |
| Z Joe's Sea/Steak \| **River N** | 26 |
| Kamehachi \| **multi.** | 21 |
| Z Keefer's \| **River N** | 25 |
| Lockwood \| **Loop** | 19 |
| L. Woods Tap \| **Lincolnwood** | 20 |
| Z Mercat \| **S Loop** | 26 |
| Mesón Sabika \| **Naperville** | 23 |
| Z mk \| **Near North** | 27 |
| Z Naha \| **River N** | 27 |
| Z N9ne Steak \| **Loop** | 24 |
| Z NoMI \| **Gold Coast** | 27 |
| Z one sixtyblue \| **W Loop** | 26 |
| Park Grill \| **Loop** | 20 |
| Pete Miller \| **multi.** | 22 |
| Red Light \| **W Loop** | 23 |
| Z Rosebud \| **multi.** | 22 |
| Russian Tea \| **Loop** | 22 |
| Z Ruth's Chris \| **multi.** | 25 |
| Scoozi! \| **River N** | 19 |
| Sepia \| **W Loop** | 24 |
| Z Shanghai Terrace \| **River N** | 25 |
| Z Shaw's Crab \| **multi.** | 24 |
| Z Spiaggia \| **Gold Coast** | 27 |
| SushiSamba \| **River N** | 21 |
| Z Tallgrass \| **Lockport** | 28 |
| 312 Chicago \| **Loop** | 21 |
| Z Topolobampo \| **River N** | 28 |
| Trattoria Roma \| **Old Town** | 21 |
| Vivo \| **W Loop** | 24 |
| Z Wildfire \| **multi.** | 23 |

## PRIX FIXE MENUS

(Call for prices and times)

| | |
|---|---|
| Z Arun's \| **NW Side** | 28 |
| Z Avenues \| **River N** | 26 |
| Bank Lane \| **Lake Forest** | 23 |
| Bistro 110 \| **Gold Coast** | 21 |
| Z Carlos' \| **Highland Pk** | 27 |
| Z Charlie Trotter's \| **Lincoln Pk** | 27 |
| Courtright's \| **Willow Spgs** | 25 |
| Cyrano's Bistrot \| **River N** | 22 |
| D & J Bistro \| **Lake Zurich** | 24 |
| Z Everest \| **Loop** | 27 |
| Froggy's \| **Highwood** | 22 |
| Z Gabriel's \| **Highwood** | 25 |
| La Sardine \| **W Loop** | 24 |
| Z Les Nomades \| **Streeterville** | 29 |
| Z mk \| **Near North** | 27 |
| Z Moto \| **W Loop** | 27 |
| Z North Pond \| **Lincoln Pk** | 25 |
| Z Oceanique \| **Evanston** | 27 |
| Red Light \| **W Loop** | 23 |
| Roy's \| **River N** | 25 |
| Salpicón \| **Old Town** | 26 |
| Z Seasons \| **Gold Coast** | 27 |
| Z Spiaggia \| **Gold Coast** | 27 |
| Z Spring \| **Wicker Pk** | 27 |
| Z Tallgrass \| **Lockport** | 28 |
| Z Tru \| **Streeterville** | 28 |

## QUICK BITES

| | |
|---|---|
| Aladdin's Eatery \| **Lincoln Pk** | 18 |
| Art of Pizza \| **Lakeview** | 22 |
| Artopolis \| **Greektown** | 22 |
| Azucar \| **Logan Sq** | 22 |
| Bagel \| **multi.** | 19 |
| NEW Bakin' & Eggs \| **Lakeview** | 19 |
| Bar Louie \| **multi.** | 16 |
| NEW Belly Shack \| **Humboldt Pk** | 23 |
| Berghoff \| **O'Hare Area** | 18 |
| Big Bowl \| **multi.** | 20 |
| Big Jones \| **Andersonville** | 21 |
| NEW Big Star \| **Wicker Pk** | 23 |
| Bijan's \| **River N** | 19 |
| Billy Goat \| **multi.** | 17 |
| Bin 36/Wine \| **multi.** | 21 |
| Birchwood \| **Bucktown** | 23 |
| NEW Bonsai Café \| **Evanston** | – |
| Bristol \| **Bucktown** | 23 |
| Café Selmarie \| **Lincoln Sq** | 23 |
| Chicago Pizza \| **Lincoln Pk** | 23 |
| C-House \| **Streeterville** | 21 |
| NEW Crêpe Crave \| **Wicker Pk** | – |
| NEW Crêpe Town \| **Lakeview** | – |
| NEW Cuna \| **Lakeview** | – |

| | |
|---|---|
| NEW deca \| **Streeterville** | - |
| Distinctive Cork \| **Naperville** | 21 |
| NEW DMK Burger \| **Lakeview** | 22 |
| Drawing Room \| **Gold Coast** | 23 |
| NEW Edzo's \| **Evanston** | - |
| Eleven City \| **S Loop** | 19 |
| NEW Epic \| **River N** | - |
| Epic Burger \| **Loop** | 22 |
| NEW Felony Franks \| **W Loop** | - |
| Five Guys \| **multi.** | 20 |
| Flat Top Grill \| **multi.** | 20 |
| foodlife \| **Streeterville** | 19 |
| Frankie's Scaloppine \| **Gold Coast** | 18 |
| NEW Franks 'N' Dawgs \| **Lincoln Pk** | - |
| fRedhots \| **Glenview** | 21 |
| Gold Coast \| **multi.** | 19 |
| Z Hannah's Bretzel \| **Loop** | 23 |
| Honey 1 BBQ \| **Bucktown** | 20 |
| Hot Chocolate \| **Bucktown** | 24 |
| Z Hot Doug's \| **NW Side** | 27 |
| Jerry's \| **Wicker Pk** | 22 |
| NEW J. Wellington's \| **Wicker Pk** | - |
| Lem's BBQ \| **Far S Side** | 25 |
| NEW Leo's Coney Island \| **Wrigleyville** | - |
| Maiz \| **Humboldt Pk** | 23 |
| MANA Food \| **Wicker Pk** | 27 |
| Manny's \| **multi.** | 23 |
| NEW M Burger \| **Streeterville** | - |
| Z Mercat \| **S Loop** | 26 |
| Mundial \| **Pilsen** | - |
| Nia \| **W Loop** | - |
| NEW 90 Miles \| **Logan Sq** | 22 |
| Noon-O-Kabab \| **NW Side** | 25 |
| Oak Tree \| **Gold Coast** | 17 |
| Old Jerusalem \| **Old Town** | 19 |
| Old Oak Tap \| **Ukrainian Vill** | 20 |
| NEW Old Town Social \| **Old Town** | 18 |
| Pegasus \| **SW Side** | 20 |
| Penny's Noodle \| **multi.** | 20 |
| Perry's Deli \| **Loop** | 26 |
| Pierrot Gourmet \| **River N** | 20 |
| NEW Piggery \| **Lakeview** | - |
| Pomegranate \| **Evanston** | 18 |
| Pompei Bakery \| **multi.** | 19 |
| Z Potbelly \| **multi.** | 19 |
| Puck's at MCA \| **Streeterville** | 20 |
| NEW Purple Pig \| **River N** | - |
| Quartino \| **River N** | 21 |
| NEW Rootstock \| **Humboldt Pk** | 24 |
| Roti \| **River W** | 21 |
| Russell's BBQ \| **Elmwood Pk** | 19 |
| Sarkis Cafe \| **Evanston** | 15 |

| | |
|---|---|
| Stained Glass \| **Evanston** | 23 |
| NEW State and Lake \| **Loop** | 21 |
| Stir Crazy \| **multi.** | 19 |
| Z Superdawg \| **NW Side** | 21 |
| NEW Taco Fuego \| **Lakeview** | - |
| Tapas Las Ramblas \| **Andersonville** | 23 |
| Tasting Room \| **W Loop** | 20 |
| Tempo \| **Gold Coast** | 20 |
| Trattoria Trullo \| **Lincoln Sq** | 23 |
| Uncle John's \| **Far S Side** | - |
| Uncommon Ground \| **Lakeview** | 22 |
| urbanbelly \| **Logan Sq** | 24 |
| Viand Bar \| **Streeterville** | 22 |
| Webster Wine \| **Lincoln Pk** | 20 |
| Z Wiener's Circle \| **Lincoln Pk** | 21 |
| NEW XOCO \| **River N** | 25 |

## QUIET CONVERSATION

| | |
|---|---|
| Akai Hana \| **Wilmette** | 21 |
| Amitabul \| **NW Side** | 21 |
| Aria \| **Loop** | 24 |
| Z Arun's \| **NW Side** | 28 |
| Z a tavola \| **Ukrainian Vill** | 26 |
| Bank Lane \| **Lake Forest** | 23 |
| Z Barrington Country \| **Barrington** | 25 |
| NEW Bistro Bordeaux \| **Evanston** | - |
| Café Bernard \| **Lincoln Pk** | 19 |
| Café/Architectes \| **Gold Coast** | 24 |
| Café la Cave \| **Des Plaines** | 21 |
| Cafe Matou \| **Bucktown** | 23 |
| Café 103 \| **Far S Side** | - |
| Cafe Pyrenees \| **Libertyville** | 21 |
| Café Selmarie \| **Lincoln Sq** | 23 |
| Z Café Spiaggia \| **Gold Coast** | 25 |
| Cape Cod Room \| **Streeterville** | 22 |
| Z Carlos' \| **Highland Pk** | 27 |
| Z Charlie Trotter's \| **Lincoln Pk** | 27 |
| NEW Cibo Matto \| **Loop** | 24 |
| Cité \| **Streeterville** | 20 |
| D & J Bistro \| **Lake Zurich** | 24 |
| erwin cafe \| **Lakeview** | 23 |
| Z Everest \| **Loop** | 27 |
| Gaetano's \| **Forest Pk** | 24 |
| Gale St. Inn \| **Mundelein** | 22 |
| Gaylord Indian \| **Schaumburg** | 22 |
| Geja's Cafe \| **Lincoln Pk** | 21 |
| Glen Prairie \| **Glen Ellyn** | 23 |
| Inovasi \| **Lake Bluff** | - |
| Itto Sushi \| **Lincoln Pk** | 24 |
| Jacky's on Prairie \| **Evanston** | 21 |
| Jilly's Cafe \| **Evanston** | 21 |
| Klay Oven \| **River N** | 20 |

| La Crêperie | Lakeview | 21 |
| Z La Gondola | Lakeview | 24 |
| Lawry's | River N | 24 |
| Le P'tit Paris | Streeterville | 20 |
| Z Les Nomades | Streeterville | 29 |
| Z Le Titi/Paris | Arlington Hts | 26 |
| Le Vichyssois | Lakemoor | 26 |
| Z Lovells | Lake Forest | 23 |
| Z North Pond | Lincoln Pk | 25 |
| Z Oceanique | Evanston | 27 |
| One North | Loop | 15 |
| Pierrot Gourmet | River N | 20 |
| NEW Prairie Fire | W Loop | - |
| Z Pump Room | Gold Coast | 22 |
| Quince | Evanston | 23 |
| Rhapsody | Loop | 20 |
| Z RL | Gold Coast | 23 |
| Russian Tea | Loop | 22 |
| Z Seasons | Gold Coast | 27 |
| 1776 | Crystal Lake | 22 |
| Z Shanghai Terrace | River N | 25 |
| Z Signature Room | Streeterville | 18 |
| South Gate | Lake Forest | 20 |
| South Water | Loop | 16 |
| TABLE 52 | Gold Coast | 24 |
| Z Tallgrass | Lockport | 28 |
| Tasting Room | W Loop | 20 |
| NEW Terzo Piano | Loop | 21 |
| Trattoria No. 10 | Loop | 24 |
| Tre Kronor | NW Side | 23 |
| Z Tru | Streeterville | 28 |
| Village | Loop | 21 |
| Vinci | Lincoln Pk | 21 |
| Vivere | Loop | 22 |
| Zealous | River N | 25 |

## RAW BARS

| NEW Balsan | Gold Coast | - |
| NEW Benny's | River N | - |
| Z Bob Chinn's | Wheeling | 23 |
| Brasserie Jo | River N | 22 |
| Brazzaz | River N | 22 |
| C-House | Streeterville | 21 |
| Davis St. Fish | Evanston | 19 |
| NEW deca | Streeterville | - |
| Half Shell | Lakeview | 24 |
| Mitchell's | Glenview | 21 |
| Z N9ne Steak | Loop | 24 |
| Niu | Streeterville | 19 |
| Z Pappadeaux | Arlington Hts | 21 |
| Riva | Streeterville | 20 |
| Z Shaw's Crab | multi. | 24 |
| Tin Fish | Tinley Park | 23 |

## ROMANTIC PLACES

| Abigail's | Highland Pk | 24 |
| Ai Sushi | River N | 24 |
| aja | River N | - |
| Alhambra | W Loop | 16 |
| Z Avenues | River N | 26 |
| Azucar | Logan Sq | 22 |
| NEW Balsan | Gold Coast | - |
| Z Barrington Country | Barrington | 25 |
| NEW Bistro Bordeaux | Evanston | - |
| Z Bistro Campagne | Lincoln Sq | 25 |
| Bistrot Margot | Old Town | 20 |
| Blue 13 | River N | 24 |
| BOKA | Lincoln Pk | 25 |
| Briejo | Oak Pk | 14 |
| NEW Browntrout | North Ctr/St. Ben's | 24 |
| Café Absinthe | Bucktown | 23 |
| Café la Cave | Des Plaines | 21 |
| Z Carlos' | Highland Pk | 27 |
| NEW Ceres' Table | Uptown | - |
| Z Charlie Trotter's | Lincoln Pk | 27 |
| Chez Joël | Little Italy | 24 |
| NEW Cibo Matto | Loop | 24 |
| Cité | Streeterville | 20 |
| Z Coco Pazzo | River N | 25 |
| Courtright's | Willow Spgs | 25 |
| Z Crofton on Wells | River N | 26 |
| NEW Cuna | Lakeview | - |
| D & J Bistro | Lake Zurich | 24 |
| Drawing Room | Gold Coast | 23 |
| NEW Elate | River N | 21 |
| NEW Epic | River N | - |
| Z Eve | Gold Coast | 22 |
| Z Everest | Loop | 27 |
| Fiddlehead | Lincoln Sq | 20 |
| Fiorentino's | Lakeview | 22 |
| Gaetano's | Forest Pk | 24 |
| Geja's Cafe | Lincoln Pk | 21 |
| Gioco | S Loop | 25 |
| Glen Prairie | Glen Ellyn | 23 |
| Il Mulino | Gold Coast | 25 |
| Z Japonais | River N | 24 |
| Jilly's Cafe | Evanston | 21 |
| Kiki's | Near North | 25 |
| NEW Kith & Kin | Lincoln Pk | - |
| La Crêperie | Lakeview | 21 |
| Landmark | Lincoln Pk | 20 |
| NEW Lan's Bistro | Old Town | - |
| La Tache | Andersonville | 22 |
| Le Bouchon | Bucktown | 24 |
| Z Le Colonial | Gold Coast | 24 |
| L'Eiffel | S Barrington | 21 |

| | |
|---|---|
| Le P'tit Paris \| **Streeterville** | 20 |
| **Z** Les Nomades \| **Streeterville** | 29 |
| **Z** Le Titi/Paris \| **Arlington Hts** | 26 |
| Le Vichyssois \| **Lakemoor** | 26 |
| **NEW** LM \| **Lincoln Sq** | 22 |
| **NEW** LOKaL \| **Bucktown** | - |
| **Z** L2O \| **Lincoln Pk** | 27 |
| Maijean \| **Clarendon Hills** | 28 |
| Marigold \| **Uptown** | 23 |
| **NEW** Masu Izakaya \| **Lincoln Pk** | - |
| May St. Market \| **W Loop** | 24 |
| **NEW** Melanthios \| **Lakeview** | - |
| **NEW** Mercadito \| **River N** | 22 |
| **NEW** Mezé \| **W Loop** | - |
| **Z** mk \| **Near North** | 27 |
| Mon Ami Gabi \| **multi.** | 22 |
| Mythos \| **Lakeview** | 23 |
| **Z** Nacional 27 \| **River N** | 23 |
| **Z** Naha \| **River N** | 27 |
| Natalino's \| **W Town** | 23 |
| Niche \| **Geneva** | 28 |
| **Z** NoMI \| **Gold Coast** | 27 |
| **Z** Oceanique \| **Evanston** | 27 |
| Pane Caldo \| **Gold Coast** | 23 |
| Paramount Room \| **Near W** | 24 |
| **NEW** Pasha \| **W Loop** | - |
| **NEW** Pelago \| **Streeterville** | 26 |
| Piccolo Sogno \| **Near W** | 24 |
| **NEW** Prairie Fire \| **W Loop** | - |
| **NEW** Prasino \| **La Grange** | - |
| Prosecco \| **River N** | 24 |
| **Z** Pump Room \| **Gold Coast** | 22 |
| **NEW** Purple Pig \| **River N** | - |
| Quince \| **Evanston** | 23 |
| **NEW** RendezVous \| **Lincoln Sq** | - |
| Rhapsody \| **Loop** | 20 |
| **Z** Riccardo \| **Lincoln Pk** | 27 |
| **Z** RL \| **Gold Coast** | 23 |
| **NEW** Sable \| **River N** | - |
| **Z** Seasons \| **Gold Coast** | 27 |
| Sepia \| **W Loop** | 24 |
| **Z** Shanghai Terrace \| **River N** | 25 |
| **Z** Signature Room \| **Streeterville** | 18 |
| sola \| **Lakeview** | 25 |
| **NEW** Southern \| **Bucktown** | - |
| **Z** Spring \| **Wicker Pk** | 27 |
| **NEW** Sprout \| **Lincoln Pk** | 28 |
| Stained Glass \| **Evanston** | 23 |
| SugarToad \| **Naperville** | 19 |
| Sunda \| **River N** | 23 |
| **NEW** Sushi Taiyo \| **River N** | - |
| TABLE 52 \| **Gold Coast** | 24 |
| **Z** Tallgrass \| **Lockport** | 28 |
| Tasting Room \| **W Loop** | 20 |

| | |
|---|---|
| Taxim \| **Wicker Pk** | 22 |
| Topo Gigio \| **Old Town** | 23 |
| Trattoria Trullo \| **Lincoln Sq** | 23 |
| Trattoria 225 \| **Oak Pk** | - |
| **Z** Tru \| **Streeterville** | 28 |
| Vermilion \| **River N** | 22 |
| Vinci \| **Lincoln Pk** | 21 |
| **NEW** Vintage 338 \| **Lincoln Pk** | - |
| Vivo \| **W Loop** | 24 |
| Wave \| **Streeterville** | 13 |
| Webster Wine \| **Lincoln Pk** | 20 |
| Wildfish \| **Arlington Hts** | 21 |
| Zak's Place \| **Hinsdale** | - |
| Zhivago \| **Skokie** | 16 |
| Zocalo \| **River N** | 20 |

## SENIOR APPEAL

| | |
|---|---|
| Andies \| **Ravenswood** | 18 |
| Ann Sather \| **multi.** | 21 |
| Army & Lou's \| **Far S Side** | 26 |
| Bacchanalia \| **SW Side** | 24 |
| Bagel \| **multi.** | 19 |
| Berghoff \| **Loop** | 18 |
| Bruna's \| **SW Side** | 26 |
| Café 103 \| **Far S Side** | - |
| Cape Cod Room \| **Streeterville** | 22 |
| Carson's Ribs \| **River N** | 22 |
| Czech Plaza \| **Berwyn** | 22 |
| Dave's Italian \| **Evanston** | 17 |
| Davis St. Fish \| **Evanston** | 19 |
| Del Rio \| **Highwood** | 20 |
| Edelweiss \| **Norridge** | 19 |
| Francesco's \| **Northbrook** | 24 |
| Gale St. Inn \| **multi.** | 22 |
| Hackney's \| **multi.** | 18 |
| Jacky's on Prairie \| **Evanston** | 21 |
| La Cantina \| **Loop** | 21 |
| **Z** La Gondola \| **Lakeview** | 24 |
| Lawry's \| **River N** | 24 |
| Le P'tit Paris \| **Streeterville** | 20 |
| Le Vichyssois \| **Lakemoor** | 26 |
| Lou Mitchell's \| **Loop** | 23 |
| **Z** Margie's Candies \| **Bucktown** | 22 |
| Miller's Pub \| **Loop** | 17 |
| Mirabell \| **NW Side** | 21 |
| Myron & Phil Steak \| **Lincolnwood** | 21 |
| **NEW** Nagoya \| **Naperville** | - |
| Next Door \| **Northbrook** | 23 |
| Nick's Fishmarket \| **Rosemont** | 23 |
| Oak Tree \| **Gold Coast** | 17 |
| **Z** Original/Walker Pancake \| **multi.** | 24 |
| **Z** Pump Room \| **Gold Coast** | 22 |
| Rist. al Teatro \| **Pilsen** | - |

| | |
|---|---|
| ☑ Rosebud \| **Loop** | 22 |
| Russell's BBQ \| **Elmwood Pk** | 19 |
| Russian Tea \| **Loop** | 22 |
| Sabatino's \| **NW Side** | 24 |
| **NEW** Sarks/Park \| **Lincoln Pk** | - |
| South Gate \| **Lake Forest** | 20 |
| Tre Kronor \| **NW Side** | 23 |
| Tufano's Tap \| **University Vill** | 20 |
| Village \| **Loop** | 21 |
| White Fence \| **Romeoville** | 22 |
| Zhivago \| **Skokie** | 16 |

## SINGLES SCENES

| | |
|---|---|
| Adobo \| **Old Town** | 21 |
| Bar Louie \| **multi.** | 16 |
| BOKA \| **Lincoln Pk** | 25 |
| Café Iberico \| **River N** | 22 |
| ☑ Carnivale \| **Loop** | 23 |
| Clubhouse \| **Oak Brook** | 21 |
| Drawing Room \| **Gold Coast** | 23 |
| Fleming's \| **Lincolnshire** | 23 |
| ☑ Gibsons \| **multi.** | 26 |
| Landmark \| **Lincoln Pk** | 20 |
| LuxBar \| **Gold Coast** | 20 |
| Market \| **W Loop** | 18 |
| Mike Ditka's \| **Gold Coast** | 22 |
| Moody's Pub \| **Edgewater** | 19 |
| ☑ N9ne Steak \| **Loop** | 24 |
| **NEW** Old Town Social \| **Old Town** | 18 |
| P.J. Clarke's \| **Gold Coast** | 17 |
| Red Light \| **W Loop** | 23 |
| Rockit B&G \| **River N** | 19 |
| Scoozi! \| **River N** | 19 |
| Stanley's \| **Lincoln Pk** | 18 |
| Sullivan's Steak \| **multi.** | 22 |
| SushiSamba \| **River N** | 21 |
| Tavern/Rush \| **Gold Coast** | 21 |
| **NEW** 33 Club \| **Old Town** | 20 |
| Trader Vic's \| **Gold Coast** | 17 |
| Wave \| **Streeterville** | 13 |

## SLEEPERS

(Good food, but little known)

| | |
|---|---|
| Azucar \| **Logan Sq** | 22 |
| Carlos & Carlos \| **Arlington Hts** | 24 |
| Czech Plaza \| **Berwyn** | 22 |
| Drawing Room \| **Gold Coast** | 23 |
| Evergreen \| **Chinatown** | 23 |
| Filippo's \| **Lincoln Pk** | 24 |
| Habana Libre \| **W Town** | 22 |
| Kansaku \| **Evanston** | 22 |
| Lem's BBQ \| **Far S Side** | 25 |
| Maijean \| **Clarendon Hills** | 28 |
| Maiz \| **Humboldt Pk** | 23 |
| Montarra \| **Algonquin** | 24 |

| | |
|---|---|
| Nosh \| **Geneva** | 24 |
| Paramount Room \| **Near W** | 24 |
| Pasta Palazzo \| **Lincoln Pk** | 22 |
| Ras Dashen \| **Edgewater** | 23 |
| Rumba \| **River N** | 23 |
| Shui Wah \| **Chinatown** | 24 |
| Swordfish \| **Batavia** | 27 |
| Tango \| **Naperville** | 22 |
| Tapas Las Ramblas \| **Andersonville** | 23 |
| Topaz Café \| **Burr Ridge** | 23 |
| Trattoria Gianni \| **Lincoln Pk** | 26 |
| Trattoria Isabella \| **W Loop** | 26 |
| Tub Tim Thai \| **Skokie** | 24 |
| Victory's Banner \| **Roscoe Vill** | 24 |
| Viet Bistro \| **Rogers Pk** | 25 |

## TEEN APPEAL

| | |
|---|---|
| Ann Sather \| **multi.** | 21 |
| Aurelio's Pizza \| **multi.** | 23 |
| Bacino's \| **multi.** | 22 |
| Bandera \| **Streeterville** | 22 |
| Big Bowl \| **multi.** | 20 |
| ☑ Cheesecake Factory \| **multi.** | 19 |
| Chicago Pizza \| **Lincoln Pk** | 23 |
| **NEW** Ciao Napoli \| **Logan Sq** | - |
| Counter \| **Lincoln Pk** | 20 |
| Edwardo's Pizza \| **multi.** | 20 |
| **NEW** Edzo's \| **Evanston** | - |
| EJ's Place \| **Skokie** | 22 |
| Epic Burger \| **Loop** | 22 |
| **NEW** Felony Franks \| **W Loop** | - |
| Five Guys \| **Rogers Pk** | 20 |
| Flat Top Grill \| **multi.** | 20 |
| ☑ Giordano's \| **multi.** | 23 |
| Gold Coast \| **multi.** | 19 |
| Grand Lux \| **River N** | 20 |
| Hackney's \| **multi.** | 18 |
| Hard Rock \| **River N** | 12 |
| Harry Caray's \| **River N** | 20 |
| ☑ Heaven on Seven \| **multi.** | 23 |
| ☑ Hot Doug's \| **NW Side** | 27 |
| HUB 51 \| **River N** | 21 |
| Ina's \| **W Loop** | 23 |
| Joy Yee \| **multi.** | 20 |
| Kroll's \| **S Loop** | 19 |
| **NEW** Leo's Coney Island \| **Wrigleyville** | - |
| ☑ Lou Malnati's \| **multi.** | 24 |
| Lou Mitchell's \| **Loop** | 23 |
| LuLu's \| **Evanston** | 21 |
| L. Woods Tap \| **Lincolnwood** | 20 |
| ☑ Margie's Candies \| **Bucktown** | 22 |
| Mity Nice Grill \| **Streeterville** | 17 |
| Nookies \| **multi.** | 20 |

| | |
|---|---|
| 🅩 Original Gino's \| **multi.** | 22 |
| 🅩 Original/Walker Pancake \| **multi.** | 24 |
| Penny's Noodle \| **multi.** | 20 |
| Pizzeria Uno/Due \| **River N** | 22 |
| 🆕 Pizzeria Serio \| **Roscoe Vill** | - |
| Pompei Bakery \| **multi.** | 19 |
| 🅩 Potbelly \| **multi.** | 19 |
| R.J. Grunts \| **Lincoln Pk** | 19 |
| Robinson's Ribs \| **multi.** | 21 |
| Russell's BBQ \| **Elmwood Pk** | 19 |
| Sarkis Cafe \| **Evanston** | 15 |
| Stanley's \| **Lincoln Pk** | 18 |
| Stir Crazy \| **Northbrook** | 19 |
| 🅩 Superdawg \| **NW Side** | 21 |
| Tamales \| **Highland Pk** | 20 |
| Tempo \| **Gold Coast** | 20 |
| Toast \| **multi.** | 22 |
| Trader Vic's \| **Gold Coast** | 17 |
| Uncle Julio's \| **Old Town** | 18 |
| 🅩 Wiener's Circle \| **Lincoln Pk** | 21 |
| Wishbone \| **multi.** | 21 |

## TRENDY

| | |
|---|---|
| 🅩 avec \| **W Loop** | 26 |
| 🆕 Belly Shack \| **Humboldt Pk** | 23 |
| 🆕 Big Star \| **Wicker Pk** | 23 |
| 🅩 Blackbird \| **W Loop** | 27 |
| Blue 13 \| **River N** | 24 |
| BOKA \| **Lincoln Pk** | 25 |
| 🅩 Bonsoirée \| **Logan Sq** | 26 |
| Bristol \| **Bucktown** | 23 |
| 🅩 Carnivale \| **Loop** | 23 |
| 🆕 Ceres' Table \| **Uptown** | - |
| 🆕 Cuna \| **Lakeview** | - |
| 🅩 David Burke Prime \| **River N** | 25 |
| 🆕 DMK Burger \| **Lakeview** | 22 |
| Drawing Room \| **Gold Coast** | 23 |
| Duchamp \| **Bucktown** | 17 |
| 🆕 Elate \| **River N** | 21 |
| 🆕 Epic \| **River N** | - |
| 🅩 Eve \| **Gold Coast** | 22 |
| 🆕 Folklore \| **Ukrainian Vill** | - |
| Fred's \| **Gold Coast** | 19 |
| 🅩 Frontera Grill \| **River N** | 27 |
| 🆕 Gemini Bistro \| **Lincoln Pk** | 21 |
| 🅩 Gibsons \| **Gold Coast** | 26 |
| Gioco \| **S Loop** | 25 |
| graham elliot \| **River N** | 24 |
| Great Lake \| **Andersonville** | 23 |
| 🅩 Green Zebra \| **W Town** | 26 |
| 🆕 Hearty \| **Wrigleyville** | - |
| Hot Chocolate \| **Bucktown** | 24 |
| 🅩 Hot Doug's \| **NW Side** | 27 |

| | |
|---|---|
| HUB 51 \| **River N** | 21 |
| 🆕 Isacco \| **St. Charles** | - |
| 🆕 Jam \| **Ukrainian Vill** | 21 |
| 🅩 Japonais \| **River N** | 24 |
| 🆕 Kin \| **River W** | - |
| 🆕 Kith & Kin \| **Lincoln Pk** | - |
| La Madia \| **River N** | 23 |
| Landmark \| **Lincoln Pk** | 20 |
| 🆕 Longman & Eagle \| **Logan Sq** | - |
| LuxBar \| **Gold Coast** | 20 |
| 🅩 mado \| **Bucktown** | 25 |
| MANA Food \| **Wicker Pk** | 27 |
| Marché \| **W Loop** | 23 |
| Marigold \| **Uptown** | 23 |
| 🆕 Masu Izakaya \| **Lincoln Pk** | - |
| May St. Market \| **W Loop** | 24 |
| 🆕 Mercadito \| **River N** | 22 |
| 🅩 Mercat \| **S Loop** | 26 |
| 🅩 Mia Francesca \| **Lakeview** | 26 |
| Mirai Sushi \| **Wicker Pk** | 25 |
| Miramar Bistro \| **Highwood** | 17 |
| 🅩 mk \| **Near North** | 27 |
| 🅩 Naha \| **River N** | 27 |
| 🆕 Nightwood \| **Pilsen** | 23 |
| 🅩 N9ne Steak \| **Loop** | 24 |
| 🅩 NoMI \| **Gold Coast** | 27 |
| 🅩 one sixtyblue \| **W Loop** | 26 |
| Opera \| **S Loop** | 20 |
| Osteria/Pizzeria Via Stato \| **River N** | 23 |
| Otom \| **W Loop** | 22 |
| Paramount Room \| **Near W** | 24 |
| Park 52 \| **Hyde Pk** | 19 |
| Perennial \| **Lincoln Pk** | 24 |
| Prosecco \| **River N** | 24 |
| Province \| **W Loop** | 23 |
| 🅩 Publican \| **W Loop** | 25 |
| 🆕 Purple Pig \| **River N** | - |
| Quartino \| **River N** | 21 |
| Real Tenochtitlán \| **Logan Sq** | 20 |
| Red Light \| **W Loop** | 23 |
| 🆕 Revolution Brewing \| **Logan Sq** | - |
| 🆕 Rootstock \| **Humboldt Pk** | 24 |
| 🆕 Sable \| **River N** | - |
| 🅩 Schwa \| **Wicker Pk** | 29 |
| Sepia \| **W Loop** | 24 |
| sola \| **Lakeview** | 25 |
| 🆕 Southern \| **Bucktown** | - |
| Spacca Napoli \| **Ravenswood** | 23 |
| 🅩 Spring \| **Wicker Pk** | 27 |
| 🆕 Sprout \| **Lincoln Pk** | 28 |
| 🆕 State and Lake \| **Loop** | 21 |

| | |
|---|---|
| Sunda | **River N** | 23 |
| Sura | **Lakeview** | 20 |
| SushiSamba | **River N** | 21 |
| ☑ sushi wabi | **W Loop** | 27 |
| Taxim | **Wicker Pk** | 22 |
| Tocco | **Bucktown** | 12 |
| urbanbelly | **Logan Sq** | 24 |
| Veerasway | **W Loop** | 21 |
| Zapatista | **S Loop** | 20 |

## VIEWS

| | |
|---|---|
| Athena | **Greektown** | 21 |
| Atwater's | **Geneva** | 20 |
| ☑ Avenues | **River N** | 26 |
| Chief O'Neill's | **NW Side** | 18 |
| Cité | **Streeterville** | 20 |
| Courtright's | **Willow Spgs** | 25 |
| **NEW** deca | **Streeterville** | - |
| Drake Bros.' | **Gold Coast** | - |
| ☑ Everest | **Loop** | 27 |
| Flatwater | **River N** | 16 |
| Fred's | **Gold Coast** | 19 |
| Fulton's | **River N** | 19 |
| ☑ Gage | **Loop** | 22 |
| Lobby | **River N** | 28 |
| ☑ Mercat | **S Loop** | 26 |
| ☑ NoMI | **Gold Coast** | 27 |
| ☑ North Pond | **Lincoln Pk** | 25 |
| OPA Estiatorio | **Vernon Hills** | 25 |
| Park Grill | **Loop** | 20 |
| Puck's at MCA | **Streeterville** | 20 |
| Riva | **Streeterville** | 20 |
| ☑ Rosebud | **Naperville** | 22 |
| ☑ Seasons | **Gold Coast** | 27 |
| ☑ Shanghai Terrace | **River N** | 25 |
| ☑ Signature Room | **Streeterville** | 18 |
| ☑ Sixteen | **River N** | 22 |
| Smith & Wollensky | **River N** | 23 |
| ☑ Spiaggia | **Gold Coast** | 27 |
| Tasting Room | **W Loop** | 20 |
| Tavern/Rush | **Gold Coast** | 21 |
| ZED 451 | **River N** | 21 |

## VISITORS ON EXPENSE ACCOUNT

| | |
|---|---|
| aja | **River N** | - |
| ☑ Alinea | **Lincoln Pk** | 29 |
| ☑ Arun's | **NW Side** | 28 |
| ☑ Avenues | **River N** | 26 |
| Bice | **Streeterville** | 21 |
| ☑ Blackbird | **W Loop** | 27 |
| ☑ Bob Chinn's | **Wheeling** | 23 |
| Brazzaz | **River N** | 22 |
| Cape Cod Room | **Streeterville** | 22 |
| ☑ Capital Grille | **Streeterville** | 25 |

| | |
|---|---|
| ☑ Carlos' | **Highland Pk** | 27 |
| ☑ Catch 35 | **Loop** | 24 |
| ☑ Charlie Trotter's | **Lincoln Pk** | 27 |
| ☑ Chicago Chop | **River N** | 25 |
| C-House | **Streeterville** | 21 |
| **NEW** Cibo Matto | **Loop** | 24 |
| ☑ Coco Pazzo | **River N** | 25 |
| Courtright's | **Willow Spgs** | 25 |
| ☑ Crofton on Wells | **River N** | 26 |
| Custom House | **Printer's Row** | 25 |
| ☑ David Burke Prime | **River N** | 25 |
| Entourage | **Schaumburg** | 20 |
| **NEW** Epic | **River N** | - |
| ☑ Everest | **Loop** | 27 |
| Fred's | **Gold Coast** | 19 |
| ☑ Gene & Georgetti | **River N** | 24 |
| ☑ Gibsons | **multi.** | 26 |
| graham elliot | **River N** | 24 |
| Il Mulino | **Gold Coast** | 25 |
| ☑ Joe's Sea/Steak | **River N** | 26 |
| ☑ Keefer's | **River N** | 25 |
| Lawry's | **River N** | 24 |
| ☑ Le Colonial | **Gold Coast** | 24 |
| ☑ Les Nomades | **Streeterville** | 29 |
| ☑ Le Titi/Paris | **Arlington Hts** | 26 |
| Lobby | **River N** | 28 |
| Lockwood | **Loop** | 19 |
| ☑ L2O | **Lincoln Pk** | 27 |
| ☑ mk | **Near North** | 27 |
| ☑ Morton's | **multi.** | 26 |
| ☑ Naha | **River N** | 27 |
| ☑ N9ne Steak | **Loop** | 24 |
| ☑ NoMI | **Gold Coast** | 27 |
| ☑ North Pond | **Lincoln Pk** | 25 |
| ☑ Oceanique | **Evanston** | 27 |
| ☑ one sixtyblue | **W Loop** | 26 |
| Palm | **Loop** | 24 |
| ☑ Pump Room | **Gold Coast** | 22 |
| **NEW** Ria | **Gold Coast** | - |
| ☑ RL | **Gold Coast** | 23 |
| Rosebud Prime/Steak | **Streeterville** | 25 |
| Roy's | **River N** | 25 |
| ☑ Ruth's Chris | **multi.** | 25 |
| Saloon Steak | **Streeterville** | 23 |
| ☑ Seasons | **Gold Coast** | 27 |
| ☑ Shanghai Terrace | **River N** | 25 |
| ☑ Shaw's Crab | **multi.** | 24 |
| ☑ Signature Room | **Streeterville** | 18 |
| ☑ Sixteen | **River N** | 22 |
| Smith & Wollensky | **River N** | 23 |
| ☑ Spiaggia | **Gold Coast** | 27 |
| ☑ Spring | **Wicker Pk** | 27 |
| ☑ Takashi | **Bucktown** | 26 |

| | |
|---|---|
| Z Tallgrass \| **Lockport** | 28 |
| Z Topolobampo \| **River N** | 28 |
| Trader Vic's \| **Gold Coast** | 17 |
| Z Tru \| **Streeterville** | 28 |
| Vivere \| **Loop** | 22 |
| Zealous \| **River N** | 25 |

## WINE BARS

| | |
|---|---|
| Z avec \| **W Loop** | 26 |
| Bin 36/Wine \| **Wicker Pk** | 21 |
| Broadway Cellars \| **Edgewater** | 21 |
| Cab's Wine Bar \| **Glen Ellyn** | 24 |
| Café Bernard \| **Lincoln Pk** | 19 |
| Cafe Pyrenees \| **Libertyville** | 21 |
| Cyrano's Bistrot \| **River N** | 22 |
| Devon Seafood \| **River N** | 21 |
| Fleming's \| **Lincolnshire** | 23 |
| Flight \| **Glenview** | 17 |
| Fontana Grill \| **Uptown** | - |
| Frasca Pizza \| **Lakeview** | 20 |
| NEW Orvieto Pizza \| **Lincoln Pk** | - |
| Quartino \| **River N** | 21 |
| Rhapsody \| **Loop** | 20 |
| NEW Rootstock \| **Humboldt Pk** | 24 |
| RoPa \| **Rogers Pk** | - |
| San Gabriel \| **Bannockburn** | 17 |
| South Water \| **Loop** | 16 |
| Stained Glass \| **Evanston** | 23 |
| Tasting Room \| **W Loop** | 20 |
| NEW Vintage 338 \| **Lincoln Pk** | - |
| Volo \| **Roscoe Vill** | - |
| Webster Wine \| **Lincoln Pk** | 20 |

## WINNING WINE LISTS

| | |
|---|---|
| Z Alinea \| **Lincoln Pk** | 29 |
| Z Arun's \| **NW Side** | 28 |
| Z avec \| **W Loop** | 26 |
| Z Avenues \| **River N** | 26 |
| Bin 36/Wine \| **multi.** | 21 |
| NEW Bistro Bordeaux \| **Evanston** | - |
| Bistrot Margot \| **Old Town** | 20 |
| Z Blackbird \| **W Loop** | 27 |
| Bluebird \| **Bucktown** | 20 |
| BOKA \| **Lincoln Pk** | 25 |
| Bristol \| **Bucktown** | 23 |
| Cab's Wine Bar \| **Glen Ellyn** | 24 |
| Campagnola \| **Evanston** | 25 |
| Z Capital Grille \| **Streeterville** | 25 |
| Z Carlos' \| **Highland Pk** | 27 |
| Chalkboard \| **Lakeview** | 22 |
| Z Charlie Trotter's \| **Lincoln Pk** | 27 |
| C-House \| **Streeterville** | 21 |
| NEW Cibo Matto \| **Loop** | 24 |
| Courtright's \| **Willow Spgs** | 25 |

| | |
|---|---|
| Custom House \| **Printer's Row** | 25 |
| Cyrano's Bistrot \| **River N** | 22 |
| Del Rio \| **Highwood** | 20 |
| Distinctive Cork \| **Naperville** | 21 |
| Duchamp \| **Bucktown** | 17 |
| NEW Elate \| **River N** | 21 |
| NEW Epic \| **River N** | - |
| Z Eve \| **Gold Coast** | 22 |
| Z Everest \| **Loop** | 27 |
| Fiddlehead \| **Lincoln Sq** | 20 |
| Fleming's \| **Lincolnshire** | 23 |
| Flight \| **Glenview** | 17 |
| Fogo de Chão \| **River N** | 24 |
| Fornetto Mei \| **Gold Coast** | 20 |
| Z Gabriel's \| **Highwood** | 25 |
| Geja's Cafe \| **Lincoln Pk** | 21 |
| Glen Prairie \| **Glen Ellyn** | 23 |
| graham elliot \| **River N** | 24 |
| Z Green Zebra \| **W Town** | 26 |
| Jacky's on Prairie \| **Evanston** | 21 |
| Z Japonais \| **River N** | 24 |
| Koda \| **Far S Side** | - |
| La Madia \| **River N** | 23 |
| La Sardine \| **W Loop** | 24 |
| Le P'tit Paris \| **Streeterville** | 20 |
| Z Les Nomades \| **Streeterville** | 29 |
| Z Le Titi/Paris \| **Arlington Hts** | 26 |
| Lockwood \| **Loop** | 19 |
| Z L2O \| **Lincoln Pk** | 27 |
| May St. Market \| **W Loop** | 24 |
| Z Michael \| **Winnetka** | 28 |
| Miramar Bistro \| **Highwood** | 17 |
| Z mk \| **Near North** | 27 |
| Z Moto \| **W Loop** | 27 |
| Z Naha \| **River N** | 27 |
| Niche \| **Geneva** | 28 |
| Z NoMI \| **Gold Coast** | 27 |
| Z North Pond \| **Lincoln Pk** | 25 |
| Z Oceanique \| **Evanston** | 27 |
| Z one sixtyblue \| **W Loop** | 26 |
| Pane Caldo \| **Gold Coast** | 23 |
| Perennial \| **Lincoln Pk** | 24 |
| Piccolo Sogno \| **Near W** | 24 |
| Prosecco \| **River N** | 24 |
| Province \| **W Loop** | 23 |
| Z Publican \| **W Loop** | 25 |
| NEW Purple Pig \| **River N** | - |
| Quince \| **Evanston** | 23 |
| Rhapsody \| **Loop** | 20 |
| NEW Ria \| **Gold Coast** | - |
| Salpicón \| **Old Town** | 26 |
| Sam & Harry's \| **Schaumburg** | - |
| Z Seasons \| **Gold Coast** | 27 |
| Sepia \| **W Loop** | 24 |

Menus, photos, voting and more – free at ZAGAT.com

# MILWAUKEE

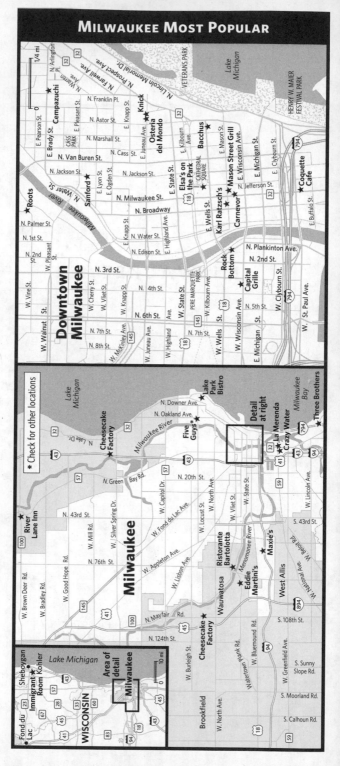

# MILWAUKEE MOST POPULAR

**Downtown Milwaukee**

Cempazuchi
Knick
Osteria del Mondo
Bacchus
Mason Street Grill
Roots
Sanford
Elsa's on the Park
Carnevor
Karl Ratzsch's
Coquette Cafe
Rock Bottom
Capital Grille

**Milwaukee**

Lake Park Bistro
Detail at right
Three Brothers
Cheesecake Factory
Five Guys
La Merenda
Crazy Water
River Lane Inn
Ristorante Bartolotta
Maxie's
Eddie Martini's
Wauwatosa
West Allis
Cheesecake Factory

Sheboygan
Kohler
Immigrant Room
Lake Michigan
Area of detail
Milwaukee
WISCONSIN
Fond du Lac
Brookfield

*Check for other locations

# Top Ratings

## MOST POPULAR

1. Sanford | *American*
2. Lake Park Bistro | *French*
3. Coquette Cafe | *French*
4. Eddie Martini's | *Steak*
5. Bacchus | *American*
6. Karl Ratzsch's | *German*
7. Capital Grille | *Steak*
8. Mason St. Grill | *American*
9. La Merenda | *Eclectic*
10. Rist. Bartolotta | *Italian*
11. Cheesecake Factory | *American*
12. Maxie's* | *Creole*
13. Rock Bottom* | *American*
14. Five Guys | *Burgers*
15. Immigrant Room* | *American*
16. Osteria del Mondo* | *Italian*
17. Carnevor | *Steak*
18. Cempazuchi* | *Mexican*
19. Crazy Water* | *Eclectic*
20. Knick* | *Eclectic*
21. Three Brothers* | *Serbian*
22. Elsa's on the Park | *American*
23. Roots* | *Californian*
24. River Lane Inn | *Seafood*

## TOP FOOD

29 Roots | *Californian*
   Sanford | *American*
   Eddie Martini's | *Steak*
28 Lake Park Bistro | *French*
   Osteria del Mondo | *Italian*

   Rist. Bartolotta | *Italian*
27 La Merenda | *Eclectic*
26 River Lane Inn | *Seafood*
   Coquette Cafe | *French*
   Hinterland Erie St. | *American*

## BY CUISINE

### AMERICAN (NEW)
29 Sanford
26 Hinterland Erie St.
25 Bacchus

### AMERICAN (TRAD.)
24 Original/Walker Pancake
23 Mason St. Grill
   Elsa's on Park

### ECLECTIC
27 La Merenda
25 Crazy Water
21 Knick

### FRENCH
28 Lake Park Bistro
26 Coquette Cafe

### ITALIAN
28 Osteria del Mondo
   Rist. Bartolotta
24 Mimma's Café

### STEAKHOUSES
29 Eddie Martini's
25 Capital Grille
   Five O'Clock Steak

## BY LOCATION

### DOWNTOWN
28 Osteria del Mondo
25 Capital Grille
   Bacchus

### EAST SIDE
29 Sanford
28 Lake Park Bistro
24 Original Pancake

### OUTLYING AREAS
24 Original Pancake
23 Fleming's
   Immigrant Room

Excludes places with low votes; * indicates a tie with restaurant above

| THIRD WARD | WAUWATOSA |
|---|---|
| 26 Coquette Cafe | 29 Eddie Martini's |
| Hinterland Erie St. | 28 Rist. Bartolotta |
| 23 Nanakusa | 20 Maggiano's |

## TOP DECOR

| | |
|---|---|
| 28 Lake Park Bistro | 25 Rist. Bartolotta |
| 27 Roots | Hinterland Erie St. |
| Sanford | 24 Capital Grille |
| 26 Eddie Martini's | Mason St. Grill |
| Bacchus | 23 Karl Ratzsch's |

## TOP SERVICE

| | |
|---|---|
| 29 Sanford | 25 Osteria del Mondo |
| 28 Eddie Martini's | Capital Grille |
| 27 Lake Park Bistro | Immigrant Room |
| Rist. Bartolotta | Bacchus |
| 26 River Lane Inn | 24 Crazy Water |

## BEST BUYS

In order of Bang for the Buck rating.

1. Potbelly Sandwich
2. Five Guys
3. Original Pancake
4. Elsa's on Park
5. Edwardo's Pizza

6. Cubanitas
7. Cempazuchi
8. Rock Bottom
9. La Merenda
10. Maxie's

# MILWAUKEE
# RESTAURANT
# DIRECTORY

### ☑ Bacchus ⑤ American
25 | 26 | 25 | $61

**Downtown** | Cudahy Tower | 925 E. Wells St. (Prospect Ave.) |
414-765-1166 | www.bacchusmke.com

With a "fabulous" Cudahy Tower setting (including a glassed-in
conservatory with lake views) as a backdrop for chef Adam Siegel's
"wonderful" American fare brought by a "marvelous staff", this
Downtown sibling of Lake Park Bistro and Ristorante Bartolotta is
built to "impress"; while some surveyors "save" it "for a special
night out", power-lunchers and others "keep coming back" for an
"experience" they deem "worth the price."

### Benihana  *Japanese/Steak*
18 | 18 | 20 | $36

**Downtown** | 850 N. Plankinton Ave. (bet. Kilbourn Ave. & Wells St.) |
414-270-0890 | www.benihana.com
See review in Chicago Directory.

### Bosley on Brady ⑤ *Seafood/Steak*
- | - | - | M

**East Side** | 815 E. Brady St. (bet. Cass & Marshall Sts.) | 414-727-7975 |
www.bosleyonbrady.com

A "casual" "Key West theme" stokes the "inviting atmosphere"
of this "neighborly", moderately priced East Sider on "trendy
Brady Street", where a "well-trained, enthusiastic staff" ferries
"luscious, fresh and creative" seafood and steakhouse fare; the
"upbeat" decor is "delightfully warm", and there's also alfresco
sidewalk seating in summer.

### ☑ Capital Grille, The  *Steak*
25 | 24 | 25 | $63

**Downtown** | 310 W. Wisconsin Ave. (4th St.) | 414-223-0600 |
www.thecapitalgrille.com
See review in Chicago Directory.

### Carnevor ⑤ *Steak*
24 | 21 | 23 | $63

**Downtown** | 724 N. Milwaukee St. (Mason St.) | 414-223-2200 |
www.carnevor.com

Milwaukee Street moguls take meat-ings at this Downtown
"steakhouse with a nightclub vibe", a "business-dinner heaven"
where rib-eyes and Kobe beef are among the "excellent" offerings
served in a "modern", earth-toned setting; of course you'll "dig
deep" into your wallet, but carnivores concur the portions are
"huge" enough to leave them "in a vegetative state"; N.B. valet
parking is a necessity.

### Cempazuchi Ⓜ *Mexican*
23 | 18 | 19 | $27

**East Side** | 1205 E. Brady St. (Franklin Pl.) | 414-291-5233 |
www.cempazuchi.com

"Beautiful mole sauces" – including a different one served weekly
over turkey – are a highlight of the "incredible, simply prepared
dishes" offered at this East Side Mexican also known for "authentic
fish tacos" and some of the "best margaritas in Milwaukee"; the
"*Dia de los Muertos* decor" adds to the "friendly, bustling" atmosphere and in summer, the "cozy setting" spills onto the sidewalk for
people-watching "trendy Brady Street"-style.

### Cheesecake Factory  *American*  | 19 | 19 | 18 | $28 |

**Glendale** | Bayshore Mall | 5799 N. Bayshore Dr. (Port Washington Rd.) | 414-906-8550

**Wauwatosa** | 2350 N. Mayfair Rd. (North Ave.) | 414-257-2300

www.thecheesecakefactory.com

See review in Chicago Directory.

### ☑ Coquette Cafe ⓢ *French*  | 26 | 22 | 24 | $38 |

**Third Ward** | 316 N. Milwaukee St. (St. Paul Ave.) | 414-291-2655 | www.coquettecafe.com

"Lovely" French bistro fare is "la différence" at this "Third Ward gem" of "real integrity" that draws Francophiles for "romantic dinners for two" and "lunch with clients" with its "superb steak frites" and "terrific" seasonal menus; the "cute" dining room with area rugs is like being "in Paris" (except for "no attitude" from the staff) with "reasonable prices" completing a package that patrons call "wonderful"; N.B. owner Sanford D'Amato passed the reins to two former protégés post-Survey, which is not reflected in the scores.

### Crawdaddy's Ⓜ *Cajun/Creole*  | ▽ 16 | 18 | 17 | $29 |

**Southwest Side** | 6414 W. Greenfield Ave. (bet. 64th & 65th Sts.) | 414-778-2228 | www.crawdaddysrestaurant.com

Cajun-Creole fare brings a touch of N'Awlins to the Southwest Side at this "general all-around good-time place" that dishes out "delightful" crawfish étouffée, gumbo and other regional bites; naturally it's "noisy" in the "big" room decorated with Louisiana artwork, and disappointed diners declare the "menu seems tired and the staff even more so", but at least it won't break the bank with its moderate prices.

### Crazy Water  *Eclectic*  | 25 | 18 | 24 | $40 |

**Walker's Point** | 839 S. Second St. (Walker St.) | 414-645-2606 | www.crazywaterrestaurant.com

"Once a bar", this "cozy" Walker's Point Eclectic "off the beaten path" has a "homey feeling" and a "great vibe" say locals who "watch" chef-owner Peggy Magister "working in her tiny makeshift kitchen"; a "casualness that's not intimidating" extends to the staff as well as moderate prices, so patrons profess it deserves "all the accolades."

### Cubanitas ⓢ *Cuban*  | 20 | 16 | 16 | $21 |

**Downtown** | 728 N. Milwaukee St. (bet. Mason St. & Wisconsin Ave.) | 414-225-1760 | www.getcubanitas.com

"Casual , tasty" Cuban fare is "at the heart of" this "hip, affordable" "slice of Havana" Downtown (little sister of Italian Osteria del Mondo) that compatriots call a "real treat"; though some speculate it "needs a shakeup" (especially in the service area), mojitos and summer sidewalk seating on modish Milwaukee Street up the pleasure quotient.

### Dream Dance Steak ⓢⓂ *American/Steak*  | - | - | - | E |

**Downtown** | Potawatomi Bingo Casino | 1721 W. Canal St. (16th St.) | 414-847-7883 | www.paysbig.com

An "incredible" 600-label wine list caps off the experience at this over-21-only steakhouse in Downtown's Potawatomi Bingo Casino where chef Jason Gorman's Wisconsin-inflected New American cuisine receives a "deft, skilled presentation", coaxing cognoscenti to whisper it's a "best-kept secret"; a staff that's "attentive" but not "overbearing" also gets kudos, though surveyors are "tempted to hit the slots afterward to make up for the outsize bill"; N.B. there's a separate restaurant entrance.

### ⦾ Eddie Martini's ⦿ Steak | 29 | 26 | 28 | $65 |

**Wauwatosa** | 8612 W. Watertown Plank Rd. (86th St.) | 414-771-6680 | www.eddiemartinis.com

"Forget the image of a smoke-filled supper club", this Wauwatosa "standout" is "elegant" say fans who call the clubby classic their "all-time favorite" (and show it with improved scores) for "huge steaks" (e.g. the 22-ounce bone-in rib-eye) and "wonderfully fresh, inventive" seafood; sure it's expensive but "you get what you pay for", and an "attentive", "knowledgeable staff" seals the deal for "a special night."

### Edwardo's Natural Pizza  Pizza | 20 | 11 | 15 | $19 |

**West Side** | 10845 W. Bluemound Rd. (Hwy. 100) | 414-771-7770 | www.edwardos.com

See review in Chicago Directory.

### Elsa's on the Park ● American | 23 | 22 | 21 | $24 |

**Downtown** | 833 N. Jefferson St. (Wells St.) | 414-765-0615 | www.elsas.com

An "interesting crowd" fills this "Milwaukee tradition" situated in a Downtown building dating to 1890, where the decor is "sleek" and "modern" and the "reasonably priced" roster of "inventive" American bar bites includes "pork-chop sandwiches" and "burgers worth the trip"; it's open for lunch, dinner and "late-night" noshing, just be sure to "dress to be seen" at this "upscale" Karl Kopp-owned spot.

### Envoy  American | - | - | - | M |

**Downtown** | Ambassador Hotel | 2308 W. Wisconsin Ave. (bet. 23rd & 24th Sts.) | 414-345-5015 | www.envoymilwaukee.com

Situated inside the painstakingly "restored" Ambassador Hotel (from 1927), this Downtown New American benefits from the "beautiful architecture" of its "art deco" surroundings and decor; a "helpful staff" adds to the "pleasant experience" even if the mid-priced menu draws mixed reviews ("average" vs. "reliable").

### Five Guys  Burgers | 20 | 10 | 16 | $11 |

**East Side** | 2907 N. Oakland Ave. (Locust St.) | 414-964-5303

**Delafield** | Shoppes at Nagawaukee | 2900 Golf Rd. (Rte. 83) | 262-646-4897

**Glendale** | Bayshore Town Ctr. | 5800 N. Bayshore Dr. (Glen Bay Ave.) | 414-962-3560

**Pewaukee** | Pewakee Commons | 1279 Capitol Dr. (Willow Grove Dr.) | 262-691-7566

www.fiveguys.com

See review in Chicago Directory.

| | FOOD | DECOR | SERVICE | COST |
|---|---|---|---|---|

**Five O'Clock Steakhouse** 🅢🅜 *Steak*　　25 | 18 | 21 | $48

**Central City** | 2416 W. State St. (24th St.) | 414-342-3553 |
www.fiveoclocksteakhouse.com

"Ordering dinner" at the bar "before you're seated" is part of the
"old-school" experience at this "reliable" Central City steakhouse
"straight from the '40s", where carnivores "step back in time" with
"classic" touches like a "relish tray" complementing "succulent cuts of
meat" with a "crispy blackened edge"; the dark wood might give it the
ambiance of a "guys' place", but it's considered "one of Milwaukee's
finest" by "ladies too"; N.B. the suburban Chicago branch has closed.

**Fleming's Prime**　　　　　　　23 | 23 | 22 | $60
**Steakhouse & Wine Bar** *Steak*

**Brookfield** | Brookfield Square Mall | 15665 W. Bluemound Rd.
(Moorland Rd.) | 262-782-9463 | www.flemingssteakhouse.com
See review in Chicago Directory.

**Heaven City** 🅢🅜 *American*　　　- | - | - | M

**Mukwonago** | S91 W27850 National Ave./Hwy. ES (Edgewood Ave.) |
262-363-5191 | www.heavencity.com

Ghost hunters and history buffs feast at this Mukwonago blend of the
past and present; the art deco decor smacks of Prohibition times
(and infamous mobster Al Capone, who is said to have hidden out
here), while the midpriced menu (bone-in rib-eye, sashimi-grade
tuna) is up-to-date New American; N.B. the long-established Tapas
Tuesday features live flamenco music.

**Hinterland Erie**　　　　　　26 | 25 | 24 | $51
**Street Gastropub** 🅢 *American*

**Third Ward** | 222 E. Erie St. (Water St.) | 414-727-9300 |
www.hinterlandbeer.com

Admirers of this "creative" New American situated in a Third Ward
storefront call its "expensive" seasonal menu emphasizing fish and
local game "superbly crafted" and give service a thumbs-up too; the
wood-filled modern quarters include a lounge that's an "excellent
spot to grab a cocktail", and there's sidewalk dining in summer.

**Il Mito Enoteca** 🅜 *Italian*　　▽ 25 | 18 | 21 | $36

**Wauwatosa** | 6913 W. North Ave. (69th St.) | 414-443-1414 |
www.ilmito.com

"Wonderful", "affordable" fare from "enthusiastic" chef-owner
Michael Feker "dazzles with flair" at this Wauwatosa Italian where a
staff that's "attentive but not pushy" navigates the warm, wood-filled,
exposed-beam quarters; on weekends, the "pleasant experience"
often includes live opera; N.B. a cooking school is adjacent.

**Immigrant**　　　　　　　　23 | 22 | 25 | $59
**Room & Winery, The** 🅢🅜 *American*

**Kohler** | American Club | 419 Highland Dr. (School St.) | 920-457-8888 |
www.destinationkohler.com

Diners feel as if they've "stepped back in time" at this New American
"tucked away" in the "dark" downstairs of a historic building at

Kohler's American Club resort, where the "expensive", "superb" cuisine is "presented with a modern twist" by staffers who are "masters of hospitality"; the six dining rooms are decorated in different ethnic themes honoring the original immigrant tenants, and there's also a winery bar with a regional cheese room; N.B. jackets are required in the dining room area.

### Jackson Grill 🛇 Ⓜ *American*   ∇ 23 | 18 | 22 | $42

**South Side** | 3736 W. Mitchell St. (38th St.) | 414-384-7384 | www.jacksongrillmilwaukee.com

The "time machine back to the 1950s" stops at this South Side American "classic", a "quintessential urban supper club" "chock-full of regulars" who regard it as the "friendliest, homiest place in Milwaukee"; everything on the menu (including steaks and ribs) is "first-rate, properly prepared and lovingly dished out" in "copious servings" that embody "what Wisconsin is all about."

### Jake's Fine Dining 🛇 *Steak*   - | - | - | E

**Pewaukee** | 21445 Gumina Rd. (Capital Dr.) | 262-781-7995 | www.jakes-restaurant.com

"On a winter day", patrons procure a table near the "huge fireplace" at this 50-year-old Pewaukee "steak haunt" where the "classic comfort-food menu" (including the "much-imitated, never-surpassed onion rings") includes "selections for more modern tastes"; to "longtime fans", it feels "comfortably like the bar down the street."

### 🌀 Karl Ratzsch's 🛇 *German*   25 | 23 | 24 | $41

**Downtown** | 320 E. Mason St. (bet. B'way & Milwaukee St.) | 414-276-2720 | www.karlratzsch.com

For a "sauerbraten and spaetzle fix", this Downtown "classic" is a "destination of choice" dishing out "substantial" portions of "excellent", "hearty" "old-world" German "favorites" including "wonderful roast goose" in a Bavarian-inspired room that "oozes gemütlichkeit"; the ski-lodge decor is "a little over-the-top" ("where else can you dine under chandeliers made from antlers?") and some find prices a bit "high for comfort food", but good service helps make it "worth the trip"; N.B. a pianist performs on weekends.

### Kil@wat Restaurant *American*   ∇ 21 | 23 | 18 | $47

**Downtown** | InterContinental Milwaukee | 139 E. Kilbourn Ave. (Water St.) | 414-291-4793 | www.kilawatcuisine.com

Located in the InterContinental hotel near the Milwaukee Repertory Theater, this "upscale" New American is a "perfect" choice for "well-prepared", "tasty" fare (including lobster pot pie) before catching a "Downtown show"; the "bar is a spot to see and be seen" before heading to the colorful orange-and-lime dining room, where a few find the service "too casual."

### King & I, The *Thai*   ∇ 20 | 17 | 19 | $25

**Downtown** | 830 N. Old World Third St. (bet. Kilbourn Ave. & Wells St.) | 414-276-4181 | www.kingandirestaurant.com

Thai "with some ingenuity" draws loyal subjects to this affordable Downtowner whose roster of dishes (pad Thai, curry) is "consis-

| | FOOD | DECOR | SERVICE | COST |
|---|---|---|---|---|

tent" and "satisfying"; patrons preach "when they say 'hot', they mean it", but that adds to the "adventure"; N.B. there's a weekday lunch buffet.

### Knick, The ☻ *Eclectic* | 21 | 21 | 22 | $33 |

**Downtown** | Knickerbocker Hotel | 1028 E. Juneau Ave. (Astor St.) | 414-272-0011 | www.theknickrestaurant.com

"One of the New York-iest spots in town", this Downtowner at the Knickerbocker Hotel is "always a good bet" for "sophisticated" Eclectic fare that's offered from lunch through "the late-hour munchies" and delivered by a staff that "goes out of its way to please"; moderate prices and modern decor with curved booths are other reasons surveyors "love hanging out here."

### ☑ Lake Park Bistro *French* | 28 | 28 | 27 | $55 |

**East Side** | Lake Park Pavilion | 3133 E. Newberry Blvd. (Lake Dr.) | 414-962-6300 | www.lakeparkbistro.com

A "beautiful view of Lake Michigan" and the park from the historic Lake Park Pavilion provides the setting "for romance" – and Milwaukee's top-rated Decor – at this East Side "French gem" where the "world-class" cuisine of chef Adam Siegel "matches any in Chicago or New York City" and is accompanied by "outstanding service" and an "attainable wine list"; fans of this "beauty" from restaurateur Joe Bartolotta feel transported "to the French country-side" whether seated "at the bar on a weeknight" or in the dining room during a "special evening out."

### La Merenda ☒ *Eclectic* | 27 | 19 | 22 | $32 |

**Walker's Point** | 125 E. National Ave. (1st St.) | 414-389-0125 | www.lamerenda125.com

"Not much on decor" but still "festive" and colorful, this "warm and comfortable" Walker's Point "little neighborhood gem" provides "outstanding", "well-presented" "international tapas" on an Eclectic menu of "creative" small plates; price points are "well within budget reach" "for larger groups", though it's also "perfect for a first date" or a "quick bite."

### Le Rêve | ▽ 27 | 19 | 22 | $29 |
### Patisserie & Café ☒ *Dessert/French*

**Wauwatosa** | 7610 Harwood Ave. (Menomonee River Pkwy.) | 414-778-3333 | www.lerevecafe.com

Francophiles feel the "formidable" pull of this "perfect little French cafe" from the "luscious pastries in the counter display case" to the "freakishly high ceiling" and "European decor" that make "you think you're in Paris" (rather than a restored century-old Wauwatosa bank building); the "excellent", "reasonably priced" bistro bites (e.g. crêpes, quiche, steak frites) are made even better by the "brisk but friendly white-aproned service."

### Maggiano's Little Italy *Italian* | 20 | 19 | 21 | $32 |

**Wauwatosa** | Mayfair Mall | 2500 N. Mayfair Rd. (North Ave.) | 414-978-1000 | www.maggianos.com

See review in Chicago Directory.

|  | FOOD | DECOR | SERVICE | COST |
|---|---|---|---|---|

## Mangia ⓜ *Italian* — ▽ 25 | 17 | 22 | $42

**Kenosha** | 5717 Sheridan Rd. (bet. 57th & 58th Sts.) | 262-652-4285 | www.kenoshamangia.com

Italian fare that's "excellent" and "consistent" makes this Kenosha trattoria "worth the drive", and its "interesting menu" – including seasonal selections and an antipasto bar – is delivered by a "friendly, knowledgeable staff" under the eye of co-owner Tony Mantuano; the rustic Italian-style surroundings include an outdoor patio, prompting patrons to praise it as a "perfect" "meeting place" between Milwaukee and Chicago.

## ⓩ Mason Street Grill *American* — 23 | 24 | 24 | $55

**Downtown** | Pfister Hotel | 425 E. Mason St. (bet. Jefferson & Milwaukee Sts.) | 414-298-3131 | www.masonstreetgrill.com

"Excellent steaks and chops" coupled with "good value" and "knowledgeable service" draw meat eaters to this American in Downtown's historic Pfister Hotel, where the "seafood is top-rate too", making for an all-around "solid stop"; patrons "grab a counter seat" facing the kitchen to "see how the food is prepared" or head for the "sleek", "upscale" dining room with light-brown leather and wood to spend a "pleasant" "evening lingering"; N.B. for the lounge lizards, there's live piano and vocals.

## Maxie's Southern Comfort *Creole* — 23 | 18 | 22 | $30

**West Side** | 6732 W. Fairview Ave. (68th St.) | 414-292-3969 | www.maxies.com

"Bustling" and "boisterous", this West Side "value" offers a "solid menu" of Cajun-Creole fare dished out "on the site of an old butcher shop" kitted out with bordello-red walls; the Southern charm extends to a "helpful staff", while a raw bar adds "flair in a meat-and-potatoes town" and "happy-hour specials" fuel the "festive" vibe.

## Meritage ⓩⓜ *Eclectic* — - | - | - | E

**West Side** | 5921 W. Vliet St. (60th St.) | 414-479-0620 | www.meritage.us

Pilgrims who venture "off the beaten path" to the West Side proclaim this Washington Heights Eclectic a "delicious destination" for chef-owner Jan Kelly's dishes "using an abundance of local and organic ingredients" in a "creative menu" that blends "tastes from all over the world"; P.S. the "outdoor patio is a summertime must."

## Milwaukee Chophouse *Steak* — ▽ 22 | 22 | 22 | $48

**Downtown** | Hilton Milwaukee City Ctr. | 633 N. Fifth St. (bet. Michigan St. & Wisconsin Ave.) | 414-226-2467 | www.milwaukeechophouse.com

The "old Milwaukee steakhouse legends" have nothing on this Downtowner, the fine-dining hub of the Hilton Milwaukee City Center where cuts are "cooked spot-on"; count in the "comfortable", "relaxed" atmosphere and "knowledgeable staff" and this beef boutique is "worth a special trip"; N.B. there's also a 30-seat private dining room.

| | FOOD | DECOR | SERVICE | COST |
|---|---|---|---|---|

**Mimma's Café** *Italian*　　　24 | 19 | 24 | $35

**East Side** | 1307 E. Brady St. (Arlington Pl.) | 414-271-7337 |
www.mimmas.com

With Brady Street as a backdrop, this East Side Italian stalwart
makes patrons "feel at home" with chef-owner Mimma Megna
"sending out little surprises" alongside "excellent pasta" and "outstanding specials" at moderate prices; while some call the elegantly
casual decor featuring marble columns "adorable", others contest
it's "seen better days"; N.B. the wine list offers 300 labels.

**Mo's: A Place for Steaks** ⊠ *Steak*　　23 | 23 | 24 | $62

**Downtown** | 720 N. Plankinton Ave. (Wisconsin Ave.) | 414-272-0720 |
www.mosrestaurants.com

"Big-city" flair accompanies the "fantastic" fare at this Downtown
steakhouse that carnivores claim "would fit right into" the Chicago
scene; in addition to "exceptional" cuts such as filet mignon and rib-
eye plus a long list of sides, the "quality" extends to the service in
the traditional wood-filled digs (and is reflected in improved scores
in all areas), so naturally it comes with "high tabs."

**Mr. B's: A Bartolotta Steakhouse** *Steak*　▽ 26 | 20 | 25 | $53

**Brookfield** | 18380 W. Capitol Drive (bet. Brookfield Rd. & Mountain Dr.) |
262-790-7005 | www.mrbssteakhouse.com

Surveyors sate their "carnivorous side" at this "traditional" chophouse in Brookfield offering "quality" steaks and other "hearty" fare
along with the "touches we have come to expect" from its parent
Bartolotta Restaurant Group (Bacchus, Lake Park Bistro, Ristorante
Bartolotta), including "excellent service" for a meal that's "wonderful
from start to finish"; N.B. a post-Survey move to a nearby location
(not reflected in the Decor score) has netted increased seating (plus
a patio) and expanded parking and the bar areas, while retaining the
trademark green-checked tablecloth ambiance.

**Nanakusa** Ⓜ *Japanese*　　　23 | 22 | 21 | $36

**Third Ward** | 408 E. Chicago St. (Milwaukee St.) | 414-223-3200 |
www.dinenanakusa.com

"Endless options" from hot dishes to "excellent" sushi and sashimi (the
"maki rolls truly shine") are offered at this midpriced Third Ward
Japanese where diners can sit in the 16-seat "tatami room" or the
modern main room; the "quiet atmosphere" is "perfect for a romantic
evening", and there's also an extensive wine and "sake selection."

**North Star American Bistro** *American*　22 | 18 | 21 | $31

**Brookfield** | 19115 W. Capitol Dr. (Brookfield Rd.) | 262-754-1515
**Shorewood** | 4515 N. Oakland Ave. (Kensington Blvd.) | 414-964-4663
www.northstarbistro.com

These "unpretentious", moderately priced Brookfield and
Shorewood American siblings offer "lots of choices" including "interesting" creations (e.g. bourbon salmon, lamb shank) that work
for a "special meal" or "family" dining in "casual" "neighborhood
bistro" settings; N.B. the monthly wine club offers tastings and
savings on featured wines.

|  | FOOD | DECOR | SERVICE | COST |
|---|---|---|---|---|

**NSB Bar and Grill** *American* — 19 | - | 19 | $35
(fka North Shore Bistro)
**North Shore** | River Point Vill. | 8649 N. Port Washington Rd.
(Brown Deer Rd.) | 414-351-6100 | www.northshorebistro.com
This North Shore "neighborhood hangout" underwent a major
face-lift post-Survey, shrinking the banquet hall–like dining room to
a small, intimate space with richly colored walls and cozy banquettes; its midpriced New American menu remains "reliable" for
salad, burger and sandwich fans, and has been hipped up with new
nightly specials (to wit: shrimp boil, prime rib).

**Original Pancake House, The** *American* — 24 | 16 | 20 | $17
**East Side** | 2621 N. Downer Ave. (E. Belleview Pl.) | 414-431-5055
**Brookfield** | 16460 W. Bluemound Rd. (Dechant Rd.) |
262-797-0800
www.originalpancakehouse.com
See review in Chicago Directory.

**Z Osteria del Mondo** ⊠ *Italian* — 28 | 21 | 25 | $53
**Downtown** | Knickerbocker Hotel | 1028 E. Juneau Ave. (Astor St.) |
414-291-3770 | www.osteria.com
Chef/co-owner Marc Bianchini's Northern Italian "standards with
flair" are "as close to authentic as you'll find in the Midwest" at this
Downtown "favorite" (and sibling of Cubanitas) that's been "consistent over the years" for "fine dining" in a "comfortable" Tuscan-
themed setting; acolytes advise "trust the server" and say "sure it's
expensive – especially for Milwaukee", but the "prix fixe menus are
a great deal"; N.B. there's an outdoor patio and a cigar lounge too.

**Palms Bistro & Bar** Ⓜ *American* — ∇ 20 | 18 | 19 | $32
**Third Ward** | 221 N. Broadway (bet. Buffalo & Chicago Sts.) |
414-298-3000 | www.palmsbistrobar.com
Situated inside a late-19th-century Cream City brick building, this
"pearl of the Third Ward" is known for its salads as well as its
"unique approach with seafood dishes" and other New American
fare served in a bistro setting with local artwork lining the walls; the
"open-air" dining at sidewalk tables appeals in summertime, but
"friendly service" and "solid value" are year-round staples;
N.B. extensive happy-hour specials run Tuesday–Friday.

**Pasta Tree** *Italian* — ∇ 20 | 19 | 23 | $35
**East Side** | 1503 N. Farwell Ave. (Curtis Pl.) | 414-276-8867
"Excellent pastas and sauces" at moderate prices lure loyalists to
this "*romantico*" 30-year-old Italian in the East Side, where a pair of
dining rooms with tin ceilings and antique chandeliers are the setting for "quiet, intimate meals"; N.B. in summer, a secluded garden
patio offers additional tables.

**P.F. Chang's China Bistro** *Chinese* — 20 | 19 | 19 | $31
**Wauwatosa** | Mayfair Mall | 2500 N. Mayfair Rd. (North Ave.) |
414-607-1029 | www.pfchangs.com
See review in Chicago Directory.

|  | FOOD | DECOR | SERVICE | COST |
|---|---|---|---|---|

## Polonez M *Polish*

| - | - | - | I |

**South Side** | 4016 S. Packard Ave. (Tesch St.) | 414-482-0080 |
www.foodspot.com/polonez

Diners decamp at this off-the-beaten-path South Sider for "true, European, old-world" Polish specialties ("mmm, sausages and pierogi"); the affordable, "excellent" menu meanders into *czarnina* (duck-blood soup) and bigos (Hunter's stew) territory, the bar stocks *Polski* beer and a mural of folk costumes adds color to the otherwise functional decor; N.B. live accordion music enlivens the Sunday all-you-can-eat brunch.

## Potbelly Sandwich Works *Sandwiches*

| 19 | 13 | 17 | $10 |

**Downtown** | 135 W. Wisconsin Ave. (Plankinton Ave.) |
414-226-0014
**Brookfield** | 17800 W. Bluemound Rd. (bet. Brookfield & Calhoun Rds.) |
262-796-9845
www.potbelly.com
See review in Chicago Directory.

## ☑ Ristorante Bartolotta *Italian*

| 28 | 25 | 27 | $55 |

**Wauwatosa** | 7616 W. State St. (Harwood Ave.) | 414-771-7910 |
www.bartolottaristorante.com

"Awesome" Italian flavors make it easy to "pretend you are in a small bistro in Rome" rather than "Downtown Wauwatosa" (in an old Pabst Brewery saloon, no less) at this "charming, noisy trattoria" that also offers an "extensive wine list" (all Italian labels) and "well-trained staff"; old family photos lining the walls provide a contrast with the "upscale sensibility" that surveyors expect from "the [Joe] Bartolotta empire" (which includes Lake Park Bistro and Bacchus).

## River Lane Inn ☑ *Seafood*

| 26 | 18 | 26 | $42 |

**North Shore** | 4313 W. River Ln. (Brown Deer Rd.) |
414-354-1995

While the look of this longtime North Shore seafood specialist located inside a late 1800s building may be "dark and unchanged", its repertoire of moderately priced seafood items – many listed on the chalkboard roster of daily specials – is "fresh and creatively prepared"; fin fans say "you can't go wrong with anything on the menu", and further adding to its "steady-as-she-goes" status is the "experienced staff" and "friendly bartenders who pour an ample drink."

## Riversite, The ☑ *American*

| - | - | - | E |

**Mequon** | 11120 N. Cedarburg Rd. (Mequon Rd.) |
262-242-6050

In its peaceful setting along the Milwaukee River, this Mequon American offers "stylish, inventive and delicious" cuisine from longtime chef Thomas Peschong to loyal patrons who especially "love the seafood and creative starters"; the room boasts 20-ft. ceilings and chandeliers, making for an upscale experience that's always "worth a visit"; N.B. a tapas menu is featured on Tuesday nights.

|  | FOOD | DECOR | SERVICE | COST |
|---|---|---|---|---|

**Rock Bottom Brewery** *American*     17 | 17 | 17 | $24

**Downtown** | 740 N. Plankinton Ave. (bet. Wells St. & Wisconsin Ave.) | 414-276-3030 | www.rockbottom.com

"It's all about" the "hearty" "appetizers and beer" for some patrons of this Downtown Traditional American "neighborhood hangout", but its "diverse" menu offers "something for everyone" too; the "brewery warehouse" atmosphere is "adult and family-friendly at the same time" and though foes find it "chain-ish" and "mediocre throughout", fans call it a "good sports bar for the price"; P.S. there's a "great roof deck for drinks in summer."

**☑ Roots Restaurant & Cellar** *Californian*     29 | 27 | 22 | $38

**Brewers Hill** | 1818 N. Hubbard St. (Vine St.) | 414-374-8480 | www.rootsmilwaukee.com

You can "see the staff snipping herbs" at this green-minded Brewers Hill Californian – voted No. 1 for Food in the Milwaukee Survey – that's a "must-go" for chef John Raymond's "exceptional" midpriced menu using "local ingredients" (some "homegrown") in "adventurous", "seasonal" creations; the "cozy" yet "fabulous digs" include a two-level patio, gracious gardens and a "beautiful view of the Downtown skyline", and the "reliable wine list" is another "step up"; N.B. the lower-level Cellar offers casual options.

**Sake Tumi** *Asian*     - | - | - | M

**Downtown** | 714 N. Milwaukee St. (bet. Mason St. & Wisconsin Ave.) | 414-224-7253 | www.sake-milwaukee.com

"Diverse little Restaurant Row" (Milwaukee Street) is the setting for this Downtown Asian, where "excellent rolls and sushi" ("tasty" Korean creations too) are served in a narrow, contemporary space; romantics say it suits "for a date", plus "you can hit the bars on Water Street afterwards to round out the evening"; N.B. since parking "can be a deterrent", consider valet.

**Sala da Pranzo** *Italian*     - | - | - | M

**East Side** | 2613 E. Hampshire Ave. (Downer Ave.) | 414-964-2611 | www.sala-dapranzo.com

Locals and profs from the nearby university call this "family-owned and -operated" East Side trattoria a "real hidden gem" for saltimbocca, pastas and other midpriced Italian fare; eclectic artwork adorns the walls, and those who "wished" for it to be "open on Sundays" are likely glad to hear that brunch is now offered then.

**☑ Sanford** **☒** *American*     29 | 27 | 29 | $74

**East Side** | 1547 N. Jackson St. (Pleasant St.) | 414-276-9608 | www.sanfordrestaurant.com

Co-owner and chef Sanford D'Amato's nationally recognized New American, residing in the East Side storefront home of his family's old grocery store, is "as impressive as any top New York restaurant" say surveyors who again vote it Most Popular and No. 1 for Service in Milwaukee; "superb and imaginative", this "little neighborhood gem" pays "attention to every detail", from its "marvelous" cuisine – including a seven-course surprise tasting menu – to its "down-to-earth, professional" service to decor that mixes "modern" (a single chartreuse wall) and historical (old black-and-white family photos); while not cheap, it's a "great value considering what you get."

### Sebastian's 🖲 M  *American*                    ⎦⎦⎦ M

**Caledonia** | 6025 Douglas Ave. (5 Mile Rd.) | 262-681-5465 | www.sebastiansfinefood.com

This casual midpriced New American has been pleasantly "surprising" patrons for the last decade in quiet Caledonia; the "nice Midwestern" staff serves signature potato-crusted grouper and dry-aged meats in a dining room with high ceilings and hardwood floors – nothing fancy because this off-the-beaten-path place is all "about the food."

### Singha Thai  *Thai*                          ⎦ - ⎦ I

**West Side** | 2237 S. 108th St. (Lincoln Ave.) | 414-541-1234

This West Side Thai serves up "some extraordinary dishes in every category" on its "huge menu" (the noodle dishes alone "are worth a drive"); service and ambiance are another story, but the lackluster "strip-mall location" just "simplifies" the decision to order "carryout."

### NEW Smyth  *American*               ▽ 24 | 27 | 26 | $44

**Walker's Point** | Iron Horse Hotel | 500 W. Florida St. (6th St.) | 414-831-4615 | www.theironhorsehotel.com

Rustic 100-year-old warehouse decor including Cream City brick is the backdrop for "smitten" surveyors at this "stylish" Walker's Point New American "'in' place" inside the motorcycle-friendly Iron Horse Hotel, where the "energy is electrifying" and chef Tom Schultz shows a "great understanding of culinary trends and what Milwaukeeans want to eat" (e.g. veal osso buco and foie gras); while the cuisine is both "innovative and comforting", the "interesting wine list" and "knowledgeable staff" make the meal even "more special."

### Tess M  *Eclectic*                          ⎦ - ⎦ E

**East Side** | 2499 N. Bartlett Ave. (Bradford Ave.) | 414-964-8377

"Cozy rooms in winter" and a "wonderful summer patio" (with open-air and heated spots) draw East Siders to this "neighborhood charmer" with a small, "quirky, casual" storefront setting; "outstanding" Eclectic dishes such as Madeira beef tenderloin and equally impressive service help justify the slightly pricey tabs.

### Third Ward Caffe M  *Italian*                ⎦ - ⎦ M

**Third Ward** | 225 E. St. Paul Ave. (bet. B'way & Water St.) | 414-224-0895

Located in historically significant Commission Row, this Third Ward "stalwart" for "pre-theater dining" offers Northern Italian fare including over 20 kinds of pasta and seasonal specials in a trattoria atmosphere; sidewalk seating adds to the appeal.

### Three Brothers M⇗  *Serbian*               24 | 12 | 20 | $32

**South Side** | 2414 S. St. Clair St. (Russell Ave.) | 414-481-7530

"Crowds of lifelong" loyalists "still" fill this 60-year-old South Side family-owned "must"-go where borek and other "excellent", "au-

FOOD DECOR SERVICE COST

thentic" midpriced Serbian fare is served in a historic former Schlitz tavern by a staff displaying "warm hospitality"; the atmosphere is "lively", though regulars warn "don't go in a hurry as this food takes time" – but it's an "experience you won't forget."

### Triskele's 🗷Ⓜ *American*  | - | - | - | M |

**Walker's Point** | 1801 S. Third St. (Maple St.) | 414-837-5950 | www.triskelesrestaurant.com

For "delightful" "comfort food" "at comfortable prices", try this Walker's Point "up-and-comer" dishing out New American fare including housemade chicken sausage and Tuesday night all-you can-eat mussels; the setting includes booth seating and has a "neighborhood" vibe underscored by "friendly service."

### Umami Moto 🗷 *Asian*  | ▽ 24 | 25 | 19 | $50 |

**Downtown** | 718 N. Milwaukee St. (bet. Mason St. & Wisconsin Ave.) | 414-727-9333 | www.umamimoto.com

"Pretty people" populate this sleek Milwaukee Street place "to be seen" with an "amazing" interior design boasting wavelike walls, river-stone pillars and pale-green tile as a backdrop for executive chef Dominic Zumpano's "imaginative", "beautifully prepared" Asian fusion menu; though it's costly, the fare "hits all the high points for taste" ("love the sliders"), plus service is "friendly" and "helpful."

### Wasabi Sake Lounge *Japanese*  | - | - | - | M |

**Brookfield** | 15455 W. Bluemound Rd. (bet. Fairway Dr. & Moorland Rd.) | 262-780-0011 | www.wasabisakelounge.com

"Fresh" sushi and sashimi attract a fish-loving following to this moderately priced Brookfield Japanese located in a strip mall; the open setting aims for Downtown New York style, and patrons are gregariously greeted by sushi chefs when they arrive; N.B. happy hour brings $5 sushi rolls.

### Zarletti 🗷 *Italian*  | 22 | 19 | 18 | $42 |

**Downtown** | 741 N. Milwaukee St. (Mason St.) | 414-225-0000 | www.zarletti.net

The pre-show and pre-nightlife crowd gathers at this "bustling Milwaukee Street" Downtowner dispensing "delicious" Italian fare "from cocktails to desserts" for slightly pricey tabs; "attentive" servers work the modern space that some call "beautiful", others "sterile", and "sidewalk dining" is an added attraction in "decent weather."

# MILWAUKEE
# INDEXES

# Cuisines

Includes names, locations and Food ratings.

## AMERICAN

| | |
|---|---|
| ⊠ Bacchus \| **Downtown** | 25 |
| Cheesecake Factory \| **multi.** | 19 |
| Dream Dance \| **Downtown** | - |
| Elsa's on Park \| **Downtown** | 23 |
| Envoy \| **Downtown** | - |
| Heaven City \| **Mukwonago** | - |
| Hinterland \| **Third Ward** | 26 |
| Immigrant Room \| **Kohler** | 23 |
| Jackson Grill \| **S Side** | 23 |
| Kil@wat \| **Downtown** | 21 |
| ⊠ Mason St. Grill \| **Downtown** | 23 |
| North Star \| **multi.** | 22 |
| NSB Bar and Grill \| **N Shore** | 19 |
| Original/Walker Pancake \| **multi.** | 24 |
| Palms Bistro \| **Third Ward** | 20 |
| Riversite \| **Mequon** | - |
| Rock Bottom \| **Downtown** | 17 |
| ⊠ Sanford \| **E Side** | 29 |
| Sebastian's \| **Caledonia** | - |
| NEW Smyth \| **Walker's Point** | 24 |
| Triskele's \| **Walker's Point** | - |

## ASIAN

| | |
|---|---|
| Umami Moto \| **Downtown** | 24 |

## BURGERS

| | |
|---|---|
| Elsa's on Park \| **Downtown** | 23 |
| Five Guys \| **multi.** | 20 |

## CAJUN

| | |
|---|---|
| Crawdaddy's \| **SW Side** | 16 |
| Maxie's \| **W Side** | 23 |

## CALIFORNIAN

| | |
|---|---|
| ⊠ Roots \| **Brewers Hill** | 29 |

## CHINESE

| | |
|---|---|
| P.F. Chang's \| **Wauwatosa** | 20 |

## COFFEE SHOPS/ DINERS

| | |
|---|---|
| Original/Walker Pancake \| **multi.** | 24 |

## CREOLE

| | |
|---|---|
| Crawdaddy's \| **SW Side** | 16 |
| Maxie's \| **W Side** | 23 |

## CUBAN

| | |
|---|---|
| Cubanitas \| **Downtown** | 20 |

## DESSERT

| | |
|---|---|
| Cheesecake Factory \| **multi.** | 19 |
| Le Rêve \| **Wauwatosa** | 27 |

## ECLECTIC

| | |
|---|---|
| Crazy Water \| **Walker's Point** | 25 |
| Knick \| **Downtown** | 21 |
| La Merenda \| **Walker's Point** | 27 |
| Meritage \| **W Side** | - |
| Tess \| **E Side** | - |

## FRENCH

| | |
|---|---|
| Le Rêve \| **Wauwatosa** | 27 |

## FRENCH (BISTRO)

| | |
|---|---|
| ⊠ Coquette Cafe \| **Third Ward** | 26 |
| ⊠ Lake Park \| **E Side** | 28 |

## GASTROPUB

| | |
|---|---|
| Hinterland \| **Amer.** \| **Third Ward** | 26 |

## GERMAN

| | |
|---|---|
| ⊠ Karl Ratzsch's \| **Downtown** | 25 |

## ITALIAN

(N=Northern)

| | |
|---|---|
| Edwardo's Pizza \| **W Side** | 20 |
| Il Mito \| **Wauwatosa** | 25 |
| Maggiano's \| **Wauwatosa** | 20 |
| Mangia \| **Kenosha** | 25 |
| Mimma's Café \| **E Side** | 24 |
| ⊠ Osteria/Mondo \| N \| **Downtown** | 28 |
| Pasta Tree \| N \| **E Side** | 20 |
| ⊠ Rist. Bartolotta \| **Wauwatosa** | 28 |
| Sala da Pranzo \| **E Side** | - |
| Third Ward \| N \| **Third Ward** | - |
| Zarletti \| N \| **Downtown** | 22 |

## JAPANESE

(* sushi specialist)

| | |
|---|---|
| Benihana \| **Downtown** | 18 |
| Nanakusa* \| **Third Ward** | 23 |
| Sake Tumi* \| **Downtown** | - |
| Wasabi* \| **Brookfield** | - |

## KOREAN

(* barbecue specialist)

| | |
|---|---|
| Sake Tumi* \| **Downtown** | - |

## MEXICAN

| | |
|---|---|
| Cempazuchi \| **E Side** | 23 |

## PIZZA

| | |
|---|---|
| Edwardo's Pizza \| **W Side** | 20 |

## POLISH

| | |
|---|---|
| Polonez \| **S Side** | - |

Menus, photos, voting and more – free at ZAGAT.com

## SANDWICHES

Potbelly | **multi.** 19

## SEAFOOD

Bosley on Brady | **E Side** -
River Ln. Inn | **N Shore** 26

## SERBIAN

Three Brothers | **S Side** 24

## SOUTHERN

Maxie's | **W Side** 23

## STEAKHOUSES

Benihana | **Downtown** 18
Bosley on Brady | **E Side** -

🗹 Capital Grille | **Downtown** 25
Carnevor | **Downtown** 24
Dream Dance | **Downtown** -
🗹 Eddie Martini's | **Wauwatosa** 29
Five O'Clock Steak | **Central City** 25
Fleming's | **Brookfield** 23
Jackson Grill | **S Side** 23
Jake's | **Pewaukee** -
Milwaukee Chophouse | **Downtown** 22
Mo's: Steak | **Downtown** 23
Mr. B's: Steak | **Brookfield** 26

## THAI

King & I | **Downtown** 20
Singha Thai | **W Side** -

# Locations

Includes names, cuisines and Food ratings.

## Milwaukee Metro Area

### BREWERS HILL

☑ Roots | *Cal.*  29

### CENTRAL CITY

Five O'Clock Steak | *Steak*  25

### DOWNTOWN

☑ Bacchus | *Amer.*  25
Benihana | *Japanese/Steak*  18
☑ Capital Grille | *Steak*  25
Carnevor | *Steak*  24
Cubanitas | *Cuban*  20
Dream Dance | *Amer./Steak*  -
Elsa's on Park | *Amer.*  23
Envoy | *Amer.*  -
☑ Karl Ratzsch's | *German*  25
Kil@wat | *Amer.*  21
King & I | *Thai*  20
Knick | *Eclectic*  21
☑ Mason St. Grill | *Amer.*  23
Milwaukee Chophouse | *Steak*  22
Mo's: Steak | *Steak*  23
☑ Osteria/Mondo | *Italian*  28
Potbelly | *Sandwiches*  19
Rock Bottom | *Amer.*  17
Sake Tumi | *Asian*  -
Umami Moto | *Asian*  24
Zarletti | *Italian*  22

### EAST SIDE

Bosley on Brady | *Seafood/Steak*  -
Cempazuchi | *Mex.*  23
Five Guys | *Burgers*  20
☑ Lake Park | *French*  28
Mimma's Café | *Italian*  24
Original/Walker Pancake | *Amer.*  24
Pasta Tree | *Italian*  20
Sala da Pranzo | *Italian*  -
☑ Sanford | *Amer.*  29
Tess | *Eclectic*  -

### GLENDALE

Cheesecake Factory | *Amer.*  19
Five Guys | *Burgers*  20

### NORTH SHORE

NSB Bar and Grill | *Amer.*  19
River Ln. Inn | *Seafood*  26

### SHOREWOOD

North Star | *Amer.*  22

### SOUTH SIDE

Jackson Grill | *Amer.*  23
Polonez | *Polish*  -
Three Brothers | *Serbian*  24

### SOUTHWEST SIDE

Crawdaddy's | *Cajun/Creole*  16

### THIRD WARD

☑ Coquette Cafe | *French*  26
Hinterland | *Amer.*  26
Nanakusa | *Japanese*  23
Palms Bistro | *Amer.*  20
Third Ward | *Italian*  -

### WALKER'S POINT

Crazy Water | *Eclectic*  25
La Merenda | *Eclectic*  27
NEW Smyth | *Amer.*  24
Triskele's | *Amer.*  -

### WAUWATOSA

Cheesecake Factory | *Amer.*  19
☑ Eddie Martini's | *Steak*  29
Il Mito | *Italian*  25
Le Rêve | *Dessert/French*  27
Maggiano's | *Italian*  20
P.F. Chang's | *Chinese*  20
☑ Rist. Bartolotta | *Italian*  28

### WEST SIDE

Edwardo's Pizza | *Pizza*  20
Maxie's | *Creole*  23
Meritage | *Eclectic*  -
Singha Thai | *Thai*  -

## Outlying Areas

### BROOKFIELD

Fleming's | *Steak*  23
Mr. B's: Steak | *Steak*  26
North Star | *Amer.*  22
Original/Walker Pancake | *Amer.*  24
Potbelly | *Sandwiches*  19
Wasabi | *Japanese*  -

### CALEDONIA

Sebastian's | *Amer.*  -

## DELAFIELD
Five Guys | *Burgers* 20

## KENOSHA
Mangia | *Italian* 25

## KOHLER
Immigrant Room | *Amer.* 23

## MEQUON
Riversite | *Amer.* -

## MUKWONAGO
Heaven City | *Amer.* -

## PEWAUKEE
Flve Guys | *Burgers* 20
Jake's | *Steak* -

MILWAUKEE

LOCATIONS

# Special Features

Listings cover the best in each category and include names, locations and Food ratings. Multi-location restaurants' features may vary by branch.

## BRUNCH

| | | |
|---|---|---|
| Knick | **Downtown** | 21 |
| **Z** Lake Park | **E Side** | 28 |
| Polonez | **S Side** | - |
| **Z** Roots | **Brewers Hill** | 29 |

## BUSINESS DINING

| | | |
|---|---|---|
| **Z** Bacchus | **Downtown** | 25 |
| Carnevor | **Downtown** | 24 |
| **Z** Coquette Cafe | **Third Ward** | 26 |
| **Z** Eddie Martini's | **Wauwatosa** | 29 |
| Envoy | **Downtown** | - |
| Jake's | **Pewaukee** | - |
| **Z** Karl Ratzsch's | **Downtown** | 25 |
| Kil@wat | **Downtown** | 21 |
| Knick | **Downtown** | 21 |
| **Z** Lake Park | **E Side** | 28 |
| **Z** Mason St. Grill | **Downtown** | 23 |
| Milwaukee Chophouse | **Downtown** | 22 |
| Mo's: Steak | **Downtown** | 23 |
| Mr. B's: Steak | **Brookfield** | 26 |
| North Star | **Brookfield** | 22 |
| NSB Bar and Grill | **N Shore** | 19 |
| **Z** Rist. Bartolotta | **Wauwatosa** | 28 |
| River Ln. Inn | **N Shore** | 26 |
| Riversite | **Mequon** | - |
| **Z** Roots | **Brewers Hill** | 29 |
| **NEW** Smyth | **Walker's Point** | 24 |
| Umami Moto | **Downtown** | 24 |

## CELEBRITY CHEFS

Marc Bianchini
| | | |
|---|---|---|
| **Z** Osteria/Mondo | **Downtown** | 28 |

Sandy D'Amato
| | | |
|---|---|---|
| **Z** Sanford | **E Side** | 29 |

Michael Feker
| | | |
|---|---|---|
| Il Mito | **Wauwatosa** | 25 |

Jimmy Jackson
| | | |
|---|---|---|
| Jackson Grill | **S Side** | 23 |

JoLinda Klopp
| | | |
|---|---|---|
| Triskele's | **Walker's Point** | - |

Peggy Magister
| | | |
|---|---|---|
| Crazy Water | **Walker's Point** | 25 |

Mimma Megna
| | | |
|---|---|---|
| Mimma's Café | **E Side** | 24 |

Joe Muench
| | | |
|---|---|---|
| Maxie's | **W Side** | 23 |

Tom Peschong
| | | |
|---|---|---|
| Riversite | **Mequon** | - |

Thomas Schultz
| | | |
|---|---|---|
| **NEW** Smyth | **Walker's Point** | 24 |

Mark Weber
| | | |
|---|---|---|
| **Z** Mason St. Grill | **Downtown** | 23 |

Dominic Zumpano
| | | |
|---|---|---|
| Umami Moto | **Downtown** | 24 |

## CHILD-FRIENDLY

(Alternatives to the usual fast-food places; * children's menu available)
| | | |
|---|---|---|
| Benihana* | **Downtown** | 18 |
| Cempazuchi | **E Side** | 23 |
| Edwardo's Pizza* | **W Side** | 20 |
| **Z** Karl Ratzsch's* | **Downtown** | 25 |
| Knick | **Downtown** | 21 |
| Maggiano's* | **Wauwatosa** | 20 |
| Mangia* | **Kenosha** | 25 |
| Palms Bistro | **Third Ward** | 20 |
| Pasta Tree | **E Side** | 20 |
| P.F. Chang's | **Wauwatosa** | 20 |
| Rock Bottom* | **Downtown** | 17 |
| Tess | **E Side** | - |
| Third Ward* | **Third Ward** | - |

## DELIVERY/TAKEOUT

(D=delivery, T=takeout)
| | | |
|---|---|---|
| Benihana | T | **Downtown** | 18 |
| Cempazuchi | T | **E Side** | 23 |
| Crawdaddy's | T | **SW Side** | 16 |
| Elsa's on Park | T | **Downtown** | 23 |
| Knick | T | **Downtown** | 21 |
| Maggiano's | T | **Wauwatosa** | 20 |
| Mimma's Café | T | **E Side** | 24 |
| Nanakusa | T | **Third Ward** | 23 |
| NSB Bar and Grill | T | **N Shore** | 19 |
| Palms Bistro | T | **Third Ward** | 20 |
| Pasta Tree | T | **E Side** | 20 |
| Polonez | T | **S Side** | - |
| Potbelly | D, T | **multi.** | 19 |
| River Ln. Inn | T | **N Shore** | 26 |
| Rock Bottom | T | **Downtown** | 17 |
| **Z** Roots | T | **Brewers Hill** | 29 |
| Singha Thai | T | **W Side** | - |
| Third Ward | T | **Third Ward** | - |

## DINING ALONE

(Other than hotels and places with counter service)
| | | |
|---|---|---|
| Benihana | **Downtown** | 18 |
| Cempazuchi | **E Side** | 23 |

Menus, photos, voting and more – free at ZAGAT.com

☑ Coquette Cafe | **Third Ward** 26
Cubanitas | **Downtown** 20
☑ Lake Park | **E Side** 28
Nanakusa | **Third Ward** 23
NSB Bar and Grill | **N Shore** 19
Potbelly | **Downtown** 19
Rock Bottom | **Downtown** 17
Singha Thai | **W Side** -

## ENTERTAINMENT

(Call for days and times of performances)

Immigrant Room | piano | **Kohler** 23
☑ Karl Ratzsch's | piano | **Downtown** 25
NSB Bar and Grill | jazz | **N Shore** 19

## FIREPLACES

Heaven City | **Mukwonago** -
Jake's | **Pewaukee** -
Palms Bistro | **Third Ward** 20
Pasta Tree | **E Side** 20
Sebastian's | **Caledonia** -

## GAME IN SEASON

Dream Dance | **Downtown** -
Hinterland | **Third Ward** 26
Immigrant Room | **Kohler** 23
Jake's | **Pewaukee** -
NEW Smyth | **Walker's Point** 24

## HISTORIC PLACES

(Year opened; * building)

1875 | Third Ward* | **Third Ward** -
1890 | Elsa's on Park* | **Downtown** 23
1890 | Three Brothers* | **S Side** 24
1893 | Mason St. Grill* | **Downtown** 23
1900 | Rist. Bartolotta* | **Wauwatosa** 28
1900 | River Ln. Inn* | **N Shore** 26
1904 | Karl Ratzsch's | **Downtown** 25
1918 | Immigrant Room* | **Kohler** 23
1927 | Envoy* | **Downtown** -
1948 | Five O'Clock Steak | **Central City** 25
1960 | Jake's | **Pewaukee** -

## HOTEL DINING

Ambassador Hotel
Envoy | **Downtown** -
Hilton Milwaukee City Ctr.
Milwaukee Chophouse | **Downtown** 22
InterContinental Hotel
Kil@wat | **Downtown** 21

Iron Horse Hotel
NEW Smyth | **Walker's Point** 24
Knickerbocker Hotel
Knick | **Downtown** 21
☑ Osteria/Mondo | **Downtown** 28
Pfister Hotel
☑ Mason St. Grill | **Downtown** 23

## JACKET REQUIRED

Immigrant Room | **Kohler** 23

## LATE DINING

(Weekday closing hour)

Elsa's on Park | 1 AM | **Downtown** 23
Knick | 12 AM | **Downtown** 21

## MEET FOR A DRINK

(Most top hotels and the following standouts)

☑ Bacchus | **Downtown** 25
Bosley on Brady | **E Side** -
Carnevor | **Downtown** 24
Cempazuchi | **E Side** 23
☑ Coquette Cafe | **Third Ward** 26
Crawdaddy's | **SW Side** 16
Crazy Water | **Walker's Point** 25
Cubanitas | **Downtown** 20
☑ Eddie Martini's | **Wauwatosa** 29
Elsa's on Park | **Downtown** 23
Envoy | **Downtown** -
Il Mito | **Wauwatosa** 25
Jackson Grill | **S Side** 23
Knick | **Downtown** 21
☑ Lake Park | **E Side** 28
☑ Mason St. Grill | **Downtown** 23
Maxie's | **W Side** 23
Mo's: Steak | **Downtown** 23
Nanakusa | **Third Ward** 23
North Star | **multi.** 22
NSB Bar and Grill | **N Shore** 19
☑ Osteria/Mondo | **Downtown** 28
Palms Bistro | **Third Ward** 20
Rock Bottom | **Downtown** 17
Sake Tumi | **Downtown** -
NEW Smyth | **Walker's Point** 24
Tess | **E Side** -
Triskele's | **Walker's Point** -
Umami Moto | **Downtown** 24
Zarletti | **Downtown** 22

## OUTDOOR DINING

(P=patio; S=sidewalk; T=terrace; W=waterside)

Edwardo's Pizza | P | **W Side** 20
Knick | P | **Downtown** 21

| | |
|---|---|
| Maggiano's \| P \| **Wauwatosa** | 20 |
| Mangia \| P \| **Kenosha** | 25 |
| NSB Bar and Grill \| P \| **N Shore** | 19 |
| Z Osteria/Mondo \| P \| **Downtown** | 28 |
| Palms Bistro \| S \| **Third Ward** | 20 |
| Pasta Tree \| P \| **E Side** | 20 |
| P.F. Chang's \| P \| **Wauwatosa** | 20 |
| Potbelly \| P, S \| **multi.** | 19 |
| Z Rist. Bartolotta \| S \| **Wauwatosa** | 28 |
| River Ln. Inn \| P \| **N Shore** | 26 |
| Riversite \| P, W \| **Mequon** | - |
| Rock Bottom \| P, W \| **Downtown** | 17 |
| Z Roots \| P, T \| **Brewers Hill** | 29 |
| Tess \| P \| **E Side** | - |
| Third Ward \| S \| **Third Ward** | - |

## PEOPLE-WATCHING

| | |
|---|---|
| Z Bacchus \| **Downtown** | 25 |
| Carnevor \| **Downtown** | 24 |
| Z Coquette Cafe \| **Third Ward** | 26 |
| Cubanitas \| **Downtown** | 20 |
| Z Eddie Martini's \| **Wauwatosa** | 29 |
| Elsa's on Park \| **Downtown** | 23 |
| Envoy \| **Downtown** | - |
| Kil@wat \| **Downtown** | 21 |
| Knick \| **Downtown** | 21 |
| Le Rêve \| **Wauwatosa** | 27 |
| Maggiano's \| **Wauwatosa** | 20 |
| Z Mason St. Grill \| **Downtown** | 23 |
| Maxie's \| **W Side** | 23 |
| Mimma's Café \| **E Side** | 24 |
| Mo's: Steak \| **Downtown** | 23 |
| Nanakusa \| **Third Ward** | 23 |
| NSB Bar and Grill \| **N Shore** | 19 |
| Palms Bistro \| **Third Ward** | 20 |
| Pasta Tree \| **E Side** | 20 |
| P.F. Chang's \| **Wauwatosa** | 20 |
| Z Rist. Bartolotta \| **Wauwatosa** | 28 |
| River Ln. Inn \| **N Shore** | 26 |
| Rock Bottom \| **Downtown** | 17 |
| Sake Tumi \| **Downtown** | - |
| Z Sanford \| **E Side** | 29 |
| NEW Smyth \| **Walker's Point** | 24 |
| Three Brothers \| **S Side** | 24 |
| Umami Moto \| **Downtown** | 24 |

## POWER SCENES

| | |
|---|---|
| Z Bacchus \| **Downtown** | 25 |
| Carnevor \| **Downtown** | 24 |
| Z Eddie Martini's \| **Wauwatosa** | 29 |
| Envoy \| **Downtown** | - |
| Z Lake Park \| **E Side** | 28 |
| Z Mason St. Grill \| **Downtown** | 23 |

| | |
|---|---|
| Mo's: Steak \| **Downtown** | 23 |
| Mr. B's: Steak \| **Brookfield** | 26 |
| North Star \| **Brookfield** | 22 |

## PRIVATE ROOMS

(Restaurants charge less at off times; call for capacity)

| | |
|---|---|
| Z Coquette Cafe \| **Third Ward** | 26 |
| Z Eddie Martini's \| **Wauwatosa** | 29 |
| Edwardo's Pizza \| **W Side** | 20 |
| Heaven City \| **Mukwonago** | - |
| Immigrant Room \| **Kohler** | 23 |
| Maggiano's \| **Wauwatosa** | 20 |
| Mangia \| **Kenosha** | 25 |
| Mimma's Café \| **E Side** | 24 |
| Mr. B's: Steak \| **Brookfield** | 26 |
| Nanakusa \| **Third Ward** | 23 |
| Z Osteria/Mondo \| **Downtown** | 28 |
| Polonez \| **S Side** | - |
| River Ln. Inn \| **N Shore** | 26 |
| Riversite \| **Mequon** | - |
| Rock Bottom \| **Downtown** | 17 |
| Sebastian's \| **Caledonia** | - |

## PRIX FIXE MENUS

(Call for prices and times)

| | |
|---|---|
| Immigrant Room \| **Kohler** | 23 |
| Z Lake Park \| **E Side** | 28 |
| Z Sanford \| **E Side** | 29 |

## QUICK BITES

| | |
|---|---|
| Cubanitas \| **Downtown** | 20 |
| Edwardo's Pizza \| **W Side** | 20 |
| Elsa's on Park \| **Downtown** | 23 |
| Knick \| **Downtown** | 21 |
| Le Rêve \| **Wauwatosa** | 27 |
| Maxie's \| **W Side** | 23 |

## QUIET CONVERSATION

| | |
|---|---|
| Bosley on Brady \| **E Side** | - |
| Dream Dance \| **Downtown** | - |
| Z Eddie Martini's \| **Wauwatosa** | 29 |
| Envoy \| **Downtown** | - |
| Jake's \| **Pewaukee** | - |
| Z Karl Ratzsch's \| **Downtown** | 25 |
| Kil@wat \| **Downtown** | 21 |
| Milwaukee Chophouse \| **Downtown** | 22 |
| North Star \| **Brookfield** | 22 |
| Z Osteria/Mondo \| **Downtown** | 28 |
| Pasta Tree \| **E Side** | 20 |
| Polonez \| **S Side** | - |
| Riversite \| **Mequon** | - |
| Z Sanford \| **E Side** | 29 |
| Third Ward \| **Third Ward** | - |

## ROMANTIC PLACES

| | |
|---|---|
| Crazy Water | **Walker's Point** | 25 |
| Heaven City | **Mukwonago** | - |
| Il Mito | **Wauwatosa** | 25 |
| Immigrant Room | **Kohler** | 23 |
| ☑ Lake Park | **E Side** | 28 |
| Mimma's Café | **E Side** | 24 |
| ☑ Osteria/Mondo | **Downtown** | 28 |
| Pasta Tree | **E Side** | 20 |
| Riversite | **Mequon** | - |
| Third Ward | **Third Ward** | - |
| Three Brothers | **S Side** | 24 |
| Zarletti | **Downtown** | 22 |

## SENIOR APPEAL

| | |
|---|---|
| Envoy | **Downtown** | - |
| Immigrant Room | **Kohler** | 23 |
| Jake's | **Pewaukee** | - |
| ☑ Karl Ratzsch's | **Downtown** | 25 |
| North Star | **multi.** | 22 |
| Polonez | **S Side** | - |
| Riversite | **Mequon** | - |
| Three Brothers | **S Side** | 24 |

## SINGLES SCENES

| | |
|---|---|
| Carnevor | **Downtown** | 24 |
| Crawdaddy's | **SW Side** | 16 |
| Cubanitas | **Downtown** | 20 |
| Elsa's on Park | **Downtown** | 23 |
| Fleming's | **Brookfield** | 23 |
| Knick | **Downtown** | 21 |
| Mo's: Steak | **Downtown** | 23 |
| Nanakusa | **Third Ward** | 23 |
| Palms Bistro | **Third Ward** | 20 |
| Rock Bottom | **Downtown** | 17 |
| Sake Tumi | **Downtown** | - |
| Umami Moto | **Downtown** | 24 |

## SLEEPERS

(Good food, but little known)

| | |
|---|---|
| Il Mito | **Wauwatosa** | 25 |
| Jackson Grill | **S Side** | 23 |
| Le Rêve | **Wauwatosa** | 27 |
| Mangia | **Kenosha** | 25 |
| Milwaukee Chophouse | **Downtown** | 22 |
| Mr. B's: Steak | **Brookfield** | 26 |

## TRENDY

| | |
|---|---|
| ☑ Bacchus | **Downtown** | 25 |
| Carnevor | **Downtown** | 24 |
| Cempazuchi | **E Side** | 23 |
| Cubanitas | **Downtown** | 20 |
| ☑ Eddie Martini's | **Wauwatosa** | 29 |
| Elsa's on Park | **Downtown** | 23 |

| | |
|---|---|
| Kil@wat | **Downtown** | 21 |
| ☑ Lake Park | **E Side** | 28 |
| Maggiano's | **Wauwatosa** | 20 |
| Mo's: Steak | **Downtown** | 23 |
| Palms Bistro | **Third Ward** | 20 |
| ☑ Rist. Bartolotta | **Wauwatosa** | 28 |
| Sake Tumi | **Downtown** | - |
| ☑ Sanford | **E Side** | 29 |
| Umami Moto | **Downtown** | 24 |
| Zarletti | **Downtown** | 22 |

## VIEWS

| | |
|---|---|
| ☑ Bacchus | **Downtown** | 25 |
| Knick | **Downtown** | 21 |
| ☑ Lake Park | **E Side** | 28 |
| Riversite | **Mequon** | - |
| ☑ Roots | **Brewers Hill** | 29 |
| Sebastian's | **Caledonia** | - |

## VISITORS ON EXPENSE ACCOUNT

| | |
|---|---|
| ☑ Bacchus | **Downtown** | 25 |
| Carnevor | **Downtown** | 24 |
| ☑ Eddie Martini's | **Wauwatosa** | 29 |
| ☑ Lake Park | **E Side** | 28 |
| ☑ Mason St. Grill | **Downtown** | 23 |
| ☑ Rist. Bartolotta | **Wauwatosa** | 28 |
| ☑ Sanford | **E Side** | 29 |
| Zarletti | **Downtown** | 22 |

## WINNING WINE LISTS

| | |
|---|---|
| ☑ Bacchus | **Downtown** | 25 |
| Carnevor | **Downtown** | 24 |
| ☑ Coquette Cafe | **Third Ward** | 26 |
| Dream Dance | **Downtown** | - |
| ☑ Lake Park | **E Side** | 28 |
| Mangia | **Kenosha** | 25 |
| ☑ Mason St. Grill | **Downtown** | 23 |
| Milwaukee Chophouse | **Downtown** | 22 |
| ☑ Osteria/Mondo | **Downtown** | 28 |
| ☑ Rist. Bartolotta | **Wauwatosa** | 28 |
| ☑ Sanford | **E Side** | 29 |
| NEW Smyth | **Walker's Point** | 24 |

## WORTH A TRIP

| | |
|---|---|
| Caledonia | |
|   Sebastian's | - |
| Kenosha | |
|   Mangia | 25 |
| Kohler | |
|   Immigrant Room | 23 |
| Mukwonago | |
|   Heaven City | - |

# Wine Vintage Chart

This chart is based on our 0 to 30 scale. The ratings (by U. of South Carolina law professor **Howard Stravitz**) reflect vintage quality and the wine's readiness to drink. A dash means the wine is past its peak or too young to rate. Loire ratings are for dry whites.

| Whites | 95 | 96 | 97 | 98 | 99 | 00 | 01 | 02 | 03 | 04 | 05 | 06 | 07 | 08 |
|---|---|---|---|---|---|---|---|---|---|---|---|---|---|---|
| **France:** | | | | | | | | | | | | | | |
| Alsace | 24 | 23 | 23 | 25 | 23 | 25 | 26 | 23 | 21 | 24 | 25 | 24 | 26 | - |
| Burgundy | 27 | 26 | 23 | 21 | 24 | 24 | 24 | 27 | 23 | 26 | 27 | 25 | 25 | 24 |
| Loire Valley | - | - | - | - | - | 23 | 24 | 26 | 22 | 24 | 27 | 23 | 23 | 24 |
| Champagne | 26 | 27 | 24 | 23 | 25 | 24 | 21 | 26 | 21 | - | - | - | - | - |
| Sauternes | 21 | 23 | 25 | 23 | 24 | 24 | 29 | 25 | 24 | 21 | 26 | 23 | 27 | 25 |
| **California:** | | | | | | | | | | | | | | |
| Chardonnay | - | - | - | - | 23 | 22 | 25 | 26 | 22 | 26 | 29 | 24 | 27 | - |
| Sauvignon Blanc | - | - | - | - | - | - | - | - | 25 | 26 | 25 | 27 | 25 | - |
| **Austria:** | | | | | | | | | | | | | | |
| Grüner V./Riesl. | 24 | 21 | 26 | 23 | 25 | 22 | 23 | 25 | 26 | 25 | 24 | 26 | 24 | 22 |
| **Germany:** | 21 | 26 | 21 | 22 | 24 | 20 | 29 | 25 | 26 | 27 | 28 | 25 | 27 | 25 |

| Reds | 95 | 96 | 97 | 98 | 99 | 00 | 01 | 02 | 03 | 04 | 05 | 06 | 07 | 08 |
|---|---|---|---|---|---|---|---|---|---|---|---|---|---|---|
| **France:** | | | | | | | | | | | | | | |
| Bordeaux | 26 | 25 | 23 | 25 | 24 | 29 | 26 | 24 | 26 | 24 | 28 | 24 | 23 | 25 |
| Burgundy | 26 | 27 | 25 | 24 | 27 | 22 | 24 | 27 | 25 | 23 | 28 | 25 | 24 | - |
| Rhône | 26 | 22 | 24 | 27 | 26 | 27 | 26 | - | 26 | 24 | 27 | 25 | 26 | - |
| Beaujolais | - | - | - | - | - | - | - | - | 24 | - | 27 | 24 | 25 | 23 |
| **California:** | | | | | | | | | | | | | | |
| Cab./Merlot | 27 | 25 | 28 | 23 | 25 | - | 27 | 26 | 25 | 24 | 26 | 23 | 26 | 24 |
| Pinot Noir | - | - | - | - | 24 | 23 | 25 | 26 | 25 | 26 | 24 | 23 | 27 | 25 |
| Zinfandel | - | - | - | - | - | - | 25 | 23 | 27 | 22 | 22 | 21 | 21 | 25 |
| **Oregon:** | | | | | | | | | | | | | | |
| Pinot Noir | - | - | - | - | - | - | 26 | 24 | 25 | 26 | 26 | 25 | 27 | |
| **Italy:** | | | | | | | | | | | | | | |
| Tuscany | 24 | - | 29 | 24 | 27 | 24 | 27 | - | 25 | 27 | 26 | 25 | 24 | - |
| Piedmont | 21 | 27 | 26 | 25 | 26 | 28 | 27 | - | 25 | 27 | 26 | 25 | 26 | - |
| **Spain:** | | | | | | | | | | | | | | |
| Rioja | 26 | 24 | 25 | - | 25 | 24 | 28 | - | 23 | 27 | 26 | 24 | 25 | - |
| Ribera del Duero/ Priorat | 26 | 27 | 25 | 24 | 25 | 24 | 27 | 20 | 24 | 27 | 26 | 24 | 26 | - |
| **Australia:** | | | | | | | | | | | | | | |
| Shiraz/Cab. | 24 | 26 | 25 | 28 | 24 | 24 | 27 | 27 | 25 | 26 | 26 | 24 | 22 | - |
| **Chile:** | - | - | 24 | - | 25 | 23 | 26 | 24 | 25 | 24 | 27 | 25 | 24 | - |
| **Argentina:** | | | | | | | | | | | | | | |
| Malbec | - | - | - | - | - | - | - | - | 25 | 26 | 27 | 24 | - | |

# ZAGATMAP

## Chicago Transit Map

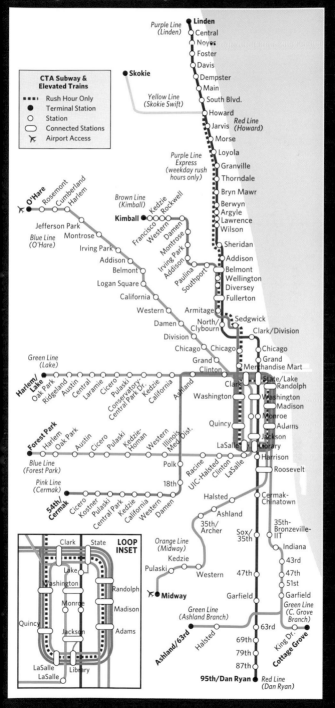

# Chicago's Most Popular Restaurants

Map coordinates follow each name. For chains, only flagship or central locations are plotted. Sections A-H show places in the city of Chicago (see adjacent map). Sections I-P show nearby suburbs of Chicago (see reverse side of map).

1 Frontera Grill (E-4)

2 Alinea (C-2)

3 Topolobampo (E-4)

4 Charlie Trotter's (B-2)

5 Gibsons (D-4, M-4)

6 Joe's Sea/Steak (E-4)

7 Blackbird (F-3)

8 Wildfire † (L-2)

9 Morton's † (D-4)

10 Tru (E-5)

11 Spiaggia (D-5)

12 Everest (G-4)

13 avec (F-3)

14 Shaw's (E-4, L-2)

15 Lou Malnati's † (E-4)

16 mk (D-3)

17 Chicago Chop House (E-4)

18 L2O (A-3)

19 Capital Grille † (E-5)

20 Giordano's † (G-3)

21 NoMI (E-4)

22 Gene & Georgetti (E-3)

23 Publican (F-2)

24 Maggiano's † (E-4)

25 Hugo's (D-4, P-1)

26 Bob Chinn's (K-4)

27 Hot Doug's (M-6)

28 Café Spiaggia (D-5)

29 Ruth's Chris* † (E-4)

30 Original Gino's † (E-5)

31 Gage (F-4)

32 Original/Walker Pancake † (O-7)

33 Les Nomades (E-5)

34 Japonais (E-3)

35 Coco Pazzo (E-3)

36 Catch 35 (F-4, P-1)

37 Cheesecake Factory † (D-5)

38 Arun's (M-6)

39 Rosebud* † (H-1)

40 David Burke's (E-4)

---

*Indicates tie with above     † Indicates multiple branches